Modern Papal Diplomacy and Social Teaching in World Affairs

This comprehensive collection offers a concise introduction to the institutional framework of the Holy See, conceptualizing papal agency and positions from a range of international theory perspectives. The authors – international scholars from political science, history, and religious studies – explore multiple fields of papal and Vatican influence, ranging from spy networks and inter-religious dialogue to social doctrine and religious freedom.

This book demonstrates that, contrary to secularization theory, the papacy is not in decline in world politics. Since World War II, the Holy See has played a steadily increasing role in international relations. Globalization supports the role of the Catholic Church as a transnational actor not only in the advanced industrial societies of the West but also increasingly across the Global South. In this volume, the authors document the legacies of John Paul II and Benedict XVI as well as the current pontificate of Pope Francis from a range of contemporary perspectives.

This book comprises research articles and commentary essays on the papacy in world politics originally published in *The Review of Faith & International Affairs.*

Mariano P. Barbato is Associate Professor of Politics at the University of Passau and Heisenberg, Germany. Currently he is the Principal Investigator of the research project 'Legions of the Pope. A case study in social and political transformation', funded by the German Research Foundation. He has published widely on religion and politics.

Robert J. Joustra is Director of the Centre for Christian Scholarship and Associate Professor of Politics and International Studies at Redeemer University College, Canada. He is an editorial fellow with *The Review of Faith & International Affairs* and author and editor of several books, including most recently *The Religious Problem with Religious Freedom: Why Foreign Policy Needs Political Theology* (2017).

Dennis R. Hoover is Editor of *The Review of Faith & International Affairs* and Senior Fellow at the Institute for Global Engagement, USA. He is editor of *Religion and American Exceptionalism* (2014), co-editor with Chris Seiple and Pauletta Otis of *The Routledge Handbook of Religion and Security* (2013), and co-editor with Douglas Johnston of *Religion and Foreign Affairs: Essential Readings* (2012).

Routledge Studies in Religion and Politics

Edited by Jeffrey Haynes, London Metropolitan University, UK

This series aims to publish high quality works on the topic of the resurgence of political forms of religion in both national and international contexts. This trend has been especially noticeable in the post-cold war era (that is, since the late 1980s). It has affected all the 'world religions' (including, Buddhism, Christianity, Hinduism, Islam, and Judaism) in various parts of the world (such as, the Americas, Europe, the Middle East and North Africa, South and Southeast Asia, and sub-Saharan Africa).

The series welcomes books that use a variety of approaches to the subject, drawing on scholarship from political science, international relations, security studies, and contemporary history.

Books in the series explore these religions, regions and topics both within and beyond the conventional domain of 'church-state' relations to include the impact of religion on politics, conflict and development, including the late Samuel Huntington's controversial – yet influential – thesis about 'clashing civilisations'.

In sum, the overall purpose of the book series is to provide a comprehensive survey of what is currently happening in relation to the interaction of religion and politics, both domestically and internationally, in relation to a variety of issues.

For more information about this series, please visit: https://www.routledge.com/Routledge-Studies-in-Religion-and-Politics/book-series/RSRP

Religion in the Context of Globalization
Essays on concept, form, and political implication
Peter Beyer

Religion and the Realist Tradition
From political theology to International Relations theory and back
Jodok Troy

Cosmopolitanism, Religion and the Public Sphere
Maria Rovisco and Sebastian Kim

Religion, Identity and Human Security
Giorgio Shani

Christians and the Middle East Conflict
Edited by John Rowe, John Dyck and Jens Zimmerman

Conservative Religious Politics in Russia and the United States
Dreaming of a Christian nation
John Anderson

European Culture Wars and the Italian Case
Which Side are you on?
Luca Ozzano and Alberta Giorgi

God and the EU
Faith in the European Project
Jonathan Chaplin and Gary Wilton

Religious NGOs in International Relations
The Construction of 'the Religious' and 'the Secular'
Karsten Lehmann

Religion at the United Nations
Value Politics
Edited by Anne Stensvold

Religion and Soft Power in the South Caucasus
Edited by Ansgar Jödicke

The Religious Problem with Religious Freedom
Why Foreign Policy Needs Political Theology
Robert Joustra

An Introduction to Religion and Politics (2nd edition)
Theory and Practice
Jonathan Fox

Religious Responses to Marriage Equality
Luke Perry

The Politics of New Atheism
Stuart McAnulla, Steven Kettell and Marcus Schulzke

Religious NGOs at the United Nations
Polarizers or Mediators?
Edited by Claudia Baumgart-Ochse and Klaus Dieter Wolf

Catholic Mediations in Southern Europe
The Invisible Politics of Religion
Xabier Itçaina

Contested Holy Cities
The Urban Dimension of Religious Conflicts
Edited by Michael Dumper

Modern Papal Diplomacy and Social Teaching in World Affairs
Edited by Mariano P. Barbato, Robert J. Joustra and Dennis R. Hoover

Modern Papal Diplomacy and Social Teaching in World Affairs

Edited by

Mariano P. Barbato, Robert J. Joustra and Dennis R. Hoover

Routledge
Taylor & Francis Group
LONDON AND NEW YORK

First published 2019
by Routledge
2 Park Square, Milton Park, Abingdon, Oxon, OX14 4RN

and by Routledge
605 Third Avenue, New York, NY 10017

First issued in paperback 2020

Routledge is an imprint of the Taylor & Francis Group, an informa business

British Library Cataloguing in Publication Data
A catalogue record for this book is available from the British Library

ISBN 13: 978-0-367-72892-2 (pbk)
ISBN 13: 978-0-367-20023-7 (hbk)

Typeset in Adobe Garamond
by RefineCatch Limited, Bungay, Suffolk

Publisher's Note

The publisher accepts responsibility for any inconsistencies that may have arisen during the conversion of this book from journal articles to book chapters, namely the inclusion of journal terminology.

Contents

Part II: Essays from the Archive

Citation Information

The chapters in this book were previously published in *The Review of Faith & International Affairs*. When citing this material, please use the original page numbering for each article, as follows:

Chapter 1

Introduction: Popes on the Rise
Mariano Barbato and Robert Joustra
This chapter was first published in its original format in *The Review of Faith & International Affairs*, volume 15, issue 4 (December 2017), pp. 1–5, a slightly edited version is included in this book.

Chapter 2

Sovereignty, Supranationalism, and Soft Power: The Holy See in International Relations
Timothy A. Byrnes
The Review of Faith & International Affairs, volume 15, issue 4 (December 2017), pp. 6–20

Chapter 3

Beyond Integration and Differentiation? The Holy See and the Pope in the System of World Politics
Mathias Albert
The Review of Faith & International Affairs, volume 15, issue 4 (December 2017), pp. 21–30

Chapter 4

Diplomacy, Papacy, and the Transformation of International Society
Thomas Diez
The Review of Faith & International Affairs, volume 15, issue 4 (December 2017), pp. 31–38

Chapter 5

Rerum Novarum *and the Right to Work: 19th-Century Lessons for 21st-Century Labor*
Robert Joustra
The Review of Faith & International Affairs, volume 15, issue 4 (December 2017), pp. 39–47

Chapter 6

Among Spies, Popes, and the Good Cyrenians: La Commission pour l'Eglise Persécutée *as a Transnational Catholic Actor in the Cold War*
Adrian Hänni
The Review of Faith & International Affairs, volume 15, issue 4 (December 2017), pp. 48–66

Chapter 7

Two "Popes" to Speak for the World: The Pope and the United Nations Secretary General in World Politics
Jodok Troy
The Review of Faith & International Affairs, volume 15, issue 4 (December 2017), pp. 67–78

Chapter 8

Papal Geopolitics: The World According to Urbi et Orbi
Petr Kratochvíl and Jana Hovorková
The Review of Faith & International Affairs, volume 15, issue 4 (December 2017), pp. 79–92

Chapter 9

Diplomatic Language in the Deepavali Messages of the Pontifical Council for Interreligious Dialogue
Melanie Barbato
The Review of Faith & International Affairs, volume 15, issue 4 (December 2017), pp. 93–104

Chapter 10

A Trajectory Towards the Periphery: Francis of Assisi, Louis Massignon, Pope Francis, and Muslim–Christian Relations
Scott M. Thomas
The Review of Faith & International Affairs, volume 16, issue 1 (March 2018), pp. 16–36

Chapter 11

Dignitatis Humanae *and the Catholic Human Rights Revolution*
Kenneth L. Grasso and Robert P. Hunt
The Review of Faith & International Affairs, volume 3, issue 3 (Winter 2005–2006), pp. 3–10

Chapter 12

Roman Catholicism and the Faith-Based Movement for Global Human Rights
Allen D. Hertzke
The Review of Faith & International Affairs, volume 3, issue 3 (Winter 2005–2006), pp. 19–24

Chapter 13

Pope John Paul II and the Dynamics of History
George Weigel
The Review of Faith & International Affairs, volume 7, issue 2 (Summer 2009), pp. 27–30

Chapter 14

Catholic Peacemaking, 1991–2005: The Legacy of Pope John Paul II
Drew Christiansen
The Review of Faith & International Affairs, volume 4, issue 2 (Autumn 2006), pp. 21–28

Chapter 15

A Diplomacy of Candor: Pope Benedict XVI on the Global Stage
Bernard J. O'Connor
The Review of Faith & International Affairs, volume 4, issue 2 (Autumn 2006), pp. 41–43

Chapter 16
Benedict XVI: Peacemaker
Drew Christiansen, S.J.
The Review of Faith & International Affairs, volume 5, issue 4 (Winter 2007), pp. 17–23

Chapter 17
Catholic Social Teaching, MacIntyre's Social Theory, and Global Development
Scott M. Thomas
The Review of Faith & International Affairs, volume 8, issue 4 (December 2010), pp. 23–34

Notes on Contributors

Mathias Albert is Professor of Political Science at Bielefeld University, Germany. His current main research interests are in the areas of world society theory/theory of international relations, as well as in youth research.

Mariano P. Barbato is Associate Professor of Politics at the University of Passau and Heisenberg, Germany. Currently he is Principal Investigator of the research project 'Legions of the Pope. A case study in social and political transformation', funded by the German Research Foundation. He has published widely on religion and politics.

Melanie Barbato is a Postdoctoral Researcher at the Institute for Religious Studies and Intercultural Theology at the University of Münster, Germany. Her research on the PCID's Deepavali messages was conducted while she was a Visiting Scholar at the American University of Rome, Italy.

Timothy A. Byrnes is Charles A. Dana Professor of Political Science at Colgate University, USA. His specialities and interests include Transnational Politics, Religion, and Politics. He was awarded the Colgate Alumni Corporation Distinguished Teaching Award in 2002.

Drew Christiansen, S.J. is Distinguished Professor of Ethics and Global Human Development in Georgetown's School of Foreign Service, USA, and a Senior Research Fellow at the Berkley Center for Religion, Peace, and World Affairs, USA. He is former Editor-in-Chief of *America*, the U.S. Jesuit weekly magazine.

Thomas Diez is Professor of Political Science and International Relations at the University of Tübingen, Germany. In September 2009, he received the Anna Lindh Award for his contribution to the field of European Foreign and Security Policy Studies.

Kenneth L. Grasso is Professor of Political Science at Texas State University, USA. He serves on the Editorial Advisory Boards of *The Catholic Social Science Review* and *The Political Science Reviewer* as well as on the Executive Editorial Board of *The Journal of Markets & Morality*. His areas of interest are religion and politics, democratic theory, liberal theory, and American constitutionalism.

Adrian Hänni is a Historian and, since 2015, a Lecturer of Political History at Distance Learning University Switzerland. His research interests include the history of propaganda, intelligence services, and terrorism, as well as the Cold War.

Allen D. Hertzke is David Ross Boyd Professor of Political Science and Faculty Fellow in Religious Freedom for the Institute for the American Constitutional Heritage at the University of Oklahoma, USA. An internationally recognized expert on religion and politics, he is a frequent news commentator.

Dennis R. Hoover is Editor of *The Review of Faith & International Affairs* and Senior Fellow at the Institute for Global Engagement, USA. He is editor of *Religion and American Exceptionalism* (2014), co-editor with Chris Seiple and Pauletta Otis of *The Routledge Handbook of Religion and Security* (2013), and co-editor with Douglas Johnston of *Religion and Foreign Affairs: Essential Readings* (2012).

Jana Hovorková is a Doctoral Degree student at the Jan Masaryk Centre for International Studies at the University of Economics in Prague, Czech Republic. She carries out her research in the geopolitics of the Catholic Church under the supervision of Professor Petr Kratochvíl, Director of the Institute of International Relations in Prague.

Robert P. Hunt is Professor of Political Science at Kean University, USA. He has written in the areas of American Constitutionalism and the development of modern political theory. His articles and reviews have appeared in a variety of publications including *First Things* and *The Catholic Social Science Review*.

Robert J. Joustra is Director of the Centre for Christian Scholarship and Associate Professor of Politics and International Studies at Redeemer University College, Canada. He is an editorial fellow with *The Review of Faith & International Affairs* and author and editor of several books, including most recently *The Religious Problem with Religious Freedom: Why Foreign Policy Needs Political Theology* (2017).

Petr Kratochvíl is Director of the Prague-based Institute of International Relations, the Czech Republic. His areas of interest are Czech foreign policy, European integration, institutional reform and EU enlargement, Russian foreign policy, political relations in the post-Soviet area, the role of religion in international relations, and the Catholic Church and international relations.

Bernard J. O'Connor was Fellow and John Henry Cardinal Newman Professor of Theology and Ecclesial Mediation at the Graduate Theological Foundation in Indiana, USA, where he served from 1996 to 2015, and was an official with the Vatican's Congregation for Eastern Churches. He lectured and published widely on ecclesiology and international diplomacy. He sadly passed away in 2015.

Scott M. Thomas is Senior Lecturer in International Relations and the Politics of Developing Countries in the Department of European Studies at the University of Bath, UK. He is also a Research Fellow in the Center for Christianity and Interreligious Dialogue at Heythrop College, University of London, UK. He has engaged with many governments around the world on the role of religion in international affairs.

Jodok Troy is a Postdoctoral Researcher in the Department of Political Science at the University of Innsbruck, Austria. His research focuses on religion, ethics, and international relations, focussing on international political theory and the policy issues of international peace and security, particularly focusing on realism and the English School.

George Weigel is Distinguished Senior Fellow and the William E. Simon Chair in Catholic Studies at the Ethics and Public Policy Center in Washington, USA. He is the author of over 20 books, including the widely translated and internationally acclaimed two-volume biography of Pope St. John Paul II: *Witness to Hope* (1999), and its sequel *The End and the Beginning* (2010).

INTRODUCTION: POPES ON THE RISE

By Mariano P. Barbato, Robert J. Joustra, and Dennis R. Hoover

Among the accounts of the Kings of Israel in the Catholic Bible, a prophet named Elisha prays for the eyes of a blinded servant (2 Kings, Chapter 6). There is nothing wrong with that servant's eyes. But what he cannot *see* are mountains "full of horses and chariots of fire all around Elisha." Here, maybe, are the Pope's divisions Joseph Stalin infamously derided. Here, too, is what foreign policy scholars have called the spiritual power of religious movements that can topple states and empires, mediate peace, and propel to war. This, certainly, is the heritage and promise of Vatican foreign policy in the world today: a force that is real, but also one that is necessarily limited, case studies of which are afresh and aplenty in our world today.

Just in the last several years, there has been a renaissance not only in the study but in the practice of Vatican diplomacy. We have found the Holy See intervening in Cuba, mediating conversations between then-President Obama and the Cuban President Raúl Castro. Vatican diplomats have been on the ground in Venezuela, attempting to mediate peace between the government of Nicolás Maduro and the opposition. The Holy See has been at the forefront of a big push at the United Nations on a new global treaty banning nuclear weapons. And this is just the front-page news. Dig into the inglorious grunt work in dusty committee rooms, and you'll find Vatican diplomats at the 2013 Geneva peace talks to end the Syrian war, at the Truth and Reconciliation process in post-Apartheid South Africa, in the Solidarity movement in Poland, and the list goes on.

But even with all these interventions, of course, the Holy See can still seem like an old-world relic in a hyper-modern world of hard power and economic globalization. What does a small quasi-sovereign mini-state really bring to the table on the "real" issues of international relations? Where, after all, are Elisha's angel legions in the failed states of Somalia, the civil war in Yemen, the desolate destruction of Mosul, and more? The Vatican might specialize in a kind of boutique moral-diplomacy, but the heavy lifting of the international order will always be left to states with carrier groups and IMF voting blocks.

Part of the argument of this volume is that this is not true. What counts as "real" and, indeed, what counts as "heavy lifting" in a world often consumed by growth rates and security dilemmas needs to be reconsidered. Just as the Vatican by its very existence challenges our common understanding of things like sovereignty and power in the international system, so its boutique diplomacy is also the "tip" of the iceberg of what the Vatican can, and has, done in foreign relations.

Legally speaking, the "Vatican" refers to two political entities of international relations: the Vatican City State and the Holy See. The minor actor is the Vatican City State founded in the Lateran Treaties between Mussolini's Italy and the Curia of Pius XI in 1929 to solve the territorial Roman question almost fifty years after the end of the Papal State in 1870. The mini-state provides the Pope with sovereign territory with such remarkable properties like St. Peter's Basilica, St. Peter's Square, the Vatican Museums and the Vatican Gardens, and a few extraterritorial real estates like a Hospital, some ancient Roman Churches, and Castel Gandolfo. The Vatican City State is a state with radio and railway stations, mail and money, and which participates in various treaties on the international stage, bringing the papal face on Euro coins (at least until Pope Francis' decision to replace the face with the coat of arms in January 2017) and on stamps as a member of the Universal Postal Union.

The "real" actor in world politics, however, is the Holy See. The Holy See is a separate legal entity that "has" a state—the Vatican City State—but is none. In Canonical law, it serves as the entity which governs the Catholic Church. Dating back to the beginning of the practice of European diplomacy, the Holy See has also full legal personality as a subject in international public law. In current practice, it is the Holy See that established diplomatic relations to almost all states and obtains a member or special status in almost all international organizations with a political mission, in contrast to more functional organizations like the Universal Postal Union in which the Vatican City State is a member.

The power of the Catholic Church, and of the Holy See, is enormous in a world that is so rapidly losing a moral vocabulary beyond profit/loss, power/order, and security/strength. The language of international diplomacy has hollowed out words which that Church still remembers: dignity, the image of God, faith, and hope. It is precisely on the back of catastrophe, of systemic and terrible evil, that the liberal-secular worldview cannot bear the weight of its own inadequacies without gesturing beyond itself. Once impelled to tone down his "prayers" for a secular crowd at the Truth & Reconciliation Commission in South Africa, Desmond Tutu tried—but halted—declaring they could not bear the weight of those proceedings apart from prayer. No purely material theory can make sense of the mystery of the human condition, its evils, or its joys, and no purely secular diplomacy is fit for the work of mediation, repentance, and reconciliation.

And yet there are also real limits. The Church speaks best and most powerfully when it does so on principle—out of the clear conviction of its confessions—and is wisely discrete on particularities, policy, and procedure. That Church has real power as convener, mediator, and prophet in a world dominated by secular elites, but peopled by the resurging religious. That Church must also see its limits where leadership will not relent, repent, or redirect. The Vatican, then, is *part* of foreign policy in what Monica Duffy Toft, Daniel Philpott, and Timothy Samuel Shah (2011) have aptly described as "God's Century"; it is not the panacea. It has real promise, but it is no silver bullet.

For these reasons we are delighted to draw together in this book a collection of recent research articles and past commentary essays on the papacy in world politics published in *The Review of Faith & International Affairs*. Most of the research articles emerged from a major conference at the Vatican in 2017 titled "Popes on the Rise! Mobilization, Media, and the Political Power of the Modern Papacy."[1] The gambit of that conference was that the Holy See made, makes, and will make substantive contributions to global policy and politics. The Vatican's mediators and its diplomats can give the world of global politics back a language it so desperately needs: a language of virtue, morality, dignity, and means—not just ends—as more than long-term expedience. Its very existence and confessions are a cap and check on unrestrained capital, tyrannical governance, and hyper-individualism. But that witness is strongest when made prophetically, and it is sometimes limited and compromised when it delves too deeply into policy. It is rhetoric—it is a witness—that can ennoble and mediate, but it cannot coerce nor prescribe. It has promise, but it also has limits. This book, then, is concerned with both the promise and limits of the Holy See in world affairs.[2]

Part I of the book begins with a research article by Timothy A. Byrnes, who structures papal politics along three spheres: (1) sovereignty and international relations; (2) supranationalism and the Church; and (3) soft power in the global public sphere. First, in the sphere of international relations the Holy See is a sovereign actor with the status of a legal person in international law and has as such diplomatic relations to most of the states and is member to many international organizations. The Holy See represents the Pope not as the sovereign of the Vatican City State but as sovereign of the Catholic Church; as such the Holy See is accepted among states as a sovereign peer. Second, being the leader of the Catholic Church turns the Pope, however, also into a supranational leader who has transnational ties in every country. In this supranational capacity, the Pope is involved in the internal affairs of almost every country and can influence in some cases the majority or a major minority of a national population. Third, the media attention allows the pope to develop a soft power capacity that reaches beyond the Catholic flock and diplomatic relations into an emerging global public sphere. Nevertheless, the soft power approach reminds us also that the pope has no means of coercion to secure a chain of command. The Pope is always as powerful as his authority or advice is accepted on the different stages he tries to perform.

Drawing on system theory, the next article by Mathias Albert explains the soft power of the Holy See in international relations through its structural position within in the world system. The Holy See has a historical tradition as hard power in diplomatic relations which explains the diplomatic and legal legacy still vibrant in the modern system. The old religiously backed legacy is not able to structurally bridge the differentiation of the modern international system and the balance of power of its units and turn the pope into a real global leader. Despite the impossibility of integrating the international system, ascribing such an integrative function to the Holy See is a useful move to bridge tensions in world politics. The Holy See is ready to represent this necessary but impossible task of integration. The ability for the impossible secures its soft power in world politics.

From the perspective of the English School in International Relations, Thomas Diez explains why and how the rise of the pope in international relations was possible and is likely to continue, while also likely to be continuously contested. In an international society that rests only on pluralist principles of sovereignty, territory, and nation, the legal entity of the Holy See is an outside relict from the past. In a world, however, that increasingly develops solidarist principles, the Holy See is no longer an alien but in tune with transnational, global, and universal ambitions. To be sure, the story of solidarism in international society and the Catholic idea of one world under God do not necessarily go together smoothly. At times, harsh contestations on what values the solidarist world should be built come up; gender issues or abortion are the most salient ones. However, also environmental issues, migration, and capitalism are contested. It is open, if, how, and to what extent the Holy See can influence these debates in the future.

Capitalism and Catholicism have a long and difficult relationship. Parts of Latin American Liberation theology once even allied with Marxism to overcome the shortcomings of capitalism. While the magisterium of the Church was ready to suppress any (mis)alliances with Marxism, papal critique on capitalism continues. Robert Joustra highlights in his contribution the continuing importance of the first social encyclical of modern times—*Rerum Novarum* (1891) of Pope Leo XIII. The encyclical laid the ground for a sophisticated and moderate stance of the Church towards the conflicts of the modern economy. Joustra shows that Leo's concept is still the blueprint of the social teaching of the popes, while it has been adapted and adjusted to newer developments during the following pontificates. Economic relationships, the popes argue, need not become conflictual, but can be built on a just relationship between labor and capital as both need each other. Labor unions play a crucial part in the papal teaching and are at the center of Joustra's example of the Right-to-Work Legislation in North America, particularly in the United States, but also in Canada.

The Holy See was not brought "back from exile" when religion arguably returned to international relations. The Holy See was always around. Adrian Hänni delves back into the time of the Cold War and the pontificate of Pius XII where he finds the remarkable story of the Commission for the Persecuted Church. Founded in 1950, the Commission was set up under the auspices of the Holy See as an umbrella organization of international lay activities to ensure that the Church behind the Iron Curtain should not be forgotten but supported. During the 1950s, the small leading circle of the Commission established a network supported by the Vatican and by Western secret services to organize a strong network of charity, propaganda, and prayer to fight communism East and West beyond the Iron Curtain.

Jodok Troy's analysis of papal human rights discourse starts also in the pontificate of Pius XII who introduced the human rights vocabulary into papal documents. In his rigorous analysis, Troy shows that the classical liberal discourse of individual rights reached a high in the pontificate of John Paul II and the context of the Cold War. Already Benedict XVI's pontificate marked a change as more universalist notions like the "right of the environment" were introduced and egalitarian demands on wealth distribution gained momentum. The pontificate of Francis remains inside the human rights discourse but accelerated the transformation to a more universal notion of human rights.

Petr Kratochvíl and Jana Hovorková lay out a papal geopolitical map by analyzing a decade of *Urbi-et-Orbi* Messages in the pontificates of Benedict XVI and Francis between 2005 and 2015. These speeches, delivered each Christmas and Easter by the Popes at St. Peter's Square and broadcasted worldwide, focus on what is important for the Pope in religious but also, deeply intertwined, in political perspective. Kratochvíl and Hovorková show that in both pontificates global de-territorialized problems of world politics, such as war, construct the earthly space in contrast to the heavenly. Both pontificates have their focus on Africa and the Middle East while neither Benedict nor Francis prioritized their continent of origin. The popes have an eye on the global challenges of the Church and world politics.

Melanie Barbato analyzes the Deepavali messages of the Holy See as a cornerstone of Christian-Hindu dialogue and as an example of high level interreligious dialogue. Deepavali, the festival of lights, is a happy occasion in the Hindu calendar when greetings among friends and relatives are exchanged. The Holy See, more specifically the Pontifical Council for Interreligious Dialogue, uses this opportunity to engage in a friendly, sometimes also critical dialogue with the Hindu community. In her rigorous analysis, Barbato shows that a shared humanity and a shared understanding as religious people are emphasized to build a bridge between the very different languages of religious discourse of the Catholic and the Hindu communities. While discussing the messages as a form of public diplomacy, she also shows that persecution of Christians in India lead to at least two different approaches in the messages—one year much more critical than is typical for these documents, and the next year with an emphasis on Hinduism's own resources of non-violence.

Scott M. Thomas examines Louis Massignon (1883–1962), one of the most important European scholars, and Catholic scholars of Islam in the 20th century. His views on Islam changed the Catholic Church's approach to Islam at the Second Vatican Council. Massignon was influenced by Francis of Assisi and his encounter with the Sultan of Egypt during the Fifth Crusade. Thomas argues that both St. Francis and Massignon were engaged in a *counter*-cultural critique of Christendom, a "trajectory towards the periphery" regarding peacemaking, Muslim-Christian relations, and interreligious dialogue, which gained for St. Francis, and for Massignon, the support of popes—and is today also reflected in Pope Francis's approach to global issues.

Part II of this book presents a selection of shorter commentaries from the essay archive of *The Review of Faith & International Affairs*. This collection includes contemporaneous reflections on the papacies of John Paul II and of Benedict XVI, as well as insightful analyses of major areas of Vatican social teaching and practice in world affairs, such as religious freedom, peacebuilding, and economic development. Contributors include a diverse and highly distinguished array of experts on global Catholicism including Kenneth L. Grasso, Robert P. Hunt,

Allen D. Hertzke, George Weigel, Drew Christiansen, Bernard J. O'Connor, and Scott M. Thomas.

Taken together, the various research articles and commentaries included in this volume shed light on the strengths and limits of the Holy See in international relations and stress jointly that the Vatican is not only an interesting object of study in its own right but a telling example how transformations in world politics are at work. Religion is a force in world affairs and secularizing processes add only a twist on that force instead of annihilating it. The Holy See's soft power in world politics seems to rest on the ability to secure its position in a small niche of the international system while playing on various stages of world politics and public diplomacy, thereby addressing and contesting continuously a wide range of crucial issues of world politics. Solving the puzzle of the unexpected rise of the Holy See in modern world politics is a task for international relations scholars that can not only help to explain the role of religious actors in world politics but can serve as a prism that improves understanding in various other fields and discourses of international relations.

At the decline of the Roman Empire, it was sometimes on the popes to defend the city against the barbarians at the gate. In 452 the Huns threatened to sack Rome when Pope Leo the Great was part of a mission sent to the Hun king Attila to beg for peace. The mission was successful. While contemporary sources gave credits to Pope Leo, historians are unable to explain Attila's reasons to withdraw. One source, Paul the Deacon, explains Attila's retreat by a vision, visible only to him, that the king of the Huns had during the negotiations with Leo. The Roman Apostle Princes Peter and Paul with swords appeared terrifically behind Leo in order to back his words with deeds. In the Apostolic Palace of the Vatican, Raffael's fresco "The Meeting between Leo the Great and Attila," painted in 1514, more than a thousand years after the encounter of Attila and Leo, celebrates the legend.

Even though no chariots of fire or heavenly legions became visible, this legend draws attention to the need and the ability of the popes to become visible as powerful international actors. Different scripts of visibility are necessary to please the various tastes of the time. Today media coverage that shows the pope backed by masses of pilgrims at St. Peter's Square or around the world encountering the pope on his visits may be the visible legions on parade which may gain him the respect of some Attilas of today.

1. Funding for the conference proceedings of Popes on the Rise! was provided by the DFG—German Research Foundation. The research articles that emerged from the conference were published in December 2017 as a special theme issue of *The Review of Faith & International Affairs* under the title "Popes on the Rise: The Modern Papacy in World Affairs" (Volume 15, Issue 4, https://www.tandfonline.com/toc/rfia20/15/4).

2. Parts of this introduction appeared on the Berkley Forum's website under "The Pope's Divisions" by Robert Joustra (February 21, 2017). https://berkleycenter.georgetown.edu/responses/the-pope-s-divisions

References

Toft, Monica Duffy, Daniel Philpott, and Timothy Samuel Shah. 2011. *God's Century: Resurgent Religion and Global Politics*. New York: Norton.

SOVEREIGNTY, SUPRANATIONALISM, AND SOFT POWER: THE HOLY SEE IN INTERNATIONAL RELATIONS

By Timothy A. Byrnes

The Holy See is a pervasive participant in international relations. Its unique legal status, its institutional reach through its leadership of the ubiquitous transnational Catholic Church, and its especially prominent moral megaphone combine to provide its singular leader, the Roman Catholic Pope, with remarkable access to multiple layers of global politics. This has long been true, of course, and Popes have played significant roles in all sorts of international political processes over the centuries. But the fact that this is still the case, despite the presumed secularizing effects of the Westphalian state system and the complex dynamics of modernity is a remarkable testament to the depth and stability of the Holy See's and Pope's political status. In some ways, indeed, we are seeing the Holy See and the Pope playing today even broader roles in international relations than they did in the past. The affirmation of the Pope's legal status on the global stage, the strengthening of the Pope's centralized institutional role in the Roman Catholic Church, and the intensity of the media's focus on the papacy's global celebrity have all reinforced the prominence and significance of a political actor who might have been expected, as the saying goes, to fade away by now.

This article will begin with an examination of the Holy See as a non-territorial, sovereign actor in international diplomacy. Casual observers may have a vague notion that the Pope participates in the diplomatic element of international relations, but most of those observers probably believe that this is grounded in the Pope's leadership of a microstate called Vatican City. This is incorrect, as incorrect as the common shorthand of referring to the Pope's diplomatic outposts around the world (182 at time of writing) as "Vatican Embassies." These 182 countries do not have diplomatic relations with Vatican City; they have diplomatic relations with the Holy See (Arangio-Ruiz 1996; Araujo 2001; Barbato 2013; Bathon 2001; Troy 2016). The Vatican City State, as such, does participate in some limited international institutional arrangements related directly to territoriality, such as the International Postal Union. But, by and large, the Pope does not act through formal diplomatic channels as the sovereign ruler of the Vatican City State (although he is that); he acts through formal diplomatic channels as the embodiment of the Holy See, as the leader, in other words, of "the supreme organ of government of the [Catholic] Church" (Cardinale 1976, 85).

This status of the Holy See as a juridical actor in international affairs has a long and complex history that I will not recount here (Graham 1959; Duchesne 1908; Hanson 1987). Suffice it to go back only as far as 1929 and the signing of the Lateran Accords by Benito Mussolini for the unified state of Italy and Pope Pius XI for the Catholic Church (Geraud and Pertinax 1929; Kertzer 2014). For many centuries, successive Popes had ruled the so-called Papal States, stretching the Church's "temporal power" across much of central Italy. This territory had been lost by 1929 to the processes of unification and consolidation of the Italian state throughout the Mediterranean peninsula. Indeed from 1870 on, three individual Popes spent over a half century as "prisoners of the Vatican," never leaving the Apostolic Palace and its immediate environs in order to graphically illustrate their refusal to accept the loss of "their" territory.

The agreements signed by Pius and Il Duce in 1929 carved out 113 acres in Rome as a "territory" under the "leadership" of the papacy. More specifically, Italy formally recognized that the Holy See has "full ownership, exclusive and absolute power, and sovereign jurisdiction over the Vatican." The understanding, at the time and since, is that the territorial integrity and legal autonomy of Vatican City exist as the logistical and geographic guarantors of the integrity and autonomy of the Holy See itself. Rule over a microstate in Rome is not the source of the Pope's legal and diplomatic standing. But rule over that microstate is the necessary condition for the endurance of that legal and diplomatic standing. The Pope is a "juridical actor" in international relations as the embodiment of the hierarchical leadership of the Catholic Church. Vatican City was created in order to make sure that the Pope would never have his status threatened by having to live and "rule" under some other state's forbearance.

I will turn shortly to the significance of this legal status, and to the many ways in which the Holy See participates, as a non-territorial sovereign entity, in diplomatic relations. But I want to stress from the beginning that this is not the only way that the Pope and the Holy See participate in world politics. I want also to draw our attention to the ways in which the Pope is able to transform into political activity and influence the simple fact that he leads a transnational church that is for all intents and purposes present throughout the globe. As the US Embassy to the Holy See once put it in a report to President George W. Bush: "the Vatican is one of the very few sovereign entities that have a presence and reach in virtually every country of the world" (*The Guardian* 2010). This means that the Pope and his Church have "interests" pretty much everywhere, and that they have institutional presence and resources in virtually any political context that one could imagine. Note also how unusual in this context is the term "sovereign" to describe an entity that has "presence and reach in virtually every country of the world."

Moreover, a related significance of this universal presence is that Catholic religious leaders and Catholic communities participate as domestic actors in a wide array of political contexts that can often have international ramifications. To be sure, there are no actual "national" or "autocephalous" churches in the Catholic tradition as there are in the Eastern Orthodox tradition (Meyendorff 1966). Unlike that tradition which encompasses the Russian Orthodox Church, the Greek Orthodox Church and several others, there is in a deep institutional sense only one Roman Catholic Church. What this means in actual ecclesiastical terms is that there is no such actual thing as the Polish Catholic Church or the US Catholic Church or the Nicaraguan Catholic Church. But the experience of Catholic leaders and believers in these three national contexts (each of which we will return to later, by the way) makes the point that "the Pope's Church" (itself an awkward phrase) involves itself at all levels of world politics, as well as at the various structural intersecting points of national politics and international relations.

Finally, I will look here at how the Pope plays a role in world politics as a function of the very fact that he is, well, the Pope. One of the best known human beings on earth, and in the words of a US Embassy report to President Obama, a spiritual leader who "wield[s] an unparalleled moral megaphone" (*The Guardian* 2010a) various Popes at various times have exercised what Nye (2004) has famously termed "soft power." "Hard power" is what we traditionally think of as state capacity, and is based in traditional measures of "military and economic might," and sometimes exercised through "inducements ('carrots') or threats ('sticks')" (5). But Nye defined a "second face of power," that "rests on the ability to shape the preferences of others" (5). This "soft power," Nye argued, involves "getting others to want the outcomes that you want [by] coopt[ing] people rather than coerc[ing] them." It is, he continued, "the ability to attract, and attraction often leads to acquiescence" (6). Today's Pope Francis seems particularly interested in playing this aspect of his papal role with gusto. While always careful to couch his pronouncements and interventions in terms of moral teaching rather than political exhortation, the former Jorge Mario Bergoglio of Argentina has aggressively and persistently inserted himself—and by extension the Church he leads—into global policy debates on issues ranging from climate change, to migration, to the role of the family, to the definitions of economic justice and injustice.

Diplomatic Relations

To start with its most formal international role, however, the Holy See currently conducts official diplomatic relations with 182 countries. That means that territorially defined states from Albania to Zimbabwe send ambassadors to Rome to represent their interests formally before the Supreme Pontiff of the Catholic Church and his institutional bureaucracy known as the Roman curia. In return, the Pope sends his own diplomatic representatives, commonly known as nuncios, to capitals in all corners of the globe. These nuncios (who also represent the Pope in his dealings with the Catholic clergy and faithful of a given country) are fully accredited members of a legitimately sovereign entity, and in many national settings they play the ceremonial role of Dean of the local diplomatic corps. On the other side of the coin, ambassadors *to* rather than *from* the Holy See are similarly accredited members of the diplomatic corps, generally working from embassies in Rome, residing in official ambassadorial residences, and working on a regular basis with members of the curial Section for Relations of States in the Secretariat of State in Vatican City.

It is tempting to dismiss all of this official scaffolding as little more than a stage set on which colorfully dressed functionaries play outdated roles in a well-choreographed but not all that meaningful ballet. But such a view would obscure the many ways and many instances in which Popes have actually used the unique access their diplomatic status affords them to bend world affairs at least a bit in their preferred direction. One example involved the Holy See's role in bestowing formal diplomatic relations in 1992 to the breakaway Yugoslav Republics of Croatia and Slovenia. Germany, and then the rest of the European Union, followed closely behind the Holy See's example (in fact Germany formally announced its intentions before the Holy See acted). But the decision by Pope John Paul II to offer recognition to Slovenia and Croatia, and the diplomatic role that his "Foreign Minister," Archbishop Jean-Louis Tauran, played in acknowledging and legitimizing the independence of the two predominantly Catholic elements of Yugoslavia, were significant political factors at the time (Cowell 1992). The subsequent Croatian Ambassador to the Holy See may be forgiven for a bit of hyperbole in terming Archbishop Tauran's support as "decisive" in terms of bringing about Croatian independence (Sunjic 1999, Personal interview with author, October 16). But less obviously self-interested parties agreed with the general thrust of the Ambassador's judgment. French President Francois Mitterrand, for one, alleged a pro-Croatian conspiracy between the Holy See and Germany, and reportedly told Archbishop Tauran personally that the Holy See's formal diplomatic recognition of independent Croatia and Slovenia was directly responsible for the breakup of the Yugoslav Federation (Weigel 1999, 652–653).

It is interesting to note here, moreover, that this was not a case of the Holy See acting as some sort of disinterested moral arbiter of political processes and structures. To the contrary, Celestine Migliore—now an Archbishop and the Pope's nuncio to Russia, but then the Holy See's Undersecretary for Relations with States—was at the time anything but shy about acknowledging that the Holy See's interest in Slovenia and Croatia's independence was grounded in the fact that the populations of those two Yugoslav Republics were predominantly Roman Catholic. Declaring that it was "normal that the Holy See would intervene in cases where the interests of Catholic states were involved," Migliore admitted (if that is the right word) that "the Holy See's favoring of Catholic communities is natural, normal" (Migliore 1999, Personal interview with author, October 15). A cable from the US Embassy to the Holy See in 2001 captured this wholly unique status when it described in telling terms the primary "'national' self-interest" of the Holy See as seeking "to protect Catholics around the world, its own position of influence, and its vast wealth" (*The Guardian* 2010). Note, again, the telling use of the phrase "national self-interest" to describe the preferences and actions of a transnational, non-territorial religious entity.

The Holy See's diplomatic role, however, goes well beyond the formal matter of legal recognition. A number of years ago, Wikileaks released a huge number of diplomatic cables that shone a unique light on how the US and many other countries conduct international affairs away from the media's lights and cameras. Included in these documents were a number of internal documents from the US State Department that highlighted the depth and breadth of interactions between the US and the Holy See as routed through the relevant embassies in Washington and Rome. So-called scene setters sent by embassy officials in Rome to the White House in anticipation of presidential audiences with Supreme Pontiffs, for example, were full scale reviews of the role played in world affairs by "The Vatican—The Supranational Power."

Particular attention was given by the authors of these memos to "areas in which we can work constructively with the Vatican" as well as "areas in which we should expect continued difficulties." A cable prepared for Barack Obama in 2009, for example, lauded the US President's upcoming visit to "the world's smallest sovereign state, and one with global clout" (*The Guardian* 2010a). The issues mentioned in the "scene setter" ran the gamut from "bioethical issues" and the global "financial crisis" through "food security," "environmental issues," and "arms reduction," to specific national and regional matters such as the "Middle East Peace Process," "Iraq and Christians," "Africa," "Cuba," and "Turkey EU Accession."

Other cables dealt with matters as diverse as the Holy See's potential influence on US–Cuba relations (a subject to which I will return), the legal, political, and financial implications of the Church's sexual abuse scandal in the US and elsewhere, and the possibility that the Bush 43 administration and "the Vatican" could work together in encouraging the international community to ban human cloning, a practice opposed at the time by both President George W. Bush and Pope John Paul II. While this issue might not rise to the status of high international politics, the interesting thing about this particular cable from the Embassy at the Holy See to the State Department was that it focused predominantly on discussion of "the opportunity the Holy See's United Nations (UN) mission had, particularly among predominantly Catholic countries to expand support for [a General Assembly] resolution banning all forms of embryonic cloning." A representative of the Holy See's Secretariat of State, in a consultation with embassy officials, "observed that while the Holy See would concentrate on the moral side of the argument, the US might be able to sway some [UN] missions by being more aggressive in making the scientific case for alternatives to embryonic stem cell research" (*The Guardian* 2010b).

Permanent Observer

I am emphasizing this discussion of votes in the General Assembly in order to highlight the truly remarkable circumstance that the Holy See —a non-territorial sovereign entity—also enjoys the status and access of being an official

Permanent Observer at the UN. One of only two so-designated Permanent Observers (the other being Palestine), this means that the Holy See "has received a standing invitation to participate as [an] observer in the sessions and the work of the General Assembly and maintain [a] permanent observer mission at Headquarters" (United Nations 2003). Again, it is important to emphasize here that the entity enjoying this Observer status is the Holy See (the ecclesiastical leadership of the Roman Catholic Church embodied in the Supreme Pontiff) and not the territorial microstate of Vatican City (Chong and Troy 2011; Gratsch 1997). This definitional matter was discussed at length, by the way, at the time the Holy See was welcomed to the UN in 1964. It was agreed by both sides that granting Observer status to Vatican City would lead to an over-emphasis on limited matters related to territorial sovereignty (Cardinale 1976, 256). Admitting the Holy See, on the other hand, would make clear that the Catholic Church, as such, was being welcomed to offer its views and extend its influence to the full range of political, social, and economic issues facing the human family.

In formal terms, being a "Permanent Observer" at the UN means that the Holy See is accorded "the rights and privileges of participation and work of the General Assembly and the international conferences convened under the auspices of the Assembly or other organs of the UN, as well as [other] United Nations conferences" (United Nations 2003). That this is a "privilege" not granted to other religious bodies or other religious or secular non-governmental organizations (NGOs) almost goes without saying. Though the Holy See cannot actually vote in General Assembly sessions, its representatives can participate in debates, have their interventions included in official recordings of proceedings, and co-sponsor resolutions "that make reference to the Holy See." But the clear "inequality of actor-ness," as one account phrased it (Chong and Troy 2011, 339), between the Holy See and other non-territorial entities is most clearly manifest in the fact that the Holy See is welcomed as a full member "state" at UN-sponsored conferences, where much of the UN's most significant work in the contemporary era actually takes place. While in the words of one critic, other NGOs "must collar delegates in hallways and restrooms to make their points" (Omang 2013, 20), Holy See representatives are "automatically considered to be a state for the purpose of the conference" (Abdullah 1996, 1844). The Pope's delegations enjoy full access to conference agendas and reports, and exercise full voting rights in the context of proceedings that often seek to operate by global consensus.

The Global Is Local

As I indicated in the opening section of this article, the international political roles of the Holy See and the Pope stretch far beyond the confines of these formal diplomatic matters, regardless of how remarkable and pervasive they are. The Pope, in addition to his leadership of the global diplomatic corps and the Roman Curia, is also the uncontested central leader of a religious community numbering over a billion souls and present in virtually every corner of the globe. This global community is overseen and led in specific national contexts by Catholic bishops who are themselves members of a global "catholic" episcopacy under the authoritative (in some limited contexts purportedly infallible!) leadership of the Supreme Pontiff of the Roman Catholic Church. What this means in practice is that the Holy See's organic connections to local bishops amount to another avenue for participation in relations among states. These local hierarchies can at times be fairly significant players in the domestic political processes of given states. And as a matter of day-to-day "governance" of the Church, the role of local bishops and/or national bishops' conferences is often shaped in significant ways by the levers of authority held at the Vatican. Three brief examples should be sufficient to make this important point.

Poland

The first involves the part that the Polish Pope, John Paul II, played in shaping the deeply significant role that Polish bishops played in the transition to democracy in Poland, and in the relationship that subsequently developed between

Poland and the rest of the "European community." It is by now a truism to argue that the Catholic Church played a significant role in precipitating the downfall of communism in Poland, or at the very least in providing crucial institutional and societal support to the trade union activists and public intellectuals who actually carried out the revolution (Osa 1997). The Catholic Church was for centuries a central player in Polish society and politics, and its role in maintaining relatively free space within which an authentic Polish national identity could withstand the indignities and imperial oppression of Soviet communism has been well documented (Michnik 1993; Szajkowski 1983). But the fact that the Roman Catholic College of Cardinals placed a living embodiment of that national identity on the throne of St. Peter in October 1978 was a crucial factor in how the Church approached communism—from Warsaw no less than from Rome—and in how the Church envisioned the geo-political status of Poland (and the rest of East Central Europe) once the ideological divisions of the European continent had been torn down.

Pope John Paul II used all the levers of his global position to advance the revolutionary events taking place in his homeland. And one of those levers, of course, was the diplomatic relationships that the Pope could engage in with significant state actors like the Reagan Administration in the US. But at the same time, Pope John Paul II also exercised the power of the papacy and influenced events in East Central Europe through his authoritative leadership of the Polish Catholic hierarchy itself. From the moment he accepted his fellow cardinals' summons to occupy the papal throne, Karol Wojtyla, as Pope John Paul II, effectively became the central figure of Polish Catholicism, institutionally and politically. He remained deeply and constantly involved in the ecclesiastical affairs of his home church; he appointed his successor as Archbishop of Krakow and in time the successor to Cardinal Stefan Wyszynski as Polish Primate as well; and just as he acted as Pope to transform the relative conciliation of his predecessor's Ostpolitik into a vision of actual revolution in the Communist states of Europe, so he also moved his brother bishops in Poland to a more open and uncompromising embrace of the possibility of real and lasting change.

Those Polish bishops were not merely the Pope's pawns, of course; they remained participants in the teaching magisterium of the Church in their one right. But over the course of roughly 25 historic years—from the founding of Solidarity in 1980 through Poland's entrance into the European Union in 2004—the political voice of the Catholic Church in Poland was amplified by the megaphone held by their leader at the Holy See and also, in substantive terms, given specific shape by his uncompromising vision of change. And in that way, his own role in these events in European history were shaped not only by Pope John Paul II's extraordinary use of papal diplomacy and soft power, but also by his organic relationship with the Church's leadership structure "on the ground" in Poland and elsewhere in East Central Europe.

The United States

The Holy See has had a long and complex relationship with the US. For much of American history, formal diplomatic relations with "the Vatican" were precluded by a powerful admixture of anti-Catholicism and devotion to a particular understanding of the separation between church and state. Franklin Roosevelt sidestepped these objections during World War II when he appointed Myron Taylor as his "personal emissary" to Pope Pius XII, holed up in a Vatican city–state that was then widely considered an indispensable listening post and Allied geostrategic asset. Harry Truman's efforts after the war to replace Taylor with General Matthew Clark as a formal ambassador to the Holy See came to naught, but in time Ronald Reagan was finally able to establish formal diplomatic relations in 1984. The story of these diplomatic relations is a fascinating one, often told by observers and participants alike (Melady 1994; Rooney 2013; Taylor 1947). But here I want to focus, as in the Polish case, not so much on the formal relationship between the Holy See and the US government, but instead on the relationship between the Holy See and the American Catholic hierarchy, and on how that relationship—and the papacy's authoritative place in it—has provided individual Popes with another avenue in which to participate in global affairs (Byrnes 1991, 92–107).

In the early 1980s, the US Catholic bishops conference embarked upon a formal collective teaching exercise that resulted in 1983 with the promulgation of a "Pastoral Letter" entitled "The Challenge of Peace: God's Promise and Our Response." The subject of the letter was nuclear weapons and the role they ought (or more accurately ought not) to play in US defense policy. Concerned by what they interpreted as a lessening commitment to nuclear arms control by the new Reagan Administration in Washington, and frankly alarmed by what they took to be an increased confidence that nuclear weapons might actually be constructively used in war, the US bishops set out to fulfill the Second Vatican Council's call to apply the lessons of the Gospel to "the signs of the times" by (a) clearly articulating the appropriate principles concerning nuclear weaponry that ought be derived from Catholic teaching on war and peace and (b) applying those principles to some of the most specific and pressing questions facing the US as it continued its decades long nuclear face-off with the Soviet Union.

"The Challenge of Peace" (NCCB/USCC 1984) was a very strongly worded call for a rejection of complacency concerning the threat of nuclear war, and an unambiguous insistence that Catholic teaching—properly understood and appropriately applied—posed a stark challenge to the US government and its policies regarding the possession and/or use of nuclear weapons. Ranging widely across the breadth of US defense doctrine, the American Catholic hierarchy (among other pronouncements) stated that "under no circumstances may nuclear weapons ... be used for the purpose of destroying population centers or other predominantly civilian targets"; (532) declared that they did "not perceive any situation in which the deliberate initiation of nuclear warfare, on however restricted a scale, can be morally justified" (533); and urged negotiations between the US and the Soviet Union to "halt the testing, production, and deployment of new nuclear systems" (548).

"The Challenge of Peace" still stands as one of the most forthright interventions by the Catholic hierarchy into a public policy debate in the history of the US. But what interests me here is not so much what the bishops had to say, but rather how what they ultimately could say was shaped by Pope John Paul II and other leading officials of the Holy See. More specifically, the American Catholic bishops were powerfully constrained in what they could actually say on this topic by what their Supreme Pontiff had said previously. Catholic bishops are by virtue of their episcopal ordinations members of the collegial magisterium of their Church. But they are not free to articulate Catholic teachings or even applications of Catholic teaching that directly contradict clear statements by the Pope. In this context, that meant that no matter how skeptical the US bishops may have been about the morality of nuclear deterrence as a centerpiece of US defense policy—and they were very skeptical indeed—they were not free to denounce the practice of nuclear deterrence itself. Just a year before the US bishops drafted their pastoral letter, Pope John Paul II had portentously declared that "in current conditions, 'deterrence' based on balance, certainly not as an end in itself but as a step on the way toward progressive disarmament, may still be judged morally acceptable" (NCCB/USCC 1984, 539). Despite enormous skepticism concerning the moral appropriateness of deterrence within the US conference, therefore, the final US pastoral letter document could not avoid concluding that "a balance of forces preventing either side from achieving superiority, can be seen as safeguarding" against the danger of nuclear war *and* the independence of vulnerable nations (540). Hemmed in by their Pope, as it were, the US bishops grudgingly offered their "strictly conditioned moral acceptance of nuclear deterrence," while also stressing that they did not "consider it adequate as a long-term basis of peace" (543).

Nicaragua

To be sure, the application of Catholic teaching to specific circumstances can show some legitimate variance from national context to national context. But as the Polish and US examples have illustrated, Popes have at their disposal several levers of internal institutional power that can allow them if they so choose to fundamentally shape those applications in ways that have ramifications in international relations as well as domestic political affairs. Perhaps nowhere was this complex dynamic more clearly played out than in the efforts that Pope John Paul II expended in setting limitations on the influence of Liberation Theology in Latin America.

Liberation Theology is a Catholic mode of thought (and related action) that was born out of the social, economic, and political inequalities of Latin America (Gutierrez 1971). Grounded in the strong belief that the Christian Gospel is inconsistent with the structures and practices that created and sustained these inequalities, and devoted to the so-called preferential option for the poor, Liberation Theology came rather quickly to define for much of the clergy and laity of the region the role that the Catholic Church should play in the revolutions (both real and symbolic) playing out in the 1970s and 1980s across Central and South America.

Pope John Paul II saw two fundamental problems with Liberation Theology, as such. The first was that he rejected any depiction and analysis of societal relations based in an understanding of inevitable conflicts between social classes. Viewing such an understanding as grounded in Marxist thought that he presumed to be antithetical to Christianity, the former Karol Wojtyla of Krakow preferred to work toward the conversion of all participants in social and economic structures and for the reconciliation of individual and communal relationships across class lines (Weigel 1999, 281–287).

Second, John Paul II harbored deep concerns about the legitimacy and appropriateness of what came to be called throughout the region "the people's church." First articulated during a period of cozy cronyism between state and church across Latin America, Liberation Theology called for and celebrated so-called Christian Base Communities, small groups of believers who met (often without the "benefit" of clerical leadership) for the purposes of religious consciousness raising, mutual support, and political mobilization. In some contexts, these CBCs became the primary organized articulation of local Catholicism, as groups of laypersons and supportive lower clergy worked to form an expression of Catholicism and "Church" that was often as distinctive politically from local bishops as it was unmoored from those bishops' formal lines of institutional authority. For Pope John Paul II, all of this represented a dangerous form of independence and autonomy that would challenge the appropriate lines of authority from the Vatican through the episcopacy, just as it would at the same time allow for very different applications of Catholic social teaching to domestic political challenges.

These dynamics were multi-faceted and provocatively complex. I cannot do them justice in a few paragraphs, nor do my purposes here require an attempt to do so. But what I do want to point out is that Pope John Paul II's efforts to reign in the political and ecclesiastical effects of Liberation Theology led him to use all of the levers of papal authority at his disposal to control and shape from the Holy See the ways in which local bishops, clergy, and laity articulated and applied Catholic teaching. The first and probably the most basic of these levers was the Pope's purposeful and clearly understood use of his power of episcopal appointment. Indeed, the simple fact that Catholic Popes personally choose and empower each and every bishop across the globe is a crucial element of the institutional centralization that is a defining feature of the Roman Church. In this case, the men that John Paul II chose to replace iconic figures like Archbishop Camara in Brazil or Archbishop Romero in El Salvador were at one in the same time practical reins on the influence of Liberation Theology in those countries and symbolic refutations of it from Rome.

Second, Pope John Paul II made aggressive use of his status as the authoritative voice of the Catholic magisterium to "silence" in practical terms liberationist voices within the Church, while at the same time sending clear signals as to what was an acceptable application of the Gospel and what was an illegitimate distortion of it. Brazilian Franciscan Leonardo Boff was not the only liberation theologian called on the carpet of the Holy See's Congregation for the Doctrine of the Faith in Rome, but his treatment there was surely the most instructive. Informed that the "relativizing logic" at the heart of his book *Church: Charism and Power* "endanger[ed] the doctrine of the faith," Father Boff was sentenced to a year of silence for "adequate reflection," and prohibited from publishing or speaking in public on matters related to his theological work (Congregation for the Doctrine of the Faith 1985).

Popes, bishops, and priests had always conflicted with each other on the finer points of theology. The very word "Inquisition" makes the historical background clear. But what was different in the modern era was that a Pope like John Paul II could not only interfere from Rome with publications or statements that he deemed problematic from an institutional or theological point of view. Now, with the possibilities offered by "television and the jet age," a Pope who was inclined to do so could "in effect, replace a local bishop," as one close observer phrased it (Hebblethwaite 1995, 115). The Pope, in other words, could travel to the local setting, publicly admonish local clergy he found wanting, and communicate directly to the local faithful what its clerical leadership was and was not authorized to do or advocate in the name of the Church. In the Spring of 1983, for example, John Paul traveled to Nicaragua and loudly (and I literally mean in the loud voice of a vigorous man) denied the Christian character of the Sandinista revolution, publicly ordered Nicaraguan priests serving in the Sandinista government to "make themselves right with the Church," and engaged in what amounted to a shouting match with Sandinista supporters protesting (during Mass!) his delineation of the ways in which Liberation Theology and the Nicaraguan revolution misappropriated the Catholic Church and its teachings (Weigel 1999, 451–457).

AT A FUNDAMENTAL LEVEL, THE POPE'S ROLE IN DEFINING AND DISCUSSING GLOBAL ISSUES IS UNLIKE THAT OF ANY OTHER MORAL LEADER OR CELEBRITY ACTIVIST

For centuries, local Catholic leaders across Latin America (with the complicity of the Holy See) had firmly placed their Church on the side of the moneyed and propertied interests in a system of systemic inequality and oppression. Obviously, this had enormous political significance in local domestic consequences. The central religious institution of many individual countries was conspiring, as it were, to keep the peasantry and the urban poor powerless and silent. Liberation Theology and its "preferential option for the poor" was (and is) an effort to reorient that emphasis and redress those wrongs by not only placing the instrumentalities of the Church on the side of the dispossessed, but also by preaching that those dispossessed are themselves *the* Church in its deepest meaning, free to organize and act as Christians independent from the Church's hierarchical structures and even in opposition to them if necessary. Pope John Paul II's effort to blunt that reorientation—or at least to channel it in ways more consistent with his own views on political economy and ecclesiology—had significant ramifications in the individual countries like Nicaragua where these struggles were being waged in day-to-day politics. But the Polish Pope's interventions in places like Nicaragua also had global political implications in an era of superpower competition where every national civil conflict was defined at least in part as a constituent element of a bipolar struggle for global influence.

Soft Power

The Pope is a global celebrity, and his words and actions receive the media and public attention common to that status. But at a fundamental level, the Pope's role in defining and discussing global issues is unlike that of any other moral leader or celebrity activist. As the embodiment of the sovereign entity known as the Holy See, the Supreme Pontiff of the Roman Catholic Church speaks and acts from the multi-faceted legal and institutional platform that I have been describing throughout this article. Pope Francis leads a global church with unparalleled geographic breadth and enormous institutional resources; he also has personal representatives at the UN, sends full participants to global inter-*state* conferences, and maintains bilateral diplomatic relations with state actors of great international scope and significant political influence.

I want to look briefly at three policy areas—climate change, refugee reception, and definition of marriage—and focus on the current Pope's efforts to marshal his institutional, legal, and moral resources in support of an exercise of soft power in favor of his preferred policy emphases. In this context, the actual effects of the Pope's words and actions—like all effects of "soft power"—are notoriously hard to gauge. Nevertheless, his every utterance is intensely covered by the global media, and his voice is greatly magnified by the institutional mechanisms and sovereign standing of his global church. One scholar (Casanova 1997) has called the Pope (any Pope) "the first citizen of the emerging global civil society" (131) and the current Pope is an active participant in several sharp public debates that at the moment straddle the borders of national policy and global norms. In that structural context, his own global standing and national institutional reach make him a moral leader whose exercise of soft power is very much worthy of our attention.

Climate Change

Given the dire warnings emanating from the transnational scientific community, it is no wonder that Catholic Popes have been speaking out for some time on this issue and its grave significance for the future of humankind. But Pope Francis has upped the ante, as it were, in a number of ways. For one thing, his statements have been more frequent and much sharper in tone than any of his predecessors were. The reality of climate change and the need to address it aggressively could be defined, in fact, as one of the central emphases of Francis' pontificate to date. The Pope has repeatedly referred to faithful stewardship of "God's creation" as one of the central responsibilities of all authentic Christians in our modern world. And in a formal encyclical entitled *Laudato Si'* Francis placed himself and the Holy See squarely on the side of those calling for profound changes in the relationship between humankind and "our common home" (Laudato Si' 2017).

What makes Francis' various statements on climate and stewardship distinctive to him and most notable, however, is the ways in which he applies to the issue his moral voice as the authoritative leader of a large, global religious community. Commemorating 2016's World Day of Prayer for the Care of Creation, for example, Francis, like many other world leaders, denounced the role that human beings are playing in contaminating the earth and squandering its resources. But turning to explicitly religious terminology that has particular resonance and significance within his own Catholic tradition, the Pope also decreed that "to commit a crime against the natural world is [to commit] a sin against ourselves and a sin against God" (Richardson 2016). Moreover, Pope Francis has repeatedly defined the scope of this "sin" as not only a violation of the Christian responsibility to steward creation, but also as a violation of *the* central Christian social obligation to protect and minister to the poor. "The world's poor," he has said, "though least responsible for climate change, are most vulnerable and already suffering its impact" (Richardson 2016). In his most authoritative statement on the subject, *Laudato Si'*, the Pope listed many ways in which various effects of the climate changes caused by the consumption practices of the complacent rich pose particular dangers to the most innocent and most vulnerable members of the human community. And he pointedly lauded "those who tirelessly seek to resolve the tragic effects of environmental degradation on the lives of the world's poorest" (Laudato Si' 2017). The first Pope from the Global South has made abundantly clear that climate change ought to be a central concern for all Christians because in his view insatiable appetites for fossil-fueled energy and purposeful disregard for the catastrophic despoiling of air and water are disrespectful responses to God's gift of creation. The Argentine Pope has made equally clear, however, that such appetites and such disregard are also tantamount to unconscionable attacks on the lives and well-being of the very people whom Christians should actively be seeking to protect, nurture, and love.

Refugees

If possible, the ways in which Francis defines the world's contemporary refugee and migration crises, and the ways in which he calls Catholics and other Christians to respond to the "stranger" at their door is even more radical in tone, even more concretely political in effect, and even more deeply grounded in the central tenets of his religion than his comments on the environment are. As he put it most bluntly in an apparently direct response to Donald Trump's oft-stated plan to build a "big beautiful wall" on the US border with Mexico: "A person who thinks only about building walls, wherever they may be, and not building bridges, is not Christian. This is not the gospel" (Yardley 2016). Francis does not speak on this issue as a political leader seeking nuance or consensus on a complex policy matter; he speaks, instead, as a religious leader articulating what he sees as the clear policy implications of a central religious teaching of his Church. Particularly in the European context where Britain's UKIP, France's National Front, and the governments of countries like Hungary and Poland have been fomenting political opposition to refugees and other migrants, the Pope has stood as a prominent voice for the simple proposition that Christians *must* as a matter of religious obligation welcome vulnerable strangers when they arrive at their borders.

"Migrants and refugees are not pawns on the chessboard of humanity," the Pope declared in a representative statement in 2013. "They are children, women, men who leave or are forced to leave their homes for various reasons" (Allen 2013). Migrants, he said during a dramatic visit to the Greek island of Lesbos in Spring of 2016, "are first of all persons who have faces, names, and individual stories," members of a human race "that before all else recognizes others as brothers and sisters" (Winters 2016). Christians *are* their brothers and sisters' keeper, the Pope is saying, and refugees are just that, brothers and sisters in need. And although the Pope does not have to satisfy a national constituency or navigate electoral politics when he addresses the question of how refugees should be treated by European states, he does have sovereign instruments at hand that allow him to offer symbolic examples of how he believes elected leaders of those states ought to behave. During his visit to Lesbos, for example, he pointedly offered three Syrian families legal asylum at the Holy See, and then ferried those refugees back to Vatican City on his plane (Witte and Faiola 2016). Very few political leaders would be free to articulate such an uncompromising position on this freighted issue. And no other religious leader would have such a legal instrument of sovereignty at his disposal.

Definition of Marriage

Lest I leave the impression that the Pope raises his sovereign religious voice only in support of policy positions associated with progressive social movements, it is also important to note the ways in which the Pope uses the prominent platforms of his celebrity and institution to advance a number of socially conservative causes as well. During Francis' pontificate to date, the most prominent example of this phenomenon has been the Pope's efforts to resist the re-definition of marriage to include same-sex unions. Many misunderstood the Pope's intentions in this regard when early in his pontificate he was quoted as saying "Who am I to judge" in the context of discussing homosexuality. The problem, however, was that Francis was responding to a very specific question about same-sex attraction among clergy—not about homosexuality in general—and that he was engaging in a particularly colorfully expressed reiteration of the Church's distinction between same-sex preference as a personal identity and same-sex activity and relationships as a concrete circumstance (Donadio 2013).

Regardless of his views on sexual preference as a matter of personal morality and Church doctrine, however, the Pope has been unambiguous in his affirmation of his Church's teaching that "there are absolutely no grounds for considering homosexual unions to be in any way similar or even remotely analogous to God's plan for marriage and family" (Crux Staff 2015). And in an action that made clear whose side the Catholic Pope is on, as it were, in the global culture war over marriage equality, Francis released a joint statement of the Patriarch of the Russian Orthodox Church expressing "regret that other forms of cohabitation have been placed on the same level as this union [between a man and a woman]."

Conclusion

Sovereignty, supranationalism, and soft power, this is the unique constellation of resources and status that the Holy See brings to its participation in global politics. Nearly a century removed from the Lateran Accords, Catholic pontiffs still preside over an independent city–state at the center of Rome that serves as the guarantor of the broadly recognized sovereignty of the Holy See. On the basis of that sovereignty, Pope Francis, like his predecessors, is able to engage in bilateral diplomatic relationships with most countries in the world, participate actively in multi-lateral institutions and conferences, and work through "official" channels of all kinds to advance the interests of his Church as he defines them. It is, to put it bluntly, an astounding platform for a religious leader, any religious leader, to possess.

At the same time, the Catholic Pontiff also sits atop a transnational Church of unparalleled scope and breadth. Often deeply enmeshed in the cultural and political lives of individual countries, Catholic Bishops Conferences and individual prelates play significant roles in national contexts as diverse as Poland, Nicaragua, the Philippines, and yes, the US. The close relationship between these national actors and the Holy See dramatically multiplies the presence of the latter on the world stage, and offers the papacy the opportunity to affect world politics by influencing the non-Church actors who are the central players on the global stage. It is not just that certain national political processes cannot be fully understood without reference to the role that the "local" Catholic Church plays in them; it is also that global debates and global diplomacy are themselves arenas of participation by the Catholic Church because national delegations to them come from places where the voice of the Holy See is clearly and powerfully expressed.

Finally, of course, the role of the Holy See is shaped and in some ways defined by the development of the modern papacy into a megaphone of global celebrity and soft power. Catholic historians will long debate the effects that John Paul II (the second longest serving Pope in history) had (and will have) on the institutional structures and doctrinal strictures of his Church. But what already seems beyond contradiction is that John Paul II's decision to define his papacy through constant travel and aggressive use of his own personal presence as an instrument of institutional centralization has had world historic consequences for the nature of the papal role in global politics.

I want to end this examination of the Pope's participation in global politics with a brief look at a circumstance that highlights both the complexity of the political dynamics at the heart of contemporary international affairs and the variety of the tools available to the transnational Catholic Church for ensuring its participation in those complex dynamics. I am referring to the Holy See's role in facilitating the resumption of formal diplomatic relations between the US and Cuba. The Holy See has served from time to time as a forum of international mediation in cases where parties to a dispute have either sought or accepted the "good offices" of the Pope as a forum, as it were, for conflict resolution. But the Holy See's role in facilitating talks between the US and Cuba illustrated with particular clarity the three paths of political participation I have been highlighting in this article. Moreover, this case also shows how these three paths can intersect with each other, and place the Holy See and the Pope at the very center of international political processes of great significance. The Holy See had diplomatic relations with the US and Cuba; local Catholic leaders in both countries played significant political roles in their respective political settings and were able to cooperate with each other as "brother bishops" in the transnational Catholic Church; and a determined Latin American Pope, trusted on all sides, had made clear through his own prominent public statements that he viewed the continuing estrangement across ninety miles of the Florida Straits to be politically nonsensical and morally unacceptable.

There is no need for me to rehearse here the tortured history of relations between the USA and

Cuba. Suffice it to say that by 2010 fifty years of fractured diplomatic relations, trade embargo, and mutual recrimination rendered the US–Cuban relationship one of the most dysfunctional bilateral relationships in the world. We now know that Barack Obama came to office in 2009 hoping to engineer a breakthrough that would restore relations with Cuba and remove from the agenda of US foreign policy (and domestic politics) one of the most intractable and confounding issues in American public life (LeoGrande and Kornbluh 2015, 418–453). Desire for a change in policy, however, was in the case of Cuba not nearly enough. Faced with enduring truculence and hostility from Havana, and hemmed in by a domestic political context that made any attempt even to communicate with the Castros unacceptable, Obama spent frustrating years probing any and all opportunities to open channels to the Cuban government that might lead to direct discussions, negotiations, and agreements. In this context, it is not surprising that President Obama ultimately accepted offers of mediation from the Holy See that included personal intervention by the Pope, clandestine meetings in Rome, and perhaps most importantly, high-level courier service by Cuban and American prelates (LeoGrande and Kornbluh 2015, 442–447).

In our age of instantaneous electronic communication—and constant threats of hacking—it is crucial to acknowledge in this case how difficult and politically risky it was for the Presidents of Cuba and the US to communicate with each other directly. Barack Obama could not call Fidel (and then Raul) Castro on the phone or e-mail them in order to suggest a thaw in relations; nor could he rely on usual diplomatic channels—even non-direct back channels—to signal a new willingness to engage with his Cuban counterparts. Any perception within politically important communities in the US that the American President was approaching the Cuban government and proposing a change in the status of the relationship between the two countries held the very real possibility of blowing up in the president's face.

But the Holy See enjoyed formal diplomatic relations with both the US and Cuba. The Pope could and did communicate in complete diplomatic confidence with both sides of the fractured relationship, encouraging them "to resolve humanitarian questions of common interest, including the situation of certain prisoners, in order to initiate a new phase in relations" (Hooper 2014). At the same time, as the first Lain American Pope in history, Francis had a particular interest in the position of Cuba on the world stage (as well as of course the status of the Church within the Communist state), and a clear desire to use his moral authority and the trust he enjoyed from both sides to advance the potential for an historic agreement. And once the Pope had taken the initiative of encouraging President Obama and President Castro to consider forging a new path, the transnational networks at the very heart of the modern Catholic Church were set in motion.

Jaime Cardinal Ortega of Havana, Theodore Cardinal McCarrick of Washington DC, and Sean Cardinal O'Malley of Boston are prominent examples of the complex identities and complex interconnections that define the modern Catholic hierarchy, identities, and interconnections that present unique opportunities for meaningful participation in International Relations. Shuttling from Rome to Washington to Havana, these three members of an exclusive transnational College of Cardinals carried and delivered messages of encouragement from their Supreme Pontiff, and received messages of wary willingness from leaders of two countries that had not had direct relations in over a half century (Hooper 2014; Vallely 2015).

Most news accounts of the Catholic Church's role in the US–Cuba thaw stress Pope Francis' personal interventions with Presidents Obama and Castro, and the Holy See's role as host to direct secret talks in Rome that led to long sought after prisoner exchanges that opened a path to resumption of diplomatic relations. Those events are clear testament to the diplomatic resources the Holy See could bring to the process and to the personal standing of Pope Francis in both Washington and Havana. But the role of the Catholic Church was more complex (and frankly more interesting) than even those emphases would imply. One of the most indispensable resources the Holy See was able to provide in this context was the service of highly trusted intermediaries who were at one and the same time citizens of the states involved and officials of the institution providing the mediation. Cardinals McCarrick and O'Malley are Americans (or perhaps, in this context, I should say *estadounidenses*) and also bishops of a global church. Cardinal Ortega is their close institutional colleague and a Cuban citizen. And all three have deep personal and professional ties with Pope Francis who heads a sovereign entity that maintains formal diplomatic relations with Cuba and the US. The story of the US–Cuba rapprochement is multi-faceted and should not be reduced in any way to the mediating role of the Holy See and members of the College of Cardinals. But the diplomatic levers that the Holy See could push in two world capitals, the prominent place that the Pope plays on the global stage, and the fascinating institutional relationships at the heart of the Holy See's leadership of the transnational Catholic Church offered Presidents Obama and Castro uniquely relevant "connections" through which they could bring a major diplomatic initiative to fruition. ❖

References

Abdullah, Y. 1996. "The Holy See at United Nations Conferences: State or Church?" *Columbia Law Review* 96 (7): 1835–1875.

Allen, J. L. 2013. "Pope Says Immigrants not Pawns on a Global Chessboard." *National Catholic Reporter*, September 24.

Arangio-Ruiz, G. 1996. "On the Nature of the International Personality of the Holy See." *Revue Belge de Droit International* 1996 (2): 355–369.

Araujo, S. J. 2001. "The International Personality and Sovereignty of the Holy See." *The Catholic University Law Review* 50 (2): 292–336.

Barbato, M. 2013. "A State, a Diplomat, and a Transnational Church." *Perspectives* 21 (2): 27–48.

Bathon, M. N. 2001. "The Atypical International Status of the Holy See." *Vanderbilt Journal of Transitional Law* 34 (3): 597–632.

Byrnes, T. A. 1991. *Catholic Bishops in American Politics*. Princeton, NJ: Princeton University Press.

Cardinale, H. E. 1976. *The Holy See and the International Order*. London: Colin Smythe.

Casanova, J. 1997. "Globalizing Catholicism and Return to a 'Universal Church'." In *Transnational Religion & Fading States*, edited by S. H. Rudolph, and J. Piscatori, 121–143. Boulder,CO: Westview Press.

Chong, A., and J. Troy. 2011. "A Universal Sacred Mission and the Universal Secular Organization: The Holy See and the United Nations." *Politics, Religion, and Ideology* 12 (3): 335–354.

Congregation for the Doctrine of the Faith. 1985. "Notification on the Book Church: Charism and Power by Father Leonardo Boff O.F.M." http://www.vatican.va/roman_curia/congregations/cfaith/documents/rc_con_cfaith_doc_19850311_notif-boff_en.html.

Cowell, A. 1992. "Vatican Formally Recognizes Independence of Croatia and Slovenia." *New York Times*, January 14.

Crux Staff. 2015. "Excerpts from the Synod's Final Report." *Crux*, October 24.

Donadio, R. 2013. "On Gay Priests, Pope Francis Asks, "Who Am I to Judge"." *New York Times*, July 29.

Duchesne, L. 1908. *The Beginnings of the Temporal Sovereignty of the Popes*. London: Kegan, Paul, Trench, Trubner & Co.

Geraud, A., & Pertinax, A. 1929. "The Lateran Treaties: A Step in Vatican Policy." *Foreign Affairs* 7 (4): 571–584.

Graham, R. A. 1959. *Vatican Diplomacy: A Study of Church and State on the International Plane*. Princeton, NJ: Princeton University Press.

Gratsch, E. J. 1997. *The Holy See and the United Nations 1945–1995*. New York: Vantage press.

Gutierrez, G. 1971. *A Theology of Liberation: History, Politics, Salvation*. Maryknoll: Orbis Books.

Hanson, E. O. 1987. *The Catholic Church in World Politics*. Princeton, NJ: Princeton University Press.

Hebblethwaite, P. 1995. *Pope John Paul II and the Church*. Kansas City: Sheed & Ward.

Hooper, J. 2014. "Pope Francis and the Vatican Played Key Roles in US-Cuba Thaw, Leaders Reveal." *The Guardian*, December 17.

Kertzer, D. I. 2014. *The Pope and Mussolini: The Secret History of Pius XI and the Rise of Fascism in Europe*. New York: Random House.

Laudato Si'. 2017. "Encyclical Letter of the Holy Father Francis on Care of Our Common Home." Accessed May 10, 2017. http://w2.vatican.va/content/francesco/en/encyclicals/documents/papa-francesco_20150524_enciclica-laudato-si.html.

LeoGrande, W. M., and P. Kornbluh. 2015. *Back Channel to Cuba: The Hidden History of Negotiations Between Washington and Havana, Updated Edition with a New Epilogue.* Chapel Hill: University of North Carolina Press.

Melady, T. P. 1994. *The Ambassador's Story: The United States and Vatican in World Affairs.* Huntington: Our Sunday Visitor Publishing Division.

Meyendorff, J. 1966. *Orthodoxy and Catholicity.* New York: Shed & Ward.

Michnik, A. 1993. *The Church and the Left.* Chicago, IL: The University of Chicago Press.

NCCB/USCC. 1984. *Pastoral Letters of the United States Catholic Bishops Volume IV 1975–1983.* Washington, DC: United States Catholic Conference.

Nye, J. S. 2004. *Soft Power: The Means to Success in World Politics.* New York: Public Affairs.

Omang, J. 2013. "Playing Hardball Against Women's Rights: The Holy See at the UN." *Conscience (Washington, D C)* 34 (2): 20.

Osa, M. 1997. "Creating Solidarity: The Religious Foundations of the Polish Social Movement." *East European Politics and Societies* 11 (2): 339–365.

Richardson, B. 2016. "Pope Francis Calls Climate Change a 'Sin'." *Washington Times*, September 1.

Rooney, F. 2013. *The Global Vatican: An Inside Look at the Catholic Church, World Politics, and the Extraordinary Relationship Between the United States and the Holy See.* Lanham: Rowman & Littlefield.

Szajkowski, B. 1983. *Next to God … Poland: Politics and Religion in Contemporary Poland.* New York: St. Martin's Press.

Taylor, M. C. 1947. *Wartime Correspondence Between President Roosevelt and Pius XII.* New York: The Macmillan Company.

The Guardian. 2010. "US Embassy Cables: Diplomat Reveals Vatican's 'Unhelpful' Role in Middle East Peace Process." December 10.

The Guardian. 2010a. "US Embassy Cables: Vatican 'Helped Secure Release' of British Sailors Captured by Iran." December 10.

The Guardian. 2010b. "US Embassy Cables: Vatican Backs US Call for 'Human Cloning Ban'." December 10.

Troy, J. 2016. "The Catholic Church and International Relations." *Oxford Handbooks Online.* doi:10.1093/oxfordhb/9780199935307.013.2.

United Nations. 2003. "Resolution 58/314." Participation of the Holy See in the Work of the United Nations.

Vallely, P. 2015. "Divine Diplomacy: The Pope's Hail Mary in Havana May Be Only the Start of the Vatican's New, More Audacious Plans." *Newsweek*, January 9.

Weigel, G. 1999. *Witness to Hope: The Biography of Pope John Paul II.* New York: Harper Collins.

Winters, M. S. 2016. "Pope Francis Champions Refugees and Migrants." *National Catholic Reporter*, April 18.

Witte, G., and A. Faiola. 2016. "Pope Francis Takes Refugees Back to Rome Following Provocative and Emotional Lesbos Visit." *Washington Post*, April 16.

Yardley, J. 2016. "Pope Francis Suggests Donald Trump Is 'Not Christian'." *New York Times*, February 18.

BEYOND INTEGRATION AND DIFFERENTIATION? THE HOLY SEE AND THE POPE IN THE SYSTEM OF WORLD POLITICS

By Mathias Albert

Within the system of world politics, the Holy See and the Pope are not easy to classify, although they clearly belong there as well. The purpose of this contribution is to approach this "difficult fit" in a theoretically informed and systematic fashion, by relating the Holy See and the Pope to both the forms of social differentiation that are characteristic of the system of world politics, as well as to the specific semantics and the symbolically generalized figure of the balance of power that characterizes the modern system of world politics. This is a decidedly more abstract way of approaching the subject than found in most of the literature inquiring into, for example, the Holy See's or the Pope's historical or contemporary relations to nation-states, their status in international law, or the role played in specific issue areas of international politics. Such an approach argues that a significant degree of papal authority in world politics stems from the fact that it has a highly specific and extraordinary way of dealing with the functional differentiation of society, as well as the operative autonomy of, among others, the systems of politics and religion that go along with functional differentiation. It extends this argument by identifying a particularly privileged "fit" between the system of world politics and papal authority.

In order to develop this argument, the present contribution is structured into three main parts: The first part will examine some of the extant literature on the Holy See and the Pope in international relations. The purpose here is not to give an overview over the state of the art, but to provide a deliberately selective reading that paves some ground for the argument to follow. The second part will then make the central argument of this contribution in three steps: A first subsection will introduce the forms of social differentiation that characterize the contemporary system of world politics. A second subsection will locate the Holy See and the Pope in this context. They are identified to be in a particular role in a functionally differentiated world society, as they provide important *semantics and representations of integration*, despite an impossibility to achieve such integration structurally under the conditions of functional differentiation. A third subsection will then outline the argument of a particularly dense link between world politics and the papacy through the historical and formal figures of a balance of power.

1. The Holy See and the Pope in an International Environment

There can be no doubt about the fact that the Holy See and the Pope carry a special status and play a special role in international politics and in international law. The literature on the subject is quite extensive, yet generally seems to converge about a range of issues and perspectives. One important aspect that makes matters rather complex in this regard pertains to distinct, yet overlapping, constituencies, organizations, and subjectivities. In this respect, there is little comparability to a "regular" sovereign territorial state. Thus, most notably, while generally – and appropriately for some purposes – most people in common parlance would not put too much into a distinction between the Holy See and "the Vatican," there are important differences in international law between the Holy See, as one of the few subjects of public international law that are not states, and Vatican State as a tiny, yet in its form nonetheless "regular" state (Haule 2006; Germelmann 2009). In legal terms, the situation is complicated further by the fact that the Holy See, despite its prime function in this respect, cannot be seen to represent the Catholic Church – as probably the still most complex organization in existence worldwide – in its entirety (and a further complication is added by the fact that the CIC institutes another entire body of law that is distinctly not "national law" in a meaningful sense; in overview: Cardinale 1976, 73–98).

In its complexity, the situation in international politics is somewhat akin to, but also in many respects different from, the situation in international law. Vatican State as a state here arguably plays little role whatsoever, whereas of course it does play a role in the sense that there are many personal overlaps with the *curiae* as the institutional host of Vatican or papal "foreign policy." It is in international politics, rather than in international law, however, that the Pope, as a symbolic figure and as a real person, is one of the key figures next to other important international players. Nonetheless, in international politics as well it seems necessary to point out that while certainly not all policies and politics of the Catholic Church are papal policies or politics, even in matters of international politics (sub-) organizational parts of the church may, and do, play independent roles.[1] The remainder of this contribution will however not deal with those. It will deal with the Holy See's and the Pope's role, and in this context usually not distinguish overtly between these two. Yet this is not to deny that differences between the two might be most pronounced in relation to varying personal styles and politics of specific popes (see, for example, Gillis 2006).

While there can be no doubt whatsoever that the Pope is an important player in international politics, there is also little doubt that it remains necessary to some extent to distinguish between political action and strategy regarding two separate realms. On the one hand, there is the realm of all issues pertaining to the Catholic Church itself, such as most notably issues of religious freedom. On the other hand, there is the realm of general political issues beyond its immediate purview, that is, issues that do not pertain to the church as a religious organization itself, but in which the Pope invests authority primarily out of a religiously founded universal understanding of obligation.

The involvement of the Holy See and the Pope in international political matters varies in degree and according to issue, and it also varies in the style of involvement (personally by the Pope, by different levels of diplomacy, through specific dioceses, etc.; see, for example, Hanson 1987; Troy 2016). On a general level, it is possible to distinguish between at least three different kinds of involvement. The most frequent kind is direct political and/or diplomatic activity. While this frequently takes place in relation to highly conflictive issues, in which the Pope plays a particular role as neutral arbiter, such as in the rapprochement talks between the US and Cuba, most of the activity in this respect is through the medium of "regular" diplomatic business, within and beyond the United Nations (Melnyk 2009) and through its diplomatic missions (Apostolic Nunciatures) in many countries of the world. A related, but separate type of involvement can be seen in cases where the Pope (or papal diplomacy) is not involved directly in talks and negotiations to a significant degree, but takes a pronounced stance on specific issues, usually for moral reasons. An important case in point here would be the statements surrounding the strong opposition to the 2003 invasion of Iraq. While related, though different, these two types of involvement to varying degrees draw on the Holy See's and the Pope's special role and status, yet can still be legitimately seen as relatively "normal" political activity if compared to the conduct of "regular" sovereign states. The third kind of involvement is of a different kind, however, as it almost completely draws on the religious authority invested in the Holy See and the Papacy: this kind of involvement relies on what could be called "world order interventions." These interventions contain far-reaching normative sketches of a good world order or some specific aspects of world politics, and are usually contained in (or are sometimes even the prime issue of) papal encyclicals.

Generalizing and simplifying to some degree, it seems fair to say that the overarching programmatic motive on which papal involvement in world politics rests is constituted by the figure of dialogue in its various forms (that is, notably, inter-national, inter-religious, or inter-civilizational dialogue). This does not mean that the Pope and the Holy See would always act as, or could analytically be framed as, neutral and external "honest broker" in all of these settings. It is, in a sense, a constitutive feature of the Pope's and the Holy See' subjectivity and their (rational) actorhood that they are also endowed with interests and self-interest; and certainly the Catholic Church could be seen as "party" in inter-religious conflictual settings as well. Nonetheless, it would seem obvious that the relation between more distanced and arbitrating involvement in specific settings on the one hand, and acting as a rational, self-interested actor, on the other hand, is different in this case when compared to most "regular" nation-states. This particularly also pertains to the way in which issues are addressed or framed: "the Holy See regards phenomena such as urbanization and migration, which political scientists and policy practitioners would likely describe in political or economic terms, primarily in terms of their social and religious implications" (Ferrari 2006, 36). This different framing invariably involves the identification of the relevant social environments and contexts and would, at first glance, already suggest that this framing is different from, and possibly also more inclusive than, the framing that governments of states provide when they frame these environments in primarily political terms. In this sense, it has been argued that "religious authorities are more likely to issue political messages when secular institutions are unwilling or incapable to take clear political decisions" (Genovese 2015, 1). However, the overall scope of Holy See/papal involvement in international politics seems too extensive to support such an argument (that incidentally is solely based on a reading of papal encyclicals) as outlining a rule of engagement – there simply is too much activity going on also in cases where secular institutions actually do take decisions.

Needless to say, given that the Pope and the Holy See have been around for a long time, there has been transformation in many respects, and the shifting relations to secular powers over the centuries do not need to be rehearsed here. Suffice to say, for the time being, that while over periods one could legitimately see the Papal States as "regular" forms of exercising political power in their contemporary political environments, in the end "world cultural" pressure that is expressed in the global harmonization of organizing political authority in the form of the nation-state also left barely a chance for the secular aspect of papal authority to *not also* be somehow manifested in a "normal" state, that is Vatican State. Given that it is unlike other states in many respects, this probably is one of the best examples for the world polity argument made in sociological neo-institutionalism, namely that a modern, rationalized world culture exerts normative pressure to globally organize each and every corner where political authority is exercised in the form of the nation-state. However, it is only the *form* and the organizational similarities that go along with it that are copied and are similar, yet these have little to do with the detailed, "de-coupled" organizational forms and practices (Meyer et al. 1997).

The Pope and the Holy See always were, and continue to be, an important factor, and important actors, in world politics. Changes over time notwithstanding, they always were, and continue to be, something "special" when compared to other and competing secular authorities of the time. Given their religious and particular grounding in the Catholic Church as one of the world's major confessions, they have always been a shaper of, and been shaped by, the transformation of the world in a wider sense. Thus, for example, when dealing with important world political questions, papal encyclicals are in one sense nothing else than programmatic statements made by any foreign ministry around the world. However, they are obviously different in kind, as they embed these questions in the context of a wider order than usually at play in governmental strategies and policies. They are not "outside" of time and society, though, but often closely interwoven with it: in that sense, the Second Vatican Council was an important part of the social sea-change of the 1960s: "The Council and its key document, the encyclical *Gaudium et Spes*, must be seen in the context of the global movement of social renewal, the 'global 68'" (Rieck and Niebuhr 2015, 45).

CHANGES OVER TIME NOTWITHSTANDING, THEY ALWAYS WERE, AND CONTINUE TO BE, SOMETHING "SPECIAL" WHEN COMPARED TO OTHER AND COMPETING SECULAR AUTHORITIES

2. World Politics in a Differentiated World Society and the Pope in World Politics

2.1. A Very Short Introduction: The Differentiation of the System of World Politics

It was hinted at already in the previous section that there might be a way different from nation-states in which the Pope and the Holy See frame, and are inserted into, the system of world politics. In order to explore this line of thought further, it is necessary to lay out the specific view of world politics as a decidedly *modern* phenomenon under the condition of functional differentiation at this point.[2]

The specific conceptual background in this context is the account of historical evolution as a development that mainly takes place *within* a comprehensive social context, that is a *world society*. In this case, world society does not connote a normatively integrated social entity (integrated by a community or a polity, as the view of society in much of classical sociological theory would have it). Rather, it refers to the social world being constituted as the entirety of communication and thus refers to the horizon of meaning in the phenomenological sense, as well as its structural consolidation and transformation. The evolution of the social world then appears as the continuation of communication and the emergence, transformation, and dissolution of media of communication and forms of social structure. The important point here is that this is the view of evolution taking place *within* the social world, and as such is markedly different from views that see nation-states – and nation-state societies – as the constitutive units of the social world (rather than results of its internal evolution), where anything social beyond them can only emerge from an interaction beyond and "above" these constitutive units: the latter would be the "Hobbesian" motive of political realism in IR, that because of its cognitive and normative power in the social world and in the social sciences has also come to be known as "methodological nationalism."

One of the most important consequences of such a "top-down," rather than a "bottom-up," view on the evolution of the social world entails the possibility of describing it by enlisting the theory of social differentiation as one of the most comprehensive theories available for picturing the form and changes of the social world. While many varieties of theories of social differentiation exist, there seem to be two commonly shared threads: *firstly*, three main forms of social differentiation can be discerned in history, namely segmentation (where a difference between segments such as clans, tribes, and families provides the main ordering principle of society); stratification (where the difference between strata such as nobility, clergy, or peasantry provides the main ordering principle); and functional differentiation (where the logics of functionally specified realms such as politics, the economy, science, law, etc., provide the main ordering principles).[3] *Secondly,* the widespread appearance and, one could argue, even primacy of functional differentiation if compared to other forms of social differentiation is usually closely associated with the idea of *modern* society. In fact, it seems that only functional differentiation supports and requires to formulate semantics of societal unity as a counter-figure to the heterogeneity of increasingly autonomous realms of politics, religion, law, education, science, etc. Certainly, the emergence of Sociology as a discipline for studying society is based on thematizing the division of labor/functional differentiation in society (and the purportedly ensuing problem of how it is "held together").

Save the fact that segmentation, stratification, and functional differentiation appear in that order historically, and save discussions about the "primacy" of one form of differentiation over the others, specific historical configurations of (world) society have always been characterized by specific mixes and a varying relative importance of the various forms of social differentiation. This also means, most notably, that even under the condition of an overall "primacy" of functional differentiation as defining characteristic of modern society, forms of social differentiation *within* the realms of society differentiated functionally do not necessarily need to reproduce such a "primacy" of functional differentiation. Thus, for example, although law might be an operatively autonomous, functionally differentiated social system, *internally* it could *primarily* be differentiated into segments (in that case: national legal systems). However, it would seem highly unlikely if any form of large-scale social system in world society would not always be structured to some degree according to all forms of social differentiation. In saying this, it is important to note that social differentiation must not be understood as something that somehow "happens to" a pre-existing, undifferentiated identity. Such would be the view of the classical tradition of sociology that sees society as an integrated whole, and can therefore only see most notably functional differentiation as something that drives it apart. However, social differentiation is not something that happens to a pre-existing, integrated entity, but it is at the same time constitutive of that entity. The very – modern – idea of a society only appears once its internal differentiation becomes visible and can be addressed as a potential issue in relation to an imagined "unity." One could actually, and seemingly paradoxically, say that modern society achieves its unity only through its differentiation.

World politics as a social system can be analyzed following these observations. However, it needs to be noted that seeing world politics under the condition of social differentiation provides for a view that is very different from a still widespread understanding of international politics or international relations as being constituted by the interaction of units as constituting a "level" of politics somehow "above" other forms of politics (e.g. domestic, local). From the perspective of a theory of social differentiation, the system of world politics is a *sub-system* of the political system. To a large degree, the political system itself is differentiated into segments (meaning national political system) and differentiated functionally (into functionally specified policy areas, such as economic, environmental, education politics, etc.). World politics in that sense would appear to be that functionally specified realm within the political system that is responsible for ordering political communication that runs across segments. This, of course, says nothing about the way in which the system of world politics itself is differentiated *internally.* Nonetheless, looking at the various expressions of different forms of social differentiation within the system, as well as expressions of combinations of these different forms, helps to make sense of the variety of forms of organizing political authority within the system of world politics at any given time. Thus, while most notably segmentation into nation-state plays a role within the system of world politics as well, there is also continuing stratification (logics of empire, distinction between great and small powers), as well as functional differentiation (global governance regimes). Logics of supranational authority/world statehood in that sense could often been seen as expressions of combined stratification and functional differentiation, and "regionalization" as combination of functional differentiation and segmentation.

The point here is that a differentiation view permits to analytically turn what might otherwise be seen as a bewildering heterogeneity into a structured, if complex, historically specific variety of forms of organizing political authority within the system of world politics. Of course, the historical view needs to be limited somewhat in this respect. It makes relatively little sense to speak of a system of world politics before the 19th century. Regular interaction between polities and dynasties at most forms a proto-system, while system formation and closure requires independence form interaction through the routinization of diplomatic exchange, the consolidation of protocol, and the reflexivity of exchange (through an imagined global public); requires a highly specific "code" for communicating something as world politics, which is provided through the figure of always also observing world politics on the basis of a "balance of power" (which will attain particular importance for the present argument in Section 2.3); and gives rise to emergent structures in the form of formal organizations, participating in the modern re-constitution of society as "society of organizations" (in this case: international organizations).

Relating the Pope and the Holy See to a system of world politics conceived in such terms could be done as a mere taxonomical exercise, establishing where and how they "fit." However, the argument pursued here is that actually more is to be gained from such an exercise, namely a more thorough understanding of the limits and possibilities of the mode of operation of the contemporary system of world politics itself. In that context, it certainly plays an outstanding role that the Pope and the Holy See mark institutions that arguably have existed longer than any other in the system of world politics, indeed also far preceding its constitution as a social system.

2.2. Pope and Holy See in the System of World Politics

The previous conceptual remarks, at first glance, would not seem to offer a ready vocabulary to analyze the Pope and the Holy See's role in the system of world politics. Quite to the contrary, given their particular status described above, they rather would seem to emphasize a range of *difficulties* in providing such an analysis. Nonetheless, it is exactly through these difficulties that it might be possible to arrive at a clearer understanding of *whence* the authority underlying the "soft power" (Byrnes in this volume; also Ryall 1998; Troy 2010) of the Pope comes from, that is its *systemic place at which it generates the legitimacy of its power.*

Within the system of politics narrowly understood, the Pope and the Holy See arguably have only a small role to play. In the segmented order of territorial nation-states, Vatican State is negligible. In the stratified order of powers – where "power" not solely, but primarily refers to traditional "hard power" attributes (such as most notably military and economic capacities) – the Holy See does not seem to feature at all. In the order of functionally specific regulation, that is in international regimes and institutions of global governance, the Holy See might play a role to varying, yet generally still small degree. However, quite obviously, as observed in both the first part of this contribution as well as in other chapters of this volume, the Holy See and the Pope do have an important role to play and they do possess factual authority and influence. This authority and influence, it is important to acknowledge, is not something that is somehow located "outside" of the system of world politics. While it may draw on sources like morality, tradition, organizational size, personality (of the Pope), etc., it needs to be exerted within the system: the fact that it does so without drawing on "traditional" resources of power is what makes this form of power "soft power."

There is one seemingly obvious way of locating the source of that soft power in case of the Pope and the Holy See. In a system that is characterized by the simultaneous presence of different forms of social differentiation, there seems to be a requirement for some form of *integrative* authority and function – and what better institution to serve that function than the Pope and the Holy See that can draw on sources of authority that are external to the system itself (in contrast to sovereignty as the major self-referential source of authority *within* the system). However, there is a problem with the intuitively convincing idea of an integrative function that bridges centrifugal forces exerted by social differentiation: it is an idea that rests on an idealized, normative idea of society as a "social whole" that is integrated and held together through common norms, values, a collective identity (most notably in the form of a "nation"), etc.; and it rests on the idea that this integrated social whole is divided and driven apart most notably by functional differentiation.[4] Such a view of society as an integrated social whole, while strongly rooted in classical sociological theory, however misses the point that it is only through and in the form of functional differentiation itself that co-constitutive with modernity society appears as a meaningful social entity that can be envisaged in terms of an integrated whole. It is, in that sense, the prime characteristic of modern society as functionally differentiated society that it has no institutions or sets of values and norms that somehow *structurally* "bridge" or even collapse functional differentiation.[5] Neither is this bridging role played by the political system, which as a functionally differentiated system performs the function of providing collectively binding decisions. Nor is this a role played by religion, that "no longer is a necessary site of arbitration that effects the relation between all societal activities to an overall sense" (Luhmann 2015).

It should be emphasized that what these observations do not imply is that a role of structurally and normatively integrating society not fulfilled by religion would be fulfilled by another function system instead. The key to understanding society as a functionally differentiated society is that there is *no* function system that can play this role. All function systems are operatively closed systems that operate according to their own "logic" (such as power in the political system, monetary value in the economic system, belief in the system of religion, truth in the system of science, etc.) and make sense of their environment on their own terms. Seemingly paradoxically, their "integration" as a social whole is only through functional differentiation. What society *does* require, however, are *semantics* and *representations of unity.* [6] These semantics and representations are provided by each function system in various forms and with varying prominence over time. They are probably most strongly anchored in the political system with a latent or manifest claim of the primacy of the state in society, and are entrenched in the figure of sovereignty; the neoliberal revolution since the 1980s could be seen as the claim of the economic system to provide such an integrating function; the prominent notion of a "knowledge society" expresses the claim of the systems of science and education to provide prime integrating functions. The system of religion in this sense is no different from other function systems in this respect. What distinguishes it from these is that, in addition to the political system, it exhibits integrative semantics and representations in a far more prominent fashion than other function systems, largely due to the fact that it can trace these semantics and representations to traditions that precede the functional differentiation of society. In the case of the Holy See and the Catholic Church, such a claim to continuity in integrative function is underpinned by an exceptionally long organizational tradition, and on the symbolic level by the preservation of scripts and artifacts.

The argument here is that the *special role* played by the Holy See also in relation to world politics is largely due to the fact that it provides powerful semantics and representations of the unity of society. This special role derives, *firstly*, from the fact that it can draw on a rich repository and on a long tradition of these semantics and representations not available to other function systems. And it derives, *secondly*, from the fact that while the political system can draw on an equally rich semantics and traditions, the overarching role of sovereignty as the representation of unity within the political system means that claims to integration in modern times have almost completely been focused on regional (that is nation-state) societies, and not (world) society as whole. This semantic and representational *specialization* of the political system has opened up a large space for semantics of "anarchy" in world politics. While there always have been, and continue to be, semantic and representational claims to unity beyond the nation-state in the political system (such as, for example, in figures of an "international community," "global commons," etc.), and while these are embodied organizationally as well (most notably in the United Nations), these claims are asymmetrically privileged in relation to semantics and representations of anarchy. It is exactly the gap left and the demands opened up by that asymmetry within the political system that accounts for the role of the Pope and the Holy See in world politics, a role that exceeds the one to be expected in purely "power political" terms.

2.3. The Challenges of Balance and the Chances of Balancing

The argument presented above only goes part of the way in explaining an influence of the Pope and the Holy See in world politics that is out of proportion to its "hard power," and introduces a conceptually dense account of why it is that in this specific case its "soft power" influence is so marked and beyond other non-state entities. The history and in particularly the organizational history and form of the Catholic Church and the papacy in this context play an important role that clearly sets its modes of influence apart from the other world religions and their representatives (Werkner and Hidalgo 2014). However, there is another factor that contributes to this particular role of the Pope in world politics that is conceptually rather fine-grained, yet important when it comes to explain this role. This factor pertains to the rather unique position of the Pope as a *constitutive player* in the game of world political balance of power, yet a player that has grown into a role of not making moves of his own. This argument can only be sketched out in this context, and would merit longer elaboration. It needs to be presented here even in short form, however, as it moves even further beyond more traditional "soft power"-accounts than the argument developed in relation to social differentiation presented above. The argument rests on the observation that the modern system of world politics is a system that relies on the "balance of power" as its basic mode of observation. This is not to say that the system of world politics is a balance of power-system in the realist sense, or due to some fixed and historically non-contingent clash of self-interest. It is only to say that always also observing oneself and others in relation to oneself and others in terms of a systemic balance of power is what characterizes world politics as a social system. Behind this systemic characteristic lies a high degree of variation regarding the boundaries of that system (witness the difference, for example, between the Concert of the early 19th century, and the East–West conflict), as well as a variety of other modes of order and observation that supplement the balance of power logic.[7] However, to be observed as part of a balance of power remains the central expression of the *recognition of actorhood* (Albert and Stetter 2015) that is required for exerting influence in the system of world politics. The struggle for recognition, and the results of this struggle, is most explicitly addressed in the form of legal subjectivity in international law, as well as in the long debates about the role of non-state actors in world politics. These struggles and debates bear witness to the relative closure of the system and the difficulty of becoming part of it.

The important point here is that although the Holy See is not able to play the balancing game when it comes to the observation of "hard" power factors, and while therefore probably not better able to "enter" the system than Greenpeace or Al-Quaida, it nevertheless is part of the self-observation of the system of world politics in terms of balance-of-power because it was never expelled from it! The loss of the Papal States might have led to a loss of status within the system, but did not lead to an exclusion from the system. The Pope and the Holy See never faced a *constitutive* struggle for recognition and actorhood in the system of world politics, and this fact goes some additional way in explaining why it can so effectively use the openings provided by functional differentiation.[8]

3. Concluding Remarks

The Pope and the Holy See play an important role in world politics. Nevertheless, it is a role that is notoriously difficult to outline in a precise way. There is a broad agreement that what is exerted in this context is a form of "soft power" that draws on a variety of resources, and is exerted through a diversity of channels. However, the workings of "soft power" remain little understood.

The present contribution seeks to provide a theoretically rich account of the specific form of soft power exerted by the Pope and the Holy See. While not discounting factors such as the influence of the Catholic Church in a broader sense, or the personalities of specific Popes, it has taken an approach that situates this soft power in the context of the specifics of the *modern* system of world politics. In this context, it has argued that it is far too simple trying to account for the Pope's influence in terms of an "integrative" power, spanning the rifts of a modern society that is differentiated functionally. Rather than providing "structural" integration, what the Pope and the Holy See provide is a semantics and representation of integration necessary under the condition of functional differentiation despite the impossibility of such a structural integration. In doing so, they can draw on its traditions and the symbolic resources of the Catholic Church as an old organization. Another important source of soft power legitimacy was identified to reside in the fact that the Pope can draw on a "hard power tradition," so to speak, that assigns it a privileged position in the system of world politics compared to other "soft power" actors. ❖

1. The Catholic Church has been described as an "atypical advocacy nongovernmental organization" in this context (Ferrari 2006, 41); the Catholic Church in this sense would seem to be not an "international" actor in any meaningful sense, but rather a "transnational actor" (Ryall 2001)
2. See Albert (2016) for an extensive elaboration; also Albert, Buzan, and Zürn (2013).
3. Sometimes it is argued that centre–periphery provides constitutes a specific form of social differentiation as well. The argument against seeing centre–periphery as a genuine for of social differentiation would be to identify it as a specific spatial expression of stratification.
4. The most "modern" and sophisticated version of this argument is provided by Habermas in his *Theory of Communicative Action* (1987), where the forces of functional differentiation pull apart – and likewise require re-integration by – the "lifeworld."
5. See Schimank and Volkmann (1999) for a concise overview over "integration" vs. "emergence" views of modern, functionally differentiated society.
6. See Shelledy (2004) for an interesting similar argument that sees the role of religion not to work across, but within different function systems (although in somewhat different terminology), in order to explain the Holy See's influence in world politics.
7. See Albert (2016) for an elaboration of this part of the argument.
8. It should added here that despite overlaps the situation does not exactly mirror international legal subjectivity. While in relation to the latter the same argument could be made regarding the Sovereign Military Order of Malta, for example, there is no equivalence whatsoever between the latter and the Holy See when it comes to the role in world politics described above.

References

Albert, M. 2016. *A Theory of World Politics.* Cambridge: Cambridge University Press.

Albert, M., B. Buzan, and M. Zürn. 2013. *Bringing Sociology to International Relations. World Politics as Differentiation Theory.* Cambridge: Cambridge University Press.

Albert, M., and S. Stetter. 2015. "Actorhood in World Politics: The Dialects of Agency/Structure Within the World Polity." In *Theorizing Foreign Policy in a Globalized World,* edited by G. Hellmann and K.-E. Jørgensen, 18–100. London: Palgrave.

Cardinale, H. E. 1976. *The Holy See and the International Order.* Gerards Cross: Colin Smythe.

Ferrari, L. L. 2006. "The Vatican as a Transnational Actor." In *The Catholic Church and the Nation-State. Comparative Perspectives,* edited by P. C. Manuel, L. C. Reardon, and C. Wilcox, 33–54. Washington, DC: Georgetown University Press.

Genovese, F. 2015. "Politics ex Cathedra: Religious Authority and the Pope in Modern International Relations." *Research and Politics* 2 (4): 1–15.

Germelmann, F. 2009. "Heiliger Stuhl und Vatikanstaat in der internationalen Gemeinschaft. Völkerrechtliche Praxis und interne Beziehungen." *Archiv des Völkerrechts* 47 (2): 147–186.

Gillis, C. 2006. *The Political Papacy. John Paul II, Benedict XVI, and Their Influence*. Boulder, CO: Paradigm Publishers.

Habermas, J. 1987. *Theory of Communicative Action*. 2nd ed. Boston, MA: Beacon Press.

Hanson, E. O. 1987. *The Catholic Church in World Politics*. Princeton, NJ: Princeton University Press.

Haule, R. R. 2006. *Der Heilige Stuhl/Vatikanstaat im Völkerrecht*. Lohmar: Eul Verlag.

Luhmann, N. 2015. *Die Religion der Gesellschaft*. 4th ed. Frankfurt am Main: Suhrkamp.

Melnyk, R. A. 2009. *Vatican Diplomacy at the United Nations. A History of Catholic Global Engagement*. Lewiston: The Edwin Mellen Press.

Meyer, J. W., J. Boli, G. M. Thomas, and F. O. Ramirez. 1997. "World Society and the Nation-State." *American Journal of Sociology* 103 (1): 144–181.

Rieck, C. E., and D. Niebuhr. 2015. "Microstate and Superpower. The Vatican in International Politics." *KAS International Reports* 10: 38–60.

Ryall, D. 1998. "How Many Divisions? The Modern Development of Catholic International Relations." *International Relations* 14 (2): 21–34.

Ryall, D. 2001. "The Catholic Church as a Transnational Actor." In *Non-state Actors in World Politics*, edited by D. Josselin and W. Wallace, 41–58. London: Palgrave.

Schimank, U., and U. Volkmann. 1999. *Gesellschaftliche Differenzierung*. Bielefeld: Transcript-Verlag.

Shelledy, R. B. 2004. "The Vatican's Role in Global Politics." *SAIS Review of International Affairs* 24 (2): 149–162.

Troy, J. 2010. "Die Soft Power des Heiligen Stuhls. Unsichtbare Legionen zwischen internationaler Gesellschaft und Weltgesellschaft." *Zeitschrift für Außen- und Sicherheitspolitik* 3 (4): 489–511.

Troy, J. 2016. *The Catholic Church and International Relations*. [ebook]Oxford: Oxford HandbooksOnline DOI:10.1093/oxfordhb/9780199935307.013.2.

Werkner, I.-J., and O. Hidalgo. 2014. *Religionen – Global Player in der internationalen Politik?* Wiesbaden: VS Springer.

DIPLOMACY, PAPACY, AND THE TRANSFORMATION OF INTERNATIONAL SOCIETY

By Thomas Diez

Gone are the days in which analysts had assumed that religion would no longer play a role in politics, let alone international politics. We live in a post-secular age, and religion is back—yet it often gets a bad press. Religion seems to be the source of conflict, violence, terrorism, and more broadly speaking limitations to individual liberties. At the same time, however, one religious actor, the Pope, has received a lot more positive attention. From the supposed contribution of John Paul II to the demise of the Soviet empire and concomitantly the Cold War (Perrone 2012) to the wave of enthusiasm for Pope Francis, the Head of the Catholic Church seems to have returned as a player to be reckoned with in international politics.

How can we understand this increasing influence of an actor that most observers regarded as marginal and on the decline only a few decades ago? What explains the return of the Pope?

The answer to this question can certainly not be reduced to a single factor. As in any other foreign policy analysis, a variety of personal and circumstantial variables have played their part in raising the Pope's profile. Thus, both John Paul II and Francis have had a massive presence in the media not least because they have sought close proximity to their people, have traveled widely, and have had a penchant for highly symbolic actions. At the same time, a globalized and diversified media, in which symbolic pictures have gained in importance over traditional text and in which the duration of news transmission across the whole globe has been reduced to zero, has made it easier for actors and institutions such as the Papacy to spread their message and place themselves on the agenda.

In this article, I want to suggest an additional yet mostly overlooked factor in the return of the Pope on the international scene: the transformation of international society. This concept is the most important contribution of the so-called English School of International Relations to the study of international politics. As I will develop in more detail in the first section, it sees states not only related to each other in a mechanical fashion determined by some material structure of the system in which they are situated. Instead, the concept of society presumes that states share common interests and values, and that they develop common norms and institutions in order to achieve these interests and realize their values. Diplomacy is one of the core institutions through which states meet each other in this society.

Yet as in any society, the structures and practices of international society possess a certain stability on the one hand while undergoing constant change on the other. Important transformations of the international society have taken place between the poles of a pluralist and a solidarist international society, where the latter differs from the former in the extent to which individuals and transnational actors are carriers of rights in this society, and thus the extent to which states (and by extension the international society as a whole) bear duties not only to their own citizens but to people outside their boundaries. I argue that despite setbacks and contestations, we have witnessed a solidarization of international society that has had a transformative impact on diplomatic practices and created a window of opportunity for actors such as the Pope to increase their influence both on the society of states and on a transnational, "world" society of individuals.

To trace this process, in the second section I chart the position of the Holy See in a traditional, pluralist international society, in which it has always been an awkward remnant of medieval, pre-international times when territory was not yet the only defining criterion of the extension of authority. This has resulted in an odd construction of the Holy See bearing traits of sovereignty while at the same time not having the status of a full member of international society, which in turns has constrained yet never completely foreclosed its actions and influence. The third section will then illustrate how the solidarization process of international society has allowed the Holy See to use its "soft power" and public diplomacy instruments to greater effect to influence an increasingly transnational public debate. As I will show, the changing constituency of international society is only one aspect in favor of the Papal rise. The norms implicit in a solidarist international society also provide a discursive context in which Christian norms in a narrowly political sense related to peace, environmental sustainability, and development have become easily translatable, whereas more personal norms on issues such as abortion or marriage have become more contested and thus marginalized in the broader international society debate.

This will lead me to some reflections on the future role of the Pope in international society, which seems to hinge on (a) the continued solidarization of this society, and (b) the degree to which the norms articulated by norm entrepreneurs within the international society at large and the Holy See coincide.

International Society and Diplomacy

In Hedley Bull's iconic definition, an international society

> exists when a group of states, conscious of certain common interest and common values, form a society in the sense that they conceive themselves to be bound by a common set of rules in their relations with one another, and share in the working of common institutions. (1977, 13)

A society in that sense implies that there is a certain degree of will and intentionality in the relations of states among each other. This stands in contrast to a mere system, in which the effects of one state's actions on another are largely mechanistic and determined by the entanglement of their transactions such as trade or the distribution of power among them. This also marks the international society as a proto-constructivist concept (Dunne 1995) and sets it apart from realist conceptions of the international.

The backbone of this international society are its institutions. We can distinguish between "primary" and "secondary" institutions (Buzan 2004, 167, 2014, 16–17). The concept of secondary institutions follows a narrow definition of institutions with a certain degree of formalization, either rooted in a founding treaty around which an international regime may form, or as a full-fledged international organization. Primary institutions, in contrast, follow a wider, sociological definition of institutions as routinized practices. They thus include practices that states routinely utilize to ensure the realization of their common interests and values.

In many ways, the idea of primary institutions is the more interesting contribution that the English School makes to our analysis of international institutions, as secondary institutions are commonly covered by other approaches as well, and of course first and foremost by neoliberalism. There is thus considerable debate about what to include as possible primary institutions. In his original list, Hedley Bull includes five such institutions: International Law, Diplomacy, Balance of Power, Great Power Management, and War. Of these, two are most interesting for our discussion: diplomacy and war. War is interesting because the Holy See has no standing army with which it could intervene to restore order in international society, which is the main function of war as an institution of international society. It is thus an institution that illustrates the position of the Holy See as a liminal actor in international society: it may take part in the discussions about war and may broker peace deals behind the scenes, but may not partake in war as such. The brokering of peace in turn illustrates the participation of the Holy See in the institution of diplomacy, although even here, as we will see, there are some constraints, and it is exactly in diplomacy that I will argue that the changing nature of international society has its biggest impact on the Pope's role in this society.

Which, then, are the common interests and values that states pursue through these institutions? In Bull's version of the international society, these are reduced to a minimal set including sovereignty and non-intervention. This may not sound like a lot—and yet, these twin values/interests have had far-reaching consequences for the organization of international society. They meant that states have not recognized non-state actors that would challenge their sovereignty as equals; that secessionist entities have been recognized only in exceptional circumstances; that violations of state territory could legitimately be countered by war; that even autocrats have found it necessary to legitimize any such violation; or that human rights have only been guaranteed through the very states that they had been developed in opposition to.

Again, this international society looks a lot like a realist conception of an international system. Yet the realist underestimates the degree to which states depend on each other in the pursuit of sovereignty and non-intervention, and have developed complex institutions, such as diplomacy and war, to ensure their continued existence. As in the case of classical realists, this version of international society furthermore has a core ethical concern that it draws from: in a communitarian fashion, it guarantees the persistence of different identities through their organization in different territories. Pluralism, therefore, is at the heart of this international society; and it is thus commonly known as a "pluralist" international society (Wheeler 1992).

Such a pluralist international society explicitly rules out cosmopolitan concerns. To Bull (1977, 85–86), the main question in voicing such concerns, in particular if they are contested, is who legitimizes the speaker–statesmen can draw on their respective constitution (whether democratic or otherwise) to claim legitimacy and are recognized by other states as legitimate representatives of their states. But a claim to human rights must ultimately reside in a natural law assumption that in itself has no further justification than belief—which is insufficient for the validity of global claims if this belief is not shared.

Against this conception of a pluralist stands that of a solidarist international society. In contrast to pluralists, solidarists presume the existence of a world society of individuals with their own rights and legitimate claims against states. As such, the values that states need to pursue are not only related to their own continued existence but to individuals outside their territories. At the very least, states need to go beyond refraining from undue interventions in other states' territories, they are also required to abstain from inflicting harm on humans—be it their own citizens or not (Linklater and Suganami 2006, 155–188). In most versions of solidarism, states furthermore have an obligation to observe human rights and prevent and respond to gross human rights violations. They have a duty, in Wheeler's words, to "save strangers" if these are existentially threatened (2000).

It is not difficult to see how international society since the 1970s, in which Bull wrote his main work, *The Anarchical Society*, has moved from the pluralist pole of the international society spectrum toward the solidarist pole. This "solidarisation" (Ahrens and Diez 2015) has included the rise of the concept of human security, the formulation of the Responsibility to Protect (R2P), the installation of the International Criminal Court, the reinforcement of Human Rights in the Vienna Declaration, and the Universal Periodic Review in the Human Rights Council, the Ottawa Convention on the Anti-Personnel Landmine Ban, to name but a few developments. None of these developments has been uncontested, or can be considered complete. The solidarization of international society is thus inherently contested, resisted, and often conflict-ridden. It is also not the path to some kind of global paradise. Instead, the normative and institutional changes implied in this process are often ambiguous. "Saving Strangers", for instance, implies on the one hand a stronger emphasis on human rights in international politics, but on the other hand also a strengthening of the institution of war in the form of humanitarian interventions. Perhaps even more problematically, it presupposes a discursive hegemony or what Ashley (1989) once called the "imposition of international purpose" in that, against Bull's concern for pluralist difference, solidarism rests on an agreement about core values that apply to all humankind.

Bound up with this process of solidarization, we have also witnessed a change in the nature of diplomacy. Diplomacy in the traditional pluralist international society has been heavily regulated. It was an institution the practices of which were confined to states, and included rules such as the extraterritoriality of embassies to the dress code and behavior at receptions. Many of these practices are still in place, and sending diplomatic notes, withdrawing ambassadors or calling ambassadors to the foreign office remains a central part of the repertoire through which states engage and communicate with each other. Yet as Holsti (2004, 206–210) notes, the institution of diplomacy has become much more complex. This involves the changes in information and communication technology. On the one hand, foreign ministries are no longer dependent on their embassies for the gathering of intelligence. On the other hand, they can communicate through other means than diplomatic notes—and these often cross the border between state and public diplomacy. State representatives, including individual foreign ministers, thus regularly now use Twitter to make their views heard. Furthermore, we have witnessed a rise in the importance of paradiplomacy—diplomacy performed by non-state actors, from subnational units (such as the German Länder) to NGOs and celebrities (e.g. Cornago 2016). This rise, in turn, has also been made possibly by technological changes that allows these actors to raise their voices in arenas that used to be closed to them.

These changes in the nature of diplomacy as an institution of international society are linked to the process of solidarization in several ways. Firstly, as solidarization includes the concerns of a "world society" of individuals in international society, the latter needs representatives from world society in its assessment, for instance, of human rights violations. Vice versa, and secondly, this intertwining of international and world society means that governments find it necessary not only to talk to other governments but "to win the hearts and minds" of people, which is the core purpose of public diplomacy. Thirdly, the speed with which international problems arise on the agenda of governments requires a reliance on a more complex network of actors other than only states.

In short, then, in whatever imperfect and contested ways, international society has moved toward a solidarist understanding, implying a transformation toward greater responsibilities toward individuals beyond a state's own territory, the increasing relevance of non-state actors, and a change in diplomatic practices. I argue that it is these changes that have allowed the Pope and the Holy See to increase its visibility and influence in international politics.

The Holy See in a Pluralist International Society

What has the role of the Pope and the Holy See been in the traditional, pluralist international society? Intriguingly, the English School itself has had little interest in the role of religion in international society, and largely confines its discussion of the Catholic Church to the historical struggles in the formation of the modern society of states. While this is indicative of the strict separation of church and state that at least some of the English School writers from Bull onwards not only observed but also endorsed, it is also a missed chance to utilize an outlier example to illustrate the core features of international society, and to think creatively about the interlinkages of world and international society.

Clearly, the universal claim of the Holy See (as opposed to the mini-state of Vatican City) is at odds with the society of states. It is a remnant of times gone past, in which religious and secular leaders competed over power and authority in Europe (and elsewhere), in which such power and authority was often overlapping, and in which authority rested in individuals —here, the Pope (Bull 1977, 9; Ipsen 1990, 82). The rise of the international society, from the Treaties of Augsburg and Westphalia to the Napoleonic re-ordering of Europe to decolonization, did away with such overlaps and created a system of mutually exclusive, clearly demarcated territories. The Holy See is thus not a fully sovereign and equal member of international society; it occupies a liminal, ambiguous status. On the one hand, it maintains diplomatic relations and is recognized as a subject of international law so that it can sign treaties and other formal legal, international documents. It is also a member of many international organizations and sub-organizations of the United Nations, including the International Atomic Energy Agency, the World Intellectual Property Organization, or the Organization for Security and Co-Operation in Europe. On the other hand, it is not a full member and "only" an observer of the United Nations and many other of its sub-organizations. It also concludes treaties with states on a bilateral basis of a specific kind, regulating the relationship, including rights and duties, between the Catholic religion and the state in each case.

THE HOLY SEE IS THUS NOT A FULLY SOVEREIGN AND EQUAL MEMBER OF INTERNATIONAL SOCIETY; IT OCCUPIES A LIMINAL, AMBIGUOUS STATUS

The exact status of the Holy See in international society has thus been contested. Those close to the Church itself often emphasize its recognition as a full subject of international law (e.g. Araujo 2001, 346). However, even they recognize that the Pope's sovereignty does not reside in the existence of territory, people, and authority, as the Montevideo criteria for state sovereignty would require, but in its "spiritual sovereignty" (Casaroli 1981, 95; Ryngaert 2011). Such spiritual sovereignty, however, is at odds with the central norms of a pluralist international society, so that other analysts have branded the international status of the Holy See as "atypical" and refer to those who "argue that the Holy See acts solely as a religious authority in the United Nations, a body where membership is supposed to be limited to independent states" (Bathon 2001, 597).

This "atypical status" leads to a degree of marginalization in a world of states. In the General Assembly, the Holy See can only speak after "proper" member states—although it is entitled to speak as the first of the observers. It can also attend even closed meetings of the General Assembly, but has no voting rights or rights to table resolutions. Holy See diplomats are often seen as exotic figures in their clergy dress, and not everyone takes their moral argumentation seriously.

Yet such a status at the margins can also be an advantage. On the one hand, it makes it easier to voice particular position without having to pay dues to the game of power politics. On the other hand, having one's foot in the door without being fully immersed in the politics of the day makes an actor attractive as a neutral mediator in conflict cases.

The Holy See has thus been far from an inactive member even of traditional pluralist international society. In particular, it has long pursued a policy of promoting peace, détente, and reconciliation across ideological blocs. Its diplomacy, at least in theory, has always been a diplomacy of peace (Casaroli 1981, 4–5). This has included mediation efforts in international conflicts such as the so-called Beagle conflict between Argentina and Chile in 1978 (Troy 2010, 505). Chong and Troy (2011) see this, together with the promotion of human rights, as a "universal sacred mission".

However, despite these diplomatic efforts, especially in the field of mediation, the role of the Pope as an actor in international society remained heavily circumscribed, and its visibility outside Church circles limited. This has changed since the 1980s.

The Holy See in a Solidarizing International Society

As I have pointed out in the introduction, the increased visibility and influence of the Pope in international society can partly be traced to personal factors. In addition, Haynes (2007, 141) points to the increasing internationalization of the Church since the Second Vatican Council, culminating in the election of a Pole, a German and an Argentinian as Pope. Likewise, technological innovation and globalization have made it easier for the Catholic Church as well to build and maintain transnational networks and promote their view of morality and the Gospel (Haynes 2001).

Yet this is only part of the story. The solidarization of international society that I have described above has brought with it two core changes that have provided the Pope with greater opportunities to voice his views and influence international politics. The first, structural change is that of the changing nature of international society to include non-state actors as both partners in developing international policies and as addressees of such policies, and the changes in diplomacy that have gone along with this. The second, normative change is that of the increased relevance of human rights, development, environmentalism, and peace—core norms in a Christian worldview.

The structural change has not altered the formal-legal position of the Holy See in the United Nations or other international organizations. However, it has meant that it has become increasingly "normal" for states to involve non-state actors in their deliberations, and that individuals have become a more central reference point for state actions. Both developments play into the hands of the Holy See. On the one hand, it no longer has to rely on its contested status to make claims in international society, but can also act as a representative of world society. Its borderline status allows it to play both parts. On the other hand, mass festivals such as the World Youth Day or encyclicals such as Francis' 2015 *Laudato Si'*, address both states and individuals and thus easily play the game of transversing the boundaries between international and world society (Troy 2010).

The normative change toward the inclusion of world society concerns in international society, meanwhile, meets a long-standing concern of the Church to strengthen a "cooperative and solidarist world society privileging the individual and not a statist balance of power" (Troy 2010, 503). Thus, while the Holy See may well have contributed to the normative changes in international politics since the 1980s, it also benefits from the significant overlaps between its own normative agenda and that of a solidarizing international society. Norms such as human security or environmental stewardship (Falkner and Buzan 2017) are fully in line with Catholic teaching and award the Pope the possibility to be heard by states and non-state actors alike.

In that sense, encyclicals that speak to current themes of international politics, from environmental protection to a wider understanding of peace, are effective communications of the concerns of at least a subgroup of world society in a solidarizing international society. In such teachings and in other public appearances, the Pope can use his authority as an actor not tainted by the geopolitical interests of states speaking on behalf of a broader global interest while at the same time being recognized as a quasi-equal in international society. Likewise, as other contributions to this special issue show, the Pope can mediate in international conflicts such as in the often-cited Beagle conflict precisely because he is recognized as an authority speaking on behalf of the individual citizen and engaging with states in the international society.

The normative overlap between the Church and a solidarist international society is of course not endless. On many issues, in particular when it comes to sexuality and family values, the norms of the Catholic Church and that of world society at large diverge. In these cases, the Pope becomes merely one actor among many who try to influence the public debate and can do so from a particularly prominent position as an actor in international and world society.

The Future of Papal Diplomacy

In this paper, I have situated the rise of the Pope in international politics since the 1980s in the broader context of a solidarizing international society. I have argued that two changes within this solidarization process have benefited the Pope and the Holy See as his diplomatic representation: a structural change in the rise of the inclusion of non-state actors as well as practices of paradiplomacy; and a normative change in the overlap of the values of a solidarist international society and the core beliefs of the Catholic Church. In an assessment of the future of Papal diplomacy and the status of the Holy See in international society, caveats must be made on both developments.

In terms of structure, the Pope's continued influence hinges on the extent to which non-state actors continue to be seen as an important party to the decision-making process in international society. The pressures of globalization and the degree to which the involvement of such actors has been institutionalized, as well as the difficulties to reign in and control social media speak in favor of a continued relevance of non-state actors. This would allow the Pope to continue to play toward the society of states through diplomatic missions and the engagement in the United Nations and other international organizations, while at the same time addressing world society through the means of public diplomacy or "soft power" (Troy 2010). However, as autocracies are on the rise again, we may well also see the curtailment of the influence of non-state actors and a return to a purely statist, pluralist international society. I do not think this is a likely scenario, but it cannot be ruled out entirely.

In terms of norms, two further issues are at stake. Firstly, the secular norms of a solidarist international society do overlap with those of the Holy See and the Catholic Church, but it is only a partial overlap. The Church has been criticized for its stance on abortion, LGTB rights, or divorce, at the same time as its engagement for peace, human rights, and environmentalism has been praised. The question thus becomes to what extent norms that are less popular in a secular, multi-religious international society can or ought to be altered or downplayed by the Holy See, or ignored by those who disagree with them.

Secondly, the norms of a solidarist international society themselves have come under fire since the enthusiasm of the first decade of the new millennium. Human security plays no longer the central role in United Nations debates that it once did, and R2P is challenged by the course of events in Libya, but also by its abuse to legitimize partisan interventions on behalf of proclaimed Russian populations in states of the former Soviet empire. Instead, autocrats who dispute these norms anyway or at least state responsibility to enforce them, have won elections in many states, including the US. The question here is whether we will witness a (further) backlash against solidarization in the years to come.

Thus, there is no guarantee that the normative context in international society remains favorable to the Holy See. Just as other actors, the Pope and other representatives of the Church need to engage continuously in a discursive struggle to shape the norms of international society. Yet within this struggle, the structural transformations implied in the solidarization process mean that in all likelihood, the Pope is a figure at the interstices of international and world society that we will have to reckon with in the foreseeable future. ❖

Acknowledgements

A previous version of this paper was presented at the conference "Popes on the Rise! Mobilization, Media, and Political Power of the Modern Papacy", Vatican, March 2017. I am grateful to the participants, the reviewers of this journal, and especially Mariano Barbato for their comments and encouragement.

ORCID

Thomas Diez http://orcid.org/0000-0001-8056-6693

References

Ahrens, Bettina, and Thomas Diez. 2015. "Soldarisation and Its Limits: The EU and the Transformation of International Society." *Global Discourse* 5 (3): 341–355.

Araujo, Robert John. 2001. "The International Personality and Sovereignty of the Holy See." *Catholic University Law Review* 50 (2): 291–360.

Ashley, Richard K. 1989. "Imposing International Purpose: Notes on a Problematique of Governance." In *Global Changes and Theoretical Challenges: Approaches to World Politics for the 1990s*, edited by Ernst-Otto Czempiel, and James N. Rosenau, 251–290. Lexington: Lexington Books.

Bathon, Matthew N. 2001. "The Atypical International Status of the Holy See." *Vanderbilt Journal of Transnational Law* 34: 597–632.

Bull, Hedley. 1977. *The Anarchical Society: A Study of Order in World Politics.* Basingstoke: Macmillan.

Buzan, Barry. 2004. *From International to World Society? English School Theory and the Social Structure of Globalisation.* Cambridge: Cambridge University Press.

Buzan, Barry. 2014. *An Introduction to the English School of International Relations.* Cambridge: Polity.

Casaroli, Agostino Kardinal. 1981. *Der Heilige Stuhl und die Völkergemeinschaft: Reden und Aufsätze.* Berlin: Duncker & Humblot.

Chong, Alan, and Jodok Troy. 2011. "A Universal Sacred Mission and the Universal Secular Organization: The Holy See and the United Nations." *Politics, Religion & Ideology* 12 (3): 335–353.

Cornago, Noé. 2016. "(Para)Diplomatic Cultures: Old and New." In *Diplomatic Cultures and International Politics: Translations, Spaces and Alternatives*, edited by Jason Dittmer, and Fiona McConnell, 175–184. London: Routledge.

Dunne, Timothy. 1995. "The Social Construction of International Society." *European Journal of International Relations* 1 (3): 367–389.

Falkner, Robert, and Barry Buzan. 2017. "Global Environmental Politics in English School Perspective: Environmental Stewardship as an Emerging Primary Institution of International Society." Paper for the 2017 Annual Convention of the International Studies Association, Baltimore, February 22–25.

Haynes, Jeff. 2001. "Transnational Religious Actors and International Politics." *Third World Quarterly* 22 (2): 143–158.

Haynes, Jeffrey. 2007. *An Introduction to International Relations and Religion.* Harlow: Pearson Longman.

Holsti, K. J. 2004. *Taming the Sovereigns: Institutional Change in International Politics.* Cambridge: Cambridge University Press.

Ipsen, Knut. 1990. *Völkerrecht.* 3rd ed. München: C.H. Beck.

Linklater, Andrew, and Hidemi Suganami. 2006. *The English School of International Relations: A Contemporary Assessment.* Cambridge: Cambridge University Press.

Perrone, Arragon. 2012. "Pope John Paul II's Role in the Collapse of Poland's Communist Regime: Examining a Religious Leader's Impact on International Relations." University of Connecticut. http://digitalcommons.uconn.edu/srhonors_theses/244

Ryngaert, Cedric. 2011. "The Legal Status of the Holy See." *Goettingen Journal of International Law* 3 (3): 829–859.

Troy, Jodok. 2010. "Die Soft Power des Heiligen Stuhls: Unsichtbare Legionen zwischen internatiionaler Gesellschaft und Welltgesellschaft." *Zeitschrift für Außen- und Sicherheitspolitik* 3 (4): 489–511.

Wheeler, Nicholas J. 1992. "Pluralist or Solidarist Conceptions of International Society: Bull and Vincent on Humanitarian Intervention." *Millennium: Journal of International Studies* 21 (3): 463–487.

Wheeler, Nicholas J. 2000. *Saving Strangers: Humanitarian Intervention in International Society.* Oxford: Oxford University Press.

RERUM NOVARUM AND THE RIGHT TO WORK: 19TH-CENTURY LESSONS FOR 21ST-CENTURY LABOR

By Robert Joustra

Since Pope Leo XIII addressed the problem of labor and capital in *Rerum Novarum (1891)* more than a hundred years have passed, the global economy has not only come into being it has increased on incredible orders of magnitude, and the world has been—it is not an exaggeration to say it—transformed by technological capitalism. Some would say that the world of that Pope, and of *Rerum Novarum*, separated from our own by rockets and moon landings, nuclear bombs and microchips, bears little resemblance to us. On the face of it, there is every reason to believe the bracing historical-economic thesis of Karl Polanyi, that we have indeed witnessed *The Great Transformation*. Yet, at least 90 years later, when Pope John Paul II penned *Laborem Exercens (1981)* we find *Rerum Novarum* at its very foundation, urgently contemporary, for what would soon become the post-Soviet world. Much of this remains true even today.

In this article it is my argument that *Rerum Novarum* provides a spiritual blueprint, in the phraseology of Bob Goudzwaard (1979), for the revitalization of organized labor in North America. That blueprint has three essential elements that are especially pressing of labor in the present day. First, in what Pope Leo XIII calls the "marvelous and manifold" efficacy of Christian institutions [RN, 19], *Rerum Novarm* recovers for us both authentic post-secular engagement with resurgent global religion (including inside North America), *and* a perspective on institutions and organizations which unsettles the typical atomized, secular account of volunteerism. In its recovery of a *moral* vocabulary for labor, *Rerum Novarum* suggests a way to think beyond the false dichotomy of individualist association, and compulsory collectivism. Second, *Rerum Novarum* helps us recover labor unions as essentially *economic* institutions, that is to say, organizations whose primary purpose is to steward the dignity of human work, and not—as *Laborem Exercens* argues—to "play politics" [LE, 20]. While union activity undoubtedly enters into politics insofar as it has a "prudent concern for the common good" its *limited* role is "first of all not to be about human rights, redistribution, or social support" but rather "about stewarding human capital and ensuring that its potential is realized and a fair return on investment is provided" (Pennings 2010). Third, this gives us a picture of labor unionism which is an essential part of, but not the totality, of true development. It also renders a variable picture for the form that unionism might take within diverging conditions in the power and distribution of capital. The *goal* of stewarding human capital, in service of its members, may require different organizing strategies. It also gives us a picture from which to discriminate between better and worse labor practice, practice which either undermines or enables said stewardship. Further, it makes labor unionism, like capital, like political, social, and civil associations, *partners* rather than rivals in building a more a just society. It recognizes, in short, that labor depends in vital ways on these other systems and institutions, and cannot survive their degradation or collapse.

In the case of Right to Work legislation, I argue these laws rely on an atomized associationalism often endemic to secular democracies, but at odds with the blueprint of *Rerum Novarum*. Somewhat tragically, in trying to undercut the overreach of labor unions politically and socially, these laws have also undercut the essential economic function of unions, specifically their powers of collective bargaining. This misbalance will tend to exaggerate not only adversarial relations between capital and labor, but also the long term sustainability of capital itself.

"The Efficacy of Christian Institutions"

The recovery of religion as refreshing a new *perspective* on labor takes place on at least two levels. In the first place, it takes place in recognizing the often overlooked *religious roots* of organized labor, a movement which has now become highly secular, in the polarizing (religion vs. secularism) sense of the term. That is to say, there is a need to recover institutional religion and its communities as protagonists rather than victims of global capitalism, as Benedict XVI says in *Caritas in Veritate (2009)* [CinV, 42]. Second, therefore, in the recovery of "the efficacy of Christian institutions" we find an urgently needed moral vocabulary for the economy and true development. We recover, in other words, the capacity to contend for the *purpose* of trade unionism that defaults to more than mere material and political monopoly on the part of its membership.

Maybe the first thing *Rerum Novarum* may properly remind us of is that labor unions have a long and studied history of encouragement and promotion in the Church. Repeated in *Laborem Exercens*, *Caritas in Veritate* and other papal documents, *Rerum Novarum* argues unapologetically that "the most important of all are workingmen's unions" [RN, 49]. *Rerum Novarum* goes on:

> It is gratifying to know that there are actually in existence not a few of these associations of this nature, consisting either of workmen alone, or of workmen and employers together, but it were greatly desired that they should become more numerous and more efficient. We have spoken of them more than once, yet it will be well to explain here how notably they are needed, to show that they exist of their own right, and what should be their organization and mode of action. [RN, 49]

Such unions, the encyclical argues, are "lesser and not independent societies, but, nevertheless, real societies" [RN, 50] anticipating in some respects the limits—and simultaneous interdependence—of discrete spheres of human life. Indeed, we read in that same section a now much abused wedding invocation from Ecclesiastes, that "it is better two should be together than one" [RN, 50] an exegetical argument for *trade unionism*, which might bleed it of some of its romance.

This, sadly, is a largely lost history in North America's labor unions. North American unionism has a historic connection not only to Catholic social doctrine, but also to a powerful social gospel tradition in the early 20th century. That legacy persists, if only in a few actual unions themselves, including the Catholic inspired 300,000 member *Centrale des syndicats democratiques* (CSD) in Quebec or the Protestant inspired 60,000 member Christian Labour Association of Canada.

Yet these are now exceptions, not the rule. The religious roots of the movement had been largely expunged already by the turn of the 20th century. The fault lines became exposed in 1919 with the Winnipeg General Strike. Some churches, especially the United Church of Canada, continued to bridge church and union worlds, but the terms of that engagement became more and more politically polarizing. Eugene Forsey argued that until "Christians learn to understand and apply the lessons of Marxism they cannot enter the Kingdom of Heaven" (Milligan 2004). The result was that the socialist radicalism ran increasingly at odds with orthodox Christian sentiment, and the movement took on class based, rather than religious undertones. The vocabulary became increasingly adversarial and rights based. In the United States, this premise became so persistent that it was eventually enshrined in actual law, in the 1935 *Wagner Act*. Canada was not far behind. Within a decade, provinces had introduced similar measures which established labor law and rules of engagement for industrial conflict.

By the *Wagner Act* we have come very far from high-minded ideas like "solidarity" and "social justice," or—perhaps more to the point—a partner framework in which "each needs the other: capital cannot do without labor, nor labor without capital," where "mutual agreement results in the beauty of good order, while perpetual conflict necessarily produces confusion and savage barbarity" [RN, 19]. Indeed, part of the hermeneutic *Rerum Novarum* may supply is that labor relations were, by the time of the *Wagner Act*, well on its way to savage barbarity, if partly for the collapse of Christian institutions and its religious supports. Concluding the thought, *Rerum Novarum* argues:

> Now, in preventing such strife as this, and in uprooting it, the efficacy of Christian institutions is marvelous and manifold. First of all, there is no intermediary more powerful than religion (whereof the Church is the interpreter and guardian) in drawing the rich and working class together, by reminding each of its duties to the other, and especially of the obligations of justice. [RN, 19]

The encyclical is even more explicit later on, arguing that "if human society is to be healed now, in no other way can it be healed save by a return to Christian life and Christian institutions" [RN, 27]. So we come to the not incidental work of recovering a moral vocabulary, and especially ends that transcend material self-interest, salved by the healing balm of Christian life. North America has struggled with terms like "social justice" to try and situate such conversations, which in some respects can be defined in both libertarian and socialist fashion. But in giving such terms concrete meaning which elicit duties and obligations *as well as* rights within a system of common concern, the mutual dependence of capital and labor, we often fall short. At times, we fall victim to the now common problems of globalization: "buy American" as a shorthand for loyalty to the "worker," by which of course we mean workers close to home, patently not "workers of the world." Free trade advocates have the luxury of defaulting to the "market," and the law of comparative advantage, but in practice the politics of this are perilous. It means empty American factories. It means, at the least, short term losses.

Can *Rerum Novarum* provide the kind of framework of meaning that helps us in balancing these competing interests? I believe it can, or at least it can provide us with a better part of that framework as it relates to labor unionism. It does this first and foremost by underwriting the priority of labor, and its essential function as an *economic* institution. Not, I hasten to add, to invoke econometrics in a quantitative sense and back away (again, this time under the guise of neutral or positivist social science) from the moral conversation. But rather *economics* as tethered to the task of integral human development, the dignity of work, and its' just returns.

The Priority of Labor

Ray Pennings, a leading neo-Calvinist on labor and economic in Canada, writes that, "of top priority is that there is really no common framework by which we understand unions in North America" (Pennings 2010). There are, he argues, two "knee-jerk" responses to unions: (1) a negative response, regarding union as prohibiting free choice; (2) a positive response, regarding unions as essential for defending worker's rights against aggressive and often amoral capital. The point, he says, is not to mediate these perspectives, but a la *Rerum Novarum* to say that both are essentially invalid or incomplete. They are invalid because they fail to recognize that the labor union is a "primarily *economic* institution whose potential can be realized around economic norms and objectives." Instead, he argues, we often conceive of them as either political or social organizations.

The recovery of trade unionism as a primarily economic institution is critical because it both focusses the task and work of unions, and it does so in ways normed by the goals of economic life (rather than political, or social life). That norm, often called stewardship, is evoked from the commonly understood etymological rooted of economics, *oikonomia*, housekeeping, or household management. This is the picture of the economic life we get from *Rerum Novarum*, which argues it is a "great mistake" to imagine classes as "naturally hostile" or that "the wealthy and the working men are intended by nature to live in mutual conflict" [RN, 19]. And that, there are duties that bind the proletarian and the worker, the faithful performance of work agreed upon, just as there are duties that bind the owner, safe and reasonable conditions of labor, and "to give to every one what is just" [RN, 20]. Invoking *Rerum Novarum*, *Laborem Exercens* says that "human work is a *key*, probably *the essential key*, to the whole social question" [LE, 3].

Fundamentally, argues John Paul II, man is the subject of work, not the reverse, and the end of that work is the dignity of man. This means that "*the primary basis of the value of work is man himself*, who is its subject" [LE, 6]. This leads, he argues, to a pivotal conclusion about the ethical nature of work:

> However, true it may be that man is destined for work and called to it, in the first place work is "for man" and not man "for work." … In fact, in the final analysis it is always man who is the *purpose of work*, whatever work it is that is done by man-even if the common scale of values rates it as the merest "service," as the most monotonous even most alienating work. [LE, 6]

The great nobility of work is a common refrain of *Laborem Exercens*, which when humans are either robbed of or dominated by does damage to the dignity of man, and the image of God. Writes John Paul II, "work is a good thing for man—a good thing for his humanity—because through work man *not only transforms nature*, adapting it to his own needs, but he also *achieves fulfilment* as a human being and indeed, in a sense, becomes more a human being" [LE, 9].

FUNDAMENTALLY, ARGUES JOHN PAUL II, MAN IS THE SUBJECT OF WORK, NOT THE REVERSE, AND THE END OF THAT WORK IS THE DIGNITY OF MAN

> This is why Pennings argues that while labor has a proper role to exercise in a variety of spheres,
>
> the primary sphere in which unions operate is the economic sphere. They ought first of all not to be about rights, redistribution, or social support. They are about (1) *stewarding human capital* and ensuring that (2) *its potential is realized* and a (3) *fair return on investment* is provided. (Pennings 2010)

This provides a very different framework for the basic goals of labor unions than the caricatures presented by Pennings above, a kind of "spiritual blueprint" for labor relations. It implies an obligation of unions to:

(1) identify and cultivate the potential of workers,
(2) to labor actively on behalf of workers to help them discern and carry out a dignified vocation, and

(3) to ensure that they are fairly treated and receive just compensation for their contribution, including a share of the rewards of their investment. (Pennings 2010)

This is a framework that we can use to judge the relative success of trade unionism, one which deals with workers in the context of their contribution, and one which depends on the underlying moral vocabulary of *Rerum Novarum* and, indeed, of the Christian gospel.

The Limits of Labor

Among the fecund theological insights on human society that the tradition of papal encyclicals offers us is the recognition of the *limits* of the discrete spheres of human activity, and the interdependence—or solidarity—that these spheres must practice together to realize a harmonious society. It will, in all likelihood, have occurred to the perceptive reader that the foregoing picture of a new paradigm for trade unionism is idealistic, in that it depends on not only an amenable capital climate and a non-adversarial political context, but also an underlying willingness to recover this highly polarizing content of Catholic social doctrine for the purpose of revitalization. These, a labor representative might fairly say, are commendable sentiments, but the grand prisoner's dilemma at the labor negotiating table means that adversarial rights-based approaches will favor the first to break rank with all this talk of "mutuality" and "interdependence" among capital and labor. But this paradigm, and in fact even the encyclicals themselves, are not this naïve. First, an allowance in both *Rerum Novarum* and *Laborem Exercens* is made for the "right to strike," to exercise a final option in the face of demonstrable and intransigent injustice. This is one fundamental limit *Rerum Novarum* recognizes to the paradigm of partnership. But second, it also recognizes that labor is only *one piece* of the renewal demanded in society, and that key as work is to the social question, it is not the only or even necessarily decisive human institution. Renewal in labor, in other words, must accompany a simultaneous realization of norms. We therefore come in eyes wide open to this paradigm as aspirational, norming our approach to organized labor, certainly, but also knowing that in a broken world the union will never be able to achieve each of these aspects perfectly, through no (potential) fault of its own efforts.

"North American unions are addicted to their rights-based approach, relying on tools of industrial conflict to play games of power," says Ray Pennings (2010), and he would know. The increasing aggression, both on the part of capital and labor, over the 20th century has conditioned a highly adversarial system whose logic can become a kind of "iron cage" from which negotiators can only with greatest of difficulty escape. The limits of this framework are reached when labor must, in deference to its above objectives, insist through the form of strike action that labor honor some essential obligation.

Rerum Novarum mentions strikes only twice, and though in the first case it does not rule them out by any means, it does remand to the state the right to break strikes if they threaten public safety [RN, 36]. In the second place, it places on the state the obligation to remove "in good time" the causes which lead to the conflict, since strikes are a "grave inconvenience" and "injurious to trade and to the general interests of the public" [RN, 39]. In both cases Pope Leo XIII recognizes that strikes are often caused by long hours, work that is too hard, and wages that are too low. In other words, in both cases the encyclical recognizes there are justified grievances.

Laborem Exercens, interpreting *Rerum Novarum*, offers a more robust defense of the need to strike. "This method [striking]," writes Pope John Paul II, "is recognized by Catholic social teaching as legitimate in the proper conditions and within just limits" [LE, 20]. He sustains that workers should be assured a right to strike, while at the same time insisting that this right not be abused, but used only as an extreme means in the breakdown between capital and labor. In fact, strikes—as with the purpose of labor unions as a whole—should be understood primarily as *for* things, not a struggle *against* others. Even if the struggle, says Pope John Paul II, takes on the character of opposition, it is only because of its first aim at "the good of social justice" not struggle for the sake of struggle, or to eliminate an adversary [LE, 20]. And there is, in addition to this larger moral aim, always a public interest.

The caveat of the "public interest" is an interesting one, in the way that it has worked itself out in labor negotiation in different developed democracies. In many Canadian provinces, for example, governments can insist on binding arbitration in cases of public interest, and for certain services deemed essential, the right to strike is entirely absent. In other European countries, by contrast, the State takes a far more activist role in mediating critical (and in some cases non-critical) contracts making, in a sense, every arbitration between capital and labor "binding."

Regardless, we can see that exception is made in the form of adversarial approaches that *may* be needed. The priority of labor as an economic institution is not to break its power to bargain vis-à-vis capital, but rather to *repoint* and *reframe* its priorities with a moral vocabulary that *makes possible* a non-adversarial partner strategy with capital.

The right to strike is one recognition this is not always possible. And, in fact, the interdependence of certain spheres on labor, especially capital and the political, will mean that major decay in any of these key, correlated spheres will almost certainly have a destructive effect on labor. Unquestionably, decay in other spheres, for example the family, will also have a major effect on labor. Labor mobility in Canada has become a major issue in the Canadian economy, and the near extinction of family life in Alberta oil sands has come to a point of crisis for both capital and labor (Pennings 2006). The problem of "mobile labor" is not a new one, but its scale and effects are only starting to be understood, especially those on parents, especially fathers, long absent from their families. It can, tragically, become the case that, as in northern Alberta, capital and labor are of one mind on this relational catastrophe, but both lack the normative power to redress it. Compensation, sadly, can prove more enabler of destructive habits, more a violation of dignity, than its recognition. But in the sphere of capital this is especially obvious, where anonymous shareholder expectations, largely held beyond account for how profit margins are increased, squeeze labor in ways that are—by the definition of *Rerum Novarum*—*economically* unsound. In these environments, it is almost impossible for labor to embrace a model of partnership, and very quickly adversarial confrontations escalate until strikes become alarmingly common. This is, of course, hardly the rule in every industry, but unreasonable demands on the part of capital, which *have* become more common, can put management in an unenviable position.

The political sphere itself can create a charged environment, especially when in an attempt to legislatively punish workers associations that have drifted into partisan work far outside of their mandate. This is the case in the so-called Right to Work campaigns across the United States, and to a lesser degree in Canada. I turn to this as a case through which to apply and evaluate the framework for labor unionism provided by *Rerum Novarum*.

Case: "The Right to Work"

The case study I use to test this approach is the contemporary crisis crystalizing around the "right to work" in North America. In the United States, currently 24 states have passed Right to Work laws.[1] Right to Work laws guarantee that no person can be compelled, as a condition of employment, to join or not to join, or to pay dues to a labor union. It is my argument[2] that the foregoing engagement with *Rerum Novarum* gives us a picture of the *moral aims* of labor unionism. I call them moral aims very specifically, to discriminate in the case of practical politics from what Charles Taylor calls *operative modes* (Taylor and Maclure 2011). Operative modes are institutional arrangements that are designed to *safeguard* moral aims, and are often interpreted or applied in variable ways, depending on context. Problems arise when operative modes are conflated with moral aims, producing a kind of backward logic that can obscure the proper aims of labor.

In the case of the Right to Work an institutional arrangement, or an operative mode, is conflated with a moral aim—namely the rights of individual preference and choice—which is not, in fact, one of the primary moral aims of the trade union. Indeed, such a libertarian picture of volunteerism may even be considered to be a transposition of secular liberality, which tends to reduce the moral aims of any institution or organization to the specific concerns of its constituent members. Having then considered the moral aims of trade unionism at length, as provided in the "spiritual blueprint" of *Rerum Novarum*, I argue in this case that so applied to the Right to Work, these laws *violate* the integrity of those moral aims, making difficult, if not impossible, the actualization of those aims. This is the basis on which we can speak of political overreach, a violation of the integrity of an independent sphere of human life which actually prevents it from realizing its own internal norms.

An "operative mode" is a variable institutional arrangement, designed to safeguard moral aims. Several have already been suggested, including the different structures through which labor and capital meet and negotiate in European countries, especially the Low Countries, compared to either America or Canada. Each of these uses slightly different operative modes, largely to secure the same moral aims, namely (in a basic sense) the harmonious relations between labor and capital. But if we consider other jurisdictions, for example India or China, we may agree that in order to secure the moral aims of labor unionism explained above, the operative mode or institutional arrangements would have to be very different. This can be for any number of reasons. India is a constitutional democracy with relatively reasonable labor laws on the books, but suffers from the extremely variable application of those laws depending on region. That is to say, the *rule of law* in India is not always and everywhere equally enforced. This is the basic argument of people like Gary Haugen and Victor Boutros at the International Justice Mission, which does indeed do a great deal of work in that country. Their complaint in *The Locust Effect* is not that India's laws and law makers are corrupt, inept, or absent, but rather that the *law enforcement* is very poor, and of extremely variable quality across the country (Haugen and Boutros 2014). The problem, as they say, is that the laws that exist are not being enforced. What is needed, in an operative sense, are labor unions *powerful* enough to compel enforcement, and the accompanying civil and social associations to sustain labor activism (freedom of speech, freedom of association, freedom of the press, freedom of religion, so forth).

China has not dissimilar problems. Han Dongfang, a world famous China labor activist, and one time architect of the Beijing Workers' Autonomous Federation (BWAF) during the Tiananmen Square protests of 1989, describes China's labor laws as among the most enlightened in the world. China has, he often remarks jokingly, the largest labor union in the world, the ACFTU (All-China-Federation of Trade Unions) with over 900,000 full time staff (Dijkema and Dongfang 2014). In his opinion, it has become a power in its own right, a political challenger to the actual communist party itself. The result is that, again, the actual laws that exist are often not enforced, or are enforced in arbitrary or nepotistic ways. The result, which is no secret to much of the world, is that a regime founded on worker's rights and interests, is a bad place to work. Here an absolute operative mode of collectivist authoritarianism intended to secure *exactly* the moral aims of harmony between capital and labor, actually precludes any such harmony. In this case, argues Han Dongfang, now an exile from China living in Hong Kong, reform of the monopolized labor system is essential to any improvement in actual worker rights. Here, unlike India, labor has become *so powerful* its survival as a particular operative mode as eclipsed its moral aims. In both cases, tragically, the actual laws themselves, were they enforced, would be a major practical improvement.

So here we see two examples where operative modes will need to be variable to accommodate the moral aims of labor unionism. What about the Right to Work in North America? Do these laws facilitate the moral aims of unions?

They do not. The reason is that the institutional arrangement provided by Right to Work laws assumes that the moral basis of trade unions is an atomistic and individualist perspective on unionism. That is to say, it assumes unions must only act on the preferences and choice of its individual members, and should dissent be registered, those members should either have their views reflected, or be given the opportunity to opt-out of collective bargaining. This understanding of volunteerism is a basic picture of secular liberalism, and seems reasonable to many at the face of it. Yet it confuses the moral aims of labor unions with those of political liberalism, and further does so in such an extreme fashion as to be untenable if actually applied back to democracy itself. American and Canadian governments regularly exercise judgment with which significant minorities, if not outright majorities, of their constituents disagree. This does not immediately invalidate their moral authority to govern. These states have *accountability* intrinsic in their mandate, and every few years the engines of democracy will provide people the opportunity to decide whether their government's judgment has become so disagreeable as to vote against them. And *even when they do* their opinions may not be reflected in a popular vote, and they will remain subject to legislation and acts of government with which they profoundly disagree. Such is the miracle of democracy.

A radical atomistic picture of voluntary association rests on a fictional presumption of perpetual ascent on the part of its individual members. Yet while this may be the largely default paradigm through which association is understood, its problems are increasingly manifest in communities whose covenants are oriented toward *more fundamental* moral aims than the particular interests of individual members. This is the case for covenants in religious communities, as in religious organizations and institutions more generally (hence, institutional religious freedom).[3] Labor unions too have concerns more basic than individual preference, namely the stewardship of human capital. Practically speaking, unions exercise this primary obligation through *collective bargaining*, a process made nearly impossible by "right to work" and its atomistic associational perspective.

Adjudication may be reached in this case by applying a kind of Westminster model to labor organizations, namely providing a political space within which open shop and competitive labor representation can flourish (the State's obligation to ensure), but foreclosing on individual defaults on a signed union covenant between open periods for renewal. This is, in fact, widely practiced in many labor environments, including North America. It is, not accidentally, largely the operative mode of politics too. The old joke that Canadians elect virtual dictators on a rotating four year basis has roots in the fact that a majority in the Canadian parliament has very little effective accountability to the population, outside of Constitutional or juridical limits, between elections. This, proud constitutional-monarchists will be quick to add, is a major advantage for coherent policy making, and stewarding the moral aims of public justice, rather than perpetual electioneering.

The Right to Work laws properly identify that establishment unions have foreclosed, in some jurisdictions, on competitive representation, but have wrongly insisted on atomized associationalism as the solution, undercutting the possibility of collective bargaining, thereby crippling labor's negotiating power, and effectively violating labor's ability to achieve its moral aims. The result has been that because labor unionism has overstepped *politically* and *socially* in their mandates, even their basic and essential *economic* function has become untenable.

There is plenty of blame to go around, naturally, but the point of this case is to demonstrate that the spiritual blueprint provided by *Rerum Novarum* can and does make practical contributions to major disputes on the role and limits of labor unionism in today's world. In fact, in providing an essential moral vocabulary for the work and aims of unions, *Rerum Novarum* gives us the ability to discriminate between better and worse labor policy and practice, and indeed benchmarks for how to think about *progress* in labor rights across various jurisdictions.

Conclusion

Rerum Novarum is not the only, but it is one of the best, sources for the recovery of a moral vocabulary through which to understand and practice present day labor unionism. Its spiritual blueprint, for (1) the identification and cultivation of the potential of workers; (2) the work on behalf of members to discern and carry out a dignified vocation (work for man, not man for work); (3) and the fair treatment and just compensation for worker contribution, including a just share of the reward of their investment, is a major intervention in today's often rights based, material adversarialism that dominates North American unionism. Recovering the moral aims of labor unions yields not only a picture by which to judge present day cases, like the operative mode of Right to Work laws, but it also gives an inspiring picture of what progress in labor might look like in highly variable settings, like India and China. Perhaps most urgently, for North Americans, it identifies the sources and benchmarks for revitalization of their own tradition of labor unions. That dream, of getting beyond "zero sum" conversations on labor, like "buy American," where labor from the developed world uses its *own* resources, talent, and power to advocate on behalf of more than its own members and society, is one that can only be realized on the back of the powerful, religious images invoked by *Rerum Novarum*, *Laborem Exercens*, and the very labor representatives who practice their logic at the negotiating table. ❖

1. Alabama, Arizona, Arkansas, Kansas, Florida, Georgia, Idaho, Indiana, Iowa, Louisiana, Michigan, Mississippi, Nebraska, Nevada, North Carolina, North Dakota, Oklahoma, South Carolina, South Dakota, Tennessee, Texas,Utah, Virginia, and Wyoming.
2. I owe a great deal to Brian Dijkema, Program Director of Work and Economics at Cardus, and Ray Pennings, Executive Vice-President of Cardus, for conversation and inspiration on this argument. Both have worked widely in the labor world, and continue to be among Canada's leading authorities on open shop and alternative unions.
3. See for example Stanely Carlson-Thies on this, and his Institutional Religious Freedom Alliance (IRFA), now merged with the Center for Public Justice (as of September 2014).

References

Dijkema, Brian, and Han Dongfang. 2014. "In Good Faith: Compromise in the Face of Revolution." *Comment Magazine*, March.

Encyclical of Pope Benedict XVI on Integral Human Development in Charity and Truth. 2009. *Caritas in Veritate*. Accessed September 10, 2014. http://www.vatican.va/holy_father/benedict_xvi/encyclicals/documents/hf_ben-xvi_enc_20090629_caritas-in-veritate_en.html.

Encyclical of Pope John Paul II on Human Work. 1981. *Laborem Exercens*. Accessed September 10, 2014. http://www.vatican.va/holy_father/john_paul_ii/encyclicals/documents/hf_jp-ii_enc_14091981_laborem-exercens_en.html.

Encyclical of Pope Leo XIII on Capital and Labor. 1891. *Rerum Novarum*. Accessed September 10, 2014. http://www.vatican.va/holy_father/leo_xiii/encyclicals/documents/hf_l-xiii_enc_15051891_rerum-novarum_en.html.

Goudzwaard, Bob. 1979. *Capitalism and Progress: A Diagnosis of Western Society*. Grand Rapids, MI: Eerdmans.

Haugen, Gary, and Victor Boutros. 2014. *The Locust Effect: Why the End of Poverty Requires the End of Violence*. Oxford: Oxford University Press.

Milligan, Frank. 2004. *Eugene A. Forsey: An Intellectual Biography*. Calgary: University of Calgary Press.

Pennings, Ray. 2006. *Working Mobile: A Study of Labour Mobility in Canada's Industrial Construction Sector*. Hamilton: Work Research Foundation.

Pennings, Ray. 2010. "Work and Love in the Global Village: Responding to *Caritas in Veritate*." *The Review of Faith and International Affairs* 8 (4): 69–73.

Taylor, Charles, and Jocelyn Maclure. 2011. *Secularism and Freedom of Conscience*. Cambridge, MA: Harvard University Press.

AMONG SPIES, POPES, AND THE GOOD CYRENIANS: *LA COMMISSION POUR L'EGLISE PERSÉCUTÉE* AS A TRANSNATIONAL CATHOLIC ACTOR IN THE COLD WAR

By Adrian Hänni

When around 1200 representatives of national and international Catholic lay organizations came together at the First World Congress of the Lay Apostolate in Rome in October 1951, the absence of delegates from Eastern Europe was obvious (Minvielle 2001, 113–167). Accordingly, the Congress explicitly commemorated the so-called persecuted church and the victims of "atheist ideologies" in its final declaration. Even Pius XII (1954, 1499) deplored, in his address to the participants of the Congress, the fate of the incarcerated priests in the countries "in which the Church is persecuted like in the first centuries of Christendom."

During the Congress, the executive committee of the Conference des Organisations Internationales Catholiques (Conference of the International Catholic Organizations, COIC) felt inspired to set up a permanent group with the objective to address the problem of the Catholic Church behind the Iron Curtain. This group, which was called *La Commission pour l'Eglise Persécutée*, forms the subject of this article.

The role of the Holy See as a political actor in the Cold War has been widely acknowledged (e.g. Rhodes 1992; Kirby [ed.] 2003b; Pollard 2014). Especially under Pope Pius XII, the East–West conflict was the main preoccupation of Vatican diplomacy, whose efforts were overwhelmingly directed toward combating communism during the former's pontificate. Pius XII himself often and vigorously denounced communist ideology in his speeches, radio messages, and encyclicals, in which he formulated the Catholic rejection of "materialistic atheism." The most dramatic public action was probably the excommunication of communists through a July 1949 decree of the Holy Office (Acta Apostolicae Sedis 1949, 334). Less visible, the Vatican even maintained what Pollard (2014, 379–383) called a "special relationship" with the United States in the early years of the Cold War, a close cooperation to subvert communism in Europe that included the sharing of intelligence (Kirby 2003a, 120; Gallagher 2008, 161–166). The fervent anti-communism of Pius XII was eventually succeeded by the "Ostpolitik" of John XXIII,[1] who sought better relations with the communist world through a move toward non-alignment in the Cold War and an opening to a dialogue with the East (Hebblethwaite 1984). The cordial relationships between the Holy See under John Paul II and the Reagan administration, including papal support for US Cold War policies and especially for Solidarity in Poland, have likewise received widespread attention (di Stefano 2008; Gayte 2011, 713–736; Wanner 2017).

However, the Holy See was not the only transnational Catholic actor engaged in the East–West confrontation. Since the early 20th century, the Catholic community has been acting in international affairs in two primary ways. In addition to the direct "top level" engagement of the Holy See, the Catholic Church has taken part in global governance less officially through a plethora of international Catholic organizations (ICOs) (Ahern 2013, 45–53). In his monograph *The Holy See and the International Order* written in the 1970s, Cardinale (1976, 266) describes the ICOs as being "among the most efficacious and flexible instruments" that the church uses in its public engagement.

Besides the Holy See, several transnational Catholic organizations and networks were accordingly engaged as political actors in the global Cold War, often in close contact and coordination with the ecclesiastic hierarchy. The *Commission pour l'Eglise Persécutée* (The Commission for the Persecuted Church, henceforth "the Commission"), which cooperated with the Holy See as well as with European intelligence services and a Russian anti-communist resistance organization, is a highly significant and in may ways unique example.[2] The following analysis of the Commission will therefore enhance our understanding of the political role played by transnational Catholic actors in the Cold War, considering that academic inquiry on the topic has focused almost exclusively on the Holy See. While doing so, the article also provides an illustrating case study how Catholic actors used religion in myriad ways during the Cold War—by drawing upon religious resources and institutions or by promoting religious practices—at a time religious themes gained a prominent place in Western propaganda and the religious was used in covert operations.[3]

The COIC and the Establishment of the Commission

The origins of the COIC, the parent body of the Commission, lie in the inter-war years. From 1927 to the outbreak of World War II in 1939, the leaders of the ICOs met annually at a private and informal conference to better harmonize their international activities and to envisage possible collaborations, especially in regards to their work with the League of Nations (Minvielle 2001, 81; Ahern 2013, 51–52). After the war, the institution was re-established, under the initiative of Pax Romana, at a meeting in the Swiss town of Fribourg in January 1948. This foundation of the COIC took place before the backdrop of an apostolic verve and intensive movement growth in late 1940s Europe, when a number of new organizations were created and the lay apostolate experienced a process of internal differentiation (Minvielle 2001, 49, 78; Grosse Kracht 2016, 63–65).[4] As the result of an effort directed by Pax Romana and the Office catholique international du cinema, the COIC got rid of its informal character in 1950 by turning into a central umbrella organization for several dozens ICOs to assure the coordination of Catholic forces and prepare common activities, without touching the autonomy of its constituent organizations (Minvielle 2001, 82). A visible sign of this change of the structure and working methods of the COIC was the opening of a permanent secretariat in Fribourg in June 1951, four months ahead of the First World Congress of the Lay Apostolate. The organizations now represented by the COIC can be classified into three categories: (1) the ICOs of Catholic Action (mass organizations);

(2) technical ICOs (e.g. Struggle against Alcoholism, Defense of Children's Rights, Catholic Cinema); (3) professional and social ICOs (e.g. intellectuals, nurses, and athletes).

The COIC thus reflected an attempt to internationalize the Catholic Action that had emerged in different national contexts in the inter-war years through a lay apostolate that was actively trying to shape the increasingly transnational and globalizing post-war societies in close accordance with the Catholic hierarchy. As an internal report of the COIC (1954, 1) explained, the organization acted upon a mandate "to launch on the global level, in cooperation with the Hierarchy, an action that can be compared to the one that is waged, inside each nation, by Catholic Action." The cooperation between the COIC and the Holy See was indeed close. The COIC leadership vowed to "act in complete concord with the ecclesiastic hierarchy and solicit from her its immense backing" (COIC 1952, 3), and since 1950 an official representative of the Holy See's Secretariat of State participated in the work of the COIC's executive committee (Minvielle 2001, 82–83).

Another sign of the pivotal influence of the Holy See was the large financial dependence of the COIC, whose operation was to a major degree bankrolled by the Vatican. Through the 1950s, the COIC received an annual amount of 20,000 US dollar (USD, ca. 180,000 2017 USD) from the Secretariat of State. In 1956, this amounted to no less than three-quarters of the COIC's total expenses, and still constituted two-thirds of the overall budget in 1960. In 1964, the Holy See's contribution had nominally increased to 22,000 USD (ca. 172,000 2017 USD) and still constituted about 62 percent of the budget.[5]

The interested involvement and strong support of the Holy See for the COIC reflected the new attitude of the Holy See toward the international Catholic movement in the post-war period more generally. As Vittorino Veronese wrote to Giovanni Battista Montini, the future Pope Paul VI, in 1947, before World War II the meetings of the leaders of the ICOs and their work with the League of Nations "were barely tolerated by the Roman Authorities, who mistrusted the laicism of certain international groups" (Goldie 1998, 47).[6] In the post-war period, the distrust prevailing in the inter-war years was replaced by a complete approval and explicit encouragements. According to Minvielle (2001, 83), the organized action of lay Catholics within the ICOs or the institutions of the United Nations (UN) was from then on considered a useful auxiliary of Vatican diplomacy.

Constituting one of a few permanent working groups within the COIC, the Commission was originally founded in 1951 to organize a vast campaign of collecting signatures and organizing protests at the UN to build up pressure on the governments of the countries under Communist rule where the church suffered from persecution (Bernard 1954, 1). This objective reflected the central theme of the COIC at the time: the collaboration of Catholics in the activities of the emerging official international organisms, especially the UN and its agencies (Minvielle 2001, 80–82).[7] However, the Commission quickly deemed such efforts ineffective. This judgment set the direction for the future: Over the next two decades, the Commission would largely reject action to directly impact political institutions but instead employ a wide range of tactics to target international public opinion by mobilizing mass audiences. "If the Catholic propaganda wants to fight effective against Marxism," its members recognized early, "it has to renounce using solely purely intellectual methods and arguments convincing for the elite" (COIC 1955, 13).

In its first three years, the Commission was a small group of four to five lay Catholics and clerics, chaired by its permanent President Jean Bernard. A priest originating from the small Grand Duchy of Luxembourg, Bernard was incarcerated in the concentration camp of Dachau for one year and a half during World War II, before taking over as the director of the Catholic daily newspaper *Luxemburger Wort* after 1945. In 1947, he was further elected President of the International Catholic Organization for Cinema (OCIC), a member organization of the COIC. Bernard would lead the OCIC for a quarter century, an effort that led film historian Lesch (2015, 85–99) to call him "[o]ne of the largely forgotten Catholic film leaders in Europe."

The Commission and Western Intelligence

However, not Jean Bernard but the editor-in-chief of the Catholic International Press Agency (KIPA), Henri Marmier, was the driving force within the Commission during its early years. During World War II, Canon Marmier, who had been teaching at the Catholic seminary in Fribourg since 1933, had written a book on "La Petite Eglise" (Marmier 1941), a secret association of secular priests in francophone Switzerland in the first half of the 19th century. Fighting for an ultramontane restoration, the members of the "Petite Eglise" strengthened their theological education to crusade against both liberal policies and radical ideas (Python 1987, 14–16, 21–23, 126–134, 140–171; Genoud 1991, 49–57; Marti 2006, 353–370). After the war, Marmier began personally applying his insights on secret networking and political mobilization. Through his activities from the shadows, he also made the decisive link to a man who would profoundly change the character of the Commission. Enter Jean Violet.

Since the early 1950s, the international lawyer Violet worked as a fixer for Antoine Pinay, a leading French politician and Prime Minister in 1952. He started building a small, informal and sometimes conspiratorial group of influential personalities around the French statesman, which consisted mainly of leading Christian-Democrats and lay Catholics from France and Germany. This transnational group, whose members shared a vision of a Catholic Europe united in its defense against the threat posed by communism, soon included the Dominican Father Yves-Marc Dubois, an agent of the Vatican intimately involved in the world of the ICOs, and Marmier (Grossmann 2014a, 2014b; Hänni 2016, 118–130).

Through a recommendation by Pinay, Violet also became an agent ("honorable correspondant") of the French foreign intelligence service SDECE[8] around the same time (Grossmann 2014a, 444–446). The fervent Catholic envisaged the situation of the Church in communist-ruled Eastern Europe as the starting-point to implement his ideas for "action psychologique" (psychological warfare). His concept preached the use of psychological insights and banked on objective information on the discrepancy between the promises and realities of communist rule (Grossmann 2014b, 91). Violet was able to convince the SDECE as well as the nascent German foreign intelligence service[9] to fund a joint undertaking that would later be known as Operation Pax and was to a major extent run through the Commission (Marmier 1955; Violet 1956, [n.d.], 11; Langemann 1980; Melnik 1989; Krop 1995, 544–548; Melnik 2008, 442). With the French and eventually also the German intelligence service starting to contribute a monthly sum of 5000–6000 French Francs (ca. 10,000 2017 USD) to Violet's operations, the Commission was so profoundly reshaped that in a public report published five years later, it was made known that "our commission, as we know it, was founded in Fribourg in September 1954" (*L'Echo des Persécutés*, January 1959, 5).

The date relates to a meeting in Fribourg on September 26 and 27, 1954, at which the Commission was restructured and enlarged. Louis Gauthier, a former director of the Kantonspolizei Fribourg (state police of Fribourg) and notorious for helping Nazis and collaborators evade justice after World War II (Van Dongen 2008, 276–277, 296–297, 311, 508), was installed as the Secretary and Vice President. Well connected in intelligence circles and thus well-placed to coordinate with the SDECE (cf. Lebec 1997, 140), Gauthier set up the Commission's office in Fribourg. In November 1954, he also traveled to Rome to inform the ecclesiastic authorities about the new developments which they fully approved (COIC 1955, 14). The Commission considered it indispensable to maintain a "close and easy contact" with the Holy See, as it considered such a direct link to the Vatican as the necessary "guarantee that its activities developed at every moment in perfect accordance with the intentions of the Church" (Bernard 1954).

Mobilizing the Masses in the West

Before the beginning of Operation Pax, the Commission had run on a shoestring annual budget of 2000 Swiss francs (ca. 4000 2017

USD), which was allotted to it by the COIC. Owing to the new financial opportunities, the activities of the Commission were greatly expanded in the years following 1954 and reached a remarkable diversity. They can be grouped in three categories corresponding in principal to the three dimensions of the Apostolate according to the French model of Catholic Action (Grosse Kracht 2016, 122): (1) social/charity; (2) political/propaganda; (3) spiritual.

Social/Charity

One pillar of the Commission's activity was the organization and coordination of material aid for Church institutions behind the Iron Curtain. In this project, the Commission cooperated with the *Mission Catholique Suisse* (Catholic Mission of Switzerland, MCS), which was conveniently based in Fribourg. From there it managed the delivery of aid packages for almost a quarter century. The MCS was an obvious partner for the Commission, not just because of their common location in Fribourg but also considering that Marmier had served for the MCS during World War II (Grossmann 2014a, 452).

The MCS was originally founded at the dawn of World War I in 1914. Conceived as a wartime institution, the Mission cared for the physical and spiritual well-being of the victims of the two world wars in close coordination with both the Catholic hierarchy as well as the Red Cross, and supported the search for missing soldiers and civilians (Marmier 1947; MCS 1962). In contrast to 1918, the Mission continued its operation into peacetime after the end of World War II and in 1948, on the demand of the Nunciature in Bern and the last Apostolic Delegate to Yugoslavia, Silvio Oddi, it began sending aid parcels to the distressed Church in Yugoslavia (MCS 1962, 1). At the beginning of the 1950s, the shipments were extended to religious houses, seminaries, convents, and concentration camps for priests in a range of countries under Communist rule—in Eastern Europe, the Soviet Union but also in Vietnam.

The originally modest charity service was greatly expanded over the decade: In 1951, the shipments reached a total weight of 2379 kilograms and in 1954 about 3000 kilograms with an approximate value of 37,000 Swiss francs (ca. 78,000 2017 USD) (MCS [n.d.], 1). When the Commission's money—originating mainly from German and French intelligence—started pouring in, the aid shipments increased quickly to 4681 kilograms in 1955 and to 8135 kilograms representing a value of circa 120,000 Swiss francs (ca. 252,000 2017 USD) in 1956 (MCS 1956a; Gauthier 1957). The cooperation and personal connection between the Commission and the MCS had been institutionalized early, when the driving force of the Mission, the infatigable Marguerite Emery, also became a permanent member of the Commission. Besides the money provided through the Commission, the MCS used to procure significant relief aid through an annual call published in the Swiss press during the Advent season through Marmier's Catholic press agency KIPA.

The parcels sent behind the Iron Curtain were filled with goods as varied as cloths, shoes, glasses, food, linen, and drugs. As the countless thank-you notes received by the MCS (MCS-283; MCS-284) testify, this aid was much needed and appreciated. In 1962, the abbess of the Benedictine abbey on the Yugoslav island of Krk even wrote gratefully: "You are the good Cyrenian who helps us to carry our cross" (MCS 1962, 3).[10] It is therefore barely surprising that the communist regimes took action against the aid deliveries in several instances, by considerably raising tariffs or imposing other impediments. In some instances, the MCS was able to circumvent the crackdown by sending checks instead of packages, for example, to Yugoslavia in 1961. In other instances, the communist authorities prevailed. For example, aid deliveries to a concentration camp for priests in Czechoslovakia had to be suspended in 1961, after the MCS had sent 50 kilogram of clothes every month since 1952 to the priests submitted to forced labor in that camp (MCS 1962).

In addition to the material aid, the Commission and the MCS also sent a plethora of religious literature to Catholic institutions behind the Iron Curtain. A delivery of 14 parcels sent to the Soviet Republic of Lithuania only during the summer of 1956 Illustrate the dimensions. The packets, which were sent to six institutions in six different cities of the small country, included a great variety of liturgical, theological, and spiritual texts (MCS 1956b). In 1958, the Commission printed thousands of catechisms, prayer books, brochures, and other religious texts worth 14,000 Swiss francs (ca. 27,500 2017 USD), and had them sent to believers behind the Iron Curtain (COIC 1959, III/5). Such deliveries were a principal component of Operation Pax (cf. Melnik 1989, 154; Krop 1995, 546–548), taking place, of course, at the intersection of the charitable work of the Commission and its distinctly political activities.

Political/Propaganda

The Commission employed a wide range of tactics of mass mobilization with the objective to alert public opinion in the West to the character and extent of the persecution of the Church in the states under communist rule. The persecution of religion was used to showcase to Christian audiences the ugly reality of communism, its atheist character and absolute incompatibility with religion with the aim to immunize these audiences not only to Communist ideology but also to any form of détente and rapprochement. To achieve these goals, various mass media were employed that ranged from traditional outlets, such as the Catholic press or the KIPA, to more innovative media like exhibitions.

An early example of the Commission's crusade for public opinion was the serial novel *Terreur sur la Chine* ("Terror on China") published in the important Swiss Catholic newspaper *La Liberté* in 1955. Using the form of the feuilleton novel, which was exceedingly popular in the post-war years, this previously unpublished story features a French Catholic returning from China reporting in a lively manner about the persecutions the Chinese Catholics were suffering (COIC 1955, 14; COIC 1956a, 37–38).

Another product illustrating the propaganda work was the so-called *Martyrologe de l'Eglise du Silence* ("Martyrology of the Church of Silence"), which the Commission printed and distributed in 1959: A large poster displayed a map of the Eurasian landmass and North Africa, on which a block of red-colored countries representing the "Church of Silence" confronted a block of white-colored countries representing the "Church of Freedom." The territory of the "Church of Silence" corresponded precisely to the countries under communist rule, while the Iron and Bamboo Curtains constituted the border to the "Church of Freedom." The other side of the poster listed, country-by-country, the large number of bishops who fell victim to communist persecution, claiming that they occupied the first place in both the hate of the communists as well as in the life of the Church and its apostolate (see MCS-271 for a copy of the Martyrology).

The Martyrology hence reduces geospatial complexity to the simple explanatory binaries of the Cold War. Through the spiritualization of space, however, its semiotics goes beyond the secular imagery and political propaganda of the 1950s. The listing of the many "martyrs" in the East constructs the space ruled by the error that is communism also as a territory of witnessing the truth. "Meditating" in front of the Martyrology, the Catholic newspaper *La Liberté* (Menoud 1959) accordingly reached the conclusion that the menace was a testimony for the urgency of a "more lively and contagious" Christianity and for the need to construct a social order "inspired ever stronger by Christianity." In Switzerland, the poster was placed on the portal of all churches in the diocese of Lausanne, Geneva, and Fribourg as well as in the Canton of Ticino, with the explicit authorization and recommendation of the bishop (Commission [n.d.]d; Charrière 1959).

More important was the monthly magazine *Echo des Persécutés* (Echo of the Persecuted), which the Commission started publishing in 1956.[11] The staunchly anti-communist bulletin soon found a readership on all five continents, concentrating in France, Spain, Italy, Switzerland, Belgium, and Luxembourg, but with some copies being shipped as far as the United States, Mexico, South America, and Australia. The driving force behind the magazine was its editor-in-chief Louis Gauthier. In the style of an intelligence operation, he set up a network of sources from centers for refugees from Eastern Europe, among Catholic diplomats from Western European nations stationed in Eastern Europe, and through discreet liaison with Catholics living in countries behind the Iron Curtain (COIC 1959, III/3; CIA 1970). Based on their reports the *Echo* published periodical information on the situation of the Church in the individual states under communist rule.

The information collected was also used to compile "intelligence reports" that were shared with French and German intelligence services. However, the quality of the Commission's reports was disputed. The CIA, who had indirect access, found them "either erroneous or of such low level as to be of no interest." When the Commission solicited support from the CIA for its activities, the US foreign intelligence service accordingly declined (CIA 1970). In addition to its reports on the situation of religion in Eastern Europe, the *Echo des Persécutés* often printed essays that attacked communism and highlighted its incompatibility with Catholicism. Titles included "Communism: The great heresy of our era," "Communism: Enemy of all Religion," "Communism is always persecutor," "Atheism, Menace for Peace," or "Marxism and Religion" (*L'Echo des Persécutés*, September 1956, 15; April 1959, 1–3; August 1959, 1–3; August 1959, 4–6; October 1960, 7–10; November 1960, 7–10; December 1960, 3–7).

The Commission further organized, financed, supported or just encouraged several exhibitions on "the Persecuted Church," especially in the large Western European Catholic countries France and Italy. These exhibitions, putting on display educational material produced by the Commission, drew large numbers of visitors and received much local attention. In 1958, the Commission obtained that a mass was held in memory of the Church of Silence in the Vatican Pavillon at the Brussels World's Fair. In the same pavillon, a *Red Book* documenting religious persecution under communist rule was put on display and prints of a papal prayer for the Persecuted Church were handed out to visitors (COIC 1959, III/4-5). The Expo 58 was the first world fair after World War II and strongly characterized by the competition of the superpowers (Kretschmer 1999, 217–230).

Another major exposition was organized by the Commission in Lyon in late 1958, creating such a "profound sensation" that it was transformed into a traveling exhibition and embarked on a "tour de France" (*L'Echo des Persécutés*, January 1959, 6; COIC 1959, III/5). Maybe the most influential exhibit took place in the Basilica Spirito Santo (Basilica of the Holy Spirit) in Ravenna, Italy, in spring 1961. The exhibition was organized by the Italian youth of Catholic Action in collaboration with the Commission to counter communist propaganda, and specifically to react to the statement made on television by the leader of the Italian Communist Party Palmiro Togliatti in October 1960 that "there is no religious persecution in the states behind the Iron Curtain" (*L'Echo des Persécutés*, December 1961, 34).

The Italian communists reacted to the success of the exhibition energetically, although somewhat desperately, by publishing a communiqué through the Associazione Nazionale Perseguitati Politici Italiani Antifascisti (National Association of Politically Persecuted Italian Anti-Fascists, ANPPIA), claiming that the persecutions documented in the exhibit were committed by the Nazis, not the communists (*L'Echo des Persécutés*, December 1961, 34–35). The clash between Catholics and communists in Ravenna was followed by a large traveling exhibition touring through Italy in 1962. On display in Rome, it was reportedly visited by a majority of the clergy gathering in The Eternal City for the Second Vatican Council (*L'Echo des Persécutés*, December 1961, 34–35; January 1962, 1–2; *Témoins*, April 1963, 20–21). Further expositions were organized, for example at the "Exposition missionnaire de Lourdes" in the Catholic pilgrimage town in southwestern France (*L'Echo des Persécutés*, July 1962, 1–2; Rives 1961). Expositions had been providing state-actors, and especially the United States government, with an important space for their public diplomacy in the Cold War (Wulf 2015). With their exhibitions on the Persecuted Church, the Commission and like-minded Catholic actors successfully appropriated this outlet for the targeting of public opinion and mass mobilization in the late 1950s and early 1960s.

The single most significant effort to target global public opinion was the *Libro Rosso della*

Chiesa Perseguitata ("Red Book of the Persecuted Church") (Galter 1956). This large collection of documents on the history of religious persecution in the communist-ruled countries in Eastern Europe and Asia was envisaged to demonstrate that religious persecution was a permanent, fundamental, and inevitable practice of atheist communism (Galter 1957, XIV). Apparently, the Commission was not itself involved in the writing of the *Red Book*, a project that from the beginning was fully approved by the Secretariat of State, but chosen as a front group for its publication and tasked with its distribution (Marmier 1956). According to Lebec (1997, 140), the author hiding behind the pseudonym of Albert Galter was Albert Giovanetti, the first deputy of Domenico Tardini, Pius XII's Pro-Secretary of State for Extraordinary Ecclastical Affairs. While this assertion cannot be verified, it is plausible considering that Giovanetti maintained close relations to Violet and his circle as well as to the Commission. Until the mid-1960s, Giovanetti was a principal contact person for the Commission at the Secretariat of State (Bernard 1964; Krop 1995, 545). When Paul VI appointed him the Holy See's first Permanent Observer to the UN in 1964, he brought Violet's close associate Yves-Marc Dubois to New York as his counselor for social affairs.

The Commission judged the *Red Book* to be "one of the best instruments in the fight against communism" (COIC 1957, IV/6). Published first in Italian and French, it was submitted to Pius XII in May 1956. The Pope received Bernard, Gauthier, and Marmier on this occasion, commending them highly for their work and underscoring its extreme importance. Thereafter, the book was presented to the diplomatic corps at the Circolo di Roma, and discussed positively by Radio Vaticana and in *L'Osservatore Romano* (Commission [n.d.]b, 1–2). In the next year and a half editions in Spanish, English, German, and Portuguese followed. Secret intelligence money provided by Violet allowed the Commission to pursue a global diffusion of the *Red Book* "on a very big scale," mainly through the Catholic press, which heavily advertised the book, and press outlets deemed "neutral but sympathizing." Special events were organized by Catholic lay organizations, and copies distributed to high-ranking politicians and members of the Catholic Hierarchy (Commission [n.d.]b, 1–2; Grossmann 2014a, 455–456). Elaborate national propaganda campaigns were set up, even in a peripheral country like Australia ("La Propagande" 1957, 26). These national dissemination campaigns were sometimes entrusted to principal organizations of Catholic Action, for example in Spain to the Junta Técnica Nacional de la Acción Católica Española (*L'Echo des Persécutés*, February 1957; Commission [n.d.]b).

Moreover, the *Red Book* was smuggled behind the Iron Curtain ("Le Rayonnement" 1957; Krop 1995, 547), and the Commission attempted to confront Soviet authorities with the book. When a delegation of the Supreme Soviet of the Soviet Union made a visit to Luxembourg in summer 1956, Bernard tried to give a copy of the *Red Book* as a gift of honor to its Vice President Justas Paleckis during a press conference. Paleckis declined with the flimsy excuse that it was not custom for his delegation to accept such a gift (*L'Echo des Persécutés*, August 1956, 17–18).

Spiritual

In addition to the rather traditional media of political propaganda outlined in the last section, the Commission also exploited specifically religious practices for anti-communist mass mobilization. Already in the Commission's very first strategy document, formulated by Marmier in December 1951, the "action through prayer" was named as one of two central modes of action besides the "action upon public opinion" (Marmier 1951). This approach was reaffirmed a few weeks later, when Bernard demanded a "two-track crusade of prayer and public action" from the members of the Commission (Bernard 1952). Promoting the practice of praying was accordingly a cornerstone of the Commission's strategy, as the spiritual aid to the persecuted church was seen as important as the material aid, and the "crusade of prayers" (*L'Echo des Persécutés*, February 1956) was deemed as effective as the crusade to alert global public opinion. The Commission organized various prayer campaigns and launched prayer calendars, often mobilizing the ICOs as a multiplier with an official mandate by the COIC (Bernard 1956; Gauthier 1956). Local and national days of common prayers for the Persecuted Church were initiated in places as far apart as Geneva, Rome, the Netherlands, and Mexico (*L'Echo des Persécutés*, March 1959, 25; August 1959, 25; October 1959, 1; December 1960, 34). So-called Sundays of the persecuted were prepared in various dioceses.

In 1955, the Secretariat of State rejected a proposal of the Commission for the Papal proclamation of a world day of prayers, including an offertory, specifically for the persecuted church (COIC 1956a, 37). But the Commission remained persistent and after several initiatives, Pope Pius XII reacted to the input by composing a *Prayer for the Church of Silence* in July 1957 (COIC 1957, IV/3-4; *L'Echo des Persécutés*, June–July 1957, 28). In the next two years, the Commission, which was officially entrusted with its dissemination (COIC 1959, III/5), translated the prayer into 19 languages and printed and distributed hundreds of thousands of copies on both sides of the Iron Curtain and even in Vietnam (Commission [n.d.]d, 1; *L'Echo des Persécutés*, November 1959, 1–2).[12] Later, a prayer of Pope John XXIII for the Persecuted Church, composed in January 1959, was widely distributed as well.

However, it would be wrong to understand the Commission's mobilization of Christians to pray for the persecuted church solely or even primarily as a mobilization to an act of creed and an appeal to God. The Commission mainly regarded the practice of prayer as an effective resource to spread its message about the communists' persecution of the Church. By portraying the "cry of distress" of Catholics under communist rule, the prayer of Pius XII and similar prayers were supposed to emotionally move its readers and "wake up the Catholics" to the "rigorous command to fight the injustice of our time" (*L'Echo des Persécutés*, November 1959, 1–2). Far from being understood as a passive appeal to a metaphysical force, the members of the Commission conceived of the prayer as a "generator of action" ("pensée génératrice d'action") ("Travailler ensemble" 1957, 2). Prayers were thus used as a specific religious resource at their disposal to mobilize lay Catholics for the struggle against communism.

Exploiting the Fissures in the Iron Curtain

The spiritual and political-propagandistic "double crusade" of the 1950s focused on the anti-communist immunization of audiences in the free world. Besides this defensive concept, the Commission also envisioned a more offensive approach. Based on the belief that the Catholic Church, with its deep roots in Central and Eastern Europe, constituted the major, and eventually insurmountable, obstacle for communism (Commission [n.d.]b), the Commission regarded Catholicism as the focal point for a roll back of the communist system.

THE COMMISSION REGARDED CATHOLICISM AS THE FOCAL POINT FOR A ROLL BACK OF THE COMMUNIST SYSTEM

Besides the material aid and especially the sending of religious texts, this offensive approach was initially pursued through the *Oeuvre académique de l'Eglise du Silence* ("Academic Work of the Church of Silence"), which enabled promising youths from communist-ruled countries, who were deemed "susceptive to re-Christianize one day their homelands" (*L'Echo des Persécutés*, November 1960, 5), to pursue their studies at the University of Fribourg. With Gauthier acting as President and Emery as Secretary, the Oeuvre académique was a front organization for the Commission, with the objective to form a Catholic elite in certain communist states and thus "to prepare the religious renaissance" (Pizzardo 1955, 1). The institution internationalized a strategy of post-war German Catholic Action—the attempt to build a new Catholic elite by supporting the university education of particularly talented students, who would later be able to influence political decision-making (Grosse Kracht 2016, 366–369)—and combined it with the strategy of student exchange programs between the two blocs, which played a major role in the Cultural Cold War after Stalin's death (Richmond 2003, 2005, 355–360). However, the Oeuvre académique remained a small operation, with the number of supported students fluctuating between 6 and 10 youths coming from Poland, Vietnam, Yugoslavia, and the Soviet Republic of Lithuania.

It was not before the 1960s that the Commission shifted the target of its main activities beyond the Iron Curtain. At this time, the focus of its double-faced action shifted from a dialogue on the Persecuted Church between Christians in the Free World, which was multiplied through the various organizations of lay Catholics, to a true dialogue and exchange with the Persecuted Church through the utilization of fissures in the Iron Curtain. At the beginning of the 1960s, the Commission also succeeded in developing new sources of funds. In 1959, the intelligence money available to the group had significantly decreased and its activities had to be reduced (Commission [n.d.]d; several other documents in COIC-N08-ET). The budget hole was now plugged primarily with a Palm Sunday offertory in the diocese of Luxembourg, which was collected annually as part of a "Sunday of the Persecuted" from 1960 onwards and placed at the disposal of the Commission (various documents in COIC-N08-ET).[13]

In its attempt to exploit the few but growing fissures in the Iron Curtain to enable a dialogue and support the Church behind the Iron Curtain, the Commission increasingly planned to coordinate existing initiatives. Primarily, although with modest success, it sought to take on a coordinating role between the growing numbers of Catholic lay organizations delivering aid to the Church behind the Iron Curtain and to expand into a central clearing house for these groups. An especially close cooperation was maintained with Entr'Aide d'Eglise, an organization led by a lay Catholic but under the control of the francophone dioceses of Belgium, which had founded it in 1957. However, the Commission also launched its own activities. Most significantly, the group set up *Radio Omega*, the first and at its time only clandestine religious radio station, which directed religious broadcasts to Russia between August 1962 and August 1965.

Radio Omega

Radio Vaticana, "the Pope's Radio" operated by the Jesuits, had joined the Cold War anti-communist crusade early on. Modest broadcasts in Russian and several Eastern European languages started already during the 1940s. In 1950, radio officials announced expansion plans to counter the "Moscow-inspired atheist propaganda being poured into the ears of bewildered Catholics in Iron Curtain countries" (Nelson 1997, 107–109). Radio Vaticana turned its attention particularly on the persecution of the Catholic Church in Eastern Europe, transmitting the regular program *La chiesa del silenzio* (The Church of Silence), and from 1957 on *Radiogiornale* (Radio News), which was directed especially at Eastern Europe (Pollard 2010, 196–197). In 1962, Radio Vaticana broadcasted overall 39.75 hours in 17 languages to countries under communist rule ("Section Radio" 1962, 10). Presumably, these broadcasts were jammed behind the Iron Curtain and according to Pollard (2014, 374), they had a deeper impact on public opinion in the West than they had on people in Eastern Europe. In any case, until as late as 1967 the emphasis of Radio Vaticana was on the technical, not the content, and the station was staffed and structured accordingly (Nelson 1997, 107–108).

The Commission, for its part, shared this critical evaluation of Radio Vaticana's effect behind the Iron Curtain at the time. It also felt that the station, because of its specific Roman Catholic character, could by principle not offer a complete response to the cultural and spiritual hunger of the people under communist rule (*Eglise-Témoin*, November 1967). The other radio stations transmitting religious broadcasts behind the Iron Curtain—primarily the BBC, Radio Madrid, Radio Free Europe, and Radio Liberty—were judged even more critically by the Commission, which lamented their various shortcomings ("Section Radio" 1962, 10–11). Accordingly, the Commission decided to explore the possibility to direct its own broadcasts behind the Iron Curtain at a meeting in November 1959

(Commission [n.d.]d, 2). After a lengthy period of planning and preparation—which included consultations with the Secretariat of State, several bishops and even Cardinal Jozsef Mindszenty, the leader of the Catholic Church in Hungary confined to the US Embassy in Budapest at the time—Radio Omega went on air on August 1, 1962.[14]

The radio section of the Commission was led by Father Jan Fierens from the CICM[15] missionary congregation in the Belgian town of Scheut. Fierens had worked as a missionary in China from 1937 to 1953, where he was apprehended first by the Japanese occupiers and later by Mao Zedong's government. After being detained six years either under house arrest, in prison or in a concentration camp, Fierens was expelled and sent on missions in Haiti and the United States by his congregation. Back in Europe, he taught a course on "the psychology of the apostolate in Communist milieus" at the International University of Social Sciences in Rome before accepting a full time position for the Commission to organize its radio project in late 1961 (Bernard 1962a, 1–2; Commission 1963a). After Louis Gauthier had died unexpectedly—and some say mysteriously (Krop 1995, 546)—in August 1962, Fierens also took over as Secretary and moved the Commission's Secretariat to Brussels, where the radio section was already located.

Radio Omega's Russian language short wave broadcasts into the Soviet Union, one hour daily, were technically executed by the National Alliance of Russian Solidarists (NTS) through a transmitter that this militantly anti-communist organization of Russian exiles, seeking to overthrow the Soviet regime, had been using since 1950 to broadcast its clandestine Radio Free Russia. The Commission paid the NTS for this service, which sometimes also included translation work, around 8000–10,000 Swiss francs (ca. 15,000–18,500 2017 USD) every month (Bernard 1962b; de Habicht 1962, 2, 1963b, 1963c; de Reymaeker 1963a, 1963b). Overall, Radio Omega was run with a budget of more than 1.5 million Belgian Francs (between 300,000 and 350,000 2017 USD) (Commission [n.d.]c). This money was raised specifically for the clandestine radio operation and not covered with the Commission's regular budget. A main contributor of funds was the Holy See through the Secretariat of State (Commission 1963b, 8–12). In turn, the Vatican desired to be kept informed closely on the operation and expected to be consulted on every strategic decision (various documents in COIC-N08-ET, particularly de Habicht 1964). Hence, the Holy See indirectly also supported the NTS with its financial contribution. Additionally, Fierens was able to raise significant funds, through personal contacts, from sources in the United States, whose identities are unfortunately not revealed by the available source material (Sugranyes de Franch 1961a, 1961b).

The broadcasts of Radio Omega can be described as religious, spiritual, and cultural. The program of a typical week illustrates their character quite well.

> *Monday*: a religious instruction: explication of the bases of religion and the great Christian truths
>
> *Tuesday*: the Bible, presented as the spiritual food that can be found in the Holy Scripture
>
> *Wednesday*: Broadcast of "response to objections", in the sense in which John XXIII understands apostolic action: "to provide for the people's present needs, by showing the value of the teaching of the Church [...]."
>
> *Thursday*: musical broadcasts, demonstrating that the religious conviction, if vivid, is looking for its musical expression in every country
>
> *Friday*: a Christian and dynamic response to the problems posed in life
>
> *Saturday*: Information; what is happening in the world from a religious standpoint? The most important religious news of the week

> *Sunday*: a very intense Communion with our persecuted brothers, by means of liturgical prayer. (Commission 1962)

The Sunday Communion was held according to Orthodox liturgy and the Saturday broadcasts were predominantly ecumenical as well. To produce these broadcasts, Radio Omega maintained a working relationship with an Orthodox priest. Fierens and his team also received some limited support, in some cases unofficially, from a number of ICOs. Especially Pax Romana produced or reviewed some texts. On the other hand, the Commission in some instances shared its scripts with other radio stations broadcasting to Russia such as the BBC (Commission 1963b, 12–16).

Members of the Commission kept insisting that the *content* of their broadcasts was apolitical and purely religious. However, the documents of the Commission leave no doubt that the broadcasts were designed to have political *effects* as well. The Christian message, envisaged to reach also non-Christian audiences, was undeniably intended to support the ideological struggle against atheist communism and to contribute, bit by bit, to the subversion of the Soviet regime. As an internal strategy paper (Commission [n.d.]a, 2) demands: "Our broadcasts also have to help the convinced communists to understand that their ideal [for society] can be better realized by Christianity than through their atheist vision of the world."

The politically charged connections through Radio Omega, between the ICOs and the Catholic Hierarchy on one side and a clandestine movement that had been sending sabotage and espionage teams into the Soviet Union on the other side, led to a major controversy about the broadcasts at the COIC's General Assembly held in the Swiss town of Appenzell in May 1963. Many ICO representatives protested, fearing repercussions for Catholics living in the Soviet bloc countries (Commission 1963b, 8–16). The COIC leadership reacted with the demand to legally separate Radio Omega from the Commission. This, however, was a sheer formality only enhancing the cover of Radio Omega, which had never publicly mentioned its connections to the Commission, the COIC or the Vatican anyway. In practice, the operation continued unchanged for more than two years, and certain ICOs like Pax Romana continued collaborating unofficially.

In contrast to the major Western radio stations broadcasting behind the Iron Curtain (Woodard 2010, 51–66), Radio Omega avoided Soviet jamming most of the time. Its relatively limited reach offers a potential explanation for this remarkable success. Other smaller radios such as Radio France International were likewise not jammed in the Soviet Union (Nelson 1997, 110).[16] However, an episode in March 1964 points toward a different explanation. One afternoon NTS activists, probably somewhat annoyed by the success of Radio Omega through the transmitter of its Radio Free Russia, interrupted the program for a short political announcement. Radio Omega protested immediately but the damage was done. For the next ten days its broadcasts were jammed ("Notes sur Radio Omega" 1969). This shows that the Soviet authorities were closely monitoring Radio Omega but that they decided, for strategic or economic reasons, not to disturb the broadcasts as long as their content was strictly religious.

In the mid-1960s, the Commission had consequently reached the conclusion that the "radio apostolate" was both desirable and possible. Nevertheless, the broadcasts through the relatively small NTS transmitter could only reach a restricted audience in the Soviet Union. On these grounds, Radio Omega was dismantled between the end of August 1965 and early 1966. Whether Fierens himself reached the conclusion that the expenses for the radio operation were no longer justified, as he stated publicly somewhat later (*Eglise-Témoin*, November 1967), or whether the financial backers jumped off remains an open question.

Positive Anti-communism and the "Fascinating Apostolate"

In 1956, at the time of the Red Book and the height of Operation Pax, the Commission had argued that no dialogue was allowed to take place with the Communists ("Dialogue" 1956, 1). Its magazine *L'Echo des Persécutés* maintained the image of an "irreconcilable opposition," claiming that the morals of what was called the *homo sovieticus* were incompatible with Christian morals (Kaciurine and Smeerson 1956, 14). Now, in spring 1963, the Commission fundamentally changed its strategy and started calling forcefully for contacts between East and West resulting in a constructive dialogue with convinced Communists. This dialogue was conceived as a dialogue between the people in the West and the people in the East, taking place in personal face-to-face conversations between two individual human beings. The Christians were expected to enter these conversations with an open, prudent, and confidant attitude with the aim to convince the Communists, at the end of a truly dialogic process, that their "ideal and idealism, the good of man in society, finds a more complete realization in Christianity than in Marxism" (Fierens 1963, 19).

This opening toward East–West contacts and a dialogue with communists was to a large degree the result of Fierens replacing Gauthier as the driving force of the Commission. However, it is highly significant that the radical change of strategy came at the very moment John XXIII wrote his revolutionary encyclical *Pacem in Terris*[17] (Hebblethwaite 1984, 67–88). Promulgated on April 11, 1963, this inherently political text—which was followed by a media offensive through Radio Vaticana, *L'Osservatore Romano* and other outlets—likewise advocated an opening toward the East and a dialogue. And in the same spirit as the Commission justified it, the Pope made it clear that the dialogue with the East was not a naïve negotiating of positions or a convergence. Rather, it was aimed to convince the erring communists of the truth of Catholic doctrine and that peace was possible only on the basis of Catholicism (Brechenmacher 2017).

Pursuing this new approach, which was based on the belief that communism was reversible, the Commission developed what Jan Fierens later termed himself "positive anti-communism," as opposed to the "negative anti-communism" that it replaced. "Positive" was this re-conceptualization of anti-communism in three ways: (1) regarding the process, as it made positive contributions to a dialogue; (2) in regards to content, which focused on a positive vision of a Christian social order and actively accepted positive aspects in Communism; (3) in respect of the outcome insofar as it supported the Christianization of society (*Eglise-Témoin*, October 1969, 3). This positive anti-communism constituted nothing less than a new, third way approach toward the Soviet bloc, between the hard-line anti-communism that rejected all contacts with the East and the anti-communism that was prepared to accept "peaceful co-existence" with few reservations. Especially considering the ongoing hardship of the Church behind the Iron Curtain, the Commission was not willing to endorse peaceful co-existence, which was still perceived as a threat. Later, in the early 1970s, some secular Cold War actors in the West would pursue an analogue shift from "negative" to a "positive" form of anti-communism, as Scott-Smith (2012) has demonstrated in regards to Interdoc, a Western propaganda and psychological warfare network closely connected to European intelligence services. Their secularized version of positive anti-communism would focus on the propagation of "Western values" instead of Christianity.

To provide Catholics with the preparation necessary to succeed in this "fascinating apostolate," the Commission studied and taught the psychological conditions of the apostolic dialogue, its laws and mechanisms. Through an empirical, systematic approach, Fierens and his colleagues attempted to "know and make known" the mentality of the people behind the Iron Curtain—not the mentality of their leaders the Western Kremlinologists had been studying. Especially, they were interested in the psychology of the Russian youth (summary analysis of the numerous texts published in *Eglise-Témoin*).

Starting in the mid-1960s, the Commission promoted tourism—in concrete terms: holidays of Western Christians in Eastern Europe—as the main instrument to enable the constructive dialogue. This choice of focus was based on the observation that tourism was not just another fissure in the Iron Curtain, but in fact the only mode of East–West contact on a vast scale. In contrast to the multiplying quantity, the Commission diagnosed a lack of quality of these interactions. The cause of this "propagandistic problem" was seen in a lack of preparation of Western tourists that resulted in ignorance and hence naïve behavior. From 1965 onwards, the preparation of Christian tourists traveling behind the Iron Curtain became a central activity of the Commission: it edited respective guides published ahead of the summer holiday seasons and distributed them with great success through major travel agencies and the Catholic mass organizations (especially *Eglise-Témoin*, July 1965 ["Le Tourisme à l'Est"]; *Eglise-Témoin*, June 1966 ["Tourisme vers l'Est: Qui est votre guide?"]; "Résolutions adaptées" 1966, 7).

Conclusion

Over two crucial decades, the activities of the Commission had combined in a truly original way the strategies of the Cultural Cold War and the secret Cold War of intelligence agencies with modes of action developed by Catholic Action and other forms of the lay apostolate. The Commission pursued a comprehensive defensive-offensive approach to the ideological contest of the Cold War, seeking to influence public opinion both in the West and in the East. In the early 1970s, the Commission phased out its activities mainly in the light of two developments. On the one hand, there was a reconstruction of the work of the COIC, during the course of which its system of commissions and working groups was fundamentally re-created (various documents in COIC-N37). On the other hand, there was a waning interest for the "Church of Silence" in the West, as different political concepts, especially the surging human rights discourse, became dominant.[18]

A transnational Catholic actor, the Commission has cooperated closely and multifariously with ICOs and the Holy See, and was integrated into a transnational network of Catholic aid organizations for the "Persecuted Church" behind the Iron Curtain. From this position, the Commission used religious themes, discourses, practices, institutions, and spaces in myriad ways for its political fight against communism. Particularly in the 1950s, the "Commission against Communism," as the group was widely known (de Habicht 1963a, 2), exploited religious persecution in the communist world as a propaganda theme. To alert public opinion in the West to the ugly reality of communism, its atheist character and absolute incompatibility with religion, the Commission often utilized specific religious spaces, especially churches, where common prayers were organized, services held or exhibitions put on display. In the 1960s, the Commission directed clandestine religious radio broadcasts to the Soviet Union and advocated an evangelizing dialogue with communists behind the Iron Curtain.

However, the group not only facilitated the transfer of religious semantics and practices into the political realm. The political activities of the Commission and the Catholic actors it cooperated with effected a feedback dynamic, resulting in a political-religious exchange process that modified the religious field as well.[19] First, by charging it likewise with political semantics, mainly through the widespread individual and common prayers, Sunday masses, and ways of the cross for the Persecuted Church. Second, by influencing internal theological and ecclesiological self-interpretations. Especially, the production of a new canon of martyrs was understood by some Catholics in the West as a new testimony for the truth of Christianity, and as a result reinforced their faith and conviction to engage in the apostolate. The Commission therefore built an intersection of the religious and the political fields of society, where the heterogeneous practices and communication processes analyzed in this article interacted. ❖

1. There is a controversy within the literature whether, by the end of his pontificate, Pius XII already sought to move from his alliance with the West and advocate "co-existence." While Coppa (2003, 63) claims that by "1958 and the end of Pius XII's pontificate, the Vatican was moving to reach some sort of accommodation with the Soviet system," Pollard (2014, 413–414) asserts that "there is little evidence that, in the last few years of his reign, he did much that would have prepared the ground for his successor's 'Opening to the East.'" See also Brechenmacher (2017), who tends to side with Coppa.

2. The major holdings of primary sources on the Commission are the archives of the COIC at the Bibliothèque cantonale et universitaire in Fribourg, Switzerland (henceforth COIC). They are processed in this article for the first time. Particularly relevant is a folder in Box N08 named "Eglise-Témoin 1960-64" (henceforth COIC-N08-ET). Further relevant source material on the Commission is found among the records of the Misssion Catholique Suisse at the State Archives of Fribourg, Switzerland (henceforth MCS). Useful introductory overviews over the Commission, although without regard to the main holdings of primary sources, are provided by Grossmann (2014a, 451–458); Grossmann (2014b, 91–92). The "Commission pour l'Eglise Persécutée" was renamed "Commission Delta" in 1963 and called "Commission Eglise-Témoin" from 1964 onwards.
3. For an excellent overview over the "Religious Cold War" see Kirby (2013). Kirby concludes that religion offered the West "a stick with which to beat, and a means of subverting, the new communist regimes" (564).
4. As Minvielle reports, between 1945 and 1957 a dozen of new OIC were set up, often through the federation of movements already organized on the national level. In 1955, there were 30 OIC and about 1000 national Catholic groups, of which on average 50 new organizations had been created a year.
5. The other two relevant categories of revenues were contributions by the COIC's member organizations as well as external donations. The COIC's revenues and expenses are rather well documented by its archival depositions. For the numbers presented here see especially COIC (1956b), COIC (1960), and COIC (1963).
6. Veronese was the international Vice President of Pax Romana and the leader of Italian Catholic Action in the 1940s.
7. From 1947 onwards, an increasing number of COIC member organizations were granted "consultative status" at various UN agencies. See Ahern (2013, 52–53).
8. Service de Documentation Extérieure et de Contre-Espionnage, established in November 1944. In 1954, the SDECE was headed by Pierre Boursicot and subordinated to the President of the Conseil de la République, the upper house of the French legislature. The SDECE was replaced by the Direction Générale de la Sécurité Extérieure (DGSE) in 1982, which still operates today.
9. The Gehlen Organization, which was formally established as the Bundesnachrichtendienst (BND), the West German foreign intelligence service, in April 1956.
10. The good Cyrenian refers to Simon of Cyrene, the man compelled by the Romans to carry the cross of Jesus taken to his crucification.
11. The *Echo des Persécutés* was renamed *Témoins* in April 1963. Starting from January 1964, the magazine was called *Eglise-Témoin.*
12. The languages in which Pius XII's *Prayer for the Church of Silence* was printed were German, English, Spanish, French, Italian, Dutch, Hungarian, Polish, Czech, Slovakian, Romanian, Croatian, Slovenian, Albanian, Russian, Ukrainian, Belarusian, Lithuanian, and Vietnamese. For the text of Pius XII's *Prayer for the Church of Silence* and various material relating to its dissemination see MCS-272.
13. In 1960, the offertory of the "Sunday of the Persecuted" in Luxembourg brought the Commission more than 600,000 Luxembourg Franc (>100,000 2017 USD). See Bernard (1960).
14. If not indicated otherwise, the following section on Radio Omega is based on a summary analysis of the documents in COIC-N08-ET.
15. Congregatio Immaculati Cordis Mariae, engl. Congregation of the Immaculate Heart of Mary, a Catholic religious order established in 1862 by the Belgian priest Theophiel Verbist.
16. The Russian service of Radio France International started in 1963, the year after Radio Omega first went on air. See Brunnquell (1992, 96).
17. A copy of the encyclical can be found at http://w2.vatican.va/content/john-xxiii/en/encyclicals/documents/hf_j-xxiii_enc_11041963_pacem.html (accessed June 15, 2017).
18. Tellingly, the Commission itself took up the "human rights" discourse, e.g. through devoting the February 1972 issue of *Eglise-Témoin* to "Human Rights in the Soviet Union."
19. For useful theoretical reflections on a "histoire croisée" of the multifaceted and complex transfers between the "religious field" and the "political field" see Graf and Grosse Kracht (2007, 33–37).

References

"Acta Apostolicae Sedis: Commentarium officiale". 1949. "Annus XXXXI, Series II, Vol. XVI." Accessed June 15, 2017. http://www.vatican.va/archive/aas/documents/AAS-41-1949-ocr.pdf.

Ahern, Kevin J. 2013. "Structures of Grace: Catholic Nongovernmental Organizations and the Mission of the Church." Ph.D. diss., Boston College.

Bernard, Jean. 1952. "Commission pour l'Eglise Persécutée." Letter to the members of the Commission, 6.2.1952. Records of the Mission Catholique Suisse, State Archives of Fribourg, Switzerland, Box 268 (henceforth MCS-268).

Bernard, Jean. 1954. "Conférence des Organisations Internationales Catholiques: Commission pour l'Eglise Persécutée." MCS-268.

Bernard, Jean. 1956. "Notre Campagne de Prières Inter-O.I.C." *L'Echo des Persécutés*, January 1956, 3–4.

Bernard, Jean. 1960. "Letter [probably to Mieczyslaw de Habicht], 7.5.1960." Archives of the COIC, Box N08, Folder "Eglise-Témoin 1960-64", Bibliothèque cantonale et universitaire, Fribourg, Switzerland (henceforth COIC-N08-ET).

Bernard, Jean. 1962a. "Editorial." *L'Echo des Persécutés*, October/November 1962, 1-3.

Bernard, Jean. 1962b. "Letter to Mieczyslaw de Habicht, 27.11.1962." COIC-N08-ET.

Bernard, Jean. 1964. "Letter to Mieczyslaw de Habicht, Permanent Secretary of the COIC, 2.6.1964." COIC-N08-ET.

Brechenmacher, Thomas. 2017. " 'Pacem in terris' (1963) und das Erbe Pius' XII", paper presented at the conference "Popes on the Rise! Mobilization, Media, and Political Power of the Modern Papacy", Campo Santo Teutonico, Rome, 22-26 March.

Brunnquell, Frédéric. 1992. *Fréquence monde: du Poste Colonial à RFI.* Paris: Hachette.

Cardinale, Hyginus Eugene. 1976. *The Holy See and the International Order.* Toronto: MacMillan.

Central Intelligence Agency (CIA). 1970. *Report on Sint Unum and La Commission pour l'Eglise Persécutée, Attached to a Memorandum from Henry Kissinger to President Richard Nixon,* February 1970. NSC Files, Series: Country Files—Europe, Box 732, Folder "Vatican—Vol. I," Nixon Presidential Library, Yorba Linda, CA.

Charrière, François. 1959. "Appel de S.E. Mgr François Charrière, evêque de Lausanne, Genève et Fribourg en faveur de l'affiche sûr l'Eglise du Silence." Published in *L'Echo des Persécutés,* July 1959, 4.

Conference des Organisations Internationales Catholiques (henceforth COIC). 1952. "Conference des Présidents des Organisations Internationales Catholiques: Session Ordinaire de Fribourg, 1952." 29.2.1952. COIC-C50.

COIC. 1954. "Rapport du Comité de Continuité à l'Assamblée de la COIC, Paris, 12-15 Mars 1954." C.C. 94-XII-54. COIC-N31.

COIC. 1955. "Rapport General sur les activités de la COIC pour l'année 1954." C.C. 130-XVII-55, COIC Permanent Secretariat. COIC-N32.

COIC. 1956a. "Rapport General sur les activités de la COIC pour l'année 1955." C.C. 159-XXI-56, COIC Permanent Secretariat. COIC-N32.

COIC. 1956b. "Comité de Continuité, Paris, 24 et 25 Octobre 1956: Rapport intérimaire sur la situation financière de la trésorerie." C.C. 176-XXIII-56, Permanent Secretariat COIC. COIC-N32.

COIC. 1957. "Elements du Rapport General sur les activités de la COIC pour l'année 1956." C.C. 182-XXIV-57, COIC Permanent Secretariat. COIC-N08-ET.

COIC. 1959. "Rapport General du Comité de Continuité sur les activités de la COIC en 1958." C.C. 231-XXIX-59, COIC Permanent Secretariat. COIC-N33.

COIC. 1960. "Comité de Continuité, Paris, 21-22 février 1960." C.C. 255-XXXII-60, Permanent Secretariat COIC. COIC-N33.

COIC. 1963. "Prévisions budgétaires de la conference des O.I.C. pour l'année 1964." C.C. 317-63. COIC-N35.

Commission pour l'Eglise persécutée (henceforth Commission). 1962. "'Omega' et la 'Section Radio'." COIC-N08-ET.

Commission. 1963a. *Report of the Meetings of the Commission in Brussels, 18 & 19 February 1963.* Published in *Témoins,* April 1963, 5-23.

Commission. 1963b. "Compte-Rendu de la Commission 'Delta'," Appenzell, 18–21 May 1963, Strictly Confidential. COIC-N08-ET.

Commission. [n.d.]a. "Internal Document of the Commission's Radio Section." COIC-N08-ET.

Commission. [n.d.]b. "La Diffusion du Livre Rouge." Internal Note. MCS-269.

Commission. [n.d.]c. "O.I.C. Commission pour l'Eglise Persécuté: Budget 1963." COIC-N08-ET.

Commission. [n.d.]d. "Rapport sur l'activité de la Commission pour l'Eglise persécutée durant l'année 1959." COIC-N08-ET.

Coppa, Frank J. 2003. "Pope Pius XII and the Cold War: The Post-war Confrontation Between Catholicism and Communism." In *Religion and the Cold War,* edited by Dianne Kirby, 50–66. Basingstoke: Palgrave Macmillan.

de Habicht, Mieczyslaw. 1962. "Letter to Jan Fierens, 12.12.1962." COIC-N08-ET.

de Habicht, Mieczyslaw. 1963a. "Letter to Jean Bernard, 5.2.1963." COIC-N08-ET.

de Habicht, Mieczyslaw. 1963b. "Letter to Jan Fierens, 19.3.1963." COIC-N08-ET.

de Habicht, Mieczyslaw. 1963c. "Letter to Jan Fierens, 26.4.1963." COIC-N08-ET.

de Habicht, Mieczyslaw. 1964. "Letter to Jean Bernard, 27.5.1964." COIC-N08-ET.

de Reymaeker, R. 1963a. "Letter to Mieczyslaw de Habicht, Secretariat Radio Section, Commission, 25.2.1963." COIC-N08-ET.

de Reymaeker, R. 1963b. "Letter to Mieczyslaw de Habicht, 22.4.1963." COIC-N08-ET.

"Dialogue avec le Communisme?". 1956. *L'Echo des Persécutés,* February 1956, 1–2.

di Stefano, Andrea. 2008. "Stati Uniti-Vaticano: Relazioni Politiche e Aspetti Diplomatici, 1952-1984." PhD diss., University of Teramo.

Fierens, Jan. 1963. "Les Conditions Psychologique du Dialogue." *Témoins*, Mai 1963, 4–20.

Gallagher, Charles R. 2008. *Vatican Secret Diplomacy: Joseph P. Hurley and Pope Pius XII*. New Haven: Yale University Press.

Galter, Albert. 1956. *Libro rosso della Chiesa perseguitata*. Milan: Ancora.

Galter, Albert. 1957. *Rotbuch der verfolgten Kirche*. Recklinghausen: Paulus.

Gauthier, Louis. 1956. "Rappel Important à propos de notre champagne de prières." *L'Echo des Persécutés*, September 1956.

Gauthier, Louis. 1957. "Activité de la Mission Catholique Suisse en 1956 en faveur des couvants derrière le rideau de fer." Report, 15.1.1957. MCS-263.

Gayte, Marie. 2011. "The Vatican and the Reagan Administration: A Cold War Alliance?" *Catholic Historical Review* 97 (4): 713–736.

Genoud, François. 1991. "La 'Petite Eglise' (1810-1844), une société secrète de prêtres face à l'autorité." *Schweizerische Gesellschaft für Wirtschafts- und Sozialgeschichte* 9: 49–57.

Goldie, Rosemary. 1998. *From a Roman Window: Five Decades of the World, the Church and the Laity*. Melbourne: HarperCollins.

Graf, Friedrich Wilhelm, and Klaus Grosse Kracht. 2007. "Religion und Gesellschaft im Europa des 20. Jahrhunderts." In *Religion und Gesellschaft: Europa im 20. Jahrhundert*, edited by Friedrich Wilhelm Graf, and Klaus Grosse Kracht, 1–44. Köln: Böhlau.

Grosse Kracht, Klaus. 2016. *Die Stunde der Laien? Katholische Aktion in Deutschland im europäischen Kontext 1920-1960*. Paderborn: Ferdinand Schöningh.

Grossmann, Johannes. 2014a. *Die Internationale der Konservativen: Transnationale Elitenzirkel und private Aussenpolitik in Westeuropa seit 1945*. München: Oldenbourg.

Grossmann, Johannes. 2014b. "Winning the Cold War: Anti-Communism, Informal Diplomacy, and the Transnational Career of Jean Violet." *New Global Studies* 8 (1): 87–101.

Hänni, Adrian, et al. 2016. "Ein Forum konservativer Machteliten im transatlantischen Raum: Der Cercle im Zeitalter des Kalten Kriegs." In *Wie Eliten Macht organisieren: Bilderberg & Co.: Lobbying, Thinktanks und Mediennetzwerke*, edited by Björn Wendt, 118–130. Hamburg: VSA.

Hebblethwaite, Peter. 1984. *John XXIII: Pope of the Council*. London: Geoffrey Chapman.

Kaciurine, M. C., and M. A. Smeerson. 1956. "L'Athéisme dans l'enseignement de la littérature." *L'Echo des Persécutés*, March/April 1956, 13–17.

Kirby, Dianne. 2003a. "Harry Truman's Religious Legacy: The Holy Alliance, Containment and the Cold War." In *Religion and the Cold War*, edited by Dianne Kirby, 77–102. Basingstoke: Palgrave Macmillan.

Kirby, Dianne (ed.). 2003b. *Religion and the Cold War*. Basingstoke: Palgrave Macmillan.

Kirby, Dianne. 2013. "The Religious Cold War." In *The Oxford Handbook of the Cold War*, edited by Richard H. Immerman, and Petra Goedde, 540–564. Oxford: Oxford University Press.

Kretschmer, Winfried. 1999. *Geschichte der Weltausstellungen*. Frankfurt a.M. Campus.

Krop, Pascal. 1995. *Les secrets de l'espionnage français de 1870 à nos jours*. Paris: Payot & Rivages.

Langemann, Hans. 1980. "Confidential Note from the Director Department I F of the Bavarian State Ministry of the Interior to Georg Waltner, Private Secretary to the Bavarian Interior Minister Gerold Tandler, Munich, 7.3.1980." Published in *Der Spiegel*, October 1980, 23.

"La Propagande pour le Livre Rouge". 1957. *L'Echo des Persécutés*, October 1957, 26.

Lebec, Éric. 1997. *Histoire secrète de la diplomatie vaticane*. Paris: Albin Michel.

"Le Rayonnement du Livre Rouge de l'Eglise Persécutée". 1957. *L'Echo des Persécutés*, June/July 1957, 1–2.

Lesch, Paul. 2015. "Jean Bernard's Fight for 'Good' Cinema in Luxembourg." In *Moralizing Cinema: Film, Catholicism and Power*, edited by Daniel Biltereyst, and Daniela Treveri Gennari, 85–99. New York: Routledge.

Marmier, Henri. 1941. *La "Petite Eglise" du diocèse de Lausanne et Genève*. Fribourg: Imprimerie St-Paul.

Marmier, Henri. 1947. "Le Saint-Siège et son œuvre d'assistance en faveur des victimes de la guerre (1939–1945)." *International Review of the Red Cross* 29 (343): 602–613.

Marmier, Henri. 1951. "Rapport de M. le Chanoine Marmier, Fribourg." Conférence Internationale des Présidents: Commission en faveur de l'Eglise persécutée, 19.12.1951. MCS-268.

Marmier, Henri. 1955. "Letter to Josef Jansen, 14.11.1955." Nachlass Josef Jansen (01-149), 003/2, Archiv für Christlich-Demokratische Politik, Sankt Augustin, Germany.

Marmier, Henri. 1956. "A Propos du Livre Rouge sur les Pérsecutions Réligieuses." Confidential Note, 13.3.1956. MCS-269.

Marti, Pierre. 2006. "Les prêtres de la 'Petite Eglise': Réseaux et stratégies épistolaires écclesiastiques dans le premier XIXe siècle." In *La correspondence familiale en Suisse romande au XVIIIe et XIXe siècles: Affectivité, sociabilité, résaux: Actes du colloque de Neuchâtel, 27-28 mai 2005*, edited by Philippe Henry, and Jean-Pierre Jelmini, 353–370. Neuchâtel: Alphil.

Mission Catholique Suisse (henceforth MCS). 1956a. "Au secours des maisons réligieuses derrière le rideau de fer." Report. MCS-268.

MCS. 1956b. "Envoie de livres effectués en Lithuanie par les soins de la Mission Catholique Suisse." Report. MCS-269.

MCS. 1962. "La Mission Catholique Suisse en faveur des victimes de la guerre." Report on the activities of the MCS, March 1962. MCS-263.

MCS. [n.d.]. "Note concernant l'activité de la Mission Catholique Suisse en faveur des couvants derrière le rideau de fer." MCS-268.

Melnik, Constantin. 1989. Les beaux coups de nos services secrets." *Le Figaro Magazine*, 27 May, 150–160.

Melnik, Constantin. 2008. *Les espions: réalités et fantasmes*. Paris: Ellipses.

Menoud, Alphonse. 1959. "En méditant devant une carte." *La Liberté*, 20 June.

Minvielle, Bernard. 2001. *L'apostolat des laïcs à la veille du Concile (1949-1959): histoire des Congrès mondiaux de 1951 et 1957*. Fribourg: Editions universitaires.

Nelson, Michael. 1997. *War of the Black Heavens: The Battles of Western Broadcasting in the Cold War*. Syracuse, NY: Syracuse University Press.

"Notes sur Radio Omega". 1969. *Eglise-Témoin*, January 1969, 20–21.

Pius XII. 1954. "Ansprache an die Teilnehmer des Weltkongresses für das Laienapostolat, 14.10.1951." In *Aufbau und Entfaltung des gesellschaftlichen Lebens: Soziale Summe Pius XII*, edited by Arthur-Fridolin Utz, and Joseph-Fulko Groner, 1493–1505. Fribourg: Paulus.

Pizzardo, Giuseppe. 1955. "Letter from Cardinal Pizzardo to the Deans of Catholic Universities, 17.5.1955." MCS-274.

Pollard, John F. 2010. "Electronic Pastors: Radio, Cinema, and Television, from Pius XI to John XXIII." In *The Papacy Since 1500: From Italian Prince to Universal Pastor*, edited by James Corkery, and Thomas Worcester, 182–203. Cambridge: Cambridge University Press.

Pollard, John F. 2014. *The Papacy in the Age of Totalitarianism, 1914-1958*. Oxford: Oxford University Press.

Python, Francis. 1987. *Mgr Etienne Marilley et son clergé à Fribourg au temps du Sonderbund, 1846-1856*. Fribourg: Editions Universitaires.

"Résolutions adaptées par l'Assemblée Generale des OIC à propos de la Commission Eglise-Témoin: Tourisme et Radio". 1966. *Eglise-Témoin*, September 1966, 2–9.

Rhodes, Anthony. 1992. *The Vatican in the Age of the Cold War, 1945-1980*. Norwich: M. Russell.

Richmond, Yale. 2003. *Cultural Exchange and the Cold War: Raising the Iron Curtain*. University Park: Pennsylvania State University Press.

Richmond, Yale. 2005. "Cultural Exchange and the Cold War: How the West Won." *The Polish Review* 50 (3): 355–360.

Rives, A. 1961. *L'Eglise du Silence*. Lourdes: Exposition missionnaire de Lourdes.

Scott-Smith, Giles. 2012. *Western Anti-communism and the Interdoc Network: Cold War Internationale*. Basingstoke: Palgrave Macmillan.

"Section Radio". 1962. *L'Echo des Persécutés*, October-November 1962, 5-12.

Sugranyes de Franch, Ramon. 1961a. "Letter from Sugranyes de Franch, President of the COIC, to Jean Bernard, 5.7.1961." COIC-N08-ET.

Sugranyes de Franch, Ramon. 1961b. "Letter to Jean Bernard, 27.11.1961." COIC-N08-ET.

"Travailler ensemble". 1957. *L'Echo des Persécutés*, March 1957, 1–3.

Van Dongen, Luc. 2008. *Un purgatoire très discret: la transition "helvétique" d'anciens nazis, fascistes et collaborateurs après 1945*. Paris: Perrin.

Violet, Jean. 1956. "Letter to Franz Josef Strauss, 26.9.1956." Nachlass Franz Josef Strauss, BMVg 852, Archiv für Christlich-Soziale Politik, Munich.

Violet, Jean. [n.d.]. "Exposé sommaire." Private archive.

Wanner, Tassilo. 2017. *Heilige Allianz? Die Aufnahme diplomatischer Beziehungen zwischen den Vereinigten Staaten und dem Heiligen Stuhl*. Wiesbaden: Springer VS.

Woodard, George W. 2010. "Cold War Radio Jamming." In *Cold War Broadcasting: Impact on the Soviet Union and Eastern Europe*, edited by A. Ross Johnson, and Eugene Parta, 51–66. Budapest: Central European University Press.

Wulf, Andrew James. 2015. *U.S. International Exhibitions During the Cold War: Winning Hearts and Minds Through Cultural Diplomacy*. Lanham, MD: Rowman & Littlefield.

TWO "POPES" TO SPEAK FOR THE WORLD: THE POPE AND THE UNITED NATIONS SECRETARY GENERAL IN WORLD POLITICS

By Jodok Troy

Despite recent studies on leadership, the discipline of International Relations is still reluctant to engage in studies of individual agency in the international structure.[1] Two prominent examples are the leader of the Catholic Church, the pope, and the United Nations (UN) Secretary-General (UNSG). Neither of them is a leader in control of considerable hard power, yet both exemplify the puzzle of how institutions, individuals, and moral authority relate in leadership. I argue that it is a combination of individuals in institutions that leads to unexpected and unintended effects such as the evolution of the papacy and the UNSG as instances of moral authorities. While pointing out their potential for moral leadership, this article presents a conceptual framework of how to perceive the Pope and the UNSG in world politics. The article unfolds in three sections: in the first, I look at the potential of comparing the two positions in terms of moral leadership and their emphasis of the common good. In a literature review, I then outline the current state of the literature on the two positions and what it misses. The remainder of the paper proposes a conceptual framework on how the two positions fit into the current literature and what promising future research for International Relations it conceals.

Servant of God, Servant of Governments

In many regards, both positions, the papacy and the UNSG, represent an anachronism. The individuals that represent them are elected in dubious ways, influenced by variables hard to grasp, and both are heirs of political developments that shaped the establishment of positions and institutions that have long since changed. Nevertheless, the pope and the "secular Pope," the UNSG, are two individuals whose voices are given particular attention in world politics. They are quite similar as both depend on the character of the office holder and the institution. It is thus not only about authority and autonomy of the organization arising out of delegated, moral, and expert authority (Barnett and Finnemore 2004, 20–29; Hall 1997). Rather, like executive heads,[2] the Pope and the UNSG are in authority and an authority themselves (see also Barnett and Finnemore 2004, 25). Eventually, such positions lead to good leadership which is "valued as a moral necessity" (Burns 2003, 2).[3]

Popes since 1945	UNSGs since 1945
Pius XII (1939–1958)	Trygve Lie (1946–1952)
St. John XXIII (1958–1963)	Dag Hammarskjöld (1953–1961)
Paul VI (1963–1978)	U Thant (1961–1971)
John Paul I (1978)	Kurt Waldheim (1972–1981)
St. John Paul II (1978–2005)	Javier Perez de Cuellar (1982–1991)
Benedict XVI (2005–2013)	Boutros Boutros-Ghali (1993–1996)
Francis (2013–)	Kofi Annan (1997–2006)
	Ban Ki-Moon (2007–2016)
	António Gutierrez (2017–)

'Vous êtes mon homologue laïque," Pope Pius XXII told UNSG Dag Hammarskjöld (Lipsey 2013, 153), who himself considered the UN a "secular church" (Foote 1962, 47).[4] Pope John XXIII (1963) addressed in his encyclical *Pacem in Terris* "all men and women of goodwill" and Hammarskjöld argued that "all men and women of good will can influence the course of history in the direction of the ideals expressed in the Charter" (Foote 1962, 45). In his most recent encyclical, Pope Francis (2015) even speaks to "every person living on this planet." Putting forward such broad claims suggests that both individuals perceive themselves as moral authorities, working for the common good.

Moral authority invoking the common good is not only a publicly called for demand, but a necessity of human conduct in a globalized world. The world is facing a growing "enlargement of human expectations" as UNSG Cuéllar (1995, 168) called it. This makes the pope and the UNSG disputed but appealing figures of moral authority. While there is no way to foresee the end of the current papacy, Francis seems to be an indicator that supports the main thesis of this article: it is the combination of institutions and individuals that shapes their positions and establishes the power of moral leadership that eventually transforms institutions (Franco 2013a, 2013b; Ivereigh 2015).

There are extensive studies on the power and the moral authority of the UNSG (Chesterman 2007; Kille 2007, 2006), less so and mainly historical ones on the pope (Coppa 1998, 2008, 2014; Hall 1997; Riccards 1998). This is surprising, as research points out that via their leaders, institutions can have unexpected and unintended effects beyond their formal codified mission statement (Barnett and Finnemore 1999). This, however, is only possible if institutions are, first, assumed to be moral agents within a social practice and, second, if the leaders' followers are taken into account of the potential and extent of moral authority (Kellerman 2008): "The very notion of an individual moral agent presupposes the existence of a collective practice with its associated ethic embedded in it" (Frost 2003, 98 original in italics; see also Frost 1996). Agency, then, takes shape in and due to sociality. Nonetheless, modest emphasis has been placed on leadership and transformative action. Leaders engage in transformative action if they override existing structures and create something unusual based on their agency (Menaldo 2013; Saunders 2009).[5]

Many definitions of leadership focus on traits-based leadership. They define a leader as "someone who helps a group create and achieve shared goals" (Nye 2008, 18). Often it is charisma that drives moral authority as charismatic authority is "a rule over men, whether predominantly external or predominantly internal, to which the governed submit because of their belief in the extraordinary quality of the specific *person*" (Weber, Gerth, and Mills 1946, 295). Likewise, role theory and micro foundations of behavioural International Relations hold that the positions have changed because key individuals have changed the role of that position in the institution (Harnisch, Frank, and Maull 2011; Walker, Malici, and Schafer 2011; see also Hudson 2005).

Moreover, definitions of leadership distinguish between leadership and executive tasks to "differentiate the responsibilities and authority." However, executive leadership is about "determining an organization's goals and mobilizing constituents to achieve those goals" (Schroeder 2014, 3). Most broadly, the literature on leaders (e.g. Byman and Pollack 2001; Chiozza and Goemans 2011; Isaak 1975) and leadership (e.g. George 1969; Hermann 1980) point out particular moments when the impact of individual leaders on the course of events is most likely. This is when political institutions are unstable, young, in crisis, collapse, institutional constraints are limited and the issue or situation is peripheral, unusual, or ambiguous (Mingst and Arreguín-Toft 2013, 180–181).

Institutions, Agency, and the Pope's and UNSG's Moral Leadership

I argue that a combination of individuals in institutions leads to the influence and possession of moral authority beyond constitutional arrangements and external structural constraints and opportunities. A parallel look at the pope and the UNSG facilitates such an understanding of agency and leadership. While stressing a comparative perspective (Helms 2012), this provides additional insights into ontological and epistemological developments and produces more general results on moral leadership.[6]

There are two basic caveats to this argument. First, comparing the pope and the UNSG brings up shortcomings in terms of structural comparability and technicalities. However, apart from choosing them because of their normative attributes, both can be compared because of the nature of the organizations in which they are embedded.[7] The character of agents, institutional constraints, and external effects influence the two institutions and their individual agency. Whereas in-house constraints (e.g. the Curia, the Security Council) can candidly be located, the impact of external influences is hard to evaluate. Second, despite the similarities between the pope and the UNSG, there are limiting parameters of a comparison in the formulation of their power (i.e. political and religious leader vs. administrative official).[8] The most important one is that the pope, the "Vicar of Christ" and absolute monarch is, ipso facto, leader of the Catholic Church. The UNSG is chief administrative officer of the UN. Even more so, his potential for moral leadership is constrained by structural forces rooted in a world of states (Thakur 2017, 11).

One might argue that the UNSG is an administrative officer and mediator, whereas the pope is a religious and political leader. However, popes and UNSGs have been engaged in in-house (i.e. "catholic") and external (i.e. "political") mediation. The political engagement of John Paul II during the Cold War comes to mind. But also his successors, Benedict XVI (e.g. on the cultural foundation of Europe) and Francis (e.g. on improving Cuban–US relations) (Álvarez 2014) intermingled in international politics beyond rhetorical appeals. Another example is Pope Francis' attempt to escape existing political rivalries, avoiding mirroring the formerly East–West tensions. Instead, he is shifting the focus on geopolitics to Latin America like Pope John Paul II did for Eastern Europe (Flamini 2014; Levine 2016). A particular case in point is Francis' allegedly "giving up" on human rights and referring instead more to social justice, structural problems, and collective solutions that individual rights probably are not able to solve (Moyn 2015). Another example is the prevailing international trend of enforcing responsibility and accountability (Ainley 2008; Sikkink 2011). This trend has been pushed (e.g. by Ghali and Pius XII) and restrained (e.g. by Hammarskjöld and Francis) by popes and UNSGs alike.

Individuals in Institutions

The literature on leadership does not address that what and how leaders do something is as important as what they are and what resources they command. Whereas "[p]ower does not equal leadership" (Nabers 2011, 88), the opposite is also true: leadership does not equal "hard" power. Examples are John Paul II and Dag Hammarskjöld. In both cases, it was also their charisma which led to transformative leadership. Their performance did not only change the institution due to their delegated, expert, and moral authority. Their charisma became the impetus for institutional change and policy outreach and, ultimately, account for transformative leadership. This is the case for Hammarskjöld's efforts (e.g. the independent international civil service), John XXIII's initiatives (e.g. the initiation of the second Vatican Council), or John Paul II's public stance on matters of the Cold War (e.g. the help to initiate protests against communist regimes) (Weigel 1992).

Popes and UNSGs laid out strategic plans and visions, yet their implementing strategies differed widely. Hammarskjöld had a vision of an independent Secretariat and civil service which he implemented (Childers and Urquhart 1994; Hammarskjöld 1960; Orford 2011, chapter 2; Sending 2015, 47–53; Sinclair 2015). John XXIII's vision of peace and engaging in the crises in the nuclear age is another example (Flamini 1980; Zizola 1978). Some chose follower-oriented strategies, while others chose opposition-oriented strategies (i.e. mobilizing those opposed to the vision). Some of them exercised self-restraint while working on their vision (e.g. Hammarskjöld changed the organization of the Secretariat, John XXIII initiated the Second Vatican Council), some did not (e.g. Boutros-Ghali, John Paul II). Some accompanied their implementation strategies with institutional and administrative changes (e.g. Hammarskjöld, John Paul II), some not (e.g. Boutros-Ghali, John XXIII).[9]

Studies on the impact of individuals reveal limits when it comes to the pope's and the UNSG's host institutions. Both institutions, the Holy See and the UN, are not "new." Consider the cases of Hammarskjöld and John XXIII: the UN Secretariat at that time was young and institutional constraints were limited (e.g. via the Security Council at the beginning of the term). The conditions Hammarskjöld encountered where unusual and ambiguous (e.g. the joint intervention of France and Great Britain over the Suez Canal crisis and the subsequent installation of the first UN peacekeeping mission). The same is true for the tenure of John XXIII. Although the papacy was not young, unstable, or in a state of crisis, the institutional constraints (e.g. via the Curia) were rather limited. What is more, in the Cuban Missile Crisis John XXIII encountered an unusual situation that enabled him to mediate between Khrushchev and Kennedy (Flamini 1980).[10] The same circumstances enabled U Thant to assist in the Cuban Missile crisis by establishing a communication line between the great powers (Dorn and Pauk 2009).

Looking at the pope and the UNSG demonstrates the lacuna in the literature on leadership of individuals in institutional contexts and their social setting (Battilana 2006; Helms 2014). Although few studies pay attention to the two positions, "[d]ecision making does matter" (Hagan 2001) and "who leads matters" (Hermann et al. 2001). This is even more the case regarding the pope and the UNSG (Cox 1969; Kille 2006; Kille and Scully 2003). Popes and UNSGs, however, might be good "statesmen" and leaders only in the capacity of their offices in the Holy See and in the UNSG Secretariat (Claude 1971, 210). Studies on the UNSGs point out that personal leadership style is paramount (Kille 2006) but principal-agent theories are offering too less of an explanation of the autonomy of UNSGs (Karns 2012).

The papacy and the UNSG Secretariat are potentially shaped by their office holders, internal factors of the institutions, and by variables outside the immediate scope and influence of the institutions and their representatives. Popes often have little international experience and tend to depend on their secretaries of state. The UNSG, on the other hand, is a professional diplomat and servant of many masters. In both cases it is also the "rational-legal authority that [International Organizations] embody also gives them power independent of the states that created them and channels that power in particular directions" (Barnett and Finnemore 1999, 699).

Possessing agency, that is possessing internal powers and capacities (Barnes 2000, 5), is not only based on the pope's and the UNSG's weak material and institutional power (i.e. head of state, administrational officer, agenda setter, etc.). It is also based on their normative power provided by their institutions. Claude (1971, 191) observed that while there may be powerful members (such as in the Curia or the Security Council) of international organizations, the staff headed by a secretary or secretary general "*is* the organisation" (see also Mathiason 2007). As such, both positions and the "normative power" they entail matter in world politics as they are prone for moral leadership.

Moral Leadership

The similarity between the pope and the Secretary-General illustrates, first, how both exercise their posts out of a combination of weak material capability and normative power. Focusing on the normative role of power adds another facet to the discussion on power beyond military capabilities. Evaluating the moral power of the pope and the UNSG takes into account "the socially diffuse production of subjectivity in systems of meaning and signification" (Barnett and Duvall 2005, 43). Second, in recognizing the similarity between the two, the nature of institutions and their office holders are evidence of a mutual relationship of secular and religious world political representation and normative claims therein (Agensky 2017; May et al. 2014; Wilson 2010). Third, looking at them illustrates that both struggle between policy positions of interventionism and restraint.

In representing transnational institutions,[11] the pope and the UNSG claim to speak for the world's population. The UNSG speaks in his legal right as chief administrative officer as set up in the Charter (United Nations, art. 1,4), to "be a centre for harmonizing the actions of nations". In the words of the first UNSG Lie (1954, 88), he is a "spokesman," for the world interest (see also Chesterman 2015, 506). As such, he has the responsibility to heighten international awareness as UNSG Boutros-Ghali (1996, 88) termed it. The pope, on the other hand, is "the Vicar of Christ, and the pastor of the universal Church on earth" (Code of Canon Law, Can. 331) and "obtains full and supreme power in the Church" (Code of Canon Law, Can. 332 §1). He acts on the grounds that "the Church believes she can contribute greatly toward making the family of man and its history more human" (Second Vatican Council 1965, Art. 40)—a statement similar to the spirit of the Charter of the UN. In any case, each of them has the "constitutional licence to be as big a man as he can" (Claude 1971, 211)—they are potentially moral leaders.

In a globalized world political leadership requires a "bold and noble vision for the community" where the UNSG must have the "elusive ability to make others connect emotionally and intellectually to a larger cause that transcends their immediate self-interest" (Thakur 2006, 333). This is not least since the UN is framed as a "focal point of an emerging 'world-oneness'" (Pedersen 2010, 339). This is equally true for the Catholic Church, which already in its name proposes to be a unifying authority. Nevertheless, both institutions are representative of the growing pluralization of their constituency on the global scale—religious and secular, modern and anti-modern (e.g. Berger 2014). Moreover, neither of the two commands any traditional hard material power. However, it is not the "lack of an army to command, but [the] lack of a party to lead and a body politic to rally behind" (Claude 1971, 207–08). Looking at single individuals illustrates that they build their office on a vision of the common good and a "body politic to rally behind."

What is presented as crucial in world politics by the pope and the UNSG as moral leaders is the paramount value both attribute to peace and human rights (e.g. Claude 1996; Matlary 2001). This can be seen by the inter-Christian formulation of the 1948 universal *Human Rights Declarations* and the declaration of the later Popes John XXIII and Paul VI (Nurser 2005, 172, FN 45; Glendon 2001, 132, 217). Eventually, their rhetorical engagement to foster peace and human rights propelled their practical engagement in world politics more broadly.

The Pope and the UNSG in World Politics

The pope and the UNSG demonstrate executive leadership and entrepreneurial power (Haack and

Kille 2012; Kille 2006) by deploying "ideas and information to produce significant structural change" (Goddard 2009, 251). The two institutions and their leaders are "self-directed actors" (Oestreich 2012) in possession of autonomous agency. This aspect also offers insights to international political conduct in focusing on moral stewardship under structural constraints. To give one example: Why is it that the "silent diplomacy" of Hammarskjöld was not carried on to this extent by his successors (Ask and Mark-Jungkoist 2005; Fröhlich 2008; Jones 2004; Jordan 1983; Stahn and Melber 2014), let alone that it became a part of the institutional structure? In a similar way, the shuttle diplomacy of Pope John Paul II, lobbying for political transformation via a conception of anti-politics,[12] was not carried on by his successor (see also Christiansen 2006).

RELIGION AND POLITICS HAVE ALWAYS BEEN INTERMINGLED AND MUTUALLY CONSTITUTIVE

International leadership, as pointed out above, is about particular individuals in particular institutions (Frost 2003, 84), the ideas they promote, and how they attribute and give the office meaning by those ideas. The rhetorical emphasis of international law as a guarantor for international order is something both leaders emphasize (Johnston 2003; Pontifical Council for Justice and Peace 2004, para. 434). The two individuals act in world politics not on behalf of a particular nation but for collectives and thus transcend inter-national and intra-national boundaries.[13]

Collective practices are an overlooked element that ground themselves not only on the formal, constitutional practice, but on elements that go beyond such a practice.[14] The question, for example, is not only why John Paul II contributed to the downfall of Communism, but rather how he managed to do so at all and how his actions influenced the conceptualization of the papacy. Inquiring such questions not only provides insights to the papacy and the UNSG but likely also produce general outputs as they are entrepreneurs and followers of normative trends. The pope and the UNSG are nuances in the split between conservative and liberal ideals in world politics. The persistence of nationalism, the "rise of the rest," and great power aspirations are evidence for prevailing conservative paradigms. Aspirations for global governance, development of principles in favour of human rights such as the *Responsibility to Protect*, cosmopolitanism and the focus on world society are evidence for the latter (Bernstein and Pauly 2007; Meyer et al. 1997; Phillips 2013). The UN Charter always struggled between conservative and liberal poles and so does the papacy, particularly since the end of the Second World War.

"Papal Interventionism" (Walsh 2000) is nothing new. Protecting "fundamental rights of individuals and the rights of people in their quest for authentic self-determination" (Araujo 2007, 368) led the popes to harsh criticism of military interventions (e.g. John Paul II on Operation Desert Storm and Iraqi Freedom). At the same time, this rhetorical emphasis of the popes led the Church to rethink just war theory (Heft 2011) and increased the approval rate of humanitarian interventions. This is evident in the speeches of the UNSGs and popes since the end of the Second World War. Pope Pius XII, for example, could not remain neutral any longer during the Cold War (Kent 2002) and neither could the UNSGs. Eventually, both individuals have been entrepreneurs and followers of international norms, engaging in their life cycles (Finnemore and Sikkink 1998), either pushing or hindering them.

This conceptual framework illustrates that the nature of institutions and their office holders are evidence for a mutual relationship between secular and religious world political representation and normative claims therein. The values and ideas that secularism wanted to ban influence how we live in this global age (Thomas 2010). Religion and politics have always been intermingled and mutually constitutive (Agensky 2017; Hurd 2008; Thomas 2014; Walzer 2007, 147–67). The UN is a case in point where religious norms diffuse into the secular sphere via institutional and individual translation (Bettiza and Dionigi 2014; Dionigi 2016). The "secular church" UN (Lash 1962, 543) can act as an institutional translator, rephrasing religious norms and ideas into secular language. All the same, the UN reaches with its own agenda based on the Charter and subsequent texts into the sacred realm (Barnett and Stein 2012; Luomaaho 2011).[15] The UN stands, as Hammarskjöld once remarked, "outside—necessary outside—all confessions but it is, nevertheless, an instrument of faith. As such, it is inspired by what unites and not by what divides the great religions of the world" (Foote 1962, 56–57).[16]

Conclusion

This article argued, using the example of the pope and the UNSG, that institutions can have effects via their leaders beyond their formal mission statement, often translated as moral leadership. If those individuals link agency and responsibility, they can outgrow constitutional arrangements and external constraints. It is a combination of individuals in institutions that leads to unexpected and unintended effects such as the evolution of the papacy and the UNSG as instances of moral authorities and sometimes even transformative leadership. This requires future empirical research to bolster those preliminary and explanatory propositions presented in this conceptual framework. ❖

Acknowledgements

I would like to thank the journal's editors and reviewers as well as the reviewers of the project for their comments, suggestions, and interest. I also would like to thank The Europe Center at Stanford University for hosting me as a visiting scholar (2016–2018).

Funding

This work was supported by the Austrian Science Fund [project J3906-G16].

Notes

1. E.g. Horowitz, Stam, and Ellis (2015), Saunders (2014), Sandal (2017), Byman and Pollack (2001).
2. I am aware that, in a formal sense, neither the UNSG nor the pope is an "executive officer."
3. Regardless the demand for a global leader, in case of the UNSG, this demand "has not generally been matched by a supply of high-quality candidates" (Chesterman 2015, 506).
4. For a similar notion of the UN (as the "cathedral of the international community, the organizational repository of the community's collective beliefs") see Barnett (1997, 541).
5. Transforming leadership, then, implies a "metamorphosis" whereas "change" in the context of leadership simply means to substitute (Burns 2003, 24) and transforming the structure around it to infer roles.
6. Gordenker (1966/1967, 6) stressed this aspect at the example of Pope Paul VI and UNSG U Thant.
7. This is to ignore for now the fact that the pope is also head of a micro state.
8. Lord Gladwyn (1972, 257), first acting UNSG, pointed out this problem in attesting Hammarskjöld to be a leader but with the fault that he

   > thought that he almost regarded himself as a Lay Pope. If he did, he should have realized that the Secretariat was not exactly the equivalent of a Papal Chancery. Even less was the General Assembly a College of Cardinals. He could not, in fact, have anything like the apparatus that is at the disposal of the Holy Father. Nor was there any generally acceptable philosophy which could illuminate his path. The Charter does not really indicate the things that states should do in order to achieve grace. It lays down rather what they should not do in order to avert disaster.

9. In the case of the pope this can also be located at the installment of like-minded cardinals to increase the chances that they will eventually elect a pope that continues their efforts (e.g. Goodstein, Pearce, and Pecanha 2016). This is different from the election of the UNSG which is predominantly a matter of the permanent members of the Security Council without any realistic chance of the office holder to influence the choosing of his successor.
10. One prominent output of the Pope's engagement was the encyclical *Pacem in Terris* (John XXIII 1963, especially part III).
11. Here I refer to "institutions" as formal organizations with "prescribed hierarchies and the capacity for purposive action" (Keohane 1988, 384).
12. Griffith (2001) characterizes the ideal-type pope as one who "acts politically, but at the same time throws the politics of his acts into question."
13. Again, the Pope does so, but insignificantly (i.e. for the State of the Vatican City).

14. Hammarskjöld captured this aspect in the following remarks: "The principles of the Charter are, by far, greater than the Organization in which they are embodied, and the aims which they are to safeguard are holier than the policies of any single nation or people" (Security Council Official Records 1956, 1–2).
15. This is also the case regarding religion within the UNO's vast bureaucratic framework (e.g. Haynes 2014; Religion Counts 2002).
16. The Charter does not encompass a reference to God or religious values yet its Preamble makes it clear that "nations express their faith in the dignity and worth of the human person."

References

Agensky, Jonathan C. 2017, January 12. "Recognizing Religion: Politics, History, and the 'Long 19th Century'." *European Journal of International Relations*, 1–27.

Ainley, Kirsten. 2008. "Individual Agency and Responsibility for Atrocity." In *Confronting Evil in International Relations: Ethical Responses to Problems of Moral Agency*, edited by Renée Jeffery, 37–60. New York: Palgrave Macmillan.

Araujo, Robert J. 2007. "John Paul II – A Man of God and a Servant of Man: The Pope at the United Nations." *Ave Maria Law Review* 2: 367–398.

Ask, Sten, and Anna Mark-Jungkoist. 2005. *The Adventure of Peace: Dag Hammarskjöld and the Future of the UN*. New York: Palgrave Macmillan.

Álvarez, Andrés B. 2014. "Vatican: The Key Steps that Led to the Thaw in US-Cuba Relations." *Vatican Insider La Stampa*. Accessed December 19. http://vaticaninsider.lastampa.it/en/world-news/detail/articolo/castro-obama-us-cuba-detente-thaw-38184/.

Barnes, Barry. 2000. *Understanding Agency: Social Theory and Responsible Action*. London: Sage.

Barnett, Michael. 1997. "Bringing in the New World Order: Liberalism, Legitimacy, and the United Nations." *World Politics* 49: 526–551.

Barnett, Michael, and Raymond Duvall. 2005. "Power in International Politics." *International Organization* 59: 39–75.

Barnett, Michael N., and Martha Finnemore. 1999. "The Politics, Power, and Pathologies of International Organizations." *International Organization* 53 (4): 699–732.

Barnett, Michael, and Martha Finnemore. 2004. *Rules for the World: International Organizations in Global Politics*. Ithaca, NY: Cornell University Press.

Barnett, Michael, and Janice G. Stein. 2012. *Sacred aid: Faith and Humanitarianism*. Oxford: Oxford University Press.

Battilana, J. 2006. "Agency and Institutions: The Enabling Role of Individuals' Social Position." *Organization* 13 (5): 653–676. doi:10.1177/1350508406067008.

Berger, Peter L. 2014. *The Many Altars of Modernity: Toward a Paradigm for Religion in a Pluralist Age*. Boston, MA: de Gruyter.

Bernstein, Steven F., and Louis W. Pauly. 2007. *Global Liberalism and Political Order: Toward a New Grand Compromise?* Albany: State University of New York Press.

Bettiza, Gregorio, and Filippo Dionigi. 2014. "How do Religious Norms Diffuse? Institutional Translation and International Change in a Post-secular World Society." *European Journal of International Relations*. doi:10.1177/1354066114542663.

Boutros-Ghali, Boutros. 1996. "Global Leadership After the Cold War." *Foreign Affairs* 75 (2): 86–98.

Burns, James M. 2003. *Transforming Leadership: A New Pursuit of Happiness*. New York: Grove Press.

Byman, Daniel L., and Kenneth M. Pollack. 2001. "Let Us Now Praise Great Man: Bringing the Statesman Back in." *International Security* 25 (4): 107–146.

Chesterman, Simon, ed. 2007. *Secretary or General? The UN Secretary-General in World Politics*. Cambridge: Cambridge University Press.

Chesterman, Simon, ed. 2015. "The Secretary-General We Deserve?" *Global Governance* 21: 13–505.

Childers, Erskine, and Brian Urquhart. 1994. *Renewing the United Nations System: Development Dialogue*. Uppsala: Dag Hammarsköld Foundation.

Chiozza, Giacomo, and H. E. Goemans. 2011. *Leaders and International Conflict*. Cambridge: Cambridge University Press.

Christiansen, Drew. 2006. "Catholic Peacemaking, 1991–2005: The Legacy of Pope John Paul II." *The Review of Faith & International Affairs* 4 (2): 21–28. doi:10.1080/15570274.2006.9523246.

Claude, Inis L. 1971. *Swords Into Plowshares: The Problems and Progress of International Organization*. 4th ed. New York: Random House.

Claude, Inis L. 1996. "Peace and Security: Prospective Roles for the Two United Nations." *Global Governance* 2: 289–298.

Code of Canon Law. http://www.vatican.va/archive/ENG1104/_INDEX.HTM.

Coppa, Frank J. 1998. *The Modern Papacy, 1798–1995. Longman History of the Papacy.* London: Addison Wesley Longman.

Coppa, Frank J. 2008. *Politics and the Papacy in the Modern World.* Westport, CT: Praeger.

Coppa, Frank J. 2014. *The Papacy in the Modern World: A Political History.* London: Reaktion Books.

Cox, Robert W. 1969. "The Executive Head: An Essay on Leadership in International Organization." *International Organization* 23 (2): 205–230. doi:10.1017/S002081830003157X.

Cuéllar, Javier P. de. 1995. "Reflecting on the Past and Contemplating the Future." *Global Governance* 1: 149–170.

Dionigi, Filippo. 2016. "Dag Hammarskjöld's Religiosity and Norms Entrepreneurship: A Post-secular Perspective." *Politics and Religion* 9 (1): 162–186. doi:10.1017/S1755048315000930.

Dorn, A. W., and Robert Pauk. 2009. "Unsung Mediator: U Thant and the Cuban Missile Crisis." *Diplomatic History* 33 (2): 261–292. doi:10.1111/j.1467-7709.2008.00762.x.

Finnemore, Martha, and Kathryn Sikkink. 1998. "International Norms Dynamics and Political Change." *International Organization* 52 (4): 887–917.

Flamini, Roland. 1980. *Pope, Premier, President: The Cold War Summit That Never was.* New York: Macmillan.

Flamini, Roland. 2014, July/August. "Peter and Caesar: Is Pope Francis Shifting the Vaticans's Worldview?" *World Affairs*, 25–33.

Foote, Wilder, ed. 1962. *Dag Hammarskjöld: Servant of Peace* (A Selection of His Speeches and Statements). New York: Harper & Row.

Franco, Massimo. 2013a. "The First Global Pope." *Survival* 55 (3): 71–77. doi:10.1080/00396338.2013.802853.

Franco, Massimo. 2013b. "The Possible Revolution of Pope Francis." *Survival* 55 (6): 115–122. doi:10.1080/00396338.2013.862939.

Frost, Mervyn. 1996. *Ethics in International Relations: A Constitutive Theory.* Cambridge: Cambridge University Press.

Frost, Mervyn. 2003. "Constitutive Theory and Moral Accountability: Individuals, Institutions, and Disperse Practices." In *Can Institutions Have Responsibilities? Collective Moral Agency and International Relations*, edited by Toni Erskine, 84–99. Houndmills, NY: Palgrave Macmillan.

Fröhlich, Manuel. 2008. *Political Ethics and the United Nations: Dag Hammarskjöld as Secretary-General.* London: Routledge.

George, Alexander L. 1969. "The 'Operational Code': A Neglected Approach to the Study of Political Leaders and Decision-making." *International Studies Quarterly* 13 (2): 190–222.

Gladwyn, Hubert M. G. J. B. 1972. *The Memoirs of Lord Gladwyn.* New York: Weybright Talley.

Glendon, Mary A. 2001. *A World Made New: Eleanor Roosevelt and the Universal Declaration of Human Rights.* New York: Random House.

Goddard, Stacie E. 2009. "Brokering Change: Networks and Entrepreneurs in International Politics." *International Theory* 1 (2): 249–281. doi:10.1017/S1752971909000128.

Goodstein, Laurie, Adam Pearce, and Sergio Pecanha. 2016. "Pope Francis' Race against Time to Reshape the Church." *The New York Times*, November 18. Accessed February 14, 2017. https://goo.gl/9no7VK

Gordenker, Leon. 1966/1967. "U Thant and the Office of U.N. Secretary-General." *International Journal* 22 (1): 1–16.

Griffith, Paul. 2001. "The Future of the Papacy: A Symposium." *First Things (New York, N Y)* (111): 35–36. http://goo.gl/UW6CMC.

Haack, Kirsten, and Kent J. Kille. 2012. "The UN Secretary-General and Self-directed Leadership: Development of the Democracy Agenda." In *International Organizations as Self-directed Actors: A Framework for Analysis*, edited by Joel E. Oestreich, 29–59, 64. Abingdon: Routledge.

Hagan, Hoe D. 2001. "Does Decision Making Matter? Systemic Assumptions vs. Historical Reality in International Relations Theory." *International Studies Review* 3 (2): 5–46.

Hall, Rodney B. 1997. "Moral Authority as a Power Resource." *International Organization* 51 (4): 591–622.

Hammarskjöld, Dag. 1960. "The International Civil Servant in Law and in Fact: Lecture Delivered to Congregation at Oxford University." http://www.un.org/Depts/dhl/dag/docs/internationalcivilservant.pdf.

Harnisch, Sebastian, Cornelia Frank, and Hanns Maull. 2011. *Role Theory in International Relations: Approaches and Analyses.* New York: Routledge.

Haynes, Jeffrey. 2014. *Faith-based Organizations at the United Nations.* New York: Palgrave Macmillan.

Heft, James L. 2011. "John Paul II and the 'Just War' Doctrine: 'Make Peace Through Justice and Forvigeness Not War'." In *Religion, Identity, and Global Governance: Ideas, Evidence and Practice*, edited by Patrick James, 203–219. Toronto: University of Toronto Press.

Helms, Ludger, ed. 2012. *Comparative Political Leadership*. Houndmills: Palgrave Macmillan.

Helms, Ludger, ed. 2014. "Global Political Leadership in the Twenty-First Century: Problems and Prospects." *Contemporary Politics* 20 (3): 261–277. doi:10.1080/13569775.2014.911499.

Hermann, Margaret G. 1980. "Explaining Foreign Policy Behavior Using the Personal Characteristics of Political Leaders." *International Studies Quarterly* 24 (1): 7–46.

Hermann, Margaret G., Thomas Preston, Baghat Korany, and Timothy M. Shaw. 2001. "Who Leads Matters: The Effects of Powerful Individuals." *International Studies Review* 3 (2): 83–131. doi:10.1111/1521-9488.00235.

Horowitz, Michael C., Allan C. Stam, and Cali M. Ellis. 2015. *Why Leaders Fight*. New York: Cambridge University Press.

Hudson, Valerie M. 2005. "Foreign Policy Analysis: Actor-specific Theory and the Ground of International Relations." *Foreign Policy Analysis* 1 (1): 1–30. doi:10.1111/j.1743-8594.2005.00001.x.

Hurd, Elizabeth S. 2008. *The Politics of Secularism in International Relations*. Princeton, NJ: Princeton University Press.

Isaak, Robert A. 1975. *Individuals and World Politics*. North Scituate, MA: Duxbury Press.

Ivereigh, Austen. 2015. *The Great Reformer: Francis and the Making of a Radical Pope*. New York: Atlantic Books.

Johnston, Ian. 2003. "The Role of the UN Secretary-General: The Power of Persuasion Based on Law." *Global Governance* 9 (4): 441–458.

John XXIII. 1963. "Pacem in Terris." Vatican. http://goo.gl/CBNTTj.

Jones, Dorothy V. 2004. "The World Outlook of Dag Hammarskjöld." In *In Ethics and Statecraf: The Moral Dimension of International Affairs*, edited by Cathal J. Nolan, 2nd ed, 133–146. Westport, CT: Praeger.

Jordan, Robert S., ed. 1983. *Dag Hammarskjöld Revisited: The UN Secretary-General as a Force in World Politics*. Durham, NC: Carolina Academic Press.

Karns, Margaret P. 2012. "The Roots of UN Post-conflict Peacebuilding: A Case Study of Autonomous Agency." In *International Organizations as Self-directed Actors*, edited by J. E. Oestreich, 60–88. Abington: Routledge.

Kellerman, Barbara. 2008. *Followership: How Followers are Creating Change and Changing Leaders*. (Leadership for the Common Good). Boston, MA: Harvard Business School Press.

Kent, Peter C. 2002. *The Lonely Cold War of Pope Pius XII: The Roman Catholic Church and the Division of Europe, 1943–1950*. Montréal, QC: McGill-Queen's University Press.

Keohane, Robert O. 1988. "International Institutions: Two Approaches." *International Studies Quarterly* 32 (4): 379–396.

Kille, Kent J. 2006. *From Manager to Visionary: The Secretary-General of the United Nations*. New York: Palgrave Macmillan.

Kille, Kent J., ed. 2007. *The UN Secretary-General and Moral Authority: Ethics and Religion in International Leadership*. Washington, DC: Georgetown University Press.

Kille, Kent J., and Roger M. Scully. 2003. "Executive Heads and the Role of Intergovernmental Organizations: Expansionist Leadership in the United Nations and the European Union." *Political Psychology* 24 (1): 175–198. doi:10.1111/0162-895X.00321.

Lash, Joseph P. 1962. "Dag Hammarskjöld's Conception of His Office." *International Organization* 16 (3): 542–566.

Levine, Daniel H. 2016. "What Pope Francis Brings to Latin America." CLALS Working Paper Series 11. Unpublished manuscript, last modified February 17, 2017. https://lsa.umich.edu/content/dam/polisci-assets/Docs/What%20Pope%20Francis%20Brings.pdf. Religion and Democratic Contestation in Latin America.

Lie, Trygve. 1954. *In the Cause of Peace: Seven Years with the United Nations*. New York: The Macmillan Company.

Lipsey, Roger. 2013. *Hammarskjöld: A Life*. Ann Arbor: University of Michigan Press.

Luoma-aho, Mika. 2011. "Millenarian Development Goals: Commentary on the Political Theology of the Millennium Declaration." In *The Future of Political Theology: Religious and Theological Perspectives*, edited by Péter Losonczi, Mika Luoma-aho, and Aakash Singh, 173–185. Farnham: Ashgate.

Mathiason, John. 2007. *Invisible Governance: International Secretariats in Global Politics*. Bloomfield, CT: Kumarian.

Matlary, Janne H. 2001. "The Just Peace: The Public and Classical Diplomacy of the Holy See." *Cambridge Review of International Affairs* 14 (2): 80–94. doi:10.1080/09557570108400358.

May, Samantha, Erin K. Wilson, Claudia Baumgart-Ochse, and Faiz Sheikh. 2014. "The Religious as Political and the Political as Religious: Globalisation, Post-secularism and the Shifting Boundaries of the Sacred." *Politics, Religion & Ideology* 15 (3): 331–346. doi:10.1080/21567689.2014.948526.

Menaldo, Mark. 2013. *Leadership and Transformative Ambition in International Relations.* (New Horizons in Leadership Studies). Cheltenham: Edward Elgar.

Meyer, John W., John Boli, George M. Thomas, and Francisco O. Ramirez. 1997. "World Society and the Nation-State." *American Journal of Sociology* 103 (1): 144–181.

Mingst, Karen A., and Ivan M. Arreguín-Toft. 2013. *Essentials of International Relations.* 6th ed. New York: W. W. Norton & Company, Incorporated.

Moyn, Samuel. 2015. "Pope Francis has Given Up on Human Rights: That's a Good Thing." *The Washington Post.* https://goo.gl/51vZ5f.

Nabers, Dirk. 2011. "Identity and Role Change in International Politics." In *Role Theory in International Relations: Approaches and Analyses*, edited by Sebastian Harnisch, Cornelia Frank, and Hanns Maull, 74–92. New York: Routledge.

Nurser, John. 2005. *For all Peoples and all Nations: The Ecumenical Church and Human Rights.* Washington, DC: Georgetown University Press.

Nye, Joseph S. 2008. *The Powers to Lead: Soft, Hard, and Smart.* Oxford: Oxford University Press.

Oestreich, Joel E., ed. 2012. *International Organizations as Self-directed Actors: A Framework for Analysis 64.* New York: Routledge.

Orford, Anne. 2011. *International Authority and the Responsibility to Protect.* Cambridge: Cambridge University Press.

Pedersen, Kusumita P. 2010. "Sri Chinmoy's Work at the United Nations: Spirituality and the Power of Silence." *CrossCurrents* 60: 339–351.

Phillips, Andrew. 2013. "The Wars on Terror, Duelling Internationalisms and the Clash of Purposes in a Post-Unipolar World." *International Politics* 50 (1): 77–96. doi:10.1057/ip.2012.29.

Pontifical Council for Justice and Peace. 2004. *Compendium of the Social Doctrine of the Church.* Vatican: Libreria Editrice Vaticana.

Pope Francis. 2015. "Laudato si." http://goo.gl/yhVFvJ.

Religion Counts. 2002. "Religion and Public Policy at the UN." https://goo.gl/o4xeyj.

Riccards, Michael P. 1998. *Vicars of Christ: Popes, Power, and Politics in the Modern World.* New York: Crossroad.

Sandal, Nukhet A. 2017. *Religious Leaders and Conflict Transformation: Northern Ireland and Beyond.* Cambridge: Cambridge University Press.

Saunders, Elisabeth. 2009. "Transformative Choices: Leaders and the Origins of Intervention Strategy." *International Security* 34: 119–161.

Saunders, Elizabeth N. 2014. *Leaders at War: How Presidents Shape Military Interventions.* Ithaca, NY: Cornell University Press.

Schroeder, Michael B. 2014. "Executive Leadership in the Study of International Organization: A Framework for Analysis." *International Studies Review* 16 (3): 339–361. doi:10.1111/misr.12147.

Second Vatican Council. 1965. "Pastoral Constitution Gadium et Spes." http://www.vatican.va/archive/hist_councils/ii_vatican_council/documents/vat-ii_cons_19651207_gaudium-et-spes_en.html.

Security Council Official Records. 1956. "Eleventh Year, 751st Meeting." http://goo.gl/yl1tyb.

Sending, Ole J. 2015. *The Politics of Expertise: Competing for Authority in Global Governance.* Ann Arbor: University of Michigan Press.

Sikkink, Kathryn. 2011. *The Justice Cascade: How Human Rights Prosecutions are Changing World Politics.* New York: W.W. Norton & Co.

Sinclair, G. F. 2015. "The International Civil Servant in Theory and Practice: Law, Morality, and Expertise." *European Journal of International Law* 26 (3): 747–766. doi:10.1093/ejil/chv045.

Stahn, Carsten, and Henning Melber. 2014. *Peace Diplomacy, Global Justice and International Agency: Rethinking Human Security and Ethics in the Spirit of Dag Hammarskjöld.* Cambridge: Cambridge University Press.

Thakur, Ramesh C. 2006. *The United Nations, Peace and Security: From Collective Security to the Responsibility to Protect.* Cambridge: Cambridge University Press.

Thakur, Ramesh C. 2017. "Choosing the Ninth United Nations Secretary-General: Looking Back, Looking Ahead." *Global Governance* 23: 1–13.

Thomas, Scott M. 2010. "A Globalized God: Religion's Growing Influence in International Politics." *Foreign Affairs* 89 (6): 93–101.

Thomas, Scott M. 2014. "Culture, Religion and Violence: Rene Girard's Mimetic Theory." *Millennium: Journal of International Studies* 43 (1): 308–327.

United Nations. "Charta of the United Nations." http://www.un.org/en/documents/charter/.

Walker, Stephen G., Akan Malici, and Mark Schafer. 2011. *Rethinking Foreign Policy Analysis: States, Leaders, and the Microfoundations of Behavioral International Relations.* New York: Routledge.

Walsh, Michael. 2000. "Catholicism and International Relations: Papal Interventionism." In *Religion and Global Order,* edited by John L. a. M. W. Esposito, 100–118. Cardiff: University of Wales Press.

Walzer, Michael. 2007. *Thinking Politically: Essays in Political Theory.* Selected, edited, and with an introduction by D. Miller. New Haven, CT: Yale University Press.

Weber, Max, Hans H. Gerth, and C. W. Mills. 1946. *From Max Weber: Essays in Sociology.* New York: Oxford University Press.

Weigel, George. 1992. *The Final Revolution: The Resistance Church and the Collapse of Communism.* New York: Oxford University Press.

Wilson, Erin K. 2010. "Beyond Dualism: Expanded Understandings of Religion and Global Justice." *International Studies Quarterly* 54 (3): 733–754. doi:10.1111/j.1468-2478.2010.00607.x.

Zizola, Giancarola. 1978. *The Utopia of Pope John XXIII.* New York: Orbis.

PAPAL GEOPOLITICS: THE WORLD ACCORDING TO URBI ET ORBI

By Petr Kratochvíl and Jana Hovorková

The Catholic Church (or the Church, in this article) is, despite appearances, one of the most influential geopolitical actors in the world. Its leaders are seen as moral and political authorities by the believers as well as many others and the dominant ecclesial narratives about space and politics have a tremendous impact on the geopolitical imaginations of humanity. While there are a multiplicity of different voices coming from the Church, its hierarchical structure makes the position of the Catholic Church more intelligible than, say, the position(s) of Protestantism which is split into a great number of individual denominations, or that of other religious traditions where a formal head comparable to the Pope is missing.

This clear hierarchy also applies Church documents. From the point of view of Catholic theology, certain papal pronouncements and the documents issued by the ecumenical councils are considered the most relevant among the many texts produced by the Church (cf. the reference in First Vatican Council: Aeternus 1870). However, from the point of view of society at large, other pronouncements may gain an even wider media coverage and thus influence the public even more strongly. Among these, the papal messages Urbi et Orbi which are delivered every Christmas and Easter constitute the most influential series of regular media appearances which are followed by millions of people all across the globe. And the interest in these messages is strong and stable: For instance, the Christmas Message of 2004 was broadcast to 72 countries with 114 television networks (CathNews 2004), in 2006 it was beamed to 63 countries (Deutsche Welle 2006), and the Message of Pope Francis at Christmas 2013 was broadcast to 70 countries (Rai 2013).

Although the intended contents of the Messages are primarily religious, they also reveal a substantial amount of information about the geopolitical views of the Popes and, by extension, the Church under their leadership—which areas are relevant, which are not, what parts of the world are worth focusing on, where is the center and what constitutes the periphery, who is powerful and who is weak. Focusing on this geopolitical context of the Messages, we will compare the contents of the Messages delivered by Pope Benedict XVI and Pope Francis. We will proceed in three steps. First, we will introduce our approach to the study of geopolitics of the Catholic Church, which, following Ó Tuathail, builds on the three pillars of exploring the discursivity, perspectivalism and hegemony in the Church's discourse. Second, we will briefly describe our research design. Third, our findings will be presented. We will assess the spatial relevance, spatial agency and spatial closeness expressed in the Messages, followed by a short conclusion.

The Church, Mental Maps and Critical Geopolitics

The Church and its political activities have gradually become a popular topic for those who deal with the religious turn in IR (for instance Berger 1999; Philpott 2000, 2002, 2009; Kubálková 2000, 2003, 2009; Fox 2001; Haynes 2001; Hatzopoulous and Petito 2003; Hurd 2004; Leustean 2005; Thomas 2005; Fox and Sandler 2006; Philpott and Shah 2006; Kratochvíl 2009; Wilson 2013; Kratochvíl and Doležal 2015). The theoretical background from which these scholars usually approach the topic is very diverse. There are those who deal with a variety of key traditional IR theories in relation to religion (Haynes 2011, 2012) and those who focus on particular theoretical approaches, such as social constructivism (Hassner 2009) or phenomenology, hermeneutics and poststructuralism (Kubálková 2009) or draw upon the English school (Thomas 2001). Others take more sociological approaches, such as focusing on the micro-level of individuals (Leustean 2005).

Our own theoretical perspective is indebted to critical geopolitics, in particular, Geraóid Ó Tuathail (1992, 1994, 1996a, 1998, 1999, 2006), but we also draw on John Agnew (2006, 2010a, 2010b) and on Dalby (1991). Critical geopolitics is focussed on discourses (cf. Ó Tuathail 1996a) which means that it is concerned with producing, transforming and even annihilating spaces for political action. Clearly, spatio-political changes can be achieved not only by moving physical objects (such as our bodies or armies, by erecting fences or by digging trenches), but also by discursive practices, i.e. by speaking and writing about space in its relation to (international) politics.[1] This also means that discursive geopolitics is very practical: it does not have to explore the academic discourses about geopolitics (even though these may be of interest too), but the official discursive politics of space as it is practiced by the top representatives of the Church. It is this discursive production of space that Ó Tuathail calls "practical geopolitics" (1999, 113–114).

As we intend to produce a depiction of the spatial representation of the Church's place in the world as it is perceived by the Popes, we will also build on the notions of "geographical mental maps" (Da Vinha 2012, 12) which can be understood as "a conceptual instrument for foreign policy analysis" (Da Vinha 2012, 12). For our research, the idea of mental map is crucial as

> [t]he aim is, through a careful analysis of the language [...] used in public speeches, diplomatic notes, treaty texts, cartographic annexes and the like, to determine the key geographical concepts and related images that [...] officials more or less consciously entertain in making, conducting, and justifying foreign policy. (Henrikson 1980, 509)

A caveat is in place here: For post-structuralist students of geopolitics, mental maps can have a broader meaning. They are usually interpreted in the Lacanian sense of "the orders of the imaginary and the symbolic not the real. In other words, we are dealing with the systematic refusal of the [too complex] real" (Ó Tuathail 1994, 270). Imaginary maps of meaning thus consist only of those elements of reality which are understood as meaningful, whereas the seemingly unimportant elements of reality are discarded. While we are, broadly speaking, interested in mental maps as such, we focus here on geographic mental maps, i.e. those parts of the mental maps that give a spatial imagery to the relations of power and meaning mental maps describe (cf. Ó Tuathail 1994, 270; Da Vinha's 2012, 13).

As we are focusing on a small number of highly influential individuals, we also employ the concept of the "geographic mind" and the "geographic field" of an individual. The geographic mind describes the spatial imagination of a particular person, the ideas about which parts of the world are relevant/irrelevant, close/distant, central/peripheral, etc. While the geographic mind does not have to necessarily work on such binary oppositions, dichotomies of this kind are frequently present as they may reflect the person's ideas about spatio-political hierarchies and the relations of dominance and submission.

Geopolitics of the Catholic Church: Discursivity, Perspectivalism, and Hegemony

In its more than two decades of existence, critical geopolitics has been through a lively debate about which topics should be thematized (Dodds 2001; Sturm 2008; Agnew 2010b; Jones and Sage 2010; Kuus 2010). Among the topics that emerged as worth exploring is also religion (Ó Tuathail 2000; Agnew 2006; Dijkink 2006; Proctor 2006; Wallance 2006; Sturm 2013). One may trace two perspectives in the religion-related geopolitical research (Sturm 2013): religious geopolitics, which studies how religion is employed in the politics of state, and geopolitics of religion, which asks what sort of geopolitics is conducted by religious communities and leaders themselves. The former point of view is much more popular among students of critical geopolitics. Interestingly, Catholicism is thematized very rarely from both the perspective of religious geopolitics (De Busser 2006) and that of geopolitics of religion (Ó Tuathail 2000; Agnew 2010a; Olson 2013).

Every kind of geopolitical practice is characterized by three basic elements: discursivity (that is the rhetorical constitution of the political space), truth-claims derived from a particular source of authority (perspectivalism) and hegemony (the overarching simplifying narrative that binds the geopolitical construction into a coherent whole).

Discursivity is an essential part of performing "geopolitics" since, in this way, the author of the utterance constructs the world, including its spatial arrangement, through language. While mental maps do not always have to be expressed discursively, to explore them we need their external expressions, i.e. discursive depictions of these maps. We started from our own preliminary assessment of what kind of mental maps we could expect from the top leaders of the Church. These characteristics are both general, i.e. pertaining to the Church as such, and particular, i.e. related to the person of the speaker. The general focus ranges from the regions with large Catholic populations (such as Latin America, Philippines etc.) to regions of particular religious relevance (such as the Holy Land and Rome/Vatican as the seat of the Pope). The personal focus can be shaped by the region of the Pope's birth, by his education, life experience and even theological preferences.

The second feature lies in presenting the authority's truth whereas the authority itself is not necessarily revealed (which Ó Tuathail calls Cartesian perspectivalism; Ó Tuathail 1996b, 3). Perspectivalism differentiates between the outside world and the "I/eye" of the subject (Ó Tuathail 1996b, 3). In modern geopolitics, this distinction between the mind and the world leads to the subjective view's transformation, thus universalizing a certain perspective "into a supposedly scientific method of establishing objectivity and certainty" (Ó Tuathail 1996b, 3). Since the scientific truth-claim is thus not presented as the speaker's, but the authority's, further arguments are not necessary and the truth of the statement is not questioned: It is automatically taken for true and its validity for granted. Thus "objectivity" is introduced: One is "authorized" by the authority to present its truth. In other words, one's view of reality becomes objective because of the supreme authority whose truth is presented. In this context, it is not important that critical geopolitics is skeptical of objectivity in human affairs;[2] the problem lies in the alleged objectivity's goal to suppress and discredit alternative views which might pose a challenge to the established geopolitical order and erode the established hierarchies which are often oppressive. In Ó Tuathail's words, "knowledge is always situated knowledge, articulating the perspective of certain cultures and subjects while marginalizing that of others" (Ó Tuathail 1999, 108).

The task of critical geopolitics thus lies, in the first step, in revealing the supreme authority. It means suspending the claim from its unquestionable validity, truth and objectivity which the supreme authority seems to have endowed it with. Are religious actors somehow different as far as the supreme authority is concerned? Thomas argues that for secular actors the "ultimate authority is located in humanity" (Thomas 2001, 517), i.e. it is this-wordly and rational-moral, whereas religious actors refer to God or another transcendentally grounded religious-moral authority as their supreme source of knowledge/revelation. We are, however, convinced that this view is only partially applicable as we can easily discover rational-moral reasoning in religious texts as well and the construction of papal mental maps can also combine immanent and transcendental sources of authority. Also, as the below-discussed differences between the two Popes shows, the reference to the same ultimate authority may result in divergent assessments of reality as well as entirely different mental maps.

As for the third aspect, i.e. hegemony, Ó Tuathail and Agnew (1992, 195) claim that "geopolitical reasoning works by the active suppression of the complex geographical reality of places in favor of controllable geopolitical abstractions." In other words, geopolitical practitioners make the world smaller and simpler so that it is easier to manage and control. This "simplification of the world" is heavily dependent on Cartesian perspectivalism as it constitutes the core of discursive hegemony. Vice versa, perspectivalism's robustness depends on the strength of the hegemonic narratives. The mutual reinforcement means that actors who refer to certain authorities and base their arguments on these authorities will only rarely doubt these authorities as this would undermine both their claim and their position.

Although all the three elements are typical for all kinds of modern geopolitical enterprises, we believe that they are even more pronounced in the geopolitical practices of religious/faith-based actors. Since religious actors often lack material power and large, state-like territories, it is only logical that ideational/discursive constructions gain greater prominence. In a similar vein, arguments based on allusions to authority are more frequent and the hegemonic narratives even more forcefully put forward. The two features of modern geopolitical practices (discursivity and perspectivalism) are thus very explicit in the Urbi et Orbi messages, and for this reason, we dedicate our attention mainly to uncovering the third principle of Ó Tuathail's, i.e. hegemony.

Research Design

Critical geopolitics does not use its own methods and instead makes use mainly of discourse analysis and ethnographic methods (Sturm 2008). In line with this claim, we draw upon Milliken's (1999) approach to the study of discourse in international relations, Fairclough's (2001) analytical framework and Ruth Wodak's concept of basic discursive strategies used by political actors (Wodak and Meyer 2009). However, as these approaches are rather complex and sometimes need some modification to fit in our research design, we choose mainly those elements of the aforementioned approaches that are instrumental in revealing the hegemonic aspects of the Church's geopolitical practice.

First of all, we are interested in Milliken's productivity and "objects," i.e. places and groups which are "produced" as such (Milliken 1999, 229). Hence, we are looking for places charted in Pope Benedict's and Francis' mental maps in terms of spatial relevance and groups in terms of spatial agency. Here, we follow the binary oppositions of relevant/irrelevant for places and self/others for groups (Milliken 1999). For spatial relevance, we employ slightly modified principles of content analysis, for the spatial agency we refer to certain aspects of Fairclough's agency (2001, 2003) and use Milliken's concept of the publics (audiences) (1999). Moreover, we investigate spatial closeness both in spatial relevance and agency, i.e. we point out the binary opposition of close/distant. In doing so, we draw upon certain aspects of Wodak's strategies of predication (Wodak and Meyer 2009) and seek to further specify Fairclough's agency (2001, 2003). To make hegemonic features of spatiality evident, we investigate the nature of the space constructed (earthy/heavenly, religiously/non-religiously defined, Christian/Catholic/other) and it's dimensions.

As far as our corpus is concerned, we investigate the Urbi et Orbi Messages which were pronounced from 2005 to 2015; our research includes 15 Messages by Pope Benedict XVI (Christmas 2005–Christmas 2012) and 5 by Francis (Easter 2013–Easter 2015); see the Appendix.

Spatial Relevance

De-territorialisation: Reduction of the World to Spaces of Problems

The starting question revolves around the distinction between references to concrete territories and to de-territorialized issues. In the analyzed speeches, de-territorialized references are virtually always reduced to problems, global matters that need to be addressed: wars and violence, terrorism, natural disasters, poverty, migration, misuse of children and women, epidemics, moral crises, religious persecution, economic crises, social marginalization, etc. As the problem orientation is so prevalent in the Messages, it seems that the earthly world is produced mainly through de-territorialized issues —the earthly dimension is shrunk to an earthly world of problems.

Interestingly, while further reductions occur both in Benedict's speeches and in those uttered by Francis, these reductions are substantially different in each case. For Pope Benedict, religious freedom plays a dominant role, while Pope Francis' Urbi et Orbi are of a less religious nature. As a result, due to the religiously conceived Messages, Benedict's earthly world of problems is further reduced to a religious or even a Christian space. Hence, for Benedict, the world is defined by a series of problematic spaces where religious freedom is violated. The world is a space of moral crisis and where Catholic Christianity and its moral values are present, they are under constant attack. In the Messages by Pope Francis, these reductions are also present, but to a much lesser degree. In particular, the distinction between the agency of the self in the religious space and the agency of the others in the morally corrupt space is not as pronounced; instead, the earthly de-territorialized problems are tackled without this translation into the religious/irreligious binary. Hence, while discursive hegemonies are imposed by both Popes, Benedict tends to reduce the complexity much more forcefully, first to the world of problems, and second to a world of moral crisis assailing the believers.

Territorial Issues

The focus on problems is also replicated in the Popes' mental maps of relevant territories as problems are often the starting point to which territorial predicates are added (the conflict in Ukraine, in Syria, etc.). As war is the key issue, the relatively peaceful parts of the world are absent from the mental map: Europe and North America are often entirely omitted in contrast to Asia and Latin America and especially to the Middle East and Africa. Again, however, substantial differences between the Popes are visible:

(1) Benedict's larger vs. Francis' smaller territorial units

In contrast to his successor, Pope Benedict XVI refers more to continents or greater territorial units than states. This feature is more palpable in the Urbi et Orbi Messages pronounced especially in the initial years of his pontificate. In the course of time single countries are charted in the map more frequently, but the phrases "besides other states," "and other states" put them into the context of larger units with more or less common characteristics. This is not the case with Pope Francis: cornerstones of his mental map are states, rarely paying attention to continents or regions.[3]

(2) Benedict's problem orientation vs. Francis' specificity

In general, both Benedict XVI and Francis inscribe states in their mental map, even though Benedict tends to lump them together into greater units. For Benedict, however, states serve as examples of specific expressions of de-territorialized problems, such as war and famine. This is also why he often alludes to "others states" to which the particular problem might be applied. Francis, on the other hand, speaks about concrete, much more explicitly territorialized problems. Often, he presents a definitive list of states without the ambition to include other parts of the world than those he speaks about explicitly.

(3) Fixation of specific problematic territories

The basic rule of mentioning problematic countries or regions applies virtually universally in the Messages. However, some countries are mentioned only exceptionally, in the connection with a recent outburst of violence or a disaster: For instance, for Francis, this would be Mali (2013a), the Philippines (2013b), Venezuela (2014a), Pakistan (2014a), Guinea, Sierra Leone and Liberia (all 2014a, 2014b), Kenya (2015a), Iran (2015a) or Yemen (2015a). Other territories become more fixed as points of almost a ritual invocation, permanent fixtures on the Popes' mental maps. Examples of such territories include Syria (beginning with Benedict's Urbi et Orbi for Christmas 2011; Benedict 2011) and Ukraine (beginning with Francis' Urbi et Orbi for Easter 2014; Francis 2014a).

(4) Dominance of Africa and the Middle East

All in all, both Popes clearly focus primarily on Africa and the Middle East. Hence, our expectation that Francis would tend to talk more about Latin America and Benedict about Europe was wrong: In Pope Benedict's XVI mental map, Africa and the Middle East represent 74 percent of all territorial allusions (Africa: 41 percent, Middle East: 33 percent). The percentage is even higher in the map of his successor—87 percent (Africa: 54 percent, Middle East: 33 percent). The rest of the world is more present in Benedict's XVI map and its variety is definitely higher than in Francis' map: Asia represents 16 percent, Latin America 8 percent[4], Europe 1 percent[5] and even Oceania 1 percent. Francis' rest of the world consists of Asia (only 4 percent), Latin America (solely 2 percent) and Europe (7 percent[6]).

In territorial terms, both Benedict XVI and Francis construct a space where Africa and the Middle East are dominant problematic regions, with Francis being even more focused on the two and excluding the other regions from his Messages even more frequently. While the dominance of Africa and the Middle East result in part from thematizing problems related to conflicts, tensions and violence, the Popes' concern for Africa might refer to the assumption that Africa (together with Asia) is the future of the Church (Mastrofini 2006). The salience of the Middle East for the Church is obvious as well: it is a region with a tradition of religious variety implying the presence of diverse religious communities, Christian and Catholic ones included, and a region with sacred places which are of high importance for the Church.

It is, however, worth noting that this territorial focus is at odds with the de-territorialized binary construction of the world or religion vs. the world of moral crisis. For both Benedict and Francis, moral crisis is usually spatially tied to the West (Europe and North America). And yet, in the territorial parts of the Messages, it is the more religious and often more Catholic parts of the world that are seen as suffering the greatest problems (Tables 1 and 2).

(5) Spiritualization of the Holy Land

Unsurprisingly, the Holy Land is a perennial part of both Benedict's and Francis' mental maps.[7] However, both Popes eschew official terms such as the State of Israel and the State of Palestine and prefer talking about the Israelis and Palestinians, employing the religious term Holy Land and various Christian circumlocutions. Given the more

Table 1. Mental Map of Pope Benedict XVI based on his Messages Urbi et Orbi (Christmas 2005–Christmas 2012).

Sudan/Darfur (8)	Democratic Republic of Congo (6)	Somalia (5)	Nigeria (3)	Madagascar (3)	Niger (1)
					Côte d'Ivoire (1)
					Egypt (1)
			Great Lakes (2)	Horn of Africa (2)	Kamerun (1)
					Angola (1)
		Zimbabwe (2)	North Africa (2)	Mali (2)	South Sudan (1)
	Guinea (2)				Kenya (1)
		Kivu (1)	Eritrea (1)	Ethiopia (1)	Libya (1)
Holy Land (15)	Iraq (12)	Lebanon (6)			
		Pakistan (3)			
	Syria (3)				
Sri Lanka (4)	Afghanistan (4)	Korean Penisula (3)	Philippines (2)	China (2)	
			East Timor (1)	Myanmar (1)	
		Thailand (1)	Tibet (1)		
Venezuela (2)	Honduras (1)	Costa Rica (1)			
	Chile (1)	Nicaragua (1)			
Haiti (2)	Colombia (1)				
	Guatemala (1)				
Balcan Penisula (1)					
Solomon Islands (1)					

Note: Data based on the analyzed Messages available from http://www.vatican.va

forthright nature of Francis' Messages, one might also expect that he would be more explicit about this particular conflict too. Yet this is not so—indeed, the opposite is true: the detachment of the references to the Holy Land and its spiritualization is more pronounced in Francis' Messages who always puts the reference first, before the others, while this was not the norm for Pope Benedict. The diplomatic approach which leads to the religiously careful rhetoric thus spiritualizes the country, removes the Holy Land from the world of secular problems and suppresses the violent dimension of the conflict. The symbolic and spiritual relevance of the Holy Land is further reinforced by the ritual invocation of the Land —irrespective of whether the conflict was in its more violent phase or not, both Popes always mentioned the Holy Land in their speeches.

(6) Catholic strongholds vs. problematic and ambitious territories

Another assumption of ours was that Catholic strongholds, i.e. territories with the highest share of the Catholics,[8] would

Table 2. Mental Map of Pope Francis based on his Messages Urbi et Orbi (Easter 2013–Easter 2015).

Nigeria (5)	Democratic Republic of Congo (4)	Central African Republic (4)	South Sudan (4)	Guinea (2)	Liberia (2)
				Sierra Leone (2)	Libya (2)
	Mali (1)	Sudan (1)	Kenya (1)	Somali Penisula (1)	
Holy Land (5)	Syria (5)	Iraq (5)	Pakistan (1)		
			Yemen (1)		
			Iran (1)		
Philippines (1)	Korean Penisula (1)				
Venezuela (1)					
Ukraine (3)	Lampedusa (1)				

Note: Data based on the analyzed Messages available from http://www.vatican.va

be included in the Popes' mental maps. But, at least as far as these maps are articulated in the Messages, this assumption is not confirmed. Instead, here also, the problem orientation prevails: territories facing problems are the key units of reference in both papal mental maps. While countries with a high number of Catholics are mentioned, they are certainly not disproportionately stressed: Democratic Republic of Congo (which represents 5.1 percent in Benedict's map[9] and 7.4 percent in Francis' map), Nigeria (2.5 percent; 9.3 percent), Venezuela (1.7 percent; 1.9 percent), Philippines (1.7 percent; 1.9 percent) and Columbia (0.8 percent; 0 percent).

To sum up, Benedict's geographic mind tends to a certain state-centric universalism, the tendency to include as many countries as possible, but also to perceiving the world as a world of conceptual issues, of problems.[10] His map becomes larger, more enumerative, ordered by problem categories, but also more difficult to manage and control. As for Pope Francis, his geographic mind is not concerned with exhaustive lists or types of problems, instead, he tends to a certain particularism. His map is simpler, more targeted but easier to manage and control. In terms of perspectivalism and hegemony, it is clearly Pope Benedict who aims at a more ordered, classified and universalist spatial representation, with the world ordered according to well-established, problem-based principles. Paradoxically, the efforts at exhaustiveness often lead to a more complex and less easily controllable map than is the case with the pragmatically minded Francis.

Spatial Agency

For the analysis of spatial agency, we refer to Fairclough's agency (2001, 2003) and use certain aspects of Milliken's publics (audiences) (1999). The basic spatial agency is to be expressed in the distinction of the "self" and "others" and the corresponding division of the space of the "self" and that of "others."[11]

One level of the spatial "self," agency may be represented by the audience (Milliken 1999), i.e. addressees of the Pope's words. While the obvious spatial distinction is the space (and people) of Rome and the space (and people) of the world, this plays a rather ceremonial role, without having any much impact on how the Messages are conceived and what problems are addressed. In other words, the Popes focus on the world, while Rome rarely appears beyond the introduction. Even though both Popes start with the address of "dear brothers and sisters," they have clearly different audiences in mind. For Pope Benedict's XVI the audience is religiously determined: he talks to Christians, in some cases even exclusively to Catholics. Again, a reduction is taking place here: the earthly space is reduced to the religious one, the religious to the Christian and the Christian to the Catholic. In contrast to his predecessor, Pope Francis predominantly defines the audience in broader terms, i.e. people without further specifications and the religious reduction, with its corresponding claim of religious leadership is not carried out.

As the Messages are pronounced in the "we"-form, one may speak about an inclusive audience (as there are clear examples of this not being a simple majestic plural); despite being addressed as "you," the audience becomes part of "us." The very point of departure for understanding the "self" is the role of the Pope as he is the representative of the "self," the speaker who enunciates the objectified truths. Pope Benedict XVI often assumes the role of a Christian leader, speaking on behalf of Christian communities, which is again consistent with his general focus on religious matters. Pope Francis' Urbi et Orbi show less religious accents and Pope Francis clearly sees himself as a "defensor hominis" (Casanova 1996, 362). The reduction to earthly problems is thus expressed differently—for Benedict, the relevant spaces are those inhabited by agents who either suffer or cause religious persecution and discrimination; for Francis, the relevant spaces are much broader, and the agents are involved in a number of socio-economic problems and wars.

Surprisingly, Benedict's agents are more active, they are often called upon to take action by themselves. In spite of the religious orientation of his Messages, their actions are not always explicitly dependent on the initiation by transcendental agents. Francis, on the other hand, while more broadly critical of the world's problems, expects less action from the afflicted and instead typically relies on divine intervention. Both Popes also include the international community and representatives of nations in their mental maps. In addition, Pope Benedict XVI introduces religious leaders. In other words, authorities extend the earthly space of "others," regarded as ordinary people, adding the dimension of international and domestic politics. Both Popes await their role in (re)solving problems in the world either as primary agents or as secondary ones, i.e. following the agency of transcendental "others."

Spatial Closeness

Pointing out the binary opposition of close/distant in spatial relevance, we draw upon certain aspects of Wodak's strategies of predication (Wodak and Meyer 2009). For discerning closeness and distance of spatial agency, we again use a modified notion of Fairclough's agency (2001, 2003).

Benedict's XVI Distance vs. Francis' Closeness

While spatial relevance and spatial agency can be uncovered relatively easily, spatial closeness or distance is more difficult to ascertain. To do so, we applied predicate analysis (Wodak and Meyer 2009), but even then the task is not simple for a number of reasons. Most importantly, predicates are employed rarely and not used in de-territorialized issues, solely in territorialized ones. In both the mental maps, there are no objects labeled as distant pointing out to an obvious periphery: if predicates are employed, they are of a positive nature. Hence, we may only assume that distance is expressed by the absence of allusions to a territory. But as territories are primarily defined as "problematic spaces," this absence may also indicate that a particular part of the world is peaceful and prosperous.

Both Benedict and Francis use the positive predicate "beloved" in their Messages, expressing their personal or emotional relations to the place or country. Pope Benedict XVI mentions it only twice in his total 15 Messages, whereas Pope Francis 8 times in the 5 analyzed Messages. Both Popes use the word "beloved" in connection with a territorialized aspect, i.e. either with a state or region or with a people living in a concrete territory. It is the people of Haiti (Benedict 2010) and the Land of Egypt (Benedict 2012b) which are beloved to Pope Benedict XVI. Pope Francis labels Syria, Iraq and Ukraine as beloved more times.[12] One may conclude there are only a few objects in Benedict's XVI mental map which are close and the intensity of the closeness is very low,[13] whereas the relative closeness is higher and more intensive[14] and also more stable in Francis' mental map. The predicate "noble" is worth mentioning. It is used to express the notion that the object is distant, but it is connected with positive esteem, i.e. with an aspiration to get closer despite the present distance, with a desired closeness. For instance, Pope Benedict XVI used the word "noble" for the people of China in his Message pronounced at Christmas in 2012.

To conclude, the expressed closeness or aspiration to a less distant relation seems to reflect a hegemonic dimension: 72 percent of the Haitian are baptized Catholics, Egypt is "blessed by the childhood of Jesus" (Benedict 2012b), in Syria, Iraq and Ukraine there are Christian communities, and finally China is considered the future of the Catholic Church, together with the whole Asian continent (Mastrofini 2006). One may sum up the background of the closeness in the mental map as the assurance of the Christian presence in the world or the spatial expansion of the Catholic faith, or both.

Closer "You" vs. Distant "Them"

When dealing with closeness or distance in the spatial agency, we further elaborate the concept of Fairclough's agency (2001, 2003) in terms of a finer distinction between "them" and "you": the former expresses a greater distance, the latter marks objects which are closer. When investigating the category of "others" constituted in opposition to the "self," "others" facing problems are usually considered "them" in general, but rather "you" as members of Christian communities.[15] More distance, i.e. as "them," is evident in the treatment of others, when conversion to Christianity is foreseen, as it will be this conversion that would bring the people closer to the speakers (interestingly, this position is put forward much more forcefully by Benedict than Francis). Transcendental "others" are not unreachable, they are definitely understood as "you." Distancing is strongly present when authorities are addressed or mentioned. Paradoxically, while the Popes are also undoubtedly authorities of sorts, they never see themselves as part of the group of authorities which can contribute to solving the world's problems.

WHILE POPES ARE CERTAINLY AUTHORITIES/LEADERS AS WELL, THEY DO NOT PRESENT THEMSELVES AS SUCH

Conclusion

The Urbi et Orbi Messages create a very distinctive spatial order. The dominant hegemonic move is the simplification of the world to the series of "spaces of problems," which need to be tackled. In the case of Pope Benedict, this tendency is so strong that the problem orientation overshadows references to concrete territories; these territories are mentioned as examples of broader problematic issues (such as war). As far as references to particular territories are concerned, these are mostly not related to the specific relevance of such territories to the Church (in terms of the Catholic population), but reflect the perceived global distribution of "problems." As a result, the Middle East and Africa are mentioned most frequently. An interesting case is the Holy Land, which is almost ritually mentioned, but as a sort of a place between the earthly and the spiritual space. But this also means that unlike in other cases, the conflict there is addressed, but all the references are meticulously de-politicized.

The simple division of the spiritual, heavenly sphere with its transcendental actors and the earthly space of problems is further complicated in two ways. First, even the earthly sphere often undergoes, particularly in Pope Benedict's Messages, a double reduction—from the space of problems to the space of religiously defined problems (such as persecution because of faith) and to Christian/Catholic problems. Hence, the spiritual becomes present in the secular domain, but it is usually seen as persecuted, oppressed, or otherwise threatened. Second, while transcendental agents may intervene in the secular matters, often, secular authorities are invoked and asked to take measures to tackle the injustice. Religious communities are present in the earthly sphere as well, but they are typically victims, often described in passive terms, as secondary agents at best (i.e. following the lead of God or relying on divine providence).

The differences among the Popes also pertain to the definition of the "self" and the "others," which also translates into different representations of the "we" and different ways of approaching these problems. Pope Benedict clearly sees himself as a religious leader and his "we" is most frequently the Church; Pope Francis, on the other hand, presents himself as a "defensor hominis," speaking on behalf of the "people." An interesting disassociation is taking place here—while Popes are certainly authorities/ leaders as well, they do not present themselves as such. The identification with the oppressed goes so far that Pope Francis even adopts their passive stance—it is the "others" who can change things, mainly the transcendental agents are called upon, sometimes secular powers are addressed. But while the Messages call for the solution of the pressing problems, they almost never indicate which specific earthly actors should do this and, even more importantly, how this should be done. ❖

Funding

This work was partially supported by Jan Masaryk Centre for International Studies, University of Economics in Prague, Czech Republic.

1. To mark the difference between the former (physical actions) and the latter (discursive practices), Ó Tuathail uses the term "geopolitics," i.e. a hyphenated form, for geopolitics being done discursively.
2. '[T]he "view from nowhere" [...] is an illusion' (Antonsich 2000, 6–7).
3. The only exception is Africa constructed in his Urbi et Orbi pronounced at Easter 2013 as "scene of violent conflicts" (Francis, 2013a).
4. It is worth mentioning that Benedict XVI charts several Central American countries into his map: Haiti, Honduras, Costa Rica, Nicaragua and Guatemala.
5. Europe is present thanks to the Balkan Penisula which is mentioned only once (Benedict XVI, 2007).
6. The presence of Europe results from tensions in Ukraine (mentioned in three Messages: Francis 2014a,2014b; Francis 2015) and from refugees coming to the Italian island of Lampedusa (mentioned in one Message: Francis, 2013b).
7. The Holy Land is mentioned in all analysed Messages, i.e. in all 15 Benedict's XVI and all 5 Francis' Urbi et Orbi.
8. Fifteen countries with the highest number of the baptised are the following: Brazil, Mexico, Philippines, USA, Italy, France, Columbia, Spain, Democratic Republic of Congo, Argentina, Poland, Peru, Nigeria, Venezuela and Germany (Secretaria Status 2016).
9. In the map consisting of states and geographical regions, i.e. in the same map as described in paragraph 4.
10. In his Christmas Urbi et Orbi in 2009, Benedict XVI presents cases from all the continents even (Benedict XVI, 2009).
11. With the exception of Pope Benedict's XVI Message pronounced at Christmas 2009 in which the separation of "self" and "others" is explicitly expressed in addressing the audience, i.e. at the very beginning of the Message.
12. Syria is called beloved in four analysed Messages, Iraq in two and Ukraine also in two Messages.
13. Only two objects in fifteen Messages, the expression "beloved" is used only twice.
14. Three objects in five Messages, the predicate "beloved" is employed eight times.
15. See for example Christian communities in Iraq (Benedict XVI, 2010) and in Africa (Benedict XVI, 2012a).

References

Agnew, J. 2006. "Religion and Geopolitics." *Geopolitics* 11 (2): 183–191.

Agnew, J. 2010a. "Deus Vult: The Geopolitics of the Catholic Church." *Geopolitics* 15 (1): 39–61.

Agnew, J. 2010b. "Still Trapped in Territory?" *Geopolitics* 15 (4): 779–784.

Antonsich, M. 2000. *Dis-placing or Re-placing Hegemonic Geopolitical Discourse? Reading/Writing Gearóid Ó Tuathail's "Critical Geopolitics"* [Online]. Accessed December 10, 2015. https://www.academia.edu/2286337/Dis-placing_or_re-placing_hegemonic_geopolitical_discourse_Reading_writing_Gear%C3%B3id_%C3%93_Tuathail_s_critical_geopolitics

Benedict XVI. 2007. *Urbi et Orbi Message of His Holiness Pope Benedict XVI. Christmas 2007* [Online]. Accessed April 5, 2016. http://w2.vatican.va/content/benedict-xvi/en/messages/urbi/documents/hf_ben-xvi_mes_20071225_urbi.html

Benedict XVI. 2009. *Urbi et Orbi Message of His Holiness Pope Benedict XVI. Christmas 2009* [Online]. Accessed April 5, 2016. http://w2.vatican.va/content/benedict-xvi/en/messages/urbi/documents/hf_ben-xvi_mes_20091225_urbi.html

Benedict XVI. 2010. *Urbi et Orbi Message of His Holiness Pope Benedict XVI. Easter 2010* [Online], Accessed April 5, 2016. http://w2.vatican.va/content/benedict-xvi/en/messages/urbi/documents/hf_ben-xvi_mes_20100404_urbi-easter.html

Benedict XVI. 2011. *Urbi et Orbi Message of His Holiness Pope Benedict XVI. Christmas 2011* [Online]. Accessed April 5, 2016. http://w2.vatican.va/content/benedict-xvi/en/messages/urbi/documents/hf_ben-xvi_mes_20111225_urbi.html

Benedict XVI. 2012a. *Urbi et Orbi Message of His Holiness Pope Benedict XVI. Easter 2012* [Online]. Accessed April 5, 2016. http://w2.vatican.va/content/benedict-xvi/en/messages/urbi/documents/hf_ben-xvi_mes_20120408_urbi-easter.html

Benedict XVI. 2012b. *Urbi et Orbi Message of His Holiness Pope Benedict XVI. Christmas 2012* [Online]. Accessed April 5, 2016. http://w2.vatican.va/content/benedict-xvi/en/messages/urbi/documents/hf_ben-xvi_mes_20121225_urbi.html

Berger, P., ed. 1999. *The Desecularisation of the World: Resurgent Religion and World Politics*. Grand Rapids: William B. Eerdmans.

Casanova, J. 1996. "Global Catholicism and the Politics of Civil Society." *Sociological Inquiry* 66 (3): 356–373.

CathNews. 2004. "Christmas Mass to Reach 72 Countries." *Catholic World News*, December 23. http://cathnews.acu.edu.au/412/141.html

Da Vinha, L. 2012. "Charting Geographic Mental Maps in Foreign Policy Analysis: A Literature Review." *Human Geographies* 6 (1): 5–17.

Dalby, S. 1991. "Critical Geopolitics: Discourse, Difference, and Dissent." *Environment and Planning D: Society and Space* 9 (3): 261–283.

De Busser, C. 2006. "From Exclusiveness to Inclusiveness: The Changing Politico-territorial Situation of Spain and its Reflection on the National Offerings to the Apostle Saint James from the Second Half of the Twentieth Century." *Geopolitics* 11 (2): 300–316.

Deutsche Welle. 2006. *Pope Pleads for Lasting Peace in Middle East* [Online]. Accessed July 29, 2016. http://www.dw.com/en/pope-pleads-for-lasting-peace-in-middle-east/a-2290712

Dijkink, G. 2006. "When Geopolitics and Religion Fuse: A Historical Perspective." *Geopolitics* 11 (2): 192–208.

Dodds, K. 2001. "Political Geography III: Critical Geopolitics After Ten Years." *Progress in Human Geography* 25 (3): 469–484.

Fairclough, N. 2001. "Critical Discourse Analysis as a Method in Social Scientific Research." In *Methods of Critical Discourse Analysis*, edited by R. Wodak and M. Meyer, 121–138. London: Sage.

Fairclough, N. 2003. *Analysing Discourse: Textual Analysis for Social Research.* Oxon: Routledge.

First Vatican Council. 1870. *Pastor Aeternus* [Online]. Accessed July 29, 2016. http://www.ewtn.com/library/COUNCILS/V1.htm#6

Fox, J. 2001. "Religion as an Overlooked Element of International Relations." *International Studies Review* 3 (3): 53–73.

Fox, J., and S. Sandler. 2006. *Bringing Religion into International Relations.* New York: Palgrave Macmillan.

Francis. 2013a. *Urbi et Orbi Message of Pope Francis. Easter 2013* [Online]. Accessed June 16, 2015. http://w2.vatican.va/content/francesco/en/messages/urbi/documents/papa-francesco_20130331_urbi-et-orbi-pasqua.html

Francis. 2013b. *Urbi et Orbi Message of Pope Francis. Christmas 2013* [Online]. Accessed June 3, 2015. http://w2.vatican.va/content/francesco/en/messages/urbi/documents/papa-francesco_20131225_urbi-et-orbi-natale.html

Francis. 2014a. *Urbi et Orbi Message of Pope Francis. Easter 2014* [Online]. Accessed June 18, 2015. http://w2.vatican.va/content/francesco/en/messages/urbi/documents/papa-francesco_20140420_urbi-et-orbi-pasqua.html

Francis. 2014b. *Urbi et Orbi Message of His Holiness Pope Francis. Christmas 2014* [Online]. Accessed April 4, 2015. http://w2.vatican.va/content/francesco/en/messages/urbi/documents/papa-francesco_20141225_urbi-et-orbi-natale.html

Francis. 2015. *Urbi et Orbi Message of His Holiness Pope Francis. Easter 2015* [Online]. Accessed June 19, 2015. http://w2.vatican.va/content/francesco/en/messages/urbi/documents/papa-francesco_20150405_urbi-et-orbi-pasqua.html

Hassner, R. E. 2009. *War on Sacred Grounds.* Ithaca, NY: Cornell University Press.

Hatzopoulous, P., and P. Petito, eds. 2003. *Religion in International Relations: The Return from Exile.* New York: Palgrave Macmillan.

Haynes, J. 2001. "Transnational Religious Actors and International Politics." *Third World Quarterly* 22 (2): 143–158.

Haynes, J. 2011. *Religion, Politics and International Relations: Selected Essays.* New York: Taylor & Francis.

Haynes, J. 2012. *Religious Transnational Actors and Soft Power.* Farnham: Ashgate.

Henrikson, A. 1980. "The Geographical 'Mental Maps' of American Foreign Policy Makers." *International Political Science Review* 1 (4): 495–530.

Hurd, E. S. 2004. "The Political Authority of Secularism in International Relations." *European Journal of International Relations* 10 (2): 235–262.

Jones, L., and D. Sage. 2010. "New Directions in Critical Geopolitics: An Introduction." *GeoJournal* 75: 315–325.

Kratochvíl, P. 2009. "The Religious Turn in IR: A Brief Assessment." *Perspectives. Review of International Affairs* 2: 5–11.

Kratochvíl, P., and T. Doležal. 2015. *The European Union and the Catholic Church.* Hampshire: Palgrave Macmillan.

Kubálková, V. 2000. "Toward an International Political Theology." *Millennium: Journal of International Studies* 29: 675–704.

Kubálková, V. 2003. "Toward an International Political Theology." In *Religion in International Relations: The Return from Exile*, edited by F. Petito and P. Hatzopoulos, 79–105. New York: Palgrave Macmillan.

Kubálková, V. 2009. "A 'Turn to Religion' in IR?" *Perspectives. Review of International Affairs* 20: 353–354.

Kuus, M. 2010. *Critical Geopolitics* [Online]. Accessed December 12, 2014. http://www.isacompss.com/info/samples/criticalgeopolitics_sample.pdf

Leustean, L. N. 2005. "Towards an Integrative Theory of Religion and Politics." *Methods and Theory in the Study of Religion* 17 (4): 364–381.

Mastrofini, F. 2006. *Geopolitica della chiesa cattolica.* Roma-Bari: Gius, Laterza & Figli.

Milliken, J. 1999. "The Study of Discourse in International Relations: A Critique of Research and Methods." *European Journal of International Relations* 5 (2): 225–254.

Olson, E. 2013. "Gender and Geopolitics in 'Secular Time'." *AREA* 45 (2): 148–154.

Ó Tuathail, G. 1994. "Problematizing Geopolitics: Survey, Statesmanship and Strategy." *Transactions of the Institute of British Geography* 19: 259–272.

Ó Tuathail, G. 1996a. *Critical Geopolitics. The Politics of Writing Global Space.* London: Routledge.

Ó Tuathail, G. 1996b. "An Anti-geopolitical Eye: Maggie O'Kane in Bosnia, 1992-93." *Gender, Place, and Culture* 3: 171–186.

Ó Tuathail, G. 1999. "Understanding Critical Geopolitics: Geopolitics and Risk Security." In *Geopolitics, Geography and Strategy,* edited by C. S. Gray and G. R. Sloan, 107–124. London: Frank Cass.

Ó Tuathail, G. 2000. "Spiritual Geopolitics. Fr. Edmund Walsh and Jesuit Anti-communism." In *Geopolitical Traditions. A Century of Geopolitical Thought,* edited by K. Dodds and D. Atkinson, 187–210. London: Routledge.

Ó Tuathail, G., and J. Agnew. 1992. "Geopolitics and Discourse Practical Geopolitical Reasoning in American Foreign Policy." *Political Geography* 11 (2): 190–204.

Ó Tuathail, G., and S. Dalby, eds. 1998. *Rethinking Geopolitics.* London: Routledge.

Ó Tuathail, G., S. Dalby, and P. Routledge, eds. 2006. *The Geopolitics Reader.* Oxon: Routledge.

Philpott, D. 2000. "The Religious Roots of Modern International Relations." *World Politics* 52: 206–245.

Philpott, D. 2002. "The Challenge of September 11 to Secularism in International Relations." *World Politics* 55 (1): 66–95.

Philpott, D. 2009. "Has the Study of Global Politics Found Religion?" *Annual Review of Political Science* 12: 183–202.

Philpott, D., and T. S. Shah. 2006. "Faith, Freedom, and Federation: The Role of Religious Ideas and Institutions in European Political Convergence." In *Religion in an Expanding Europe,* edited by T. A. Byrnes and P. Katzenstein, 34–64. Cambridge: Cambridge University Press.

Proctor, J. 2006. "Introduction: Theorizing and Studying Religion." *Annals of the Association of American Geographers* 96 (1): 165–168.

Rai. 2013. Papa Francesco benedice Roma e il Mondo, December 25. http://www.rai.it/dl/grr/notizie/ContentItem-1fb054b1-d437-470c-a5cc-50f6787fa497.html

Secretaria Status. 2016. *Annuarium Statisticum Ecclesiae.* Città del Vaticano: Libreria Editrice Vaticana.

Sturm, T. 2008. "Critical Methodological Geopolitics: Discourse Analysis/Ethnography." *Geopolitics* 13 (3): 600–609.

Sturm, T. 2013. "The Future of Religious Geopolitics: Towards a Research and Theory Agenda." *AREA* 45 (2): 134–140.

Thomas, G. M. 2001. "Religions in Global Civil Society." *Sociology of Religion* 62 (4): 515–533.

Thomas, S. 2005. *The Global Resurgence of Religion and the Transformation of International Relations.* New York: Palgrave Macmillan.

Wallance, I. 2006. "Territory, Typology, Theology: Geopolitics and the Christian Scriptures." *Geopolitics* 11 (2): 209–230.

Wilson, E. K. 2013. *After Secularism: Rethinking Religion in Global Politics.* New York: Palgrave Macmillan.

Wodak, R., and M. Meyer, eds. 2009. *Methods for Critical Discourse Analysis.* London: Sage.

Appendix

Benedict XVI (2005) *Urbi et Orbi Message of His Holiness Pope Benedict XVI. Christmas 2005* [Online]. Accessed April 4, 2016. http://w2.vatican.va/content/benedict-xvi/en/messages/urbi/documents/hf_ben-xvi_mes_20051225_urbi.html
Benedict XVI (2006a) *Urbi et Orbi Message of His Holiness Pope Benedict XVI. Easter 2006* [Online]. Accessed April 5, 2016. http://w2.vatican.va/content/benedict-xvi/en/messages/urbi/documents/hf_ben-xvi_mes_20060416_urbi-easter.html
Benedict XVI (2006b) *Urbi et Orbi Message of His Holiness Pope Benedict XVI. Christmas 2006* [Online]. Accessed April 5, 2016. http://w2.vatican.va/content/benedict-xvi/en/messages/urbi/documents/hf_ben-xvi_mes_20061225_urbi.html
Benedict XVI (2007a) *Urbi et Orbi Message of His Holiness Pope Benedict XVI. Easter 2007* [Online]. Accessed April 5, 2016. http://w2.vatican.va/content/benedict-xvi/en/messages/urbi/documents/hf_ben-xvi_mes_20070408_urbi-easter.html
Benedict XVI (2007b) *Urbi et Orbi Message of His Holiness Pope Benedict XVI. Christmas 2007* [Online]. Accessed April 5, 2016. http://w2.vatican.va/content/benedict-xvi/en/messages/urbi/documents/hf_ben-xvi_mes_20071225_urbi.html
Benedict XVI (2008a) *Urbi et Orbi Message of His Holiness Pope Benedict XVI. Easter 2008* [Online]. Accessed April 5, 2016. http://w2.vatican.va/content/benedict-xvi/en/messages/urbi/documents/hf_ben-xvi_mes_20080323_urbi-easter.html

Benedict XVI (2008b) *Urbi et Orbi Message of His Holiness Pope Benedict XVI. Christmas 2008* [Online]. Accessed April 5, 2016. http://w2.vatican.va/content/benedict-xvi/en/messages/urbi/documents/hf_ben-xvi_mes_20081225_urbi.html

Benedict XVI (2009a) *Urbi et Orbi Message of His Holiness Pope Benedict XVI. Easter 2009* [Online]. Accessed April 5, 2016. http://w2.vatican.va/content/benedict-xvi/en/messages/urbi/documents/hf_ben-xvi_mes_20090412_urbi-easter.html

Benedict XVI (2009b) *Urbi et Orbi Message of His Holiness Pope Benedict XVI. Christmas 2009* [Online]. Accessed April 5, 2016. http://w2.vatican.va/content/benedict-xvi/en/messages/urbi/documents/hf_ben-xvi_mes_20091225_urbi.html

Benedict XVI (2010a) *Urbi et Orbi Message of His Holiness Pope Benedict XVI. Easter 2010* [Online]. Accessed April 5, 2016. Available: http://w2.vatican.va/content/benedict-xvi/en/messages/urbi/documents/hf_ben-xvi_mes_20100404_urbi-easter.html

Benedict XVI (2010b) *Urbi et Orbi Message of His Holiness Pope Benedict XVI. Christmas 2010* [Online]. Accessed April 5, 2016. http://w2.vatican.va/content/benedict-xvi/en/messages/urbi/documents/hf_ben-xvi_mes_20101225_urbi.html

Benedict XVI (2011a) *Urbi et Orbi Message of His Holiness Pope Benedict XVI. Easter 2011* [Online]. Accessed April 5, 2016. http://w2.vatican.va/content/benedict-xvi/en/messages/urbi/documents/hf_ben-xvi_mes_20110424_urbi-easter.html

Benedict XVI (2011b) *Urbi et Orbi Message of His Holiness Pope Benedict XVI. Christmas 2011* [Online]. Accessed April 5, 2016. http://w2.vatican.va/content/benedict-xvi/en/messages/urbi/documents/hf_ben-xvi_mes_20111225_urbi.html

Benedict XVI (2012a) *Urbi et Orbi Message of His Holiness Pope Benedict XVI. Easter 2012* [Online]. Accessed April 5, 2016. http://w2.vatican.va/content/benedict-xvi/en/messages/urbi/documents/hf_ben-xvi_mes_20120408_urbi-easter.html

Benedict XVI (2012b) *Urbi et Orbi Message of His Holiness Pope Benedict XVI. Christmas 2012* [Online]. Accessed April 5, 2016. http://w2.vatican.va/content/benedict-xvi/en/messages/urbi/documents/hf_ben-xvi_mes_20121225_urbi.html

Francis (2013a) *Urbi et Orbi Message of Pope Francis. Easter 2013* [Online]. Accessed June 16, 2016. http://w2.vatican.va/content/francesco/en/messages/urbi/documents/papa-francesco_20130331_urbi-et-orbi-pasqua.html

Francis (2013b) *Urbi et Orbi Message of Pope Francis. Christmas 2013* [Online]. Accessed June 3, 2015. http://w2.vatican.va/content/francesco/en/messages/urbi/documents/papa-francesco_20131225_urbi-et-orbi-natale.html

Francis (2014a) *Urbi et Orbi Message of Pope Francis. Easter 2014* [Online]. Accessed June 18, 2015. http://w2.vatican.va/content/francesco/en/messages/urbi/documents/papa-francesco_20140420_urbi-et-orbi-pasqua.html

Francis (2014b) *Urbi et Orbi Message of His Holiness Pope Francis. Christmas 2014* [Online]. Accessed April 4, 2015. http://w2.vatican.va/content/francesco/en/messages/urbi/documents/papa-francesco_20141225_urbi-et-orbi-natale.html

Francis (2015) *Urbi et Orbi Message of His Holiness Pope Francis. Easter 2015* [Online]. Accessed June 19, 2015. http://w2.vatican.va/content/francesco/en/messages/urbi/documents/papa-francesco_20150405_urbi-et-orbi-pasqua.html

DIPLOMATIC LANGUAGE IN THE DEEPAVALI MESSAGES OF THE PONTIFICAL COUNCIL FOR INTERRELIGIOUS DIALOGUE

By Melanie Barbato

As the communication of religious actors, and in particular the practice of interreligious dialogue, are increasingly recognized as being of relevance also for peacekeeping and international relations (Johnston 2003; Banchoff 2012; Marshall 2013; Seib 2013), a closer look is warranted at what different actors do when they speak about "doing interreligious dialogue." Big actors like the Catholic Church are of particular interest in this respect, as their communication reaches large numbers of people and is likely to have a large impact.

In this article, I will focus on the language in the messages on the occasion of the feast of Deepavali that are sent yearly by the Pontifical Council for Interreligious Dialogue (PCID). These messages can serve as an example for the practice of high-level interreligious dialogue. The research was conducted in Rome and has produced a document analysis of the Deepavali messages between 2000 and 2016. For the data analysis, the data analysis software MAXQDA was used. The claim will be that these messages, while also containing elements of theological dialogue and calls to social activism, fulfil primarily a public diplomacy function. The paper discusses the language strategies of the messages and argues that while in general a strategy of ambiguity is followed that is typical for communication in the field of diplomacy, more direct language is at times chosen for addressing the issue of freedom of religion, which is one of the most pressing but also most sensitive issue of Hindu–Christian relations.

Catholic–Hindu interaction dates back many centuries (Kuttianimattathil 1998; Schmidt-Leukel 2005, 397–432). Official channels of high-level interreligious dialogue of the Holy See, as the international legal institutional body of the Roman Catholic Church constituted by the pope and the curia, were, however, only established with Vatican II (Renz 2014). In line with the new idea of opening up towards the world, Pope Paul VI established in 1964 the Secretariat for Non-Christians. In 1988 under John Paul II this name was changed to PCID to put a greater emphasis on the importance of dialogue as a "two-way communication" (PCID website, n.d.). Benedict XVI merged in 2006 the leadership of the PCID with that of the Pontifical Council for Culture and reassigned the PCID's president Michael Fitzgerald as Nuncio to Egypt and the Arab league. This was widely taken as a sign that interreligious dialogue was not a priority to the new pope. However, already in 2007 the PCID was reinstated as a separated dicastery under the leadership of Cardinal Jean Louis Tauran, who still holds this position.[1] The PCID issues yearly messages to the members of other faiths. The messages are posted on the PCID website and are also sent to partnering organizations. In recent years such messages were addressed to Buddhists, Muslims, Jains, Hindus and Sikhs.[2] This paper will look exclusively at the messages sent to the Hindus on the occasion of Deepavali.

Deepavali ("row of lamps") is a festival that is celebrated every year in October/ November by Hindus, Jains and other religious groups. While there are various religious stories associated with the festival, a general symbolism of light pervades the festival, which is a joyful and family-oriented occasion for Hindu communities all over the world. The Deepavali festival, due to its universal and non-sectarian outlook, offers an ideal occasion for addressing all Hindus.

My background interviews at the PCID confirmed a strong awareness of the inner diversity of the Hindu traditions and of the difficulty, if not an impossibility, of identifying concrete teachings and authoritative persons that could speak for Hinduism as a whole. The diversity of Hindu beliefs ranges from polytheism to monotheism to atheism. In Religious Studies, the constructed nature of the category "Hinduism" is the textbook example used to argue for the constructed nature of the category "religion" (Fitzgerald 2004). Even though it does not have to follow that terms like "Hinduism" have to be replaced, it is important to acknowledge that Hinduism is marked less by shared and regulated beliefs (orthodoxy) than by shared and regulated practice (orthopraxy) (Flood 1996, 12).

The PCID's Deepavali messages (from now on simply referred to as "the messages") are on average 614 words long. They have a yearly theme, such as "Collaboration between Hindus and Christians with special regard to Children" (2004), "Hindus and Christians: Together in favour of Non-violence" (2008), or "Christians and Hindus: Together in Promoting Religious Freedom" (2011). The messages are formulated as letters. They start with the salutation "Dear Hindu friends" and close with good wishes to the festival of Deepavali, or Diwali, the alternative, shortened version of the name by which it was referred to in the messages until 2009. They are signed by the PCID's president and, in most cases, the PCID's secretary.

What Type of Dialogue?

As interreligious dialogue is a term that can include a number of activities (King 2010; Cornille 2013), the question arises as to what function the messages have in the work of the PCID and the Catholic Church as a whole. When setting out on this study, I identified three potential categories of interreligious dialogue that the messages could fall into, either exclusively or in some form of combination: theological dialogue, call for social activism, and public diplomacy.

Theological or conceptual dialogue is concerned with enriching each other's understanding of religious teachings and sharing and discussing the theological answers provided by each tradition to similar or different questions concerning the world and transcendental reality. Theological dialogue differs from missionary conversation in that it has as its basis the acceptance that each person remains rooted in their own tradition.

Although the messages constitute the communication of a religious actor, theological dialogue is not the dominant form of communication in these texts. Religious languages and metaphors were used to bring across points and to stress common attitudes, but the discussion of such theological matters is usually brief (often just part of a sentence) and affirmative rather than discursive. While almost all messages refer to theological texts such as the gospels or the papal writings, the message of these quotes is usually tailored to support a claim about shared values and concerns.

Parallels on theological issues are often used as a supporting argument for joint social or environmental activism between Hindus and Christians. By social activism, I mean both activism in the respective communities and the protection of global public goods. The themes of the yearly messages reflect the intention to further social activism in a variety of fields, such as the support of the (traditional) family, socially responsible globalization, religious freedom, the wellbeing of children, environmental and human ecology. Part of the function of the messages is therefore to promote a shared vision and shared activism for a better world. However, in almost all cases the language of the messages remains on a very general level, and no concrete steps are included that would seek to apply the invoked joint activism to concrete events. While the Catholic Church has shown the ability to mobilize interreligious action through letter writing, most notably in opposition to legitimizing abortion at the UN's Population Conference in Cairo (Neale 1998), the Deepavali messages tend to draw on a more general imagery, such as the 2004 message's call to "overcome darkness through light, evil through goodness, and hatred through love," which will be recognized by many Hindus as being drawn from the Upanishads.

Vagueness, however, should not be taken as an indication that there are no issues that could be talked about, that the sender is lost for words or that the communication is superfluous or unsuccessful. Rather, it suggests that the primary goal of the communication is not the initiation of substantive theological dialogue or the initiation of concrete cooperation in the field of social or environmental activism but that the communication strategy is more orientated on gaining or maintaining "soft power" (Nye 2004) through continued, positive relations. That means that despite the messages' religious setting they are best analysed not as part of the genre "sermon" or some other typically religious format but as diplomatic communication, similar to the speeches delivered by heads of states on recurrent events, such as New Year's messages (although the primary audience are here members of the speaker's own country), or the speeches given by professional diplomats on various occasions abroad.

Characteristics and Functions of Diplomatic Language

The language of public diplomacy seeks to serve the goals of diplomacy: to establish or maintain soft power. As Hayden (2012) has shown, "soft power" can mean different things to different actors, and hence the rhetoric used as part of public diplomacy varies as much as the technological means or the concrete projects that are developed to further these ends. The approach chosen to promote one's own soft power is, as Hayden (2012, 278) points out, shaped by various factors, including how the relevant audience is rationalized in the first place. While the PCID messages address all Hindus, the intended readership is Hindu religious leaders. This cannot only be inferred from the largely cordial but formal style of the messages. The 2008 Message also directly addresses the audience midway in the text as "religious leaders." The word "leaders" is used a total of twelve times in the documents, creating a general impression that this is the peer group in which the audience moves.

In the messages, the president and secretary of the PCID represent the Catholic Church as diplomats whose primary function is neither to convince nor to gather information but to ensure that the channels of communication are kept open and filled with content that promotes good relations and the continued influence of their state or organization. The language that diplomats can use is restricted by this specific function of diplomatic communication. Just like diplomatic protocol at official events, diplomatic communication tends to be highly ritualized (Jönssen and Hall 2005, 72). This allows both parties in the encounter to be prepared for what to expect, and thereby to minimize anxiety about the possibility of having to react spontaneously in a highly political and symbolically loaded environment.

Also, diplomats are bound by the image they have to project of their country of origin or the organization they work for. Erin Boggs has observed about the role of US diplomats:

> [W]hile conducting public diplomacy, U.S. diplomats must support an image of their country's benevolent but unchallengeable power. Because the message they send must always fit into this framework, speeches delivered in the service of U.S. public diplomacy must be premeditated and heavily pre-formulated, unlike conversation in daily life. (Boggs 2015, 62)

A very similar framework applies to the messages issued by the PCID. The expressions have to show the Catholic Church's benevolence to join in dialogue and cooperation with the adherents of other religions while maintaining an unchallengeable claim to holding the truth.[3] The fine line the Catholic Church tries to tread in its verbal framing of interreligious dialogue is exemplified in the practice of praying side by side with adherents of other religions but not praying together with them in interreligious prayer (D'Costa 2013). While it is the performative function of Catholic officials to embody openness and cooperation, their actions must remain within the confines of Catholic orthodoxy. Seemingly trivial statements must therefore cohere to the structure of a complex theological and institutional framework. The reliance on familiar pattern and vocabulary can also help to create trust and support in a diverse audience, despite an unresolved inner diversity within the group, and possibly, as in the case of Hindu–Christian dialogue, also within the sender's group as well (Charteris-Black 2014, 237).

Thus, while standardized diplomatic expressions are often criticized as empty phrases and cliché, more useful interpretations go beyond the normative evaluations and inquire about the functions provided by an established pattern of speech. Drawing on this idea of ritual exchange, Villar (2006) sees diplomatic communication as a means for creating a space in which non-violent encounter is possible, and in which there is room for both one's own position and that of the other party, with the perspective of finding some form of compromise. In a historical perspective, Villar contrasts the direct and argument focused communication of the Greek with the softer and more harmony-focused communication of the Chinese empire and the Hanseatic League, a medieval confederation of market towns in the Baltic region. While the Greek cities were quick to engage in military action, the Hanseatic League and the Chinese sought to resolve conflict primarily by diffusing the tension through diplomatic communication techniques. Drawing on other writers, she argues that vagueness is not only a rhetorical figure in diplomatic discourse but its foundational function (Villar 2006, 236). Only if communication is ambiguous and uses (usually to the full knowledge of all involved) euphemisms and hyperboles to say what has to be said in the kindest possible way, can it be non-threatening and polite, thus opening up a space that all parties can enter, without relativizing the political goals to which the participating powers may lay claim or denying their preparedness to use other means to achieve these goals if needed.[4]

It could, of course, be argued that religious groups should go beyond diplomacy, and that to deserve the label "interreligious dialogue" all partners in the encounter should make themselves open and indeed vulnerable to being touched and transformed to the degree of re-evaluating established claims. However, this is not the PCID's role within the Catholic Church (Barbato 2016). While there are Catholic groups like the Focolare Movement that are involved in grass-roots encounters, interreligious workshops and sharing the charisma of their faith, the role of the PCID lies, as with any diplomatic entity, as much or even more so in protecting the interests

WHILE STANDARDIZED DIPLOMATIC EXPRESSIONS ARE OFTEN CRITICIZED AS EMPTY PHRASES AND CLICHÉ, MORE USEFUL INTERPRETATIONS GO BEYOND THE NORMATIVE EVALUATIONS AND INQUIRE ABOUT THE FUNCTIONS of the Catholic Church as in facilitating communication and encounter. Their work has therefore not to be understood as a general dialogue with "Hinduism," according to whatever definition, but as a concrete dialogue in the sense of mutual strategic communication with groups of people, especially leaders, whose shared characteristic is that they publicly self-identify as Hindus.

The Language of the PCID's Deepavali Messages

Vocabulary

Treating the messages first and foremost as a form of public diplomacy, the expectation would be that in the choice of vocabulary, words with positive connotations outweigh those with negative connotations. Indeed, the vocabulary of the messages places an emphasis on the positive. Across the theme and main text of all 17 messages from 2000 to 2016, the most frequently used nouns are "peace," "world," love, "God," and "life." It has to be noted that with the exception of "God," none of these terms are part of an exclusively religious vocabulary. Rather, they refer to the fundamental level of human needs and hopes, indicating that the messages are tailored to be of universal relevance and appeal. Within the individual message, the word "God" is often used in the proximity of such universal words, thus producing a close connection between the idea of a metaphysical reality and more general ideas human flourishing. For example, the 2011 message opens with the greeting: "May God, the source of all light, illumine your hearts, homes and communities for a life of peace and prosperity." The individual, the family and the community are here, regardless of religious affiliation and belief, entrusted to a benevolent God for the attainment of peace and prosperity. In line with Catholicism's religious inclusivism, this opening projects the message of (the Christian) God as the source for all human flourishing.

The top-20 words in the main part of the documents are, as is typical for English sentences, almost exclusively made up of little words like "the" and "is." The exceptions are the words "human," ranked 11th, and the word "religious," ranked 13th. Again, these terms are not specifically Christian, at least if one sets aside for the moment the debate on the term "religion" as a typically Western concept (Dubuisson 2003). The terms "human" and "religious" feature prominently in the texts because they point to what brings Christians and Hindus together to the table of dialogue: their shared humanity and their shared self-perception as religious people.

The word "our" is used 98 times in the messages and ranks as the ninth most frequently used of all words. The pronoun "we" is used 74 times and "you" 71 times. While "you" clearly refers to the Hindus as the recipients of the message, the case is more complicated with words like "we" and "our." They sometimes refer to the sender's Christian or Catholic community or alternatively the PCID leadership, and sometimes to Hindus and Christians jointly. In some passages, it is difficult to clearly discern which of these versions applies, and this vagueness may to a degree be intentional. For example, the 2016 message states in the second paragraph:

> With this abiding respect for the family, and keenly aware of the global challenges daily confronting us, we wish to offer a reflection on how we, Christians and Hindus together, can promote hope in families, thus making our society ever more humane.

The third paragraph then starts: "We know that the family is 'humanity's first school' and that parents are the 'primary and principal' educators of their children."

While the "we" that wishes to offer a reflection can be identified as the PCID, and the following "we" is specified as "Christians and Hindus together," it is not clear which of the two is the "us" that is confronted by daily challenges, or more importantly the "we" in the third paragraph that sets the perspective for the following discussion about the family and the importance of parents in educating their children. As Philippe-Joseph Salazar (2012, 33f) has pointed out, in diplomatic discourse the sender's position is sometimes presented as the only available option or as a naturally shared position, which also serves to hide the fact that the underlying situation may be more complex.

Besides the ones already listed, the most frequently used nouns in the messages are "people," "respect," "Pope," and "freedom." Hindu religious terms or other native Indian terms are rarely used. The Indian-origin words that appear in the messages are Deepavali/ Diwali, Vasudhaiva Kutumbakam ("the world is one family"), which is used in 2002 in the context of a Hindu describing the Assisi gathering "as a sign of the unity of the human family under the Fatherhood of God," dharma (law, religion) and sampradaya (religious tradition) in 2003, and ahimsa (non-violence) in 2008. The 2000 message refers to the *Sanatana Dharma* (eternal law, religion) and references a quote on ultimate truth with several Hindu sources.

In general, it can be said that the style of writing and choice of vocabulary are not that of a scholar of Hinduism, or even of an expert of Indian culture, but that of a benevolent and self-confident global player whose sphere of interest includes Hindus as one group among others.

Metaphors

Metaphors are often drawn from excerpts of papal speeches or writings. Almost all messages contain at least one papal quote, and almost all of these quotes contain vivid imagery, such as "humanity's first school" and "workshop of hope" for the family (2016) or "artisans of peace" for those involved in dialogue (2010).[5]

The most pervasive metaphor is that of light. 13 of the 17 messages use the image of light, in a total of 31 elements. Often, the image switches back and forth between the concrete to the metaphorical. The 2002 message, for example, opens by referring to the physical act of lighting lamps for Deepavali: "Once again it is time for you to light tiny lamps, hang colourful lanterns on your homes." In the next paragraph, the question is posed if religious festivals "are not also expressions of the desire of human beings to conquer over darkness by light, evil by good, untruth by truth and death by life?" The symbolism of light is thereby interpreted as having a moral, epistemological and soteriological dimension. This range of interpretations sets the scene for a broader call for cooperation in working for peace and respect for life. Later on, the message returns to a concrete reference to light: at the World Day of Prayer in Assisi, "representatives of different religions held lighted lamps in their hands and after their common commitment they placed the lamps on a common stand, symbolizing the convergence of hopes and efforts for peace." Light thereby becomes a symbol of interreligious dialogue and the commitment to interreligious cooperation. Affirming the role of the Pope in this dialogue, as an authority who facilitates and mediates the efforts of diverse religions, the message states in the last paragraph: "The Pope blessed them, saying: 'Go forward into the future holding high the lamp of peace. The world has need of light!'" Returning to the occasion, the message closes by wishing a "Happy Diwali."

The light metaphor suggests itself as Deepavali is the festival of light and because of its transcultural accessibility. It has also been used in the Nostra Aetate declaration on the relation of the Church to Non-Christian religions (1965):

> The Catholic Church rejects nothing that is true and holy in these religions [i.e. Hinduism, Buddhism and other religions "found everywhere"]. She regards with sincere reverence those ways of conduct and of life, those precepts and teachings which, though differing in many aspects from the ones she holds and sets forth, nonetheless often reflect a ray of that Truth which enlightens all men. Indeed, she proclaims, and ever must proclaim Christ "the way, the truth, and the life" (John 14:6), in whom men may find the fullness of religious life, in whom God has reconciled all things to Himself.

In the way it appears in the Deepavali messages, the image of light as a symbol of goodness and truth, and ultimately Christ, is vague enough to be inoffensive to non-Catholics. Speaking of light in general, rather than the more restrictive reflection of only "a ray of that Truth" also leaves open to what degree forms of

Hinduism are thought by Catholics to partake in the truth and salvific knowledge.

Modes of Speaking

Sentences and shorter meaningful units have different communicative functions. One categorization is to distinguish, among others, between phatic, referential, directive and expressive elements (Boggs 2015, 21ff).

Phatic elements set the scene and introduce a diplomatic statement. All Deepavali messages contain some reference to the festival of Deepavali as the occasion for the statement, and return to this occasion towards the end, when good wishes are expressed to the Hindu community.

Referential elements dominate the texts. While they often contain the friendly statements of diplomatic language, this mode can also serve to present a situation as without alternative and self-evident. Referential elements can therefore also have a directive purpose, such as the statement "You will agree with me in recognizing that one of the purposes of religious feasts is to make us better human persons" (Fitzgerald 2004).

Directive Formulations seek to influence and direct the addressee. In the messages directive elements are usually formulated very carefully and often indirectly rather than directly. They tend to be presented only as suggestions and the furthest possible away from a command. A typical construction puts the suggested path of action as a question in the negative form, as in 2004 message: "Could you not give added meaning to this year's *Diwali* by highlighting the plight of children […]?"

Expressive elements share some of the sender's inner world. These elements are almost non-existent in the messages unless all polite expressions such as the "warm greetings" should be counted as expressions of the PCID president's inner world.

Religious Freedom and Non-violence: The Messages of 2007 and 2008

In the last section, I have provided a general overview of the language of the messages. In this section, I will have a closer look at two messages that stem from 2007 and 2008, years that saw numerous attacks on Christians in India, including attacks on churches in Karnataka and the rape of a Catholic nun by "a member of a Hindu mob" in Orissa (BBC 2008). Religious freedom and the violence against Christians in India are the most sensitive issues in Hindu–Christian relations. It is typically rationalized by right-wing Hindus as a defence against forced conversions of poor and uneducated Hindus.[6] While aggressive and culturally insensitive Christian mission exists in India, and the injustices of the colonial era can account for a suspicion of Christian actors, Christians in India are today usually the victims and not perpetrators of religiously motivated violence.[7] Hinduism tends to offer an elastic inclusivism that allows easily for dual belonging and a culture that places more importance on orthopraxy than inner belief. The idea of conversion that demands one forsake one's previous religious affiliation is, however, often seen as an act of aggression against Hindu/Indian culture that, according to some, demands a strong reaction (Bauman 2015, 63).

When speaking to an Indian audience, Catholic leadership has to take the difficult situation of Christians into account and avoid formulations that could be seen as supportive of proselytism. At the same time, they must speak in a way that reassures Catholics in India that the leadership in the Vatican is not indifferent to their situation. As has been shown, in most messages the language strategy that has been chosen is typically diplomatic, with the addition of some positively connotated religious vocabulary and imagery. The 2007 message stands out, however, for its much stronger language. Already the title "Christians and Hindus: Determined to Walk the Path of Dialogue" points not only to a shared conviction but implies, through the use of the word "determined" that to walk the path of dialogue one has to overcome obstacles on the way.

Message of 2007

As usual, the message starts with phatic formulations: "As *Diwali* approaches, your religious feast, I am sure all of you in your respective families, neighbourhoods and communities, will be taking time to share your joy with one another." After this reference to the celebratory occasion, the first paragraph adds, however, a sentence that can be either read as a phatic, and possibly expressive, continuation of this good wish, or as a diplomatically packaged criticism. It states:

> Sensitive to your religious feelings and respectful of your ancient religious tradition, I sincerely hope that your search for the Divine, symbolized through the celebration of *Diwali*, will help you to overcome darkness with light, untruth with truth and evil with goodness.

Here the president of the PCID points out his own sensitivity to the religious feelings of others and his respect for the Hindu tradition, while expressing his sincere hope for the betterment of the other, and in no lesser terms than overcoming "evil with goodness."

The second paragraph of the message refers to the word's universal longing for peace. It states that religions "promise peace because they trace their origin to God" and asks, in the indirect formulation typical for the PCID's messages, if "we, as believers of different religious traditions" could "not work together to receive God's gift of peace." As in the first paragraph, the second paragraph closes after these general and friendly remarks with a much stronger statement: "Our respective communities must pay urgent attention to the education of believers, who can so easily be misled by deceitful and false propaganda." For a diplomatic message, this is a strong formulation indeed. In all the messages the word "must" occurs 13 times, and four of these occurrences are in the 2007 message. Not only uses this call for a peace-oriented education the strong formulation "must" but adds other very strong words: urgent, misled, deceitful, false, propaganda. The fact that the call is directed to "our respective communities" does little to soften the impression, given that in the previous paragraph the Christian side has already been associated with sensitivity and respect and the Hindu side with the need to change.

The third paragraph discusses the issue of freedom of belief. It states as a matter of fact: "There can be no coercion in religion: no one can be forced to believe, neither can anyone who wishes to believe be prevented from doing so." The focus on personal belief as the key feature of religion is, however, not how a large percentage of Hindus would see their shared identity, which is not so much based on firmly held beliefs but a civilizational awareness and shared practices, not least a more or less rigid social order. No efforts are made in the message towards developing a more "Indian" concept of religion or religious belonging. Also, the human rights discourse which is used to defend the basic right of freedom of religion is not without its critics in Asia, as Asian voices have long since called for a conceptualization of rights that is joined with duties (Ghai 1998).

As in many of the messages, the point is supported by a papal quote, in this case from the *Dignitatis Humanae* (1965), the Second Vatican Council's declaration on freedom of religion that states that "no one is forced to embrace the faith against his own will." From this quote of the declaration, the message continues: "The Catholic Church has been faithful to this teaching as Pope Benedict XVI reminded recently to the Ambassadors of India and other countries to the Holy See." It follows a quote from the "Address of His Holiness Benedict XVI to H.E. Mr Amitava Tripathi New Ambassador of the Republic of India to the Holy See" from 18 May 2006, which states the importance of religious freedom for peace.

The inclusion of this passage is remarkable, not so much for the content of the quote from the papal address but because of the expression that Benedict XVI "reminded" the ambassador of India of issues relating to religious freedom. This implies not only an imbalance of power but almost a reprimand, especially as Benedict's address to the new ambassador was at the time perceived as a diplomatic faux-pas and caused an outcry in India among more right-wing politicians and Hindu groups. Anand Sharma, India's Minister of State for External Affairs, told India's upper house of parliament that his ministry communicated with the nunciature in

New Delhi, and stated that the Pope was "not properly briefed on the secularism and religious tolerance prevailing in India" (Catholic News Agency 2006). Rajnath Singh, chairman of the then opposition party BJP, stated that the "reference to religious intolerance made to our ambassador and the request to eliminate anti-conversion laws has pained us all. In fact, activities that really go against the secular nature of the nation are conversions, not the laws that prohibit them" (Asia News 2006). In the BJP-ruled state of Madhya Pradesh, "members of the *Dharma Sena* (religious army) set fire to the pope's effigy in the district headquarters" (UCA News 2006). This context and the inclusion of the controversial statement in a festive greeting message show the willingness of the PCID at the time to break with diplomatic expectations when the issue of religious freedom was concerned. While it is difficult to ascribe personal influences to the PCID messages, the language strategy echoes that of Benedict's intellectual style, as Benedict put also in his Regensburg speech intellectual argumentation that goes "straight to the point," as in the Greek philosophical tradition, before the etiquette of interreligious diplomacy.[8]

Message of 2008

Despite being only one year later, the language strategy of the 2008 message is very different from that of the 2007 message. The theme is "Christians and Hindus: Together in favour of Non-violence." Unlike the word "determined" in the 2007 message, this theme is neutral in that it presents Christians and Hindus as collaborators for a good cause, even though overcoming violence also tends to include the effort against one's own violent dispositions.

One aspect of language that sets the 2008 message apart from all others is that it is the only one that mentions the personal name of a non-Christian. In paragraph four it refers to "Mahatma Gandhi, the Father of the Indian nation," using the honorific version of Mohandas Gandhi's name that refers to him as the "great soul." The message is also the only one after 2003 that uses Indian philosophical/ theological terminology, namely the concept of "Ahimsa (non-violence)." Already without looking at the content of the message, this suggests a language strategy that makes more effort to appeal to Hindus by addressing them on their own terms and establishing a common basis for conversation.

The function of the first paragraph is phatic, offering in a conventional way the PCID's Diwali greetings, and refers to the tradition of sharing "a reflection on a matter of common interest." After these introductory words, which culminate in the reference to Diwali as celebrating "truth, light and hope," a more substantial statement follows: "While religions are often blamed for society's ills, we know that it is rather the manipulation of religion, contrary to its fundamental beliefs, that is used to carry out so many forms of violence." This sentence leaves again the exact referent of the knowing "we" open, but it implies a shared attitude that distinguishes not most importantly between Hindus and Christians but between those who follow a religion according to "its fundamental beliefs" and those who manipulate religion to bring about violence.

In the third paragraph, Pope Benedict XVI is quoted, but this time from an Angelus prayer that calls for meeting violence and injustice "with *more* love, with *more* goodness." The message then adds the call of the Sermon on the Mount to love one's enemies and walk the extra mile with one's opponents.

In the fourth paragraph, the parallel to a similar attitude in Hinduism is drawn. In contrast to the smooth language that marks the messages usually, this paragraph appears rather clumsy. It starts by stating that in "the Hindu tradition, non-violence is one of the more important teachings." It quotes Gandhi's famous "an eye for an eye and soon the whole world is blind," which, despite popular attribution, may not be a quote by Gandhi at all (O'Toole 2010). The message then states about Gandhi: "Throughout his life, he developed among others, the concept of Ahimsa (non-violence)." The concept of ahimsa was, however, not developed by Gandhi but is key to Hindu and even more so to Jain thought, which had a strong influence on Gandhi. Gandhi is then praised as a "model for non-violence who led by example to the point of laying down his life because of his refusal to engage in violence." The last part of this sentence is at least questionable, as Gandhi was assassinated by a militant Hindu nationalist who saw Gandhi as too accommodative to Muslim interests. These statements, however, could be read less as an enumeration of historical facts about Gandhi and more as a (hyperbolic) recognition of the greatness of a democratic Hindu who was open to religious plurality.

The next paragraph links the term "non-violence" with the Christian attitude of loving one's enemy, quoting again from Pope Benedict XVI. Non-violence, the attitude the PCID wishes to see by Hindus towards Christians, is thus presented as a genuinely Hindu resource in which Hindus can take great pride, but also as perfectly in line with Christian ethics, both in terms of being rooted in the Bible and the writings of the pope.

The sixth paragraph opens up an even wider frame, as it presents non-violence as central to religion (that is, the genuine, non-manipulated form of religion). A number of directive statements follow, in which the "religious leaders" are called to "help to foster non-violence among our followers and support it in their actions." The messages state, without going into any controversial specifics: "As Hindus and Christians, especially in the present situation, let us be won over by love without reserve."

In general, the language in the 2008 message is much softer and more in line with diplomatic etiquette than in the 2007 message. While in the 2007 message religious freedom sounded like a topic that the PCID, as the pope a year before, had to lecture Hindus on, non-violence in the 2008 message is presented as a native Indian resource that could not only be upheld by Hindus who take pride in their civilization but could, especially through well-known figures such as Gandhi, also serve as an inspiration to others.

Nevertheless, in a more controversial interpretation, the language strategy of the 2008 message could also be said to follow the recommendations of the primary sources that the message draws on: to meet injustice "with more love," and to walk the extra mile with the enemy. The 2008 message could therefore be read as the attempt by the PCID to show that it is willing to deepen dialogue and respectful communication in the face of religious violence afflicted by Hindus, rather than to withdraw from it or seek retaliation, thus like Gandhi leading by example to inspire change, and inviting the Hindu side to join in.

Conclusion

This article has made the case for studying the language strategies employed by high-level religious actors. It has argued that while the PCID addresses Hindus in yearly Deepavali messages as part of its dialogue work, in fact these messages are not primarily meant as theological dialogue or a call to social action but as a form of public diplomacy. The language of the messages exhibits the typical aspects of diplomatic language: standardized vocabulary, metaphors, structure and style, vagueness, hyperboles, and euphemism. A closer look at the messages of two consecutive years showed that even so the messages exhibit a wide variety of language strategies. While the 2007 message uses strong and direct language and is quite confrontational in regard to the issue of religious freedom, the 2008 message gives much more credit to Hindus for being possible partners in the efforts for non-violent co-existence. Despite these differences, on the spectrum of Christian engagement with the feast of Deepavali, some of which has presented Hinduism entirely negatively,[9] all of the messages of the PCID clearly present a form of communication that seeks to meet the other with respect and with an interest in constructive long-term relations. ❖

---

1. An overview of the history and function of the PCID can be found in Pratt (2010).
2. Judaism is missing from this list as Jewish–Christian relations do not fall within the responsibility of the PCID.
3. Bradley (2009, 126) argues that the political influence that the Catholic Church holds rests to a significant degree on "giving out messages of certainty."
4. For the role of ambiguity in diplomatic language, see also Scott (2001) and Pehar (2001).
5. An accessible introduction to the use of metaphors in political language can be found in George Lakoff and Elizabeth Wehling (2014).

6. For a short analysis of the language and context of the Indian anti-conversion laws, see Howard (2013, 71ff).
7. A short overview of the situation of Christians in India can be found in the report *In Response to Persecution: Findings of the under Cesar's Sword Project on Global Christian Communities* (2017, 25).
8. For a comment on Benedict's diplomatic style, see O'Connor (2006).
9. An example is provided by Schmidt-Leukel (2005, 96).

References

Asia News. 2006. "BJP Leader Argues with Pope: 'Religious Intolerance Charge Unjustified'." May 23, 2006. Accessed May 30, 2017. http://www.asianews.it/news-en/BJP-leader-argues-with-pope:-religious-intolerance-charge-unjustified-6237.html.

Banchoff, Thomas. 2012. "Interreligious Dialogue and International Relations." In *Rethinking Religion and World Affairs*, edited by Timothy Samuel Shan, Alfred Stepan, and Moica Duffy Toft, 204–2014. Oxford: Oxford University Press.

Barbato, Melanie. 2016. "Why Is There Still Interreligious Dialogue." *Blog of the Critical Religion Association*. August 1, 2016. Accessed June 3, 2017. https://criticalreligion.org/2016/08/01/why-is-there-still-interreligious-dialogue/.

Bauman, Chad. 2015. *Pentecostals, Proselytization, and Anti-Christian Violence in Contemporary India*. Oxford: Oxford University Press.

BBC. 2008. "Raped Indian Nun Denounces Police." *BBC News*, October 24. Accessed May 30, 2017. http://news.bbc.co.uk/2/hi/south_asia/7689215.stm.

Boggs, Erin. 2015. *Interpreting U.S. Public Diplomacy Speeches*. Berlin: Frank & Timme.

Bradley, John. 2009. "The Political Rhetoric of the Vatican: Aims and Strategies of the Holy See as a Transnational Actor." In *Media, Religion and Conflict*, edited by Lee Marsden and Heather Savigny, 115–128. London: Routledge.

Catholic News Agency. 2006. "Indian Gov't Expresses Displeasure over Papal Comments re Religious Intolerance." May 26, 2006. Accessed May 30, 2017. http://www.catholicnewsagency.com/news/indian_govt_expresses_displeasure_over_papal_comments_re_religious_intolerance/.

Charteris-Black, Jonathan. 2014. *Analysing Political Speeches: Rhetoric, Discourse and Metaphor*. New York: Palgrave Macmillan.

Cornille, Catherine, ed. 2013. *The Wiley-Blackwell Companion to Inter-religious Dialogue*. Chichester: Wiley-Blackwell.

D'Costa, Gavin. 2013. "Interreligious Prayer Between Christians and Muslims." *Islam and Christian–Muslim Relations* 24 (1): 1–14.

Dignitatis Humanae, Declaration on Religious Freedom on the Right of the Person and of Communities to Social and Civil Freedom in Matters Religious Promulgated by His Holiness Pope Paul VI on December 7, 1965. Accessed June 10, 2017. http://www.vatican.va/archive/hist_councils/ii_vatican_council/documents/vat-ii_decl_19651207_dignitatis-humanae_en.html.

Dubuisson, Daniel. 2003. *The Western Construction of Religion: Myths, Knowledge and Ideology*. Translated by William Sayers. Baltimore, MD: The John Hopkins University Press.

Fitzgerald, Timothy. 2004. *The Ideology of Religious Studies*. Oxford: Oxford University.

Flood, Gavin. 1996. *An Introduction to Hinduism*. Cambridge: Cambridge University Press.

Ghai, Yash. 1998. "Rights, Duties and Responsibilities." In *Asian Values: An Encounter with Diversity*, edited by Josiane Cauquelin, Paul Lim, and Birgit Mayer-Koenig, 20–42. Abingdon: Routledge.

Hayden, Craig. 2012. *The Rhetoric of Soft Power: Public Diplomacy in Global Contexts*. Lanham, MD: Lexington Books.

Howard, Angela W. 2013. "Leveraging Legal Protection for Religious Liberty." In *The Future of Religious Freedom: Global Challenges*, edited by Allen D. Hertzke, 67–85. Oxford: Oxford University Press.

In Response to Persecution: Findings of the Under Cesar's Sword Project on Global Christian Communities (2017: 25). Accessed June 3, 2017. http://ucs.nd.edu/report/.

Johnston, Douglas, ed. 2003. *Faith-Based Diplomacy: Trumping Realpolitik*. Oxford: Oxford University Press.

Jönssen, Christer, and Martin Hall. 2005. *Essence of Diplomacy*. Berlin: Springer.

King, Sally B. 2010. "Interreligious Dialogue." In *The Oxford Handbook of Religious Diversity*, edited by Chad Meister, 101–114. Oxford: Oxford University Press.

Kuttianimattathil, Jose. 1998. *Practice and Theology of Interreligious Dialogue: A Critical Study of the Indian Christian Attempts since Vatican II*. Bangalore: Kristu Jyoti Publications.

Lakoff, George, and Elisabeth Wehling. 2014. *Auf leisen Sohlen ins Gehirn: Politische Sprache und ihre heimliche Macht*. 3rd ed. Heidelberg: Carl-Auer.

Marshall, Katherine. 2013. *Global Institutions of Religion: Ancient Movers, Modern Shakers.* Abingdon: Routledge.

Neale, Palena R. 1998. "The Bodies of Christ as International Bodies: The Holy See, Wom(b)an and the Cairo Conference." *Review of International Studies* 24 (1): 101–118.

Nostra Aetate Declaration on the Relation of the Church to Non-Christian Religions, Proclaimed by His Holiness Pope Paul VI on October 28, 1965. Accessed June 2, 2017. http://www.vatican.va/archive/hist_councils/ii_vatican_council/documents/vat-ii_decl_19651028_nostra-aetate_en.html.

Nye, Joseph. 2004. *Soft Power: The Means to Success in World Politics.* New York: Public Affairs.

O'Connor, Bernard J. 2006. "A Diplomacy of Candor: Pope Benedict XVI on the Global Stage." *The Review of Faith & International Affairs* 4 (2): 41–43.

O'Toole, Garson. 2010. "An Eye for an Eye Will Make the Whole World Blind: Mohandas Gandhi? Louis Fischer? Henry Powell Spring? Martin Luther King?" December 27, 2010. Accessed May 31, 2017. http://quoteinvestigator.com/2010/12/27/eye-for-eye-blind/.

PCID website. n.d. Accessed June 14, 2017. http://www.vatican.va/roman_curia/pontifical_councils/interelg/documents/rc_pc_interelg_pro_20051996_en.html.

Pehar, Dražen. 2001. "Use of Ambiguities in Peace Agreements." In *Language and Diplomacy,* edited by Jovan Kurbalija and Hannah Slavik, 163–200. Msida: DiploProjects.

Pratt, Douglas. 2010. *The Church and Other Faiths: The World Council of Churches, the Vatican, and Interreligious Dialogue.* Bern: Peter Lang.

Renz, Andreas. 2014. *Die katholishe Kirche und der interreligiöse Dialog: 50 Jahre "Nostra aetate" – Vorgeschichte, Kommentar, Rezeption.* Stuttgart: Kohlhammer.

Salazar, Philippe-Joseph. 2012. "'Diplology', or Diplomatic Rhetoric: A Case Study Regarding Iraq." *African Yearbook of Rhetoric* 3 (3): 29–36.

Schmidt-Leukel, Perry. 2005. *Gott ohne Grenzen: Eine christliche und pluarlistische Theologie der Religionen.* Gütersloh: Gütersloher Verlagshaus.

Scott, Norman. 2001. "Ambiguity Versus Precision: The Changing Role of Terminology in Conference Diplomacy." In *Language and Diplomacy,* edited by Jovan Kurbalija and Hannah Slavik, 153–162. Msida: DiploProjects.

Seib, Philip. 2013. *Religion and Public Diplomacy.* New York: Palgrave Macmillan.

UCA News. 2006. "Hindu Group Burns Pope's Effigy in Protest Against Comments on Indian Laws." May 22, 2006. Accessed May 30, 2017. http://www.ucanews.com/story-archive/?post_name=/2006/05/22/hindu-group-burns-popes-effigy-in-protest-against-comments-on-indian-laws&post_id=27404.

Villar, Constanze. 2006. *Le discours diplomatique.* Paris: L'Harmattan.

A TRAJECTORY TOWARD THE PERIPHERY: FRANCIS OF ASSISI, LOUIS MASSIGNON, POPE FRANCIS, AND MUSLIM–CHRISTIAN RELATIONS

By Scott M. Thomas

> If one day Muslim Americans will be forced to register their identities, then that is the day this proud Jew will register as a Muslim. (Khomami and Sidahmed 2016)
>
> —Jonathan Greenblatt, head of the Anti-Defamation League (ADL)

> When we were at last together he railed against injustice, particularly injustice against the *lowly.* He told me he had made a vow—at age seventy-six—that if a certain Algerian who is wanted by both the French police and the Algerian terrorists comes to the Muslim–Christian pilgrimage in Brittany later this month and is arrested, he will enter prison with him. (Emphasis added).[1]
>
> —Herbert Mason on Louis Massignon (1988, 102)

> Many times in our private conversations, Massingnon told me how great was his debt to St. Francis of Assisi, whom he considered not only one of the most 'compassionate' men in the history of civilization, but also the first Western Christian to preach, by example, as well as by words, the principle of non-violence, as opposed to the war-like ideology of the Crusades . . . . to preach the principle that only with love should we confront those who appear to be our enemies.
>
> —Giulio Bassetti-Sani (1974, 33)

Louis Massignon (1883–1962) was one of the most important scholars of Islam in the 20th century (Hourani 1991b). He has been described by a leading scholar of Shi'ite Islam as "perhaps the greatest academic scholar of Islam that the [Western] world has ever produced" (Nasr 1987,

254; Bill and Williams 2002, 88). He was professor of Islamic mysticism and sociology of Islam at the Collège de France, and also was the most important Catholic scholar of Islam in the 20th century (Hopwood 2003). His views on Islam were largely responsible for the Catholic Church's more positive approach to Islam and Muslim–Christian dialogue after the Second Vatican Council (O'Mahony 2007).

Moreover, Massignon was not only an important figure in the modern history of Islamic Studies in the West, or a seminar figure in the Catholic Church's approach to Islam. His "agendas as an Orientalist were part of the Catholic revival in France in the first half of the twentieth century" (Irwin 2007, 225). Perhaps, he was "the only Islamic scholar who was a central figure in the intellectual life of his time" (O'Mahony 2001). In other words, Massignon's thinking on Islam, Catholicism, Christianity, the Arabs, and the Middle East was an important part of the rich dialogue among French Catholic intellectuals—writers, theologians, and philosophers—in the early 20th century.[2]

However, what makes Massignon's story so compelling for a scholar of international relations is that his Christian conversion in Baghdad—back to the Catholicism of his youth—was so intimately caught up with the story of the emergence of the modern Middle East. It took place in Bagdad, in Arabic, in a Muslim-majority country (Iraq was then part of the Ottoman Empire), and through Arab Muslim friends. It was also caught up—he was arrested by Turkish soldiers as a French spy—with the events of Ottoman Empire's constitutional ("Young Turks") revolution (his closest friends were a part of it). Moreover, he gained first-hand experience of the duplicity of great power politics, as a political advisor to the French government, and as a member of the Sykes-Picot commission, which (secretly) divided up the Ottoman Empire among the great powers, and drew up the map of the modern Middle East.

However, these aspects of Massignon background—Islamic scholar, political advisor, devout Catholic, and politically engaged French Catholic intellectual—come together in another aspect of his background. He was also deeply influenced by the life of Francis of Assisi and his encounter with Malik al-Kamil, the Sultan of Egypt, during the Fifth Crusade. He consequently became a Franciscan tertiary, i.e. a member of the Third Order Franciscans, or the Secular Franciscan Order. Massignon is in good company. He is following Ramón Lull, the most famous scholar of Islam in the Middle Ages, who also became a Franciscan tertiary for the same reason (Mayer 2009).

Massignon brings to the Franciscan story a new optic, or a *rediscovery* of a very old one. He argued that although St. Francis is well known for poverty, ecology, and animals, perhaps the central concern of the most productive years of his life (1212–1221) was Muslim–Christian relations (Bassetti-Sani 1969; Bassetti-Sani 1974). He believed religion and culture were a crucial part of the solution—and not only a part of the problems—of war, poverty, and injustice in North Africa, the Middle East, and in international relations. These views—which were criticized, even ridiculed at the time by political "realists" and practical politicians of all stripes—anticipated in many ways the "religious turn" and the "postsecular" sensitivity in the study of International Relations. Firstly, descriptively, this is the unexpected resiliency of religion in modern life (although Massignon lived during the incoming tide of secularism). This is the view of those scholars since the 1990s who have recognized the global religious resurgence, and are engaged in what is called the "religious turn" in the study of International Relations. It has challenged the bias of secularism, and religion's marginalization, and investigates the key role of religion in war, peace, reconciliation, and conflict resolution (reflected in the existence and contribution of this journal).

Secondly, analytically, and this is the strongest connection to Massignon, the postsecular is a form of radical critique and theorizing on new models of politics, which recognize a positive role of religion, theology, and spirituality in peace, democracy, freedom, justice, and inclusion (Mavelli and Petito 2012). Francis of Assisi's conversion (amidst the violence of Italy's city–state system), and dramatic encounter with the Sultan (during the crusades), offer an example of such radical critique and theorizing. It provides the elements of a "Franciscan model" of peacemaking, Muslim–Christian relations, and interreligious dialogue—encounter, conversion, knowledge, and transformation, which Louis Massingnon came to articulate in his own "Franciscan" social practices in the mid-twentieth century—compassion, hospitality, and substitution, amidst the French war in Algeria, and North African decolonization, which nearly brought the collapse of the Fifth Republic. This shows in the past how one's faith—for Francis, and Malik al-Kamil, and in the present, for Massignon, and those inspired by them—at an individual level, for Muslims and Christians in the West, there is a way "to practice an *inner* journey," and at the international level, practice an *outer* journey, with social, and foreign-policy implications, which is "neither assimilating nor appropriating." It is a way to understand that *their* faith can be discovered, encouraged, and enhanced through the faith of another (O'Mahony 2001; Saxby 2006). Therefore, with the religious turn, and the postsecular sensitivity in International Relations, Francis's encounter with the Sultan, and Massignon's "Franciscan" approach to peacemaking, interreligious dialogue, and Muslim–Christian relations, now appears more perceptive and forward looking. It offers a radical way forward in the 21st century for all people of faith, and all people of good will to engage with each other (Petito 2011), and it offers a radical way forward for the study and practice of International Relations.

Toward Another Way of Living in the World

Francis of Assisi (1182/1183–1226) and the Italian City–State System

What is most significant from the viewpoint of the study of International Relations is that Francis of Assisi's transformative life story begins with a war, the main type of event that led to the creation of this scholarly area after World War I. In this case, it was a war between city-states. Francis, before he was a saint, was a soldier, and then a prisoner of war in Assisi's war against Perugia (1202) in the Italian city–state system. Francis is not the only soldier who renounced war, and became a saint (e.g. Martin of Tours was one of Francis's mimetic models). What is far more significant is the prolonged period of war—*internally* between factions, and *externally* between Assisi and Perugia. In spite of the peace treaty (1203), there was *still* an on-going, horrific, bloody, and violent period of raids, looting, and armed combat for many years (Fortini does not spare us the details and stories omitted in other accounts).[3]

What scholars call "international anarchy" is often considered to be the central problem of international relations. This does not mean chaos, but investigates how order can be achieved with the lack of a central political authority, which leads to the fear, insecurity, and uncertainly making war, and the preparation for war, an almost inevitable part of any international system (in this case the Italian city–state system). Historians who focus on the peace treaty, Fortini argues, underplay the persistence of anarchy and violence. This "minimizes the importance of Assisi's internal and external war on the origins of the new Franciscan movement. The war accompanied Francis's spiritual crisis, as well as that of his first companions," and "it continued until the approbation of the rule [i.e. the *Early Rule*, 1209/10–1220], and may well have been the factor that determined its existence" (Fortini 1981, 166). The rise of early capitalism, a money economy, growing trade (e.g. Francis and his father often attended the trade fairs, especially in Provence), and growing wealth, poverty, and inequality characterized these times. So, for Francis and his early brothers, something was profoundly wrong with the way they were living.[4] This article argues Francis and the early Franciscan movement performed the gospel in a way that demonstrated a cultural—or really *counter*-cultural—critique of Christendom, which was also reflected in Massignon's faith, life, and vocation.[5]

Francis's life story establishes the elements of a "Franciscan model" of peacemaking, Muslim–Christian relations, and interreligious dialogue elaborated in this article—encounter, conversion, knowledge, and transformation. It all begins with encounter. It was these military events—being a soldier, and a prisoner of war—and the *encounter* with Christ, speaking to him from the cross in the dilapidated Church of San Damiano outside Assisi's city walls (the "San Damiano Cross"), that sparked Francis's conversion journey. His desire still to be a chivalrous knight after his convalescence led him to head for Apulia in southern Italy to join the papal forces against the Holy Roman Empire. He stopped in route in Spoleto where that night he had the famous "dream of Spoleto," i.e. another *encounter* with Christ, which led him to finally give up his military ambitions. (The question in the dream was, does he want to follow the heavenly Lord or only the earthly prince, who is really only the servant.) He returned to face Assisi's disgrace, dejection, and humiliation, waiting for the new vocation God would show him. In other words, Francis's conversion was more than a single "event" (e.g. the San Damiano Cross), but a series of events, responding to the persistence of anarchy and violence, his even *deeper* conversions, new *knowledge*, and deeper *transformations* (e.g. "the dream of Spoleto"), which became central to his concept of peace and to the origins of the new Franciscan movement (e.g. Francis's "peace greeting").

Francis's unexpected *encounter* with the leper, a riskier encounter, was another event that was pivotal in his conversion journey, and influenced his theology and spirituality (McMichael 2012). He speaks dramatically about it, which occurred *after* "the dream of Spoleto," in his *Testament* (1–3), written shortly before he died. Francis did not forget it was through living "among the lepers" that he had understood what the Lord wanted to reveal to him (new knowledge), and so it is not surprising he would admonish the brothers later on to "live spiritually" among Muslims (deeper knowledge) (Gallant 2006). This is why some scholars connect the *encounter* with the leper, and his *encounter* with Christ in the event of the *Stigmata* (the wounds of Christ) to his *later* encounter with the Sultan of Egypt (Hoebrichts 1997; Dalarun, Cusato, and Salvati 2006).

> Francis extended his experience of reconciliation beyond the Christian world to the Muslim world. Just as he went among lepers, he later went among Muslims, and in both cases he went among them in a spirit of peace and compassion. (McMichael 2012, 130)

Louis Massignon's faith, life, vocation, and social activism have been described in a similar way (Gude 1996).

Discovering One's Own Faith Through the Faith of Another

The Encounter Between Francis of Assisi and Malik al-Kamil, Sultan of Egypt

The encounter between Francis and Malik al-Kamil Mohammad (1180–1238), the Sultan of Egypt, and the nephew of Saladin, occurred during the siege of Damietta, Egypt, at the height of the Fifth Crusade (1217–1221). The encounter, which once seemed unbelievable, is now regarded as "probably one of the best attested episodes, historically speaking, even if the exact significance is not obvious" (Vauchez 2012, 87). All accounts indicate Francis wanted quite deliberately, even felt *compelled*, to make contact with Muslims for some time—seeking, even expecting, martyrdom. Francis had made various failed attempts to meet Muslims before 1219 (Morocco, Syria). Pope Innocent III called for the Fifth Crusade at the Fourth Lateran Council (1215) to reform the Church and recover the Holy Land. What we know is that Francis and Brother Illuminato left Italy on a ship bound for Acre, Syria, probably with Italian crusader reinforcements. "What happened next has captured the imagination of his followers and admirers down to our own time" (Carmody 2008, 55–57).

A series of debates exist over nearly every event associated with Francis's encounter with the Sultan (Hoebrichts 1997; Warren 2003; Saxby 2006; Moses 2009; Tolan 2009). This has implications for how Francis and al-Kamil are interpreted, and what relevance this encounter has for Muslim–Christian relations: (i) did the Sultan's soldiers beat up Francis (and Br. Illuminato) before seeing the Sultan, (ii) was Francis on a "peace mission," variously interpreted as ending the Fifth Crusade, the *principle* of the crusades, or "peacemaking" as peaceful conversion, (iii) was the encounter a type of early "interreligious dialogue," (iv) did Francis challenge the Sultan and his Muslim clerics to a "trial by fire," (v) did Francis go to the Holy Land with a desire to convert the Muslims, which compelled him to seek martyrdom, (vi) did the Sultan offer Francis many gifts, which he rejected, and (vii) did the Sultan offer him an ivory horn, which was used in the call to prayer? The evidence simply cannot definitively answer any of these questions. This article argues Francis of Assisi, as a devout, orthodox, Catholic, and as part of his wider counter-cultural critique of Christendom, probably opposed the crusades, and preached the gospel to the Sultan since he saw peaceful conversion as an *alternative* to their violence. Moreover, Francis and al-Kamil were both, surprisingly, transformed by the encounter, and discovered how one's own faith could be encouraged, even strengthened, through the faith of another.

HE RENOUNCED THE WORLDLY VALUES OF POWER, MONEY, AND PRESTIGE—AND THE VIOLENCE OFTEN NEEDED TO GAIN THEM

What Do We Know About Francis and the Sultan – And, How Do We Know It?

Francis's own life and writings and what they reveal regarding his theology and spirituality, it is argued in Franciscan Studies, is the proper *interpretive principle*, which should be used to evaluate any other *documents*, regarding his views on war, peace, the economy, and any *events*, like the encounter with the Sultan. This article critically argues—from the perspective of International Relations theory—such contested "events" in Franciscan history or Christendom's "international affairs" are really types of social action, constructed, like *any* event in international relations, for specific social, cultural, and political purposes (section 3).

Francis's experiences of war, and being a prisoner of war—serious illness, losing close friends, and the "dream of Spoleto"—challenged his, and medieval society's existing, accepted, *cultural* meanings of personal success, meaning, and purpose. Being a knight, the crusades, was not rejected, but *transformed*, and given a higher purpose—being a knight of Christ, now devoted to Lady Poverty. And, he renounced the worldly values of power, money, and prestige—and the violence often needed to gain them (section 1). The way Francis performed the gospel life was a reflection of his "servant Christology," and the principles of the Sermon on the Mount (Robson 2012a, 2012b; Sheldrake 1995, 66, 120,134, 153). Early Franciscan spirituality symbolized the self-giving Christ, living in poverty, humility, and simplicity in the world. This was the basis of just and peaceful relationships, and the source of salvation for all those seeking forgiveness and reconciliation. The friars were to meet everyone with "the greeting of peace," which he says in his *Testament* the Lord *specifically* revealed to him (given the persistent, and multiple levels of anarchy and violence within and between Italian city–states) (Polidoro, n.d.; Schmucki 1995). The early Franciscan way of going about the world was peace, humility, and poverty (minority), and being subject to all—this is why they were called the friars *minor*. After Spoleto, there is no known incident of Francis ever again condoning violence. Quite the opposite was true—he promoted reconciliation between individuals, cities, and all of creation. And, as part of the rapid expansion of Franciscan missions, this is also why he was eventually so determined to go to the Islamic world (Daniel 2012; McMichael 2012).

What is known about Malik al-Kamil also should be *interpreted* in the context of Muslim politics, the geopolitics of the Middle East, and early Muslim–Christian relations. Al-Kamil is now emerging as a devout, virtuous, even enlightened ruler, with an interest in theology, and Sufi mysticism, even though he was an orthodox Sunni Muslim (Cusato 2008; Moses 2009). This is very important since Massignon was also greatly interested in Sufi mysticism (section 4). This may explain the *physical* evidence, the gift of the ivory horn, if it is authentic, used to call the faithful to prayer. The Sultan was affected by the brothers' simplicity, their goodness, and he received them with kindness (Munir 2008), was willing to listen to Francis, and perhaps was open to hearing the gospel, when it was presented in a way that did not insult Mohammad (contrary to the preaching of the zealous friars in Morocco, who were executed in 1220, the first Franciscan martyrs). Al-Kamil has been called a "peacemaker" by some scholars since as part of the truce negotiations (1219) he agreed to leave the Kingdom of Jerusalem to the crusaders, if they agreed to leave Egypt. In other words, the Sultan offered them the objective of the crusade without violence, to regain the Holy Places in Jerusalem, and other lands that they had lost to Saladin in 1187. Apparently, in Islamic chronicles, al-Kamil is known as the "one who opposed those Muslims who were in favor of the Fifth Crusade" (Munir 2000). However, even given the Sufi influence, before establishing al-Kamil's "peacemaking" intentions, or support for interreligious dialogue, more information is needed on his foreign-policy decision-making: (i) domestic politics, since he was in rivalry with his brother for power and influence; and (ii) geopolitics, since the Sultan's army, and the Islamic world were in fear and disarray with the growing Mongol threat (Munir 2008; Moses 2009).

What Were the Encounter's Outcomes?

Francis did not convert the Sultan (interreligious dialogue), nor did he end the Fifth Crusade (peace mission). Francis and al-Kamil, however, were unexpectedly *transformed* by their encounter. Across the religious divide, across different civilizations, at a decisive point in the Fifth Crusade, Francis and al-Kamil discovered how one's own faith could be encouraged, even strengthened, through the faith of another (Gallant 2006; Saxby 2006; McMichael 2012). We still know less about al-Kamil (in the West), but the legacy of Muslim respect for St. Francis and his encounter with the Sultan is responsible to this day for the Franciscan Custody of the Holy Places in Jerusalem (De Beer 1981).

Francis's encounter with the Sultan influenced his thinking on religious practices: (i) regarding religious books, (ii) prayer, which is why he might have received a horn from the Sultan (Hoebrichts 1997, 89), and praise, reverence, and thanksgiving (i.e. the Islamic names of God, which so impressed Ramón Lull and Massignon), and (iii) perhaps also doctrine, since both Islam and Christianity affirm God as "all-powerful," and "the creator of all," attested to in Francis's early writings, and the *Early* Rule's Chapter 16 (Lehmann 1988; Francis of Assisi 1999b).

Francis's encounter with the Sultan, in addition to his life, and writings, also needs to be interpreted amidst the early expansion of Franciscan missions. Doctrine and missionary practice were *reflexively* worked out at the same time, i.e. they were both part of the struggle to determine what it meant to live faithfully in the world. This reflexivity is reflected in the *Earlier* Rule (1209/10–1221),[6] which famously (Chapter 16) set out two approaches to mission: (i) "not to engage in argument or disputes but *to be subject to every human creature for God's sake* and to acknowledge that they are Christians," and (ii) "to announce the Word of God, when they see it pleases the Lord, in order that [unbelievers] may believe in *almighty God*, the Father, the Son, and the Holy Spirit, the *Creator of all*, the Son, the Redeemer and Savior" (Francis of Assisi 1999a, 74; Chapter 16, 5–7). A scholarly debate exists over when Chapter 16 was drafted, and inserted into the early *Rule*. Those who argue it was *after* Francis's encounter with the Sultan, fit with this section's argument on how he was transformed by the encounter. Those who argue it was *before* the encounter connect Chapter 16 to the Franciscan mission to Spain and Morocco, which ended in martyrdom (the brothers directly criticized Islam and Mohammad, but *only* after many warnings were they executed). So, "Marrakesh" is often contrasted with "Damietta," for Francis expressly did *not* offer these criticisms when he visited the Sultan. Moreover, the *early* Rule (1221), which reflects Pope Innocent III's decrees and reforms of the

Fourth Lateran Council (1215), and Francis agreed to implement them, *omits* any reference to his call for a Fifth Crusade (Hoebrichts 1997, 3–4). The opening of Chapter 22 features an admonition from the Sermon on the Mount, "Love your enemies and do good to those who hate you." If this was written *after* his encounter, then it indicates his Muslim hosts were the "enemies-turned-friends," a part of the human fraternity. What Francis *already* experienced in his encounters with the leper, the poor in Assisi, he now *extended* to the Sultan (Cusato 2008; McMichael 2012). This interpretation fits with the article's "Franciscan model"—seeing the world, and interpreting what is going on in it (domestic society and international relations)—through a radical Franciscan social epistemology and social ontology (section 3).

A "Franciscan Model" of Peacemaking, Muslim–Christian Relations, and Interreligious Dialogue

Seeing the world differently is already a way of beginning to change it (Thomas 2005, 250). Any study of the encounter between St. Francis and al-Kamil raises the question of sources, and it cannot be properly interpreted apart from the "Franciscan Question," which began with Paul Sabatier, the Swiss Protestant pastor, and his path-breaking *Life of Saint Francis of Assisi* (1894): how best to read, interpret, and relate the early Franciscan documents, with their *multiple perspectives* on the various *events* in the life of the historical Francis (Dalarun 2002). Robert Cox, a leading critical theorist, argues, "Theory is always for someone or for some purpose," and so the *images* of international relations constitute the values, interests, and perspectives scholars use to interpret the world (Cox 1981). Therefore, the use of literary and historical criticism to *interpret* Francis's encounter with the Sultan, with the problem of its variety of images, interests, and perspectives (the Franciscan Question), is similar to the difficulties of the *images*, theories, or paradigms through which *any* event is interpreted in international relations (Thomas 2005, 72–96). In other words, both types of "events" relate to the basic problems of epistemology and ontology that underlie approaches to explaining or understanding the meaning and significance of social action in history, politics, or international relations. This similarity offers a crucial perspective for examining the Franciscan tradition, and Louis Massignon's "Franciscan model" of peacemaking, interreligious dialogue, and Muslim–Christian relations (section 4).

Toward a "Franciscan" Social Epistemology: How Did Francis Gain Knowledge of His World, and How Do We Gain Knowledge of Ours?

The mainstream approach to epistemology or constructing knowledge in the social sciences is based, firstly, on naturalism, i.e. the idea that the same methods used to investigate the physical or natural sciences can be applied to the study of social action by human beings (i.e. the methods are the same for explaining a volcanic eruption like Mount Vesuvius, or a political eruption like a revolution). Secondly, it is based on positivism, i.e. the idea that "facts," objects, things, even in the social world, easily can be separated from "values" (Thomas 2010). These assumptions indicate there is (allegedly) some objective view of what is going on in the world, a world *separate* from our minds, and separate from our theories. It is based on a "correspondence theory" of language, a correspondence theory of truth, so the "truth" of a theory or a concept is determined by how well it matches or corresponds to events which take place in the world (Booth 2005, 2007). This positivist approach to the social sciences is reflected in similar approaches to history as the discovery of "what actually happened" (Evans 2000, 8, 16–28).

In contrast, critical theorists, social constructivists, emphasize the concept of social epistemology, which underlies the concepts used in this section to develop a "Franciscan model" of Muslim–Christian relations and interreligious dialogue. These scholars, indebted to the "linguistic turn" in philosophy, interrogate the connection between facts and values, words and things, and symbols and what they symbolize in international relations. They argue the "truth" about the social world cannot be gained through an (alleged) "correspondence" between our theories, concepts, and some (objective) conception of events in the world. The main reason, which Massingnon would appreciate, is that language is bound up with what "constitutes" the world, how people see, and interpret the world, rather than merely being a *reflection* of it (Lindbeck 1984; Thomas 2005, 86–91). Most critical theorists, constructivists, do *not* doubt the world exists, nor do they doubt it exists "independent" of our minds, but they *do* doubt we can get behind the ideas, words, concepts, or even doctrines (i.e. language) of *statements* about the world in order to compare them to see if they "correspond" to an objective conception of the world (Kratochwil 2000).

Our theories, concepts, beliefs, values, passions, and interests "constitute" the world, construct what the social world is like, so "in the social sciences some of the most important concepts are *constitutive* (and are used recursively) of the social world rather than simply mirroring or describing it" like in the correspondence theory of truth (Kratochwil 2006, 7–8). What for St. Francis constituted "the world" (really, his "social world") was constructed by the concepts and social practices he and his contemporaries used every day—war, crusades, martyrdom, pilgrimage, missions, holy wars, holy places, and Muslims as fanatics, demons, heretics, idolaters. We also construct our world with the concepts we use every day—the state, sovereignty, refugees, migrants, religious violence, Islamism, Islamic fundamentalism, and Muslims as "moderates" or as "radicals" or "extremists," and a "clash of civilizations" (or a dialogue between them).

The concept of social epistemology is part of the challenge to the scientific (positivist) approach to history that has distorted the quests for the historical Jesus and historical Francis of Assisi (Hall and Kratochwil 1993; Johnson 1996; Vauchez 2012, 234–238). The search for objective truth remains a popular conception of history (e.g. "what really happened at Damietta, Egypt?") (Darness and Krier 2011). All history has the character of "contemporary history," since the way the past is recounted refers to present needs and present situations (Croce 1941). This is an apt description of the interest in Francis's encounter with the Sultan. The rise of Islam in world politics has mean an "event," which "merited barely a footnote in the history of the Crusades," has become important for Franciscans, the Catholic Church, and all people concerned about Islam and international politics (Dwyer 2000). Critical theorists and constructivists argue "events" do not simply exist—in the past, or in contemporary international affairs. They are, *inevitably*, socially, religiously, and politically constructed. The multiple accounts of the Fifth Crusade and the role of Francis indicate this. First, it is a minor "event," and after the crusaders' defeat, it is constructed as a "major event"—back then, to show Francis as a model of the renewal of the Church, and now, as a peacemaker and supporter of interreligious dialogue and Muslim–Christian relations (e.g. John-Paul II's "spirit of Assisi meetings").[7]

THE CONCEPT OF A SOCIAL EPISTEMOLOGY CLARIFIES THE NEW KINDS OF KNOWLEDGE RELIGIOUS ACTORS CAN BRING TO ANALYZING WHAT IS GOING ON IN THE WORLD

The concept of a social epistemology clarifies the new kinds of knowledge religious actors can bring to analyzing what is going on in the world —in Francis's world, and in our own. The concept of a conversionary epistemology describes this "Franciscan" way of seeking the world, and constructing knowledge of it—encounter, conversion, knowledge, and transformation. This set of concepts is rooted in insights, which are fearful, painful, gained from Francis's own dramatic *encounters*—Assisi's war against Perugia, and being a prisoner of war, with the leper, with the poor—and, ultimately with the Sultan, ostensibly the enemy of Christendom. Francis, over many years, constructed knowledge of the world as a result of his encounters, even *riskier* encounters, *deeper* conversions, as he identified with the leper, the poor, the lowly, in Assisi, Umbria, and other parts of Italy. And, through them, he made a discovery—deeper, more challenging, *knowledge* about how the world really works comes from "the Other"—those on the margins, the periphery, and not the top of society. This led to even *deeper* transformations in how he engaged with the world around him—eventually meeting the Sultan. Indeed, Franciscan Studies now emphasizes Francis's *conversions* (plural), rather than a single event (section 1), a continual process, which can be described by this concept of social epistemology, or conversionary epistemology (Brunette 1997; Horan 2008; Horan 2014).

Perhaps Rowan Williams's evocative phrase "the wound of knowledge" expresses these relationships—how fear, pain, suffering, rejection, and humiliation are all parts of genuine encounter and conversion (Williams 1979). Any such encounters lead to what can only be called a kind of "conversion," for what is radically rejected is the separation of facts and values, the observer and the observed (naturalism and positivism), "all the way down" (Brown 1994), i.e. down to a person's identity and very inner being—as a knight or merchant (Francis) or as a noble (Clare). This kind of knowledge is gained *initially* by *encounters*, like those Francis experienced, that lead to "falling upward," i.e. only those who have "gone down," and experience—in some way, at some time—fear, pain, suffering, rejection, failure, and humiliation (e.g. Francis's time as a prisoner of war, his return to Assisi after the dream of Spoleto),[8] can "come up" again, and be open to new knowledge, understandings, and broader horizons (Rohr 2011; Rout 2011).

Perhaps, not so surprisingly, Pope Francis has helped the Catholic Church recover this perspective as a trajectory toward the periphery. The title of the first collection of his homilies at Santa Marta, "truth is an encounter," recognizes St. Francis's key insights on encounter, conversion, knowledge, and transformation (Bergoglio 2014; Ferrara 2015).[9] Moreover, this is also a recovery of a central message of the Second Vatican Council (Faggioli 2013). The idea that knowledge comes from the margins is also increasingly recognized in the theory of International Relations (Enloe 1996; Blainey and Inayatullah 2007).

Toward a "Franciscan" Social Ontology: Who Did Francis Include or Exclude in Understanding His World, and Who Do We Include?

The concept of social ontology helps clarify why the radicalism of Franciscan metaphysics is relevant to international relations. For Francis, and his brothers, God is both Creator and Father, and so all people, all creatures, and creation are ontological siblings. This is the core reality of the world, the deep ontological principle underlying it. Francis's famous poem, "Brother sun, Sister moon," is not only charming poetry, but a profound statement of Franciscan metaphysics (Delio 2003; Ingham 2012). It powerfully underlies Francis's *cultural* critique of Christendom, and is a key *interpretive* principle for his views on war, peace, poverty, and Muslim–Christian relations. It is also the source of Massignon's Franciscan metaphysics, and social and political action (section 4).

The concept of a social epistemology (the discovery that knowledge comes from the margins, the periphery) helps clarify why the optic of social ontology is relevant for the past, examining medieval social history, and for the present. At all times, a key question of international theory is: What kinds of *actors*, doing which *activities*, are socially and politically *constructed* by *whom*, and in whose *interests*—to be a part, or to be excluded, from domestic politics or international affairs? The new social movements of religious reform and renewal among the laity in the 13th century engaged with the poverty and peace movements to offer a prophetic witness and criticism of the crusades. This was part of a general criticism of the way the new urban money economy in the cities was linked to the violence of the feudal classes (section 1; Lawrence 1994; Dickson 2010). The profit economy was simply seen as a new form of exploitation (Little 1978; Todeschini 2009). On this reading, Francis fits into *whose* history of the Middle Ages—the vivid history of popes, kings, ladies, knights, and crusaders, or the history of the lowly, those on the margins and the periphery, lepers, the poor, the peasants, the workers, the monks, the friars, hermits, third orders, and lay confraternities? (Cantor 1991). St. Francis and the early Franciscan movement became the best-known representative of these new types of religious renewal and social movements.

The concept of social ontology, rather than seeing St. Francis anachronistically, or retrospectively, as a social activist or reformer (Dubois 1905), helps us to better understand Francis's social agency, the way he performed the gospel in his day, and challenged some of Christendom's main social and cultural practices —martyrdom, crusades, missions. However, rather than reject them, Francis *transformed* their meaning and significance as part of his counter-cultural critique of Christendom. In the Middle Ages, as in any age, ideas, concepts, theologies, and social practices do not simply mirror the social world (the correspondence theory of truth), but socially and politically construct it. They *make social reality what it is*. This means that martyrdom, crusades, and missions, from a constructivist viewpoint, did not simply exist, they *constituted* relations with the Islamic world in one way, through ideas, theologies, and social practices—chivalry, courtesy, courtly love, indulgences, religious vows, rites of penance—and *not* in some other way (Hall and Kratochwil 1993; Alkopher 2005).

Francis, by the way he performed the gospel, rather than *reject* some of these medieval social practices, *transformed* their meaning and significance: he served not an earthly king, but the "Most-High King" ("the dream of Spoleto," section 1), and he extended "courtesy" (literally courtly behavior for nobility) to *every* leper, beggar, or lowly person who crossed his path. Regarding chivalry, the crusades, he compared his band of brothers to the Knights of the Round Table, and their itinerant preaching to their quests for adventure (Whitstable 2006). He transformed (violent) crusading to (nonviolent) peaceful conversion—part of the existing criticism of social violence by the poverty and peace movements. This was the reason for going to visit the Sultan unarmed, and without any crusader protection. In his mind, he remained a "crusader" ("cross-bearer"), but he had transformed its meaning, for "surely a crusader against the standard type familiar in the world of Francis" (Cunningham 2004).

Scholars who argue Francis supported the crusades and other social practices of his day (Kedar 1984; Meir 1994; Mastnak 2002; Tolan 2009) ignore an integrated and interpretive approach to history, theology, spirituality, politics, and international relations, and how it can be applied to the early Franciscan movement (Sheldrake 1995; Frykenberg 1996). The way Francis and his brothers, and Sister Clare and her sisters, performed the gospel demonstrated another way of living in the world (section 1): an alternative to the culture of chivalry, the civic violence *within* Italian city–states and *between* them, and the violence of the crusades, with a refusal to bear arms or take oaths, two basic requirements of feudal relationships. These principles became part of the Franciscan Third Order *Rule* of 1221, the religious order Louis Massignon felt so compelled to join (Peterson 2012).

Louis Massignon – Third Order Franciscan, and the Struggle to Live Faithfully in the World

A "Franciscan Model" of Interreligious Dialogue and Muslim–Christian Relations

Massignon's close friend, the poet Paul Claudel, played a key role in the French Catholic intellectual revival. Massignon wrote to him the very first account of his conversion (1908) in Bagdad (Gude 1996, 124). His conversion back to Christianity—the Catholicism of his youth—is a remarkable example of the "Franciscan model" set out in this article. Massignon's conversion, like Francis's, began with war, violence, and encounter. The concept of social epistemology articulates this "Franciscan way" of seeing the world, and interpreting what is happening in it: "the wound of knowledge" (Williams), and "falling upward" (Rohr) reflect the suffering, rejection, and humiliation necessary for "coming up" again (conversion) to new knowledge and understanding, which almost *inevitably* is knowledge from the periphery (section 3). Massignon, like Francis, had his own dramatic military and political encounters—his arrest as a French spy by jumpy Turkish soldiers, the threat of execution before morning, suicide attempts, illness, malarial fever, all in the run-up to the Ottoman Empire's "Young Turks" constitutional revolution (Gude 1996, 51; Latham 2008). Amidst it all, was the Arab, the Muslim, *hospitality* shown to him, to the extreme point of engineering his dramatic escape from capture, allowing him to return to France (Gude 1996, 28–31). This is the kind of conversion, which radically rejects the separation of facts and values (naturalism and positivism), "all the way down" (Brown), to a person's inner being: Massignon (age 27) being a dissolute, morally lax, sexual libertine, and a young man enthralled with adventure, the Maghreb, the desert, Arabic, and Sufi mysticism. Years later, he described his time in the Middle East before his conversion as a self-styled European researcher, whose main tie to the region (an implicit criticism of T. E. Lawrence, i.e. Lawrence of Arabia), was his thirst for adventure, exploration, "the secular rage to understand."[10]

It was Claudel who first suggested to Massingnon he consider becoming a lay member of the Franciscans. Only after studying and meditating on the link between Islam and Francis did Massignon finally became a member of the Secular Franciscan Order (November 1931). He and Mary Kahil, a close, Egyptian, Melkite Catholic friend from his youth (Gude 1996, 78), went to Egypt two years later (February 9, 1934), and prayed at the abandoned Franciscan church in Damietta, Egypt where Francis had met the Sultan. They took a vow of al-*Badaliya* (the Arabic word signifying "substitution" or "to be in the place of") to ritualize their shared commitment to Islam, and offer their lives in prayer and fasting for Muslims, "not so they would be converted, but so that the will of God might be accomplished in them and through them." Massingnon met Pope Pius XI later that year in private audience, and he blessed their offering at Damietta.[11]

Peacemaking, Interreligious Dialogue, and Muslim–Christian Relations

Massignon adopted the name "Abraham" ("Ibrahim") as part of his vows to become a Secular Franciscan. It is often argued he did this in recognition of the Patriarch's central role in the history of Judaism, Christianity, and Islam (Gude 1996, 124; Grifith 1997). A lot of Massingnon's scholarly activity, even *before* his conversion, was engaged in his "correspondence theory," i.e. finding similarities, convergences between these monotheistic religions. So this view is partly correct, but his conception of the "Abrahamic faiths" was also based on the way Abraham was central to how he interpreted his conversion (Mason 1988, 26; Grifith 1997). Massignon was seeking to demonstrate what Francis arguably learned in his encounter with the Sultan, and what he had encountered through Muslim friends in Iraq: how God can work in the lives of people of other faiths, and what God expects of them. What does it mean to be faithful *within* another religious tradition, one different from your own?

Massignon's "Franciscan model" of Muslim–Christian relations was based on the link between Abraham and a radical Franciscan social ontology and metaphysics (section 3): firstly, the concept of the "Abrahamic faiths"—Jews, Christians, and Muslims are all children, descendants, of the Patriarch, so he believed in the *ontological unity* of the Semitic peoples, a unity which pre-dates the existing (and artificial) states in the Middle East, and the (artificial) modern international system; and, secondly, this meant any rivalry between them in the Maghreb and the Middle East was for him a type of "sibling rivalry," i.e. within the family, rather than a rivalry between enemies. "If the Jews arriving in Palestine and the Arabs already there were to live in peace, it was essential that they come to understand their *shared* history as children of Abraham and respect each other's cultures" (Gude 1996, 168–169). The key to the "Abrahamic Model" was not rejecting, but *transforming* it, as the "Abrahamic faiths," with the unity of Semitic peoples—what *they* share in the region, and what *they* have in common, rather than in relations with the Western powers (which are only interested in geopolitics, and the region's resources, and not the people of the region).

Moreover, Massignon's concept of the Abrahamic faiths has been expanded to recognize the "Global Family of Adam and Eve." A radical

Franciscan social ontology, and metaphysics linked to peace making, Franciscan Muslim–Christian dialogue, and interreligious dialogue (Arafat 2000). A "Exodus motif" relates to Abraham's *call* (Gen. 12), rather than to Moses crossing the Red Sea (i.e. the Exodus motif in liberation theology). Those who engage in Muslim–Christian dialogue, like Abraham, need to "leave behind us at least something of our own self," as we seek to encounter God/Allah, which was the path of Abraham (Mooren 2000). Such an Exodus motif now connects this radical "Abrahamic" social ontology, being Abrahamic siblings, to a conversionary epistemology—radically, all the way down, to "le point vierge," i.e. what Massignon called the virgin point of a person. One's own faith is discovered, renewed, enhanced through the encounter, the openness to the faith of another. It is a "Abrahamic path" of openness to "the Other."[12] Moreover, Massingnon, and some Muslim scholars, argues this was the path of the Prophet Mohammad and of Francis of Assisi (Massignon 1989a; Mooren 2000).

The concept of the "Abrahamic faiths" provided Massingnon with the basis for a set of religious or spiritual activities, or social practices that combined his deep spirituality, scholarly study of Islam and Christianity, and social and political activism: (i) venerating key figures, (ii) common religious practices, and (iii) sacred sites, sacred spaces, for pilgrimage, especially Jerusalem and the Holy Land.

Firstly, for Massingnon the veneration of key figures, as suffering intercessors, and common religious practices—prayers, fasting, pilgrimages—were an important link between Islam and Christianity, and were reinforced by his scholarly theory of correspondences. He recognized the "soft power" of religion, i.e. the way moral, religious, or spiritual example and spiritual authority can generate the kind of positive, rather than negative, forms of mimetic desire, and positive mimetic models, which can change or even transform outlooks and behavior (Thomas 2014; Haynes 2016). Massingnon recognized the ambivalence of the sacred, i.e. the powerful role of sacred actors, intercessors, martyrdom, and redemptive suffering in religion, politics, and spirituality—for peace or violence. A key correspondence for him was between the Virgin Mary (Catholicism) and Fatima (Islam), the daughter of the Prophet Mohammad, and they are now *global* models, sources of pilgrimage, and inspiring women for all those suffering trials, tribulations, and oppression (Bill and Williams 2002, 47–74). Massingnon's religious approach anticipates the "spirit of Assisi," the interreligious prayer meetings for peace started by Pope John-Paul II in 1986, the year *after* he went to Morocco and amazingly addressed 80,000 young Muslims as part of the UN's International Youth Year (John Paul II 2005). Massignon also anticipates the annual meetings of religious leaders at the Davos World Economic Summit, and now before the opening session of the U.N General Assembly.

Secondly, for Massingnon the legend of the "Seven Sleepers of Ephesus," i.e. common sacred sites, for pilgrimage—during times of war, violence, and terrorism—was a key example of common religious practices, and correspondences between religions. It is found in the *Qur'an* (Surah 18), and in ancient Syriac-Christian sources. The greater visibility of Christian persecution in the Middle East is only now making Westerners, and Western Christians, more aware of what Massingnon always knew—the deep spiritual resources of Eastern Christianity in the Middle East (O'Mahony 2004a, 2008). Coincidentally, a church commemorating them, the Church of Notre Dame, was built in Vieux–Marché, Brittany, a village not far from Massignon's summer home. Massignon, in conjunction with the Badaliya prayer association (founded after visiting Damietta, Egypt), organized the first pilgrimage of Muslims and Christians to Vieux–Marché in 1954, to pray for reconciliation and mutual understanding, just as the FLN started the armed struggle in Algeria. It became an annual event for him until he died.[13] The legend was a key part of his work for Muslim–Christian reconciliation during the worst violence in North Africa. These saints were venerated in both traditions, and pointed toward a powerful eschatological hope for justice among Shi'ite Muslims and Christians for all the poor and oppressed (O'Mahony 2004b).

Thirdly, sacred sites and sacred spaces were another aspect of Massignon's "Abrahamic" approach to Muslim–Christian relations and interreligious dialogue. He argued that Jerusalem and the Holy Places figured prominently in any solution to the Arab-Israeli conflict (Gude 1996, 188). Massingnon was committed to what can only be described as a radical form of "religious transnationalism." The Holy Land for him was just that, a "holy land," and this meant it was not "an object for the privileged [great powers] to carve up, but the seamless garment of worldwide reconciliation, a place of intimate sharing among all." All the people of Abraham should "have renounced the cult of idols" rather than be seduced by them, the cult of narrow ethnic nationalisms and modernization, as if power, wealth, and technology can solve complex problems of political and economic inequality (Gude 1996, 169). Therefore, all the peoples of Abraham should work together to share the Holy Land "as their joint home, and protect its integrity as the *religious space sacred* to Jews, Christians, and Muslims" (emphasis added) (Gude 1996, 164–165). This meant "the practice of *sacred hospitality* was incumbent upon them in *every* area of their lives" (emphasis added), and that Muslim–Christian understanding only would be achieved through *compassion* and costly sacrificial *substitution* (Gude 1996, 214–217).

Perhaps all these activities for peace, reconciliation, and interreligious dialogue, often dismissed during France's war with Algeria, terrorism, and violent decolonization, now appear more perceptive and forward looking, given the religious turn and the postsecular sensitivity in international relations. Since Massingnon's time, the role of sacred sites and sacred places in peacemaking and conflict resolution is becoming better understood (Hassner 2009, 2013; Pazos 2013; Appleby, Little, and Omer 2015).

However, Massingnon would have been skeptical of the idea of religion primarily as an *instrument*, even for peaceful political purposes. His entire faith, life, and vocation indicate that the real basis, and only basis, for peace was the struggle to live faithfully in the world. He only met Gandhi once, but was introduced to *satyagraha* and his ideas on peace through Muslims (Massignon 1989c). The way Francis of Assisi performed the gospel demonstrated another way of living in the world, given the anarchy and violence of the medieval Italian city–state system (section 1). Similarly, Massignon developed his key "Franciscan" concepts, influenced by St. Francis and his meeting with the Sultan (compassion, hospitality, and substitution) as a way of responding to the evils, to the violence, of *his* world (the carnage of World War II, the occupation of France, great power politics, Western greed for oil, and the violence of decolonization in North Africa and the Middle East).

However, these abstract concepts are only the beginning. What mattered to Massingnon is how they could be embedded as types of *religious* social practices in the Abrahamic religious traditions in the Middle East.

Compassion

Massignon believed compassion was reaching out to "the Other," and participating in their suffering (Massignon 1989d). Did Massignon have a simple faith like Francis of Assisi? A "simple" faith need not be a "simplistic" one (even Francis commended to his brothers the theology and preaching of Anthony of Padua), but for Massignon, shockingly—like St. Francis—it was to hear the gospel, and to do it. So, compassion was a faithfulness to this experience, this transference of ourselves to others, which calls people "to go out from themselves towards the other [the 'Exodus Motif' of Abraham], to love fraternally beyond their *milieu* and relationships in time and space here below, within a community directed towards the universal" (i.e. Francis's radical social ontology) (Gude 1996, 86). However, compassion was also based on actively gaining new knowledge, knowledge from the periphery, to interpret more effectively what is going on in the world. Massignon, in ways now made clear by critical theorists, social constructivists, and the linguistic turn in their study of international relations, was quite aware of how language and speech acts relate to suffering and compassion:

> When called to by the suffering of others, the word he enacted was compassion. The turning of an indifferent ear by one not deaf was to him an act of falsehood. Cultivation of falsehood in defense of *national security* was an act of dishonor. Draining the *resources* of another community to enhance one's own was an act of injustice. And the use of any *language* to deceive was a betrayal of the essence of human intercourse. Language itself [the speech acts we use (Matt. 15:18)] "reveals what is in the heart." (Mason 1988, 18)

Hospitality

The Islamic social practice, the code of *hospitality*, saved Massignon's life. This is what led to the rediscovery of his Christian faith. He came to call it "sacred hospitality" (*l'hospitalité sacrée*), and defined it as "the acceptance, the *transfer* to ourselves of the sufferings of others" (Gude 1996, 86), the admission of "the Other" to one's self (O'Mahony 2006, 160; O'Mahony and Bowe 2006). Hospitality came to prefigure for him God's stance toward human beings. For Massignon to exercise the same hospitality and compassion he had been shown, now was a way for him to show God's compassion for others. Moreover, compassion and hospitality for him were not abstract, free-floating moral concepts (following Alasdair MacIntyre), emerging from (Western) Enlightenment rationality (Thomas 2005, 85–96, 118–119). The meaning of these concepts was first shown to him in a *specific* religious tradition, i.e. the social practices embedded *within* Islam, in Arabic, and in an Arab country (Iraq as part of the Ottoman Empire). Moreover, it was through the *faith* of Muslim friends, and their hospitality, that his Christian faith had been restored. He discovered through his *encounters* (Francis's radical social ontology) "all other human beings" are to be his "brothers," especially "the most abandoned" (Gude 1996, 85–86).

Therefore, compassion, hospitality—and, with it, the sacredness of the guest, the stranger, the foreigner, and the right to asylum (highly contested political issues then, and now)—came to guide Massignon's *less visible* social activity, as a university professor during the war in Algeria and the violence of France's decolonization. These activities included teaching the Qur'an to North African migrant workers at the mosque in Paris, or voluntarily teaching them basic math and French (he did these things for over 30 years), visiting Algerian prisoners (once the FLN's armed struggle in Algeria started), and helping to found social service organizations for migrants (Mason 1988, 83; Gude 1996, 221). These same principles "fearlessly" empowered what people at the time acknowledged, his *more visible* social activism, interviews, and public speaking (what secular liberal activists could understand), but also radical religious activities (perhaps less puzzling, and more relevant in our age of postmodernism and postsecularism)—fasting, prayers, and religious pilgrimages to promote Muslim–Christian unity over the war in Algeria and violent French reprisals elsewhere in North Africa. In other words, compassion and hospitality were not abstract concepts, but contributed to a radical "Franciscan" social ontology, "experiential knowledge of the sacred," and this is what "led him to bind himself to the most abandoned of people" (Gude 1996, 86). Encounter, conversion, and *new* knowledge—for St. Francis, for Massignon, and Pope Frances—really did come from the margins, or the periphery, leading to even *deeper* transformations; and, given the French wars in North Africa, even *riskier* forms of social and political action.

Substitution

Massignon saw substitution as the ultimate expression of the hospitality he had found in Islam before his conversion, and this became the paradigm for his Christian life, to the end of his life (Gude 1996, 160). Francis's encounter with the Sultan was interpreted by Massignon as a Christian example of the concept of *abdal* in Islam, or "substitution" (Arabic *badal*, and plural *abdal* for "substitute"). This is when another person's suffering ultimately saves humanity.[14] God calls certain heroic persons *witnesses* in each generation (Gude 1996, 162, 163, 164). These witnesses—religious, or even secular—freely acquiesce to a vocation of suffering, and become *substitutes*, intercessors "for those whose evil lives wreak havoc on the world. Jesus was the first in a long line of chosen substitutes who accept personal suffering in atonement for human sin" (Gude 1996, 59, 109). Such witnesses were linked for Massignon by their thirst for justice, the reparative value of suffering, and the vindication of the oppressed (ultimately, at the last judgment) (Gude 1996, 160).

Massignon's struggle was how to express concretely the vow of substitution he took at Damietta, given the shifting events of French foreign-policy and world politics around him. The concept of substitution, and the heroic persons he identified, were an increasing source of inspiration for him, as he became absorbed with the suffering of Muslims in France's violent and torturous decolonization of North Africa and the Middle East (Gude 1996, 158–160, 123, 124). The religious value of "substitution" was personal—meeting another person in what Catholics would call "the communion of saints," carrying one another's burdens, putting oneself in another's place, even accepting another person's help (Grifith 1997). When the French government opened negotiations with the FLN at Evian in 1961, Massignon argued for prayer, meditation, substitution, and nonviolent witness. The "unity of the human race," he said, could not be achieved by "racial hatred" and practices of "bestial torture" (Gude 1996, 238).

THEIR CONCERN FOR MUSLIMS AND MUSLIM–CHRISTIAN RELATIONS IS ROOTED IN A RADICAL, MORE HOLISTIC, "FRANCISCAN" TYPE OF SOCIAL ONTOLOGY AND EPISTEMOLOGY

Conclusion

This article has wrestled with the problem of multiple perspectives, and with interpretations of key people in events in the Franciscan tradition and in modern international relations. One—the founder of this tradition—is very well known, far beyond Christian circles; and, the other, far less well known (at least in the English-speaking world). Both are increasingly controversial, and arguably have become more important with the rise of Islam in international relations. The article handles this problem with an integrated approach to the study of history, theology, spirituality, and international relations. It made a reasonable case for viewing Francis of Assisi, during the violence of the Italian city–state system and the medieval crusades to be engaged in a cultural, or really *counter*-cultural, critique of Christendom, which embraced the leper, the poor, the marginalized, and eventually the Sultan of Egypt. This critique, and "Franciscan" *trajectory toward the periphery*, was also reflected in the way Massignon, in increasingly risky ways, *lived* a set of modern "Franciscan" social practices, inspired by St. Francis—compassion, hospitality, and substitution—during French decolonization in North Africa, especially the war in Algeria, which for France was constituted as a security threat (it nearly brought the downfall of the Fifth Republic). This trajectory toward the periphery, which gained for St. Francis, and for Massignon, the support of popes, is now reflected in Pope Francis's pontificate.

Undoubtedly, it was a Franciscan identity which strongly contributed to the concern for peacemaking, for Islam, for Muslims, and Muslim–Christian relations. The "Franciscan model" set out in this article—reflected in Francis's life and his encounter with Malik al-Kamil, and Massignon's life and social and political action—indicates that their concern for Muslims and Muslim–Christian relations is rooted in a radical, more holistic, "Franciscan" type of social ontology and epistemology: it is through *initial* encounters, and then *riskier* encounters, and *deeper* conversions, that Francis and Massignon made the discovery that knowledge about how the world works comes from the lowly, those on the margins, the periphery of society (social epistemology). The model points to an expansion of *who* to engage with (social ontology), and *how* engaging with others (social epistemology), and *not* rejecting but transforming the meaning and significance of some of medieval society's social practices and some of those of modern society, can in time transform the world. ❖

Acknowledgements

I would like to thank Anthony O'Mahony, Kenneth R. Himes, OFM, and Fareed Z. Munir for their helpful comments on earlier drafts of this paper.

1. Massingnon's is referring to the legend of the "Seven Sleepers of Ephesus" found in the Qur'an and ancient Christian sources. It is commemorated by an old French church in Brittany. Massignon started a Muslim–Christian pilgrimage there for reconciliation shortly after the FLN started the armed struggle in Algeria (section 4). Herbert Mason, formerly University Professor of History and Religion, Boston University, was a life-long friend of Massignon's, and translated into English Massignon's *La Passion d'al-Hallaj / The Passion of al-Hallaj* (Massignon 1982).
2. For example, Joris-Karl Huysmans, Charles de Foucauld, Paul Claudel, Charles Pégy, Leon Bloy, Georges Bernanos, Jacques Maritain, Gabriel Marcel, François Mauriac, and Jean Danielou (Charlton 1979, 269, 292, 300–304; Mason 1988, 14, 36, 75, 82; Schloesser 2005).
3. Arnoldo Fortini (1899–1970), a historian, lawyer, and poet, was mayor of Assisi before and during World War II. He also held the Chair in Franciscan Studies at the University of Perugia. He had full access to Assisi's historical archives to write his biography of St. Francis (Fortini 1981), which Hugo argues can be classified as primary sources, even though his *interpretations* of them need to be carefully evaluated (Fortini and Conroy 1983; Hugo 2011, 50, 103–104, 121, 127, 130, 149).
4. "Something is profoundly wrong with the way we live today" (Judt 2010, 1).
5. Francis's counter-cultural critique of Christendom has to be balanced with another similarity between Francis and Massignon – they both *desired*, and *received*, the support of popes: for Francis (Innocent III, Honorius III, and Gregory IX, who before becoming pope, as Ugolino di Conti, Cardinal Bishop of Ostia, at the special request of Francis, was made Cardinal Protestor of the Order), and for Massignon (Pius XI, Pius XII, John XXIII, and Paul VI).
6. The *earlier* Rule (1221) also reflects Pope Innocent III's decrees, and reforms at the Fourth Lateran Council (1215). This is the rule that Francis initially wrote, and received only *oral* approval (i.e. without the papal seal) from Pope Innocent the III (1209/1210), which Francis and the brothers agreed to at the famous Chapter meeting in Assisi at Pentecost (1221). The later version, the *Later Rule* finally, received approval (with the papal seal) from Pope Honorius III (1223).
7. Perhaps, the earliest account (1220) is by Jacques de Vitry, the bishop of Acre, who was in the crusader camp when Francis arrived (1219). Written when the crusaders expected victory, it depicts the encounter as a minor "event," but his second account, written after the crusaders' defeat (1223–1225), constructs the encounter as a "major event" to show St. Francis as a model of Church renewal, and now, with the rise of Islam, as a peacemaker, or precursor of interreligious dialogue. Similarly, the gifts the Sultan offered Francis (an objective, observable event) were they a genuine demonstration of "hospitality," as a type of Arab *social practice*, rooted in the Islamic *tradition* (e.g. MacIntyre, Massignon), or did this show the devious Sultan trying to undermine the Franciscan practices of poverty and simplicity (the view of St. Bonaventure and other Franciscan writers)? In other words, empirical observation cannot answer these kinds of questions regarding social actions, and the answers have to be *interpreted* in view of a variety of other factors. In fact, the different accounts reflect various interests within the order, within the Church, and the way Francis's encounter with the Sultan is depicted through the centuries (Tolan 2009) offers a barometer of Muslim–Christian relations, and Europe's changing perceptions of Islam and international security.
8. Anthony Spadaro, in the Introduction to Pope Francis's homilies at St. Martha Chapel, similarly says Pope Francis's answer to the question, "how can we discern the right path," is "the way of Jesus Christ: abasement, humility, even humiliation" (Spadaro 2015, xlv).
9. However, perhaps this is not as clear as it could be in the English title of the collection of homilies (Bergoglio 2015). The English title (*Encountering Truth*) is translated *differently* from its Italian title (*La verità è un incontro*). The Preface by Federico Lombardi, the Director General of Vatican Radio, in the Italian is the *same* as the title of the book (*La verità è un incontro*), and is translated into English as "truth is an encounter," whereas this *same* phrase (in Italian) for the *English* book title is translated *differently* as "encountering truth" (which has perhaps a slightly different connotation). Does this matter? The phrase "the truth is an encounter" (rather than "encountering truth") is arguably more consistent with the message of the homilies, and Pope Francis's trajectory toward the periphery (Ferrara 2015). This article's social epistemology, and "Franciscan model" – encounter, conversion, knowledge, and transformation, also seems to fit with this intepretation.
10. T.E. Laurence, in one of his conversations with Massignon, apparently said to him, "you love the Arabs more than I do," and with this comment, Massignon knew there could be no attempt at sharing life he and Lawrence (Massignon 1989b; Hourani 1991c).
11. This led to the formal foundation of the Badaliya prayer association in 1947. Cardinal Montini (later Paul VI) joined the Badaliya Prayer Association, and John-Paul II was also inspired by it to formulate his own "spirit of Assisi" meetings in the 1980s (Gude 1996, 133–135).
12. The Abraham Path Initiative (API), now funded by the World Bank, was created by William L. Ury co-founder of the Harvard Program on Negotiation. It is a long-distance walking trail across the Middle East which connects the sites visited by the patriarch Abraham as

recorded in ancient religious texts and traditions; http://abrahampath.org. Leon McCarron, a Fellow of the Royal Geographical Society, has recent hiked the path, written a book, and made a film about the journey (McCarron 2017).

13. Massignon's annual *Badaliya Christmas newsletter* (December 8, 1954) mentions the beginning of the FLN's national liberation struggle (Gude 1996, 190–191, 218–219).

14. The concept of *badal* immersed Massignon in his study of the Sufi mystic and martyr, Mansur al-Hallaj, whom Massignon devoted his PhD dissertation, *La Passion d'al-Hallaj* (1922 edition), and studied the rest of his life. Tolan (2009) examines these Islamic sources, but omits the Catholic sources for this concept, which go back to Massignon's friends in the French Catholic intellectual revival (e.g. Huysmans and Charles de Foucauld).

References

Alkopher, Tal Dingot. 2005. "The Social (and Religious) Meanings That Constitute War: The Crusades as Realpolitik vs. Socialpolitik." *International Studies Quarterly* 49 (4): 715–738.

Appleby, R. Scott, David Little, and Atalia Omer, eds. 2015. *The Oxford Handbook of Religion, Conflict, and Peacebuilding.* Oxford: Oxford University Press.

Arafat (Syria), Imam Mohammad Bashar. 2000. "Islam and Christianity-Two Faiths and One God." *Spirit and Life: A Journal of Contemporary Franciscanism* 9 (1): 7–24.

Assisi, Francis. 1999a. "The Early Rule." In *Francis of Assisi, Early Documents: The Saint*; vol. I, edited by Regis J. Armstrong, J. A. Wayne Hellmann, and William J. Short, 63–86. New York: New City Press.

Assisi, Francis. 1999b. "'First Letter to Custodians (1220),' 'A Letter to the Rulers of the Peoples' (1220)." In *Francis of Assisi, Early Documents: The Saint*, edited by Regis J. Armstrong, J. A. Wayne Hellmann, and William J. Short, vol. I, 56–57; 60–61. New York: New City Press; hereafter FA ED I.

Bassetti-Sani, Giulio, OFM. 1969. *Per un Dialogo Cristiano-Musulmano: Mohammed, Damietta e La Verna.* Milano: Vita e Pensiero.

Bassetti-Sani, Giulio, OFM. 1974. *Louis Massignon: Christian Ecumenist.* Chicago, IL: Franciscan Herald Press.

Bergoglio, Jorge Mario/Papa Francesco. 2014. *La verità è un incontro. Omelie da Santa Marta.* Roma: Rizzoli.

Bergoglio, Jorge Mario/Pope Francis. 2015. *Encountering Truth: Meeting God in the Everyday, The Morning Homilies From St. Martha's Chapel.* New York: Image/Random House.

Bill, James A., and John Alden Williams. 2002. *Roman Catholics and Shi'i Muslims: Prayer, Passion, and Politics.* Chapel Hill: University of North Carolina Press.

Blainey, David L., and Naeem Inayatullah. 2007. "International Relations from Below." In *The Oxford Handbook of International Relations*, edited by Christian Reus-Smit and Duncan Snidal, 663–674. Oxford: Oxford University Press.

Booth, Ken. 2005. "Critical Explorations." In *Critical Security Studies and World Politics*, edited by Ken Booth, 4–10. Boulder, CO: Lynne Rienner.

Booth, Ken. 2007. *Theory of World Security.* Cambridge: Cambridge University Press.

Brown, Chris. 1994. "'Turtles All the Way Down': Anti-Foundationalism, Critical Theory and International Relations." *Millennium: Journal of International Studies* 23 (2): 213–236.

Brunette, Pierre, OFM. 1997. *Francis and His Conversions.* Quincy, IL: Franciscan Press.

Cantor, Norman F. 1991. *Inventing the Middle Ages.* New York: Quill/William Morrow.

Carmody, Maurice. 2008. *The Franciscan Story: St. Francis of Assisi and His Influence Since the Thirteenth Century.* London: Athena Press.

Charlton, D. G., ed. 1979. *France: A Companion to French Studies.* London: Methuen.

Cox, Robert W. 1981. "Social Forces, States, and World Orders: Beyond International Relations Theory." *Millennium: Journal of International Studies* 10 (2): 126–155.

Croce, Benedetto. 1941. *History as the Story of Liberty.* London: Allen & Unwin.

Cunningham, Lawrence S. 2004. "Francis Naked and Clothed: A Theological Meditation." In *Francis of Assisi: History, Hagiography, and Hermeneutics in the Early Documents*, edited by Jay M. Hammond, 165–178. New York: New City Press. esp. 169.

Cusato, Michael F. 2008. "Healing the Violence of the Contemporary World: A Franciscan Paradigm for Dialogue with Islam." *Spirit and Life: A Journal of Contemporary Franciscanism* 12 (1): 15–16.

Dalarun, Jacques. 2002. *The Misadventure of Francis of Assisi.* St. Bonaventure, NY: Franciscan Institute.

Dalarun, Jacques, Michael F. Cusato, and Carla Salvati. 2006. *The Stigmata of Francis of Assisi: New Studies, New Perspectives.* St. Bonaventure, NY: Franciscan Institute.

Daniel, E. Randolph. 2012. "Franciscan Missions." In *The Cambridge Companion to Francis of Assisi*, edited by Michael J. P. Robson, 240–272. Cambridge: Cambridge University Press.

Darness, George, and Marvin L. Krier. 2011. *In the Spirit of St. Francis & the Sultan.* New York: Orbis Press.

De Beer, Frances. 1981. "St. Francis and Islam." *Concilium* 149 (1): 11–20.

Delio, Illia, OSF. 2003. *A Franciscan View of Creation.* St. Bonaventure, NY: Franciscan Institute.

Dickson, Gary. 2010. "Medieval Revivalism." In *Medieval Christianity, People's History of Christianity*, edited by Daniel E. Bornstein, 147–178. Minneapolis, MN: Augsburg/Fortress Press.

Dubois, Leon L. 1905. *St. Francis, Social Reformer.* New York: Catholic University of America.

Dwyer, Daniel P., OFM. 2000. "'Introduction,' 'Islam and Franciscanism: A Dialogue'." *Spirit and Life: A Journal of Contemporary Franciscanism* 9 (1): 1–6.

Enloe, Cythia. 1996. "Margins, Silences and Bottom Rungs: How to Overcome the Underestimation of Power in the Study of International Relations." In *International Theory: Positivism & Beyond*, edited by Steve Smith, Ken Booth, and Marysia Zalewski, 186–202. Cambridge: Cambridge University Press.

Evans, Richard J. 2000. *In Defence of History.* London: Granta Books.

Faggioli, Massimo. 2013. "Vatican II and the Church of the Margins." *Theological Studies* 74 (1): 808–818.

Ferrara, Pasquale. 2015. "The Concept of Periphery in Pope Francis' Discourse: A Religious Alternative to Globalization?" *Religions* 6 (1): 42–57.

Fortini, Arnoldo. 1981. *Francis of Assisi*, Trans. of *Nova Vita di San Francesco* by Helen Moak. New York: Crossroad.

Fortini, Gemma, and Finbarr Conroy. 1983. "The Contribution of Arnaldo Fortini to Franciscan Studies." *Franciscan Studies* 43 (1): 261–278.

Frykenberg, Robert. 1996. *History & Belief: The Foundations of Historical Understanding.* Grand Rapids, MN: Eerdmans.

Gallant, Laurent. 2006. "Francis of Assisi Forerunner of Interreligious Dialogue: Chapter 16 of the Earlier Rule Revisited." *Franciscan Studies* 64 (1): 58–82.

Grifith, Sidney H. 1997. "Sharing the Faith of Abraham: The 'Credo' of Louis Massignon." *Islam and Christian-Muslim Relations* 8 (2): 193–210.

Gude, Mary Louise. 1996. *Louis Massignon: The Crucible of Compassion.* Notre Dame, IN: University of Notre Dame.

Hall, Rodney Bruce, and Friedrich Kratochwil. 1993. "Medieval Tales: Neorealist 'Science' and the Abuse of History." *International Organization* 47 (3): 479–491.

Hammond, Jay M., ed. 2004. *Francis of Assisi: History, Hagiography, and Hermeneutics in the Early Documents.* New York: New City Press.

Hassner, Ron E. 2009. *War on Sacred Grounds.* Ithaca, NY: Cornell University Press.

Hassner, Ron E. 2013. *War on the Battlefield.* Ithaca, NY: Cornell University Press.

Haynes, Jeffrey. 2016. *Religious Transnational Actors and Soft Power.* London: Routledge.

Hoebrichts, Jan. 1997. *Francis and the Sultan.* Quincy, IL: Franciscan Press.

Hopwood, Derek. 2003. "Albert Hourani: Islam, Christianity, and Orientalism." *British Journal of Middle Eastern Studies* 30 (2): 127–136.

Horan, Daniel P., OFM. 2008. "'Those Going Among the Saracens and Other Nonbelievers': Thomas Merton and Franciscan Interreligious Dialogue." *Merton Annual* 21 (1): 1202–1204.

Horan, Daniel P., OFM. 2014. *The Franciscan Heart of Thomas Merton: A New Look at the Spiritual Inspiration of His Life, Thought, and Writing.* Notre Dame, IN: Ave Maria Press.

Hourani, Albert. 1991a. *Islam in European Thought.* Cambridge: Cambridge University Press.

Hourani, Albert. 1991b. "Islam in European Thought." In *Islam and European Thought*, edited by Albert Hourani, 43–49. Cambridge: Cambridge University Press.

Hourani, Albert. 1991c. "T.E. Lawrence and Louis Massignon." In *Islam in European Thought*, edited by Albert Hourani, 116–128. Cambridge: Cambridge University Press.

Hugo, William R., OFM, Cap. 2011. *Studying the Life of Saint Francis of Assisi: A Beginner's Workbook.* 2nd ed. New York: New City Press.

Ingham, Mary Beth. 2012. *The Harmony of Goodness - Mutuality and Moral Living According to John Duns Scotus.* 2nd ed. St. Bonaventure, NY: Franciscan Institute.

Irwin, Robert. 2007. *For Lust of Knowing: The Orientalists and Their Enemies.* London: Penguin.

Johnson, Luke Timothy. 1996. *The Real Jesus: The Misguided Quest for the Historical Jesus and the Truth of the Traditional Gospels.* San Francisco, CA: HarperCollins.

Judt, Tony. 2010. *Ill Fares the Land: A Treatise on Our Present Discontents.* London: Penguin Books.

Kedar, B. Z. 1984. *Crusade and Mission: European Approaches Toward the Muslims.* Princeton, NJ: Princeton Univerisy Press.

Khomami, Nadia, and Mazin Sidahmed. 2016. "Jonathan Greenblatt: 'This Proud Jew Would Register as a Muslim' in database." *BBC News*, November 18. Accessed 28 August, 2017. https://www.theguardian.com/us-news/2016/nov/18/jonathan-greenblatt-muslim-registry-database-trump

Kratochwil, Friedrich. 2000. "Constructing a New Orthodoxy? Wendt's 'Social Theory of International Relations' and the Constructivist Challenge." *Millennium: Journal of International Studies* 29 (1): 73–101.

Kratochwil, Friedrich. 2006. "History, Action and Identity: Revisiting the 'Second' Great Debate and Assessing its Importance for Social Theory." *European Journal of International Relations* 12 (1): 7–8.

Latham, Ian. 2008. "The Conversion of Louis Massingnon in Mesopotamia in 1908." *Aram Periodical* (Oriental Institute, University of Oxford, Society for Syro-Mesopotamian Studies) 20 (1): 245–267.

Lawrence, C. H. 1994. *The Friars: The Impact of the Early Mendicant Movement.* London: Longman.

Lehmann, Lawrence. 1988. "Francis's Two Letters to the Custodians: Proposals for Christian-Islamic Ecumenism in Praising God." *Greyfriars Review* 2 (3): 63–91.

Lindbeck, George A. 1984. *The Nature of Doctrine: Religion and Theology in a Postliberal Age.* Philadelphia, PA: Westminster Press.

Little, Lester K. 1978. *Religious Poverty and the Profit Economy in Medieval Europe.* London: Paul Elk.

Mark of Whitstable, OFM, Cap. 2006. *Gospel Chivalry: Franciscan Romanticism.* Leominster: Gracewing.

Mason, Herbert. 1988. *Memoir of a Friend: Louis Massignon.* Notre Dame, IN: University of Notre Dame Press.

Mason, Herbert. 1989. *Testimonies and Reflections: Essays of Louis Massignon.* Notre Dame, IN: University of Notre Dame Press.

Massignon, Louis. 1982. *La Passion d' al-Hallaj / The Passion of al-Hallaj*, Trans. by Herbert Mason, 4 vols. Princeton, NJ: Princeton University Press.

Massignon, Louis. 1989a. "The Three Prayers of Abraham." In *Testimonies and Reflections*, edited by Herbert Mason, 3–20. Notre Dame, IN: University of Notre Dame Press.

Massignon, Louis. 1989b. "My Entry Into Jerusalem with Lawrence in 1917." In *Testimonies and Reflections*, edited by Herbert Mason, 32–38. Notre Dame, IN: University of Notre Dame Press.

Massignon, Louis. 1989c. "Gandhian Outlook and Techniques." In *Testimonies and Reflections*, edited by Herbert Mason, 139–154. Notre Dame, IN: University of Notre Dame Press.

Massignon, Louis. 1989d. "The Transfer of Suffering Through Compassion." In *Testimonies and Reflections*, edited by Herbert Mason, 155–164. Notre Dame, IN: University of Notre Dame Press.

Mastnak, Tomaž. 2002. *Crusading Peace: Christendom, the Muslim World, and the Western Political Order.* Berkeley: University of California Press.

Mavelli, Luca, and Fabio Petito. 2012. "The Postsecular in International Relations: An Overview." *Review of International Studies* 38 (5): 931–942.

Mayer, Annemarie C. 2009. "Charting the Attributes of God: The Common Ground of Three Religions According to Ramon Llull (1232–1316)." *International Journal for the Study of the Christian Church* 9 (2): 95–117.

McCarron, Leon. 2017. *The Land Beyond: A Thousand Miles on Foot Through the Heart of the Middle East.* London: I.B. Tauris.

McMichael, Steven J. 2012. "Francis and the Encounter with the Sultan (1219)." In *The Cambridge Companion to Francis of Assisi*, 127–142. Cambridge: Cambridge University Press.

Meir, Christopher. 1994. *Preaching the Crusades.* Cambridge: Cambridge University Press.

Mooren, Thomas, OFM, Cap. 2000. "The Exodus Motif in Christianity and Islam." *Spirit and Life: A Journal of Contemporary Franciscanism* 9 (1): 75–98.

Moses, Paul. 2009. *The Saint and the Sultan: The Crusades, Islam and Francis of Assisi's Mission of Peace.* New York: Doubleday.

Munir, Fareed Z. 2000. "Islam and Franciscanism: Prophet Mohammad of Arabia and St. Francis of Assisi in the Spirituality of Mission." *Spirit and Life: A Journal of Contemporary Franciscanism* 9 (1): 25–42.

Munir, Fareed Z. 2008. "Sultan al-Malik Muhammad Al-Kamil and Saint Francis: Interreligious Dialogue and the Meeting at Damietta." *Journal of Islamic Law and Culture* 10 (3): 305–314.

Nasr, Seyyed Hossein. 1987. *Traditional Islam in the Modern World.* London: Kegan Paul.

O'Mahony, Anthony. 2001. "Islam in Europe." *The Way: Contemporary Christian Spirituality* 14 (1): 122–135.

O'Mahony, Anthony, ed. 2004a. *Eastern Christianity: Studies in Modern History, Religion, and Politics.* London: Melisende.

O'Mahony, Anthony. 2004b. "Louis Massignon, the Seven Sisters of Ephesus and the Christian-Muslim Pilgrimage at Vieux –Marché, Brittany." In *Explorations in the Christian Theology of Pilgrimage*, edited by Craig Bartholomew and Fred Hughs, 126–148. London: Ashgate.

O'Mahony, Anthony. 2006. "Our Common Fidelity to Abraham is What Divides Us: Christianity and Islam in the Life and Thought of Louis Massignon." In *Catholics in Interreligious Dialogue: Studies in Monasticism, Theology and Spirituality*, edited by Anthony O'Mahony and Peter Bowe, OSB, 151–190. Leominster: Gracewing.

O'Mahony, Anthony. 2007. "Catholic Theological Perspectives on Islam at the Second Vatican Council." *New Blackfriars* 88 (1016): 385–398.

O'Mahony, Anthony, ed. 2008. *Christianity in the Middle East: Studies in Modern History, Theology, and Politics.* London: Melisende.

O'Mahony, Anthony, and Peter Bowe, OSB, eds. 2006. *Catholics in Interreligious Dialogue: Studies in Monasticism, Theology, and Spiritualty.* Leominster: Gracewing.

Pazos, Antón M., ed. 2013. *Pilgrims and Pilgrimages as Peacemakers in Christianity, Judaism and Islam.* London: Routledge.

Peterson, Ingrid. 2012. "The Third Order of Francis." In *The Cambridge Companion to Francis of Assisi*, edited by Michael Robson, 194–195. Cambridge: Cambridge University Press.

Petito, Fabio. 2011. "In Defence of Dialogue of Civilizations: With a Brief Illustration of the Diverging Agreement Between Edward Said and Louis Massignon." *Millennium: Journal of International Studies* 39 (3): 759–779.

Polidoro, Gianmaria, OFM. n.d. *The Greeting of Peace Revealed to St. Francis.* Assisi: Edizioni Portziuncola.

Robson, Michael, ed. 2012a. *The Cambridge Companion to Francis of Assisi.* Cambridge: Cambridge University Press.

Robson, Michael. 2012b. "The Writings of Francis." In *The Cambridge Companion to Francis of Assisi*, 34–49. Cambridge: Cambridge University Press.

Rohr, Richard. OFM. 2011. *Falling Upward: A Spirituality for the Two Halves of Life.* San Francisco, CA: Jossey-Bass.

Rout, Paul, OFM. 2011. "St Francis of Assisi and Islam: A Theological Perspective on a Christian-Muslim Encounter." *Al-Masaq: Islam and the Medieval Mediterranean* 23 (3): 205–215.

Saxby, Steven. 2006. "Francis and the Sultan: A Model for Contemporary Christian Engagement with Islam." In *Catholics in Interreligious Dialogue: Studies in Monasticism, Theology, and Spiritualty*, edited by Anthony O'Mahony and Peter Bowe, OSB, 120–150. Leominster: Gracewing.

Schloesser, Stephen. 2005. *Jazz Age Catholicism: Mystic Modernism in Post-war Paris, 1919–1933.* Toronto, ON: University of Toronto.

Schmucki, Octavian, OFM, Cap. 1995. "St. Francis of Assisi, Messenger of Peace in His Time." *Greyfriars Review* 9 (2): 147–161.

Sheldrake, Philip, SJ. 1995. *Spirituality & History: Questions of Interpretation and Method.* New edition. London: SPCK.

Spadaro, Anthony, SJ. 2015. "Introduction." In *Encountering Truth: Meeting God in the Everyday*, edited by Jorge Mario Bergoglio and Pope Francis, xvii–xlviii. New York: Image/Random House.

Thomas, Scott M. 2005. *The Global Resurgence of Religion and the Transformation of International Relations.* New York: Palgrave.

Thomas, Scott M. 2010. "Living Critically and 'Living Faithfully' in a Global Age: Justice, Emancipation and the Political Theology of International Relations." *Millennium: Journal of International Studies* 39 (2): 505–524.

Thomas, Scott M. 2014. "Culture, Religion and Violence: René Girard's Mimetic Theory." *Millennium: Journal of International Studies* 43 (1): 308–327.

Todeschini, Giacomo. 2009. *Franciscan Wealth: From Voluntary Poverty to Market Society.* St. Bonaventure, NY: Franciscan Institute.

Tolan, John. 2009. *Saint Francis and the Sultan: The Curious History of a Christian-Muslim Encounter.* Oxford: Oxford University Press.

Vauchez, André. 2012. *Francis of Assisi: The Life and Afterlife of a Medieval Saint.* New Haven, CT: Yale University Press.

Warren, Kathleen A., OSF. 2003. *Daring to Cross the Threshold: Francis of Assisi Encounters Sultan Malek al-Kamil.* Rochester, MN: Sisters of St. Francis.

Williams, Rowan. 1979. *The Wound of Knowledge: Christian Spirituality from the New Testament to St. John of the Cross.* London: Darton, Longman, Todd.

Wojtyła, Karol/John Paul II. 2005. *Testes Spei: Ioannes Paulus II ad Fratres Minores/Witness to Hope: John Paul II to the Friars Minor.* Roma: Curia generalis OFM.

DIGNITATIS HUMANAE AND THE CATHOLIC HUMAN RIGHTS REVOLUTION

By Kenneth L. Grasso and Robert P. Hunt

In his "Message to Rulers" at the conclusion of the Second Vatican Council in December, 1965, Pope Paul VI numbered *Dignitatis Humanae* among the Council's major texts.[1] In the ensuing 40 years, history has borne out this estimate of its importance. To appreciate why, it is essential first to give the document itself a close reading, to understand it in its own terms. It is also necessary to see it against the backdrop of pre-conciliar teachings of the Roman Catholic Church on the nature and scope of religious liberty and the right ordering of political life. Finally, the ongoing salience of *Dignitatis Humanae* is evident in today's debates over the very nature of religious liberty. By providing a sound philosophical, anthropological, and theological foundation for genuine religious liberty, *Dignitatis Humanae* stands as a needed bulwark against any counterfeit "religious freedom" that offers only relativism and the radical privatization of faith.

What is *Dignitatis Humanae*?

By comparison to many Vatican documents, *Dignitatis Humanae* (*DH*) is relatively short and to the point. As one of its leading architects, the great American Jesuit theologian John Courtney Murray reminds us, *DH* is actually "a document of very modest scope."[2] Its subject matter and scope are aptly conveyed by its alternative title: "Declaration on Religious Freedom: On the Right of the Person and of Communities to Social and Civil Freedom in Matters Religious." "This Vatican Synod," it proclaims in section 2,

> declares that the human person has a right to religious freedom. This freedom means that all men are to be immune from coercion on the part of individuals or of social groups and of any human power, in such wise that in matters religious no one is to be forced to act in a manner contrary to his own beliefs. Nor is anyone to be restrained from acting in accordance with his own beliefs, whether privately

> or publicly, whether alone or in association with others, within due limits.[3]

The limits in question, it continues, consist in "the just requirements of public order" (3).

"Provided that the just requirements of public order are observed," in other words, human beings have a right not merely to "privately" practice a religion, but also to "give external expression" to their religious beliefs, to publicly profess, practice, witness, and worship (3). This right, it argues, must be recognized as a civil right in "the constitutional law whereby society is governed" (2).

IT EXPLORES THE FOUNDATIONS OF RELIGIOUS LIBERTY, ARGUING THAT THIS RIGHT "HAS ITS FOUNDATION IN THE VERY DIGNITY OF THE HUMAN PERSON"

In keeping with its modest scope, *DH* consists of only two chapters preceded by a preface. The preface begins by embracing as "greatly in accord with truth and justice" the contemporary demands for "freedom in human society" (and, in particular, the right to the "free exercise of religion") and the establishment of "constitutional limits" on the powers of government, as well as the growing sense of "the dignity of the human person" in which these demands are rooted (1).

At the same time, it reiterates the Church's traditional truth claims (affirming both "that God himself has made known to mankind the way in which men are to serve Him, and thus be saved in Christ and come to blessedness" and "that [the] one true religion subsists in the catholic and apostolic Church"); and makes clear that the right with which it is concerned "has to do with immunity from coercion in civil society" (1). The right proclaimed by *DH*, in other words, concerns the nature and scope of religious freedom in the civil order, not in the Church. As an "immunity from coercion" rather than an empowerment, moreover, it doesn't assert that individuals have a moral right to propagate their beliefs, but rather their right not to be prevented from doing so by coercive action on the part of government. Finally, it avows its intention "in taking up the matter of religious freedom … to develop the doctrine of the recent Popes on the inviolable rights of the human person and on the constitutional order of society" (1).

Beyond affirming the existence of the right to religious freedom, the focus of the first chapter is essentially fourfold. First, it outlines the scope of this right, affirming that it extends not merely to individuals but to "religious bodies." Since such bodies "are a requirement of the social nature both of man and of religion itself," religious liberty encompasses the right of religious institutions and communities to "govern themselves according to their own norms; to attempt "to show the special value of their doctrine in what concerns the organization of society and the inspiration of the whole of human activity"; and "to establish educational, cultural, charitable and social organizations, under the impulse of their own religious sense" (4). "Since the family is a society in its own original right," moreover, religious freedom also encompasses the right of parents "to determine, in accordance with their religious beliefs, the kind of religious education that their children are to receive." "Unjust burdens" thus may not be placed upon parents, "whether directly or indirectly," because of their decision to have their children educated in accord with their religious convictions (5).

Second, it explores the foundations of religious liberty, arguing that this right "has its foundation in the very dignity of the human person, as this dignity is known through the revealed word of God and by reason itself," as well as in "the social nature of man" (3). "It is in accordance with their dignity as persons," the Declaration proclaims, that "men should be at once impelled by nature and also bound by a moral obligation to seek the truth, especially religious truth," and, "once it is known … to order their whole lives in accord" with its demands (2). Truth, however, must be sought after in a manner consistent with our dignity as persons—in a manner consistent with our nature "as beings endowed with reason and free will and therefore privileged to bear personal responsibility"—and, once discovered, must be adhered to by an act of "personal assent." Human beings simply "cannot discharge" their "obligations, in a manner in keeping with their own nature, unless they enjoy immunity from external coercion as well as psychological freedom" (2, 3). All people have "the right to seek truth in matters religious," in short, because all people have the duty to seek, and to order their lives in accordance with, religious truth (3). Truth, moreover, must be sought in a manner consistent with "the social nature of man [which] requires that he should give external expression to his internal acts of religion; that he should participate with others in matters religious; [and] that he should profess his religion in community" (3).

This right, it continues, is also rooted in the limits placed on the jurisdiction of the state by virtue of the state's inherently secular character. Since "the religious acts whereby men, in private and in public ... direct their lives to God transcend by their nature the order of terrestrial and temporal affairs," government "would clearly transcend the limits of its power were it to presume to direct or inhibit" such acts (3).

Third, it briefly examines the responsibilities this right imposes on government. Since "the function of government is to make provision for the common welfare" (3), of which religion is an integral part, and "the protection and promotion of the inviolable rights of man" is among "the essential duties of government," it follows that the state has a responsibility "to help create conditions favorable to the fostering of religious life, in order that the people may be truly enabled to exercise their religious rights and to fulfill their religious duties, and also in order that society itself may profit by the moral qualities of justice and peace which have their origin in men's faithfulness to God and to His holy will." In fulfilling this function, moreover, government must "see to it that the equality of citizens before the law, which is itself an element of the common welfare, is never violated for religious reasons, whether openly or covertly" (6).

Fourth, in the context of its discussion of the responsibilities of the state, *DH* explores the limits of religious liberty. Because "it is exercised in human society," the exercise of religious liberty "is subject to certain regulatory norms." These norms arise out of the need to protect "the rights of all citizens" and to resolve "conflicts of rights" in a peaceful manner, to safeguard "genuine public peace," and to exercise a "proper guardianship of public morality." Taken together, "these matters constitute" the "basic component of the common welfare" which *DH* designates as "public order," whose vindication constitutes "the special duty of government" (7).

The second chapter considers religious liberty in the light of divine revelation. While admitting that Scripture "does not affirm in so many words the right of man to immunity from external coercion in religious matters," the Declaration nevertheless affirms that the right to religious liberty is "in accord with divine revelation" which discloses "the dignity of the person in its full dimensions," and God's regard for human dignity and freedom as well as attesting to the necessary freedom of the act of faith (9, 10). It is also in harmony with "the fundamental principle" governing "the relations between the Church and governments and the whole civil order," namely, "the freedom of the Church." When "the principle of religious freedom is ... given sincere and practical application," the Church is afforded the "full measure of freedom"—a freedom that her "divine mandate" to "care for the salvation of men requires" (13). Finally, it acknowledges and expresses regret for the times when Catholics and even Church authorities have acted in a manner inconsistent with the principles affirmed by the Declaration (12).

The Declaration and the Development of Catholic Social Teaching

DH marked a dramatic expansion in the Catholic understanding of the proper scope of religious liberty.[4] Prior to the Second Vatican Council, Catholic teaching acknowledged that under conditions of religious pluralism, the goods of public peace and civic amity might well require the establishment of a far-reaching religious liberty. It also affirmed that no one may be coerced into professing or practicing Catholicism, and that non-Catholics possessed a broad right to practice their religions privately (i.e., within the family or in an inconspicuous manner). At the same time, it insisted that in an overwhelmingly Catholic society restrictions may be placed on the public expression of non-Catholic religions. Inasmuch as the public expression of erroneous religious doctrines damaged both individuals by violating their right to be protected from error, and society as a whole because the common good itself is constituted by what is true and good, government would be remiss in its responsibilities if it did nothing to stem their dissemination. Nor did such restrictions raise issues of religious freedom for the simple reason that only the true and good can be the object of a right. In the colloquial, error has no rights.

At the risk of oversimplifying, it might be said that this conception of the proper scope of religious freedom flowed from a whole series of theological and political premises: that individuals are obligated to embrace religious truth; that Catholicism is the one true religion; that religious liberty is to be understood as an empowerment, as the moral right of individuals to profess and practice their beliefs; that "total care" of the common good—understood as, in John Courtney Murray's words, the sum total of "all the social goods, spiritual and moral as well as material, which man pursues here on earth in accord with the demands of his personal and social nature"—is committed to the state; that religious truth is an integral element of this good; and that the state's total care for the common good thus encompasses the care of religion.[5]

While *DH* leaves the theological premises informing the traditional teaching untouched, it implicitly modifies the political theory underlying it. To begin with, it distinguishes between the common good in toto and that "component" of this good which is entrusted in a "special" manner to the state, affirming that the care of the common good devolves not upon the state alone, but "upon the people as a whole, upon social groups, upon government, and upon the Church and other religious communities ... in the manner proper to each" (6). Secondly, it distinguishes between the moral and juridical dimensions of religious liberty, between the question of our obligations toward religious truth, and the question of the role of the state in enforcing these obligations. Finally, it brings into play the whole subject of the implications of our dignity as persons—as beings who possess intelligence and freedom—for the pursuit of religious truth and ordering of human social life.

What emerges in *DH* is a different and dramatically broader understanding of the nature and scope of religious liberty. Religious liberty is now understood as a universal right, as a right that is enjoyed by all men and women regardless of their religious convictions (or lack thereof), a right enjoyed by Catholics and non-Catholics alike. And, it is understood as a universal right because, as Pietro Pavan notes, it is now understood as a *human* right, a right that has its foundation not in the content of an individual's religious convictions but "in the very nature of man."[6] It is a right limited, moreover, not by the far-reaching demands of the common good, but by the considerably more modest demands of public order.

If *DH* effected a dramatic transformation in the Church's teaching on the subject of religious liberty, it also represented a pivotal step in the broader development of Catholic social teaching that George Weigel has aptly called "the Catholic human rights revolution," namely, "the transformation of the Roman Catholic Church from a bastion of the *ancien régime* into perhaps the world's foremost institutional defender of human rights."[7] It is no secret that the Church greeted the rise of modern democracy with a mixture of suspicion and hostility. In large measure, the source of this hostility was to be found in the ideologies with which democracy was associated on the European continent in the 19th and early 20th centuries.

Carried to their logical conclusion (as they frequently were in the Europe of that era), the philosophical and theological premises informing what is sometimes called Enlightenment Liberalism issued in a thoroughgoing naturalism and radical individualism. Not only were these premises incompatible with Catholicism, but in practice they required the establishment of a radically monistic society informed by a secularist ethos, and from whose public life the Church—in the name of religious freedom, and separation of church and state—was systematically excluded.[8] Confronted with the rise of democracy so conceived, the Church responded by entering into a fateful alliance with the *ancien régime*, an alliance that was more than ironic given that this regime was the linear descendent of the absolutist state that had emerged from the ruins of the medieval world, and which had long been the Church's adversary.

In the period running from the pontificate of Leo XIII through the Second Vatican Council, however, Catholic social thought underwent an extensive renewal. Two historical experiences played a critically important role in stimulating this development. The first was the shattering impact of totalitarianism. The effect was a newfound consciousness of the value and dignity of the human person, and a new exploration of this venerable theme in Christian anthropology. The second was the American democratic experiment whose unfolding prompted a gradual recognition that the institutions and practices of democratic government need not be projected from the premises of Enlightenment Liberalism, nor do they necessarily entail the construction of a social order that is secularist in character.

These experiences spurred the recovery of what is sometimes called the Catholic Whig tradition, namely, a tradition in medieval and early modern Catholic social thought committed to the freedom of the Church, the supremacy of law, constitutionally limited government, and the ruler's responsibility to the community. They also gave rise to an insistence on the dignity of the human person as the fundamental principle informing a rightly ordered society. In Pius XII's classic formulation, man "is the origin and end of human society."[9]

These intellectual developments found expression in 20th-century papal thought, which gradually embraced the idea of the "juridical" (or constitutional) state, a state whose principal function is "to safeguard the inviolable rights of the human person, and to facilitate the performance of his duties."[10] This was paralleled by a reappraisal of the merits of democratic government. "The democratic form of government," Pius XII noted approvingly, "appears to many a postulate of nature imposed by reason itself."[11] By the 1950s, Catholic teaching was moving rapidly toward the affirmation of what Paul Sigmund describes as "the moral superiority of democratic government and guarantees of human rights."[12]

WHAT EMERGES IN DIGNITATIS HUMANAE IS A DIFFERENT AND DRAMATICALLY BROADER UNDERSTANDING OF THE NATURE AND SCOPE OF RELIGIOUS LIBERTY

This development crystallized in the teaching of the Second Vatican Council, and, in particular, in the Declaration which, as Weigel notes, constitutes nothing less than "the manifesto of the Catholic human rights revolution."[13] For *DH*, he writes, "the right of religious freedom is the juridical expression of the pre-political fact that there is a *sanctum sanctorum* within every person wherein coercive power ... may not tread." The state therefore "is not omnicompetent," and the recognition of this fact through the effective institutionalization of the "prepolitical human right" proclaimed by *DH* is the essential precondition of "a just *polis*"—that is, a polity "structured in accordance with the inherent dignity of the persons who are its citizens."[14]

This commitment to sharp limitations on the scope of government is reinforced by *DH*'s insistence on the communal dimensions of religious liberty. Implicit in this insistence is a "distinction between society and state"; an affirmation of the "ontological priority of social institutions ... over [the] institutions of government"[15]; and an insistence that the state is limited by the character of its functions relative to the overall economy of social life, and thus by the responsibilities of the various institutions and groups with which it shares the stage of social life.

And, if *DH* doesn't explicitly mention the subject, its affirmation of the primacy of society over the state combines with its teachings on the dignity of the human person to point toward what another Conciliar document terms the right of all citizens "to participate freely and actively in ... governing the state ... and choosing [political] leaders."[16] Implicit in the Declaration's theory of politics, as Paul Sigmund writes, is a commitment to constitutional democracy as the form of government "most in keeping with the nature of man, and with Christian values."[17]

A Distinctive Idea of Freedom

To fully grasp the importance of *DH*, it is necessary to appreciate that it articulates distinctive understandings of religious freedom and democracy, understandings with profound implications for the quest for freedom that is sweeping the contemporary world. As Robert P. George has pointed out, religious freedom can be defended on various grounds.[18] Different justifications of religious liberty, in turn, issue in different conceptions of its nature and scope as well as different understandings of its implications for government's posture toward religion and the proper role of religion in public life. Democracy, moreover, is no more a univocal concept than is religious liberty. In fact, there are a number of different models of democracy rooted in divergent understandings of politics, and animated by disparate understandings of human nature, the human good, and the structure of social relations that should govern human life. Although broadly similar in their institutional frameworks, the democratic regimes engendered by these competing theories will differ markedly in spirit and substance.

The significance of the contemporary quest for freedom, therefore, will ultimately depend on how religious liberty and democracy are understood, on which conception of religious liberty and which model of democracy come to animate it. Tragically, recent decades have witnessed the ascendancy of understandings of these concepts that are both flawed and profoundly destructive of the very values they celebrate. What are now the dominant theories of religious liberty frequently reflect a religious skepticism, subjectivism, or indifferentism that make it hard to take religion and the religious commitments of believers seriously. In Michael Sandel's apt formulation, they understand such commitments as matters of choice rather than of conscience.[19] At the same time, they tend to conceptualize this right in a highly individualistic manner that gives short-shrift to the social and communal dimensions of religious belief and practice, and thus to religious liberty's social and communal dimensions.

> THE SIGNIFICANCE OF THE CONTEMPORARY QUEST FOR FREEDOM WILL ULTIMATELY DEPEND ON HOW RELIGIOUS LIBERTY AND DEMOCRACY ARE UNDERSTOOD

Indeed, they culminate in the demand for what is sometimes called the privatization of religion. They culminate, this is to say, in the prohibition of governmental policies which, in the words of one of the Supreme Court's landmark church-state opinions, "aid one religion, aid all religions, or prefer one religion over another"[20]; and the systematic exclusion of religion and religiously-grounded moral beliefs from public life. They lead to the establishment of what Richard John Neuhaus has termed "the naked public square."[21]

DH points up a conceptually sophisticated alternative to these theories, a better, richer conception of religious liberty. It offers us a theory of religious liberty untainted by religious subjectivism, agnosticism, and indifferentism, a theory which takes its bearings from the idea that religious truth is both attainable and of overriding importance. It begins, as Francis Canavan notes, with the idea of "a universal human nature, whose natural tendencies and needs are knowable to the human mind" and "the existence of God, who is truth, and the truth about whom answers the deepest needs of human nature."[22] A right to religious liberty exists, the Declaration affirms, not because religious truth is unattainable or unimportant but because this truth itself—as it "is known through the revealed Word of God and by reason itself" (2)—demands the recognition of such a right.

At the same time, *DH* articulates an understanding of religious freedom that appreciates not just the individual but also the social and communal dimensions of religious freedom. Inasmuch as "religious bodies are a requirement of the social nature both of man and of religion itself," the right to religious liberty extends not just to "persons as individuals" but to individuals acting "in community" (3). On the one hand, it understands religious freedom, in the words of two recent writers, as more than "a wholly negative freedom," but as "containing an element of positive liberty, that is, as requiring certain positive governmental actions that would make it possible for people to live out their religious faiths."[23] On the other hand, it insists that religious liberty encompasses the right of individuals and religious bodies to attempt "to show the special value" of their beliefs in the right ordering of human social life (4).

Today's dominant understandings of democratic government are equally problematic. At the heart of these understandings is a vision of human beings as essentially sovereign wills, free and independent "selves" unbound by moral ties antecedent to choice. These assumptions are not only philosophically flawed but profoundly destructive of the intangible prerequisites of free government. This radical individualism subverts the very social and cultural preconditions on which a democratic society depends for its vitality.[24] The ascendancy of this vision of human nature and society in contemporary America's public philosophy is at least partially responsible for many of the malaises that beset the nation's body politic.

What *DH* points us toward is an alternative model of democratic government rooted in a richer vision of humanity and society, a model which, as Walter Kasper points out, accepts "some essential concerns of the political Enlightenment," while correcting and purifying the Enlightenment's understanding of human nature and freedom in the light of "the comprehensive vision of the Bible and the Christian tradition."[25] What Jacque Maritain calls "personalist democracy" (in contrast to the "individualist" models of democracy spawned by Enlightenment Liberalism) would not view human beings as radically autonomous self-creators, but as creatures—beings created by God who are obligated to make their lives and abilities serve purposes established by Him.[26] "True freedom," it insists in the words of the Declaration, realizes itself in striving "after what is true and right," fulfilling the demands of the moral order and being obedient to lawful authority (8).

While affirming the inviolable rights of the human person, it would refuse to follow Enlightenment Liberalism into the abyss of individualism and subjectivism. It insists instead that, in Canavan's words, "the teleology inherent in man's nature and supernatural destiny" supply criteria for distinguishing valid rights claims from spurious ones.[27] And, while affirming the transcendent dignity of the human person and the individual human person's status as the origin and end of all social institutions, it would also acknowledge our nature as intrinsically social beings, and conceptualize society not as a collection of discrete and insular individuals but as a community of communities. It would thus appreciate that human flourishing is inseparable from the flourishing of the groups and institutions which collectively compose civil society.

Conclusion

In 1987, John Paul II responded to a reporter's question by stating that although he "was the evangelizer of the Gospel" and not "of democracy," if "democracy means human rights it also belongs to the message of the Church."[28] This statement would have been unimaginable without the seminal redefinition of the Church's role in global politics brought about by *Dignitatis Humanae.* This Vatican II Declaration positions the Church as the patroness of human dignity and champion of religious liberty, human rights, and democracy.[29]

Simultaneously, however, the Declaration also positions the Church at the very heart of the contemporary debate—some might say "culture war"—over the meaning of the democratic revolution sweeping the world. For as patroness of human dignity, the Church must resist not only authoritarian and totalitarian regimes but the currents in thought and culture that threaten the quest for freedom from within. For this quest to be carried to a successful conclusion, it must be informed not by the false understandings of religious liberty and democracy that loom so large on the contemporary scene, but, as Murray wrote, by "the truth about man, his dignity, his duties and rights, his freedom and his obligations"[30] ❖

1. Paul VI, *Closing Speeches: Vatican Council II* (Boston: St. Paul Editions, n.d. [1965]), p. 25.
2. John Courtney Murray, "The Declaration on Religious Freedom" in *Bridging the Sacred and the Secular: Selected Writings of John Courtney Murray, S.J.*, ed. J. Leon Hooper, S.J. (Washington, DC: Georgetown University Press, 1994), p. 187.
3. Declaration on Religious Liberty [*Dignitatis Humanae*], in *The Documents of Vatican II*, ed. Walter M. Abbott, S.J. (New York: The Crossroad Publishing Co., 1989; reprint, New York: Guild Press, America Press, Association Press, 1966), section 2. This translation is by John Courtney Murray. Further citations of *Dignitatis Humanae* will be given parenthetically by section number.
4. For the pre-Conciliar teaching and its presuppositions see John A. Ryan and Moorhouse F.X. Millar, S.J., *The State and the Church* (New York: The MacMillan Co., 1922), pp. 26-61, and John Courtney Murray, "The Problem of Religious Freedom," in *Religious Liberty: Catholic Struggles with Pluralism*, ed. J. Leon Hooper (Louisville, Kentucky: Westminster/John Knox Press, 1995), pp. 128-197. Murray, of course, was the leading critic of this understanding of religious liberty.
5. Murray, *The Problem of Religious Liberty*, p. 160, 145.
6. Pietro Pavan, "Declaration on Religious Liberty," in *Commentary on the Documents of Vatican II*, vol. IV, ed. Herbert Vorgrimler (New York: Herder & Herder, 1969), p. 65.
7. *Freedom and Its Discontents: Catholicism Confronts Modernity* (Washington, DC: Ethics & Public Policy Center, 1991), p. 25.
8. For in-depth discussions of this ideology and the model of democracy it inspired, see John Courtney Murray, "The Church and Totalitarian Democracy," *Theological Studies* 13 (December 1953): 525-563; and "Leo XIII: Separation of Church and State," *Theological Studies* 14 (June 1953): 145-214.
9. Pius XII, "1944 Christmas Message" (Washington, DC: National Catholic Welfare Conference, n.d.), p. 3.
10. Pius XII, radio message, 1 June 1941, in *Acta Apostolicae Sedis* 33 (1941): 200.
11. Pius XII, "1944 Christmas Message," p. 4.
12. Paul Sigmund, "The Catholic Tradition and Modern Democracy," in *Religion and Politics in the American Milieu*, ed. Leslie Green (Notre Dame, IN: *The Review of Politics* and Office of Policy Studies, n.d.), p. 20.
13. *Catholicism and the Renewal of American Democracy* (New York: Paulist Press, 1989), p. 83.
14. *Freedom and Its Discontents*, pp. 39-40, 11.
15. Ibid., p. 40.
16. The Constitution on the Church in the Modern World [*Gaudium et Spes*], in *The Documents of Vatican II*, section 75.
17. Sigmund, "The Catholic Tradition and Modern Democracy," p. 13.
18. *Making Men Moral: Civil Liberties and Public Morality* (Oxford: Oxford University Press, 1993), p. 219.
19. See Michael J. Sandel, "Freedom of Conscience or Freedom of Choice?" in *Articles of Faith, Articles of Peace: The Religious Liberty Clauses and the American Public Philosophy*, ed. James Davison Hunter and Os Guinness (Washington, DC: The Brookings Institution, 1990), pp. 54-73.
20. Everson v. Board of Education, 330 U.S. 1, 15-16 (1947).
21. See Richard John Neuhaus, *The Naked Public Square: Religion and Democracy in America* (Grand Rapids, MI: William B. Eerdmans Publishing Co., 1984).
22. "The Catholic Concept of Religious Freedom as a Human Right," in *Religious Liberty: An End and a Beginning*, ed. John Courtney Murray, S.J. (New York: The MacMillan Co., 1966), p. 71.
23. Stephen V. Monsma and J. Christopher Soper, *The Challenge of Pluralism: Religious Freedom in Five Democracies* (Lanham, MD: Rowman & Littlefield, 1977), p. 8.
24. On this vision of the person and its impact on contemporary America, see Michael J. Sandel, *Democracy's Discontent* (Cambridge, MA: The Belknap Press of Harvard University, 1996).
25. *The Christian Understanding of Freedom and the History of Freedom in the Modern Era* (Milwaukee, WI: Marquette University Press, 1988), p. 2, 18.
26. *Scholasticism and Politics* (New York: The MacMillan Co., 1940), pp. 70-88.
27. "The Image of Man in Catholic Thought," in *Catholicism, Liberalism and Communitarianism*, ed. Kenneth L. Grasso, Gerard V. Bradley, and Robert P. Hunt (Lanham, MD: Rowman & Littlefield, 1995), p. 20.
28. *New York Times*, 6 April 1987.
29. For some suggestions as to the Church's role in the democratic revolution that has swept the globe, see Samuel Huntington, *The Third Wave Democratization in the Late Twentieth Century* (Norman, OK: University of Oklahoma Press, 1993).
30. Murray, *The Problem of Religious Freedom*, p. 176.

ROMAN CATHOLICISM AND THE FAITH-BASED MOVEMENT FOR GLOBAL HUMAN RIGHTS

By Allen D. Hertzke

Beginning in the mid 1990s a new movement burst unexpectedly onto the international stage—a faith-based quest devoted to advancing human rights through the machinery of American foreign policy. This movement of unlikely allies passed a series of landmark congressional initiatives on international religious freedom, trafficking of women and children, atrocities in North Korea, and genocide in Sudan.

In 2005 movement leaders set their sights on an even more ambitious goal: legislation aimed at implementing comprehensive long-term strategies for ending dictatorships around the world. If true to form, this legislation will pass at the end of the 109th Congress, in 2006, rounding out a decade of lobbying achievements. This movement is filling a void in human rights advocacy, raising issues previously slighted—or insufficiently pressed—by secular groups, the foreign policy establishment, and the prestige press.

The catalyst for this movement was the campaign against global religious persecution, which united a broad spectrum of religious groups and resulted in the passage of the International Religious Freedom Act of 1998 (IRFA). Facing fierce opposition from the business community, the Clinton Administration, and foreign policy "realists", the legislation was given up for dead on more than one occasion. Its "miraculous" passage propelled the heady new religious alliance to attack other human rights abuses.

The Catholic Church was central in IRFA's passage, both in preparing the groundwork (long before the specific campaign) and providing pivotal lobbying resources during the legislative battle. Without understanding the Catholic Church's commitment to religious freedom, as articulated in the Vatican II declaration on religious liberty *Dignitatis Humanae*, we cannot appreciate how the religious community succeeded in erecting a new human rights architecture in American foreign policy.

From Resistance to Embrace

Central to the transformation of the Catholic Church's posture toward the world in the last century has been the concept of the dignity of the human person made in the image and likeness of God. This idea, found in Pope Leo XIII's 1891 encyclical *Rerum Novarum* (which inaugurated modern Catholic social teaching), crystallized the

Catholic Church's voice on social justice, and provided the rationale for its ultimate embrace of democracy. Thus even before Vatican II, the Church was turning away from its earlier rejection of democratic governance. And like a great ocean liner that turns slowly but with enormous force in its new direction, the Catholic Church became a powerful engine of democratization in the last quarter of the 20th century—promoting human rights and undermining the legitimacy of authoritarian regimes. As Samuel Huntington has documented, the third great wave of global democratization that began in 1975 in Iberia and continued through the collapse of communism in Eastern Europe was almost entirely a Catholic phenomenon.[1] From Latin America to the Philippines to Poland the Church played an active role in fostering human rights and democratic dissent.

LIKE A GREAT OCEAN LINER THAT TURNS SLOWLY BUT WITH ENORMOUS FORCE IN ITS NEW DIRECTION, THE CHURCH BECAME A POWERFUL ENGINE OF DEMOCRATIZATION

Promotion of religious freedom was inextricably tied to this role, but in this case the Church's break from the past was more abrupt. As late as the 1950s the Church's official position was that since "error has no rights," Catholicism, as the true faith, should alone be sanctioned by the state. And the Church enforced that view on its priests and theologians. As Garry Wills recounts in painful detail, John Courtney Murray—who helped articulate the grounds for *Dignitatis Humanae* and served as a consultant in its drafting at Vatican II—was in the 1950s reproached, censored, and in some cases silenced as he sought to make the case for religious freedom, along with alternative forms of church-state relations and ecumenical understanding. He was even "dis-invited" to the first session of Vatican II. But with a Catholic in the White House it became untenable for the Church to resist beckoning the most celebrated American Catholic theologian to the historic meeting, and in the second session Murray creatively helped refashion Catholic teaching.[2]

But that is not the whole story, of course. Allied with Murray was one Bishop Wojtyla of Poland, whose experience defending the faith amidst the tyrannies of Nazism and Communism forged a fierce commitment to free churches as bulwarks of civil society and resistance to oppression. As one of the principal drafters of *Dignitatis Humanae*, the future Pope linked human dignity and conscience to the right of peoples to form churches and practice their faith free of government coercion.[3]

The election to the papacy of John Paul II was thus of momentous significance to our story, as the Pontiff literally became the globe's most visible promoter of religious freedom. Indeed, John Paul II placed religious freedom at the center of his vigorous defense of human rights. In a widely-cited speech before the Vatican diplomatic corps in 1996, the same year religious activists in the U.S. began mobilizing for congressional legislation, he sounded the clarion call against communist and militant Islamic regimes that "practice discrimination against Jews, Christians, and other religious groups, going even so far as to refuse them the right to meet in private for prayer." Placing such maltreatment in context, the Pope declared that "this is an intolerable and unjustifiable violation not only of all the norms of current international law, but of the most fundamental human freedom, that of practicing one's faith openly, which for human beings is their reason for living."[4] The Pope took action himself where possible, as when he named bishops for the Chinese church operating underground and in opposition to the state-sanctioned body.

The Pope also championed ecumenical efforts to document modern martyrdom in his eloquent apostolic letter, *Toward the Third Millennium* (*Tertio Millennio Adveniente*). There he noted that on the eve of the next millennium "the church has once again become a Church of martyrs," now a "common inheritance of Catholics, Orthodox, Anglicans, and Protestants." Many of these martyrs, he lamented, are "unknown soldiers" in God's cause. As much as possible, "their witness should not be lost to the Church." Local churches, therefore, "should do everything possible to ensure that the memory of those who have suffered martyrdom should be safeguarded, gathering the necessary documentation, a gesture that "cannot fail to have an ecumenical character and expression." Though he argued that this would serve as the same kind of faith inspiration as the "martyrologium" of the first centuries, John Paul's call for documentation dovetailed with strategies of human rights advocates to shine the light on abuses.[5] By placing the powerful imprimatur of the Catholic Church on the side of the cause of religious freedom, the Pope helped invite activism by his priests and bishops and smoothed their ecumenical alliances.

The fact that the United States came to embrace religious freedom as a foreign policy aim seemed to bring the issue full circle, a fact not lost on the aging pontiff when he met with President George W. Bush in 2001. Unfortunately, when the head of the globe's largest religious institution met with the leader of its superpower on July 23, 2001, their discussion of religious freedom got submerged in the media's focus on the stem cell research controversy. But in fact the Pope had thanked the president for the nation's lead in making religious freedom a key foreign policy goal: "It is significant that the promotion of religious freedom continues to be an important goal of American foreign policy in the international community. I gladly express the appreciation of the whole Catholic Church for America's commitment in this regard."[6]

The Campaign for Congressional Legislation

With the Pope preparing the way, American Catholic veterans of human rights struggles—both leading bishops and staff at the U.S. Catholic Conference—became pivotal players in the faith-based alliance in the 1990s that pressed for religious freedom legislation.

As one of the most sweeping human rights statutes on the books, IRFA is drawing increasing attention from foreign capitals and embassies.[7] It designates an office at the State Department and an Ambassador-At-Large for International Religious Freedom. It mandates that State produce a comprehensive annual report on the status of religious freedom in every country around the world, which can set into motion presidential actions against violating nations. The law also authorizes an independent commission, with staff and budget, to recommend policies, monitor violations, and hold policy makers accountable for their response. Finally, it reaches into the daily routines of foreign policy by providing better training for diplomatic personnel and fostering their ongoing contacts with vulnerable religious communities on the ground.

But beyond its specific provisions, the law embodies the growing nexus of global church communities and American advocacy. In the ecology of human rights, the struggle for the International Religious Freedom Act shaped the environment for future initiatives. *Without IRFA, no Sudan Peace Act; without the religious advocacy coalition, no human trafficking law.* The religious freedom campaign thus represents a kind of liminal moment in the politics of human rights.[8]

Viewed as something of a miracle by partisans, the legislation was the product of an intense and sometimes bitter lobby campaign. Not only were corporate lobbyists opposed to legislation that might upset business arrangements with foreign countries, but religious partisans themselves were divided over how best the American government could respond to persecution around the world. Some religious leaders sought tough and visible action against persecuting countries; others wanted to employ the quiet routines of diplomacy. Those calling for tough action were comfortable with vigorous (even unilateral) America leadership; those stressing quiet diplomacy tended to favor multilateral approaches. In all the twists and turns of the legislative process this divide was manifest. It endures as a key feature of the continuing struggle over how America will respond to human rights abuses.

These competing visions often did not correspond to the conventional ideological categories of liberal versus conservative. Indeed, the 1998 struggle over which approach to take often involved *different camps of evangelicals* and their religious allies, unfortunately complete with recrimination and claims of bad faith. When we view these events from a greater distance—when we "get up on the balcony" and look down—we can see that this collective struggle produced legislation that blended aspects of both visions, encompassing the diversity of the American religious landscape.

The Catholic Response

In the midst of this unusual struggle to define America's response to religious oppression, Catholic leaders were positioned to play a unique role. In part this involved bringing the insights of *Dignitatis Humanae* into the debate. In 1996 testimony before Congress, Cardinal McCarrick of Washington, DC echoed the Pope's view that religious liberty is the "first freedom" because it is rooted in the God-given dignity of the human person's free will and conscience. Because of this understanding, McCarrick noted how the Church not only spoke out on behalf of Catholics, but challenged persecution against Jews in the Soviet Union, Buddhists in Vietnam, Muslims in Bosnia, evangelicals in China, and adherents of traditional African faiths in Sudan.[9]

The Catholic presence also came from such prominent human rights pioneers as Nina Shea, Director of the Center for Religious Freedom at Freedom House in Washington, DC, whose story is instructive. A human rights lawyer, she took up the cause of religious persecution when she noticed that it was slighted by the major international rights groups. For over a decade she was a lonely public voice, sometimes even shunned by supposed champions of human rights on the Left.

A cradle Catholic, Shea attended parochial schools through high school, to which she attributes a sensitivity to religious freedom and human rights issues. After receiving her law degree in 1979, Shea worked for the International League for Human Rights, a global counterpart to the American Civil Liberties Union. As program director for the International League, Shea became involved in work documenting the atrocities of right-wing death squads during the civil war in El Salvador in the early 1980s. Well connected to liberal networks and human rights organizations, Shea found herself writing op-ed pieces in the *New York Times*, getting invited to give guest lectures at Harvard, and the like.[10]

That all changed when she turned her attention to abuses committed by the Marxist Sandinista government of Nicaragua, which led to condemnation of her in left-wing circles. Moreover, she discovered that concerns about religious oppression received short shrift from secular human rights groups. This experience of double standards and secular blinders motivated Shea to form a Catholic lay human rights organization devoted to religious freedom "for all creeds in all parts of the world." She ultimately merged this organization with Freedom House, the well established institute founded on the eve of the Second World War by Wendell Wilkie and Eleanor Roosevelt to promote human rights and democracy. Under the auspices of Freedom House, Shea has carved a niche for herself as a key hub of religious freedom advocacy. Her Center for Religious Freedom co-sponsored the seminal 1996 conference in Washington, DC of evangelical, Jewish, and Catholic leaders announcing their call for American action against persecution, and she remains an ongoing participant in the implementation of IRFA as a member of the U.S. Commission on International Religious Freedom.

While the initial grass roots energy for the anti-persecution campaign came from the evangelical world—spurred on by the entrepreneurial efforts of others[11] —everyone knew that official Catholic endorsement was vital. Thus lobbyists for the U.S. Catholic Conference were key players in the legislative campaign, both because of the Church's record of defending human rights and its strategic position in American politics.

Not only is the Roman Catholic Church the largest religious institution in the nation with vast international connections, but its faithful are key swing voters. At the time of the campaign Catholic Conference lobbyists and Bishops enjoyed access and strong credibility with key Democrats who would not have responded to a "Christian Right" campaign. The Catholic Church is also a large and complex organization that moves slowly and deliberately, thus its official endorsement provided a certain cache and credibility.

One advantage enjoyed by Catholic lobbyists was the long involvement of Catholic officials in international human rights and religious freedom work in Latin America, Eastern Europe, and elsewhere. Lobbyists for the Bishops have long felt that U.S. foreign policy neglected religious freedom. Thus they were immediately inclined to back legislation once certain concerns of theirs were addressed. When the U.S. Bishops Conference did endorse the House version of the legislation, as announced at the lobby kick-off meeting in February of 1998, critics had a harder time impugning the Act as a sop to the Christian Right. Because of its international connections, moreover, the Church "knew something," had useful information to present about the problem, and thus its concerns about religious persecution were hard to ignore.

ONE ADVANTAGE ENJOYED BY CATHOLIC LOBBYISTS WAS THE LONG INVOLVEMENT OF CATHOLIC OFFICIALS IN INTERNATIONAL HUMAN RIGHTS

A final role played by Catholic lobbyists was helping mediate among the religious partisans who often clashed rancorously over which approach to take in addressing the denial of religious rights. John Carr, the Church's Secretary for Social Development and World Peace, focused on "the people whose lives and rights are at risk" and remonstrated with the other partisans to get "beyond the personalities," to avoid imputations of bad will.[12]

Taken together, these diverse factors ensured a potent Catholic role in the new architecture for global human rights. Indeed, it is probably not an exaggeration to say, as one Catholic lobbyist did, that without Catholic Church backing religious freedom legislation was doomed.

Implementation and Beyond

> It shall be the policy of the United States ... to condemn violations of religious freedom, and to promote, and to assist other governments in the promotion of, the fundamental right to freedom of religion.
>
> –IRFA[13]

The architecture built by IRFA has enhanced human rights attention in American foreign policy. A new State Department Office of International Religious Freedom, a unique Ambassador-at-Large position, a vast annual reporting enterprise on the status of religious freedom around the world, and an external watchdog entity (The U.S. Commission on International Religious Freedom) not only highlight violations of religious freedom and propose remedies but promote human rights more generally.

The Catholic presence in this enterprise has been manifest both in the State Department and in the U.S. Commission. For example, of the nine members on the Commission serving through 2006, three are prominent Catholics: Nina Shea; Reverend Ricardo Ramirez, Bishop of Las Cruces, New Mexico; and Reverend Charles Chaput, Archbishop of Denver. In addition, past commissioners have included Theodore Cardinal McCarrick, Archbishop of Washington, DC (and member of the College of Cardinals), and Reverend William Francis Murphy, Bishop of Rockville Center, New York.

But perhaps the most intriguing Catholic influence came from the first director of the

State Department Office of International Religious Freedom, Tom Farr, who served from 1999 until his retirement in 2005. A veteran State Department official and Roman Catholic, Farr was committed to the issue even before the legislation passed. Drawing inspiration from Catholic social teaching, Farr staffed the work of Ambassadors Robert Seiple and John Hanford. Part of his vision was to make religious concerns "part of the wallpaper" of Foggy Bottom,[14] but along the way he helped produce uncharacteristically eloquent pleas from the "stodgy" State Department to defend "God-given" religious freedom.

Though such pronouncements drew upon the American experience, there was an unmistakable Catholic resonance as well. The introduction to the 2001 State Department report, for example, asserted that the "inviolable and universal dignity of the human person" is "at the core of U.S. human rights policy abroad, including the policy of advocating religious freedom."[15] That an official U.S. document articulated *Dignitatis Humanae*—the dignity of the human person as mandating the right to seek transcendent truth and ultimate purpose—suggests the extent to which Catholic social teaching can inform America's evolving human rights posture. ❖

---

1. Samuel Huntington, *Third Wave: Democratization in the Late Twentieth Century* (Norman: University of Oklahoma Press, 1991).
2. Garry Wills, *Why I Am a Catholic* (Boston: Houghton Mifflin, 2002), 214-221.
3. George Weigel, *Witness to Hope: The Biography of John Paul II* (New York: Harper Perennial, 2001).
4. Pope John Paul II, Annual Address to Diplomatic Corps, January 13, 1996, Vatican Information Service.
5. Pope John Paul II, "Tertio Millennio Adveniente: Toward the Third Millennium," Apostolic Letter, November 10, 1994.
6. Speech of Pope John Paul II, July 23, 2001.
7. For a good overview see T. Jeremy Gunn, "A Preliminary Response to Criticisms of the International Religious Freedom Act of 1998," *Brigham Young University Law Review*, September 2000: 841-866. For an example of the criticism see Peter Danchin, "U.S. Unilateralism and the International Protection of Religious Freedom: The Multilateral Alternative," *Columbia Journal of Transnational Law* 41, 2002.
8. Liminal is variously defined as the "threshold of a physiological or psychological response," or a subtle membrane separating states, or a threshold. *American Heritage College Dictionary* (Boston: Houghton, 1997). Because the 1998 legislation marked the threshold of a new era in human rights advocacy, but one barely discerned at the time, it represents a kind of liminal moment. Subsequent initiatives on Sudan, human trafficking, and North Korea especially show this.
9. Testimony of then Archbishop of Newark, Theodore E. McCarrick, before the Subcommittee on International Operations and Human Rights of the Committee on International Relations, U.S. House of Representatives, February 15, 1996, "Persecution of Christians Worldwide."
10. A good summary of her story is by Sheryl Henderson Blunt, "The Daniel of Religious Rights," *Christianity Today*, September 2005. Other material from this section comes from personal interviews.
11. I devote Chapter 5 of *Freeing God's Children* to the special role of Michael Horowitz in spurring the evangelical elite to action on religious persecution.
12. John Carr, Interview by Allen Hertzke.
13. International Religious Freedom Act, Public Law 105-292, 22 USC 6401, signed into law October 27, 1998.
14. Tom Farr, Interview by Allen Hertzke.
15. U.S. Department of State, *Annual Report on International Religious Freedom 2001* (Washington, DC: GPO, Dec. 2001), Introduction. As the Director of the Office, Tom Farr was responsible for assembling the nation reports and helping draft the introduction. I strongly suspect that the Catholic language can be traced to his influence.

POPE JOHN PAUL II AND THE DYNAMICS OF HISTORY[1]

By George Weigel

We are here this afternoon to discuss the international impact of a man who is neither a politician, a diplomat, or an international relations theorist, but rather a pastor, an evangelist, and a witness to basic human rights. Yet it is also appropriate that we explore "the Pope's divisions" under the auspices of the Foreign Policy Research Institute, for this institution has always understood that ideas have consequences in history, for good and for ill.

Pope John Paul II has had a considerable impact on contemporary history. Yet one may well wonder whether those who think about international relations, professionally or as an avocation, have begun to come to grips intellectually with the meaning of John Paul's international accomplishment—or what that accomplishment suggests about the contours of world politics in the 21st century.

So my plan here is to sketch, briefly, the Pope's accomplishment as I have come to understand it as his biographer, using three examples; then I shall indicate, again briefly, some lessons from this accomplishment for the future; and finally, I shall suggest where the new intellectual terrain lies for those interested in ethics and international relations.

I.

To understand John Paul II's concept of the dynamics of international relations, indeed, the dynamics of history itself, requires us to go back to the small Polish town of Wadowice, c. 1928. There, a young Polish boy named Karol Wojtyla learned the great lesson of modern Polish history: that it was through its culture—its language, it literature, its religion—that Poland the nation survived when Poland the state was erased for 123 years from the map of Europe. History viewed from the Vistula River basin looks different; it has a tangible spiritual dimension. Looking at history from that distinctive angle-of-vision teaches the observant that overwhelming material force can be resisted successfully through the resources of the human spirit—through culture—and that culture is the most dynamic, enduring factor in human affairs, at least over the long haul.

Karol Wojtyla, whom the world would later know as Pope John Paul II, applied this lesson of the priority of culture in history in resistance to the two great totalitarian powers that sought to subjugate Poland between 1939 and 1989.

He applied it to a variety of resistance activities against the draconian Nazi Occupation of Poland from 1939 until 1945. If the Nazi strategy to erase these Polish-Slavic untermenschen from the European New Order began with an attempt to decapitate Polish society by liquidating it cultural leadership, then one effective means of resistance was to keep Polish culture alive—and this Wojtyla tried to do, at the daily risk of his life, by his participation in a host of cultural resistance groups: the underground Jagiellonian University, clandestine literary, theatrical, and religious activities, a pioneering movement of civil renewal called UNIA.

> BY RESTORING TO THE POLISH PEOPLE THEIR AUTHENTIC HISTORY AND CULTURE, JOHN PAUL CREATED A REVOLUTION OF CONSCIENCE THAT PRODUCED THE NONVIOLENT SOLIDARITY RESISTANCE MOVEMENT

As a priest and bishop in Krakow, he applied a similar "culture-first" strategy to resistance against the communist effort to rewrite Poland's history and redefine Poland's culture. Wojtyla had no direct "political" involvement between 1948 and 1978; he couldn't have cared less about the internal politics of the Polish communist party. But his efforts to nurture an informed, intelligent Catholic laity were examples of what a later generation would call "building civil society"—and thus laying the groundwork for an active resistance movement with political traction.

Pope John Paul II has applied this strategy of culturally driven change on a global stage since his election on October 16, 1978.

John Paul's role in the collapse of European communism is now generally recognized, but it does not seem well understood. He was not, pace Tad Szulc, a wily diplomat skillfully negotiating a transition beyond one-party rule in Poland. He was not, pace Carl Bernstein and Marco Politi, a co-conspirator with Ronald Reagan in a "holy alliance" to effect communism's demise. He was not, pace the late Jonathan Kwitny, a Gandhi in a white cassock, running a non-violent resistance movement in Poland through a clandestine messenger service from the Vatican. Rather, John Paul shaped the politics of east central Europe in the 1980s as a pastor, evangelist, and witness to basic human rights.

Primary-source evidence for this is found in the texts of the Pope's epic June 1979 pilgrimage to his homeland, nine days on which the history of the 20th century pivoted. In those forty-some sermons, addresses, lectures, and impromptu remarks, the Pope told his fellow-countrymen, in so many words: "You are not who they say you are. Let me remind you who you are." By restoring to the Polish people their authentic history and culture, John Paul created a revolution of conscience that, fourteen months later, produced the nonviolent Solidarity resistance movement, a unique hybrid of workers and intellectuals—a "forest planed by aroused consciences," as the Pope's friend, the philosopher Jozef Tischner once put it. And by restoring to his people a form of freedom and a fearlessness that communism could not reach, John Paul II set in motion the human dynamics that eventually led, over a decade, to what we know as the Revolution of 1989.

June 1979 was not only a moment of catharsis for a people long frustrated by their inability to express the truth about themselves publicly. It was also a moment in which convictions were crystallized, to the point where the mute acquiescence that, as Vaclav Havel wrote, made continuing communist rule possible was shattered. Moreover, it was not simply that, as French historian Alain Besancon nicely put it, "people regained the private ownership of their tongues" during the Solidarity revolution. It was what those tongues said—their new willingness to defy what Havel called the communist "culture of the lie"—that made the crucial difference.

To be sure, there were other factors in creating the Revolution of 1989: the policies of Ronald Reagan and Margaret Thatcher; Mikhail Gorbachev; the Helsinki Final Act and its effects throughout Europe. But if we ask why communism collapsed when it did—in 1989 rather than 1999 or 2009 or 2019—and how it did, then sufficient account has to be taken of June 1979. This is a point stressed by local witnesses: when I first began to research this question in 1990, Poles, Czechs, and Slovaks, religious and secular alike, were unanimous in their testimony about the crucial impact of June 1979. That, they insisted, was when "1989" started.

(Parenthetically, it's worth noting that the West largely missed this. Thus the *New York Times* editorial of June 5, 1979: "As much as the visit of Pope John Paul II to Poland must reinvigorate and reinspire the Roman Catholic Church in Poland, it does not threaten the political order of the nation or of Eastern Europe." But two other Slavic readers of the signs of the times were not at all confused: Aleksandr Solzhenitsyn and Yuri Andropov both knew that the rise of John Paul II and the deployment of his "culture- first" strategy of social change was a profound threat to the Soviet order.)

John Paul applied a similar strategy to a quite different situation when he went to Chile in 1987. Fourteen years of the Pinochet government, following the crisis of the Allende regime, had created deep divisions in Chilean society. There were raw wounds in the body politic because of human rights abuses and the recalcitrance of the Left; there was, in a phrase, no "civil society," and that lack made a democratic transition impossible.

Therefore, John Paul, in collaboration with the Chilean bishops, decided that the public purpose of his 1987 pilgrimage to Chile would be to help reconstitute civil society through a reclamation of Chile's Christian culture. The great theme for the visit would be that "Chile's vocation is for understanding, not confrontation." The papal pilgrimage would, as one of its organizers put it to me, "take back the streets," which had been places of fear under Allende and Pinochet, and transform them, once again, into places of community. And people would be deliberately mixed together at the venues for the papal Masses: Chileans would be compelled, under the eye of their common religious "father," to look at each other, once again, as persons rather than ideological objects. And it seems no accident that, some eighteen months after the papal visit had accelerated the process of reconstructing Chilean civil society, a national plebiscite voted to move beyond military rule and restore democracy.

Finally, the Pope deployed a similar strategy in Cuba in January 1998. He did not mention the current Cuban regime once in five days. Rather, he re-read Cuban history through the lens of a Christianity that had formed a distinctively Cuban people from native peoples, Spaniards, and black African slaves, and he re-read the Cuban national liberation struggle of the 19th century through the prism of its Christian inspiration. Here, as in Poland in 1979, the Pope was restoring to a people its authentic history and culture. In doing so, he was also calling for a reinsertion of Cuba into history and into the hemisphere, asking the Cuban people to stop thinking of themselves as victims (the theme of Fidel Castro's welcoming address), and start thinking of themselves as the protagonists of their own destiny.

II.

Several lessons can be drawn from this analysis. First, the experience of John Paul II suggests that "civil society" is not simply institutional: a free press, free trade unions, free business organizations, free associations, etc. "Civil society" has an essential moral core.

Secondly, John Paul's strategy reminds us that "power" cannot be measured solely in terms of aggregates of military or economic capability. The "power of the powerless" is a real form of power.

In the third place, the Pope's impact demonstrates that non-state actors count in contemporary world politics, and sometimes in decisive ways. John Paul II did not shape the history of our times as the sovereign of the Vatican City micro-state, but as the Bishop of Rome and the universal pastor of the Catholic Church.

III.

Still, the present pontificate has left some gaps in our understanding that urgently need filling in the years just ahead. It is curious that this son of a soldier, who has expressed his respect for the military vocation on many occasions, has not developed the Church's just war doctrine. This was most evident during the Gulf War, but beyond such relatively conventional conflicts, there are new issues today at the intersection of ethics and world politics—the problem of outlaw states, the morality of preemption in the face of weapons of mass destruction, the locus of "legitimate authority" in the international community—that the Pope has simply not addressed, and others must.

The same can be said for "humanitarian intervention," which the Pope identified as a "moral duty" at the FAO in 1992. But this "duty" was not defined. On whom does it fall, and why? By what means is it to be discharged? What about the claims of sovereignty? These are large questions that demand the most careful reflection.

DOES THE POPE'S SUCCESS SUGGEST THAT WE ARE MOVING INTO A PERIOD IN WHICH NATION-STATES ARE OF LESS CONSEQUENCE IN "WORLD AFFAIRS"?

IV.

John Paul II has been the most politically consequential pope in centuries. But his impact did not come through the normal modalities of politics. He had no army. His success did not, in the main, come through the normal instruments of diplomacy. In terms of the history of ideas, his "culture-first" reading of history is a sharp challenge to the regnant notions that politics runs history, or economics runs history. Does the fact of the Pope's success suggest that we are moving into a period in which nation-states are of less consequence in "world affairs"? Or were the accomplishments I've outlined here idiosyncratic, the result of a singular personality meeting a unique set of circumstances with singular prescience and effect? There is much to chew on here, for students of international affairs, in the years immediately ahead. But that we have been living, in this pontificate, through the days of a giant seems clear enough. ❖

1. This essay is based on Dr. Weigel's Templeton Lecture on Religion and World Affairs, delivered on February 22, 2000 as part of a series sponsored by John M. Templeton, Jr., M.D. The essay was originally posted on the website of the Foreign Policy Research Institute (www.fpri.org/education/templetonlecture.html) and is re-published here by permission of FPRI.

CATHOLIC PEACEMAKING, 1991-2005: THE LEGACY OF POPE JOHN PAUL II[1]

By Drew Christiansen

If the fall of the Berlin wall in 1989 marked the end of the Cold War, already by 1991 it was clear the world had entered a new era in international affairs distinguished by ethnic and religious warfare, humanitarian intervention, and new demands on international organizations. But not only that. The year 1991 also marked the beginning of a period of novel departures in Vatican diplomacy, deepening and broadening prior trends in the Catholic Church's teaching on war and peace.

Of course, both before and after 1991 Pope John Paul II was busy making history in international affairs—tutoring the Solidarity labor movement, contributing to the liberation of his native Poland and the end of communism in Eastern Europe, precipitating the fall of dictators and colonial regimes in oppressed countries where he made pilgrimage, and utilizing interfaith prayer and dialogue as means to oppose outbreaks of religiously inspired violence and the notion of a "clash of civilizations."[2] But in 1991 Cardinal Agostino Cassaroli, the executor during the Cold War of Vatican *Ostpolitik*, retired.[3] Vatican foreign policy then fell under the direction of the Frenchman Archbishop Jean-Louis Tauran, who infused Vatican diplomacy with a new creative style, working closely with lay groups, like the Community of Sant'Egidio, and with bishops' conferences, like the U.S. Conference of Catholic Bishops (USCCB), to augment the Vatican's efforts.[4] Sant'Egidio is best known for its mediation leading to the end of civil war in Mozambique (1991), but was active in other troubled areas as well, including Kosovo and Algeria. USCCB was active in various conflicts in the former Yugoslavia, Guatemala, Haiti, Israel and Palestine, and Northern Ireland, and in campaigns against anti-personnel landmines and for international debt relief, among others. On these issues the conference worked with national episcopal conferences, nuncios (ambassadors) of the Holy See, and directly with the Vatican dicasteries (ministries).[5]

For the Holy See this period was a time of innovation in social teaching on international issues, too, with Pope John Paul II offering new teaching on themes like nonviolence and forgiveness in international politics and elaborating on some older ones like the priority of international law and the need for international institutions. The Church's teaching on war also evolved, promoting humanitarian intervention and opposing the use of the just war tradition to legitimate preventive war.[6]

In the wake of this dynamic period of change and the inauguration of a new papacy in 2005, the time is ripe to do some stock-taking and evaluation of Catholic approaches to peacemaking that were prominent in the period 1991-2005. I will propose that the three most significant aspects of official Catholic peacemaking in this period were: (1) the articulation of a positive Catholic conception of peace and the development of new teaching on conflict with an accent on nonviolence; (2) an increased emphasis on international law and international institutions; and (3) the use of interreligious dialogue to counter violence and religious conflict.

A "Convoy Concept" of Peace: From Just War to Justice and Nonviolence

Beginning with Pope John XXIII's landmark encyclical *Pacem in Terris* (1963), official Catholic teaching on peace has grown into a complex web of moral threads defining the positive dimensions of peace as more than "the absence of war."[7] For John XXIII, the substance of peace was the promotion, safeguarding, and defense of human rights; for Pope Paul VI it was socio-economic development, as in the famous dictum "If you want peace, work for justice" (*Populorum progressio*, 1968); and for John Paul II it was solidarity, understood as "the unswerving and persevering commitment to the common good" (*Sollicitudo rei socialis,* 1988), including both human rights and development.[8] In 1991, John Paul added nonviolence to this list, while continuing to promote development as an alternative to war (*Centesimus annus*), and finally in 2002, he added the element of forgiveness (World Day of Peace Message, "No Peace without Justice, No Justice without Forgiveness").

There are so many dimensions of this positive conception of peace that some may regard it as confused. I have found it helpful to say that the Catholic conception of peace is a "convoy concept," that is, a series of somewhat disparate but related requirements, like a series of ships in a convoy.[9] The image is helpful in that it indicates how different themes are parts of the one concept of peace. To be sure, these themes are not mutually exclusive, and conceptual boundaries do blur. In the field of socio-economic rights, for example, development overlaps with human rights. Still, while these goods are at times articulated in shifting, imprecise ways, by 2002 Catholic social teaching arrived at a rich, comprehensive, holistic conception of peace.

At the time of World War II, existing Catholic teaching approved of the just war doctrine as the exclusive basis of conscientious action in wartime. Since then Catholic teaching on war has evolved into a more complex view embracing both nonviolence and just war, placing both in the framework of a wider teaching on peace. Vatican II praised the witness of nonviolent resisters.[10] During the Cold War, John Paul II tutored and practiced nonviolence in confronting Poland's communist governments and their Soviet overlords. He later said, in his 1991 encyclical *Centesimus annus*, that he believed the lessons he learned then applied to international order. "May people learn to fight for justice without violence," he wrote, "renouncing class struggle in their internal disputes, and war in international ones[11].... Just as the time has finally come when in individual states a system of private vendetta and reprisal has given way to the rule of law, so too a similar step forward is now urgently needed in the international system."[12]

Some question the consistency of this more complex teaching, saying that these two streams of tradition, nonviolence and just war, are incompatible. But the root of both positions in Catholic thought is the obligation to resist grave injustice.[13] The obligation exists whether one employs nonviolent means or legitimately uses force. Thus, the Catholic understanding of peace necessarily entails a defense of justice, and rejects passivity in the face of grave public injustice. In addition, the avoidance of war entails not just the prevention of conflict but alleviation of the conditions that lead to conflict. In his critique of war, Pope John Paul added:

> [A]t the root of war there are usually real and serious grievances:

> injustices suffered, legitimate aspirations frustrated, poverty and the exploitation of desperate people who see no possibility of improving their lot by peaceful means.[14]

Accordingly, John Paul, like his predecessor Paul VI, called for "a concerted worldwide effort to promote development."[15]

In their 1983 pastoral letter "The Challenge of Peace" the U.S. bishops identified nonviolence as a legitimate part of the Christian tradition. The letter advanced the teaching by articulating a common presumption against the use of force in both nonviolent and just war traditions.[16] Although conservative just-war theorists still resist the presumption against the use of force, this letter both represented and advanced the growing complexity of church teaching. Ten years later in the 1993 statement "The Harvest of Justice Is Sown in Peace," this process solidified when the bishops declared that nonviolence is the basic Christian response to injustice and that the legitimate use of force is essentially an exception—a last resort employed only when repeated attempts at nonviolent correction of injustice fail. In contrast to "The Challenge of Peace," which had legitimated nonviolence as a personal calling, "Harvest" stipulated it as a *prima facie* public obligation of government officials and citizens.[17]

THE U.S. BISHOPS AFFIRMED THE GOVERNMENT'S DUTY TO DEFEND THE NATION AGAINST TERRORISM BUT NONETHELESS URGED EXTENSIVE USE OF NON-MILITARY RESOURCES

Similarly, in their response to the terrorist attacks of September 11, 2001, the U.S. bishops affirmed the government's duty to defend the nation against terrorism but nonetheless urged extensive use of non-military resources to address "the roots of terrorism." "Stopping terrorism," they admonished, "must be a priority, but foreign policy cannot be wholly subsumed under this campaign."[18] It is becoming ever clearer that the government's duty to defend the public against terrorism cannot be separated from a broader range of policy concerns. In the Catholic vision of peace, resistance to evil must be accompanied by active peacemaking, understood as the defense of human rights, the promotion of development, the advance of justice, the increase of solidarity, and the strengthening of world order.

Going hand in hand with this elevation of nonviolence in Catholic thought has been an increasing skepticism about the efficacy of war and the probability of it ever really meeting just war criteria. Unlike Saint Augustine, who considered waging war an unavoidable responsibility of political authorities and one of the "necessities," as he called them, of sinful existence, modern Catholic social teaching has increasingly regarded war as an avoidable matter of policy. For instance, in January 2003, two months before the U.S. invasion of Iraq, in his annual address to the diplomatic corps accredited to the Vatican, Pope John Paul II made clear his opposition to so-called wars of choice. "War," he said, "is never another means that one can employ for settling differences between nations.... [W]ar cannot be decided upon ... except as the very last option and in accordance with very strict conditions."[19] At the time of the 1991 Persian Gulf War, he also publicized his reservations about war as a tool of policy:

> No, never again war, which destroys the lives of innocent people, teaches how to kill, throws into upheaval the lives even of those who do the killing, and leaves behind a trail of resentment and hatred, thus making it all the more difficult to find a solution of the very problems which provoked the war.[20]

For John Paul, war is always morally suspect, especially because it does not deliver the peace it promises. He summarized his view by writing of war as "the violence, which under the illusion of fighting evil, only makes it worse."[21]

The U.S. bishops have similarly doubted the usefulness of war. In their 1993 statement "The Harvest of Justice Is Sown in Peace," they expressed their conviction that under contemporary cultural conditions, it would be nearly impossible to wage a just war:

> Moral reflection on the use of force calls for a spirit of moderation rare in contemporary society. The increasing violence of our society, its growing insensitivity to the sacredness of life, and the glorification of the technology of destruction in popular culture could inevitably impair our society's ability to apply just war criteria honestly and effectively in time of crisis.[22]

They concluded, "Ten years after 'The Challenge of Peace,' given the neglect of the peaceable virtues and the destructiveness of today's weaponry, serious questions still remain about whether modern war in all its savagery can meet the hard tests set by the just war tradition."[23]

Following the attacks on the World Trade Center and the Pentagon, the bishops wrote in "Living with Faith and Hope after September 11": "Because of its terrible consequences, military force, even when justified and carefully executed, must be undertaken with a deep sense of regret."[24] Just a month before the 2003 invasion of Iraq, the conference judged that the impending war seemed to them, in light of the available evidence, not to satisfy the conditions for a just war.[25]

Along with skepticism about the use of force in international affairs has gone a greater stringency in the application of just-war norms. "The Challenge of Peace" ruled out nuclear fighting, the first use of nuclear weapons, and nuclear retaliation to a nuclear attack. It also expressed great skepticism about the use of battlefield nuclear weapons. "The Harvest of Justice Is Sown in Peace" questioned strategies of "overwhelming and decisive force," as declared and practiced in the first Gulf War, and it warned, "Efforts to reduce the risk to a nation's own forces must be limited by judgments of military necessity so as not to neglect the rights of civilians."[26] It also called for applications of ethical restraints to air power, particularly avoiding the bombardment of civilian infrastructure, a significant problem in the Gulf War and again in the intervention in Kosovo in 1999. Before the war with Iraq, both the Holy See and the USCCB vigorously opposed the notion of "preventive war" offered by the Bush administration as a justification for its campaign. And in 2005, "The Compendium of the Social Teaching of the Church" declared that "engaging in a preventive war without clear proof that an attack is imminent cannot fail to raise serious moral and juridical questions."[27]

In my view, the capstone of this trend from a presumption of just war to a priority of nonviolence and peacebuilding is Pope John Paul II's 2002 World Day of Peace Message, a response to the events of September 11 that introduced "forgiveness" as a necessary component in alleviating conflict and securing the peace, thereby adding forgiveness to the Catholic Church's "convoy concept" of holistic peace. Indeed, throughout his ministry John Paul sought forgiveness for the historic sins of the Church, and in the Day of Pardon in 2000, he prayed for forgiveness of sins committed in the name of the Church during the previous millennium.[28] The World Day of Peace message in 2002 was a continuation of this pattern, as it contended that forgiveness is a necessary condition of a just society. Societies, in addition to individuals, he argued, "are absolutely in need of forgiveness."[29] The stability of post-conflict societies and the steadiness of renewed social relationships, the pope argued, depend on forgiveness.

In short, the approach to conflict in contemporary Catholic teaching and in the papal ministry has evolved into a doctrine of resistance to evil with a priority on nonviolent means—a doctrine that must be applied in the context of a wider vision of peace, including forgiveness between antagonists.

International Law and International Institutions

World order is an often-overlooked component of the Catholic conception of peace. In fact, the biblical and theological sources of the Church's preoccupation with world order were underscored by "The Compendium of the Social Doctrine of the Church" (2005).[30] In addition, in "The Pastoral Constitution on the Church in the Modern World" the Second Vatican Council explained that the Church's promotion of world order stems from its belief in the fundamental unity of the human family and humanity's consequent communitarian vocation.[31] The Council defined the Church itself as a "sacrament or sign of intimate union with God and of the unity of all mankind" and declared that the promotion of unity is a primary service that the Church offers to the world.[32]

Over the last fifteen years, the exigencies of ethno-religious conflict, the legitimation of humanitarian intervention, the attenuation of sovereignty, and the advance of globalization and American unilateralism in the war on terror have all contributed to the Holy See's heightened insistence on international law and the strengthening of the United Nations. The most comprehensive statement on this matter was the 2004 World Day of Peace Message, "An Ever Timely Commitment: Teaching Peace," which devoted three sections (5-7) to international law and the international order. In this message Pope John Paul II criticized the assertive unilateralism widely associated with U.S. policy and he insisted that international law is a foundation of civilized life and that neglecting to keep agreements creates conflict. He wrote:

> The violation of this principle [the bindingness of international law] necessarily leads to a situation of illegality and consequently to friction and disputes which would not fail to have lasting negative repercussions. It is appropriate to recall this fundamental rule, especially at times when there is a temptation to appeal to the *law of force* rather than to the *force of law.*[33]

Pope John Paul noted that the breakdown of international legality led to the Second World War. Implicit is a warning that disregard of international law today, and particularly evasion of the provisions for collective security in Chapter VII of the United Nations' Charter, will lead to a new period of global violence. In that spirit, the pope supported renewal of the United Nations Organization, with the help of nongovernmental organizations and civic movements, to meet the demand for "a greater degree of international ordering"[34]

Religion, Violence, and Interreligious Dialogue

The third notable area of Catholic peacemaking in recent years is interreligious dialogue about religious violence. John Paul II led the way in inviting leaders of the world religions to denounce violence perpetrated in the name of religion.[35] As he declared to the diplomatic corps in 2003, "Killing in the name of God is an act of blasphemy and a perversion of religion."[36] The days of prayer for peace called by John Paul in Assisi in 1986, 1993, and 2002, and especially the latter two, were clear efforts to reject the accusation that religion is a source of violence; to build momentum among religious leaders for peacemaking; to contribute to the restoration of peace in the former Yugoslavia; and to respond to September 11 and the war on terror.[37] While these efforts, especially the interfaith meetings at Assisi, seem to have come into question under Pope Benedict XVI, there is no doubt that they are one of the most significant achievements of Pope John Paul II's papacy.

One country rent by conflict that received sustained, personal attention from John Paul was Lebanon.[38] Formed after World War II as a haven for Maronite Christians, Lebanon was an oasis of interreligious co-existence in the Middle East. But in 1970 the PLO took refuge there after its defeat in Jordan in the fighting of "Black December." The Palestinians became a state within a state, drawing with them Lebanon's Muslim population. In 1975 civil war broke out along sectarian lines and lasted fifteen years. Five years after the Taif agreements in 1989, which brought a cessation to hostilities, there was only an uneasy peace. John Paul hoped to secure religious comity and peace in the region, promote dialogue between Christians and Muslims, and strengthen religious freedom.[39]

In 1995, in anticipation of the synods that would prepare for the year 2000 Jubilee, John Paul summoned the Synod of Bishops in a Special Assembly for Lebanon, inviting observers from the Orthodox and Muslim communities. In May 1997, the pope himself visited Lebanon to deliver the apostolic exhortation, "New Hope for Lebanon," officially closing the synod.[40] John Paul turned his back on confessionalism, the basis of pre-Civil War political accommodation in Lebanon. He urged all parties to unite in claiming their citizenship of the one Lebanese state and in supporting democratic government. He strongly encouraged interreligious dialogue as a condition of peace and voiced his hope for "conviviality" among Lebanese as a model of interreligious harmony for the Middle East and the world. In the years following the pope's visit, Catholics coalesced politically with Sunni and Druze Muslims in the hope of preserving a secular, non-confessional Lebanese state. But the rise of Hezbollah, the growth of the Shiites as the largest Muslim group, and political interference from Syria impeded the achievement of Pope John Paul's vision of interreligious harmony.

Finally, the war on terror and especially the U.S. war in Iraq increased the need for interreligious dialogue, especially with Muslims.[41] In this context, a colloquium on the spiritual resources for peace, sponsored by the Pontifical Council for Inter-religious Dialogue in 2003, identified interreligious dialogue itself as a tool for peacemaking. It also offered this summary understanding of the requirements of peacemaking:

> Opting for peace does not mean a passive acquiescence in evil or a compromising of principle. It demands an active struggle against hatred, oppression, and disunity, but not by using methods of violence. Building peace requires creative and courageous action. A commitment to peace is a labor of patience and perseverance. It involves as well a readiness to examine self-critically the relationship of our traditions to those social, economic, and political structures which are frequently agents of violence and injustice.[42]

Let this stand, too, as a summary of the direction of Catholic peacemaking in the last decade and a half, and particularly of the contribution of the late Pope John Paul II. ❖

---

1. This article is an expanded version of a talk prepared for a meeting of the Catholic Peacebuilding Network, Chicago, IL, April 19-20, 2006.
2. For the role of John Paul II in the ending communist rule in his native Poland, see Geoffrey Garton Ash, *The Magic Lantern: The Revolution of 1989 Witnessed in Warsaw, Budapest, Berlin and Prague* (Vintage, 1990) and George Weigel, *The Final Revolution: The Resistance Church and the Collapse of Communism* (Oxford, 1992). For a detailed account of John Paul's personal influence on the defense of human rights and the liberation of one colonized people, the East Timorese, see Arnold Kohen, *From the Place of the Dead: The Epic Struggle of Bishop Belo of East Timor*, introduction by the Dalai Lama (St. Martin's, 1999). Other examples of John Paul's engagement in situations of conflict may be found in *Libano: Faccio Mio L'Appello di un Popula: Interveni di Giovanni Paolo II gennaio 1989-aprile* 1990, Quaderni de "L'Osservatore Romano," no. 13, series ed. Mario Agnes (Vatican, 1990); *John Paul II for Peace in the Middle East, War in the Gulf: Gleanings from the Pages of "L'Osservatore Romano,"* Quaderni de "L'Osservatore Romano," no. 16, ed. Mario Agnes (Vatican, 1992); *La crisi iugolsava, Quaderni de "l'Osservatore Romano"*, ed. Mario Agnes, no. 19 (Vatican, [1992]); and Assisi 1993, *Giovanni Paolo II per la pace in Bosnia ed Erzegovina, Quaderni de "l'Osservatore Romano"*, ed. Mario Agnes, no. 21 (Vatican, 1993).
3. My entry "The Vatican" in the *Encyclopedia of Politics and Religion*, revised edition (Congressional Quarterly Press, *forthcoming*), provides a general description of the Vatican's role in international politics. On the Vatican's *Ostpolitik* (i.e., its policy toward Communist Eastern Europe) prior to 1989, see Eric O. Hanson, *The Catholic Church in World Politics* (Princeton, 1987), chapter 6, "Catholic Poland and *Ostpolitik*," pp. 197-233.
4. One area of conflict in which there was close cooperation between the USCC (later USCCB) and the Holy See was the Holy Land. In 1996, for example, USCC helped disseminate specially prepared documents on the future of Jerusalem, and in 1998 facilitated the organization of European, Canadian, and American bishops' conferences to support the church in the Holy Land. In 2001, that group began annual meetings of presidents of episcopal conferences in Jerusalem and elsewhere in the Holy Land to express solidarity with the church there.
5. The Holy See is the official name applied to the Catholic Church, and specifically to the pope and the Roman curia (the pope's administrative arm), in international affairs. For an interpretative survey of the role of the Holy See in world politics prior to 1988, see: Hanson, *The Catholic Church in World Politics;* Andre Dupuy, *Pope John Paul II and the Challenge of Papal Diplomacy: Anthology (1978-2003)* (Pontifical Council for

Justice and Peace/New York, Paths to Peace Foundation, 2004), and Bernard J. O'Connor, *Papal Diplomacy: John Paul II and the Culture of Peace* (Saint Augustine, 2005). This last volume includes the pope's annual addresses to the diplomatic corps up to 2003 in their entirely. The addresses provide a handy year-by-year summary of the international concerns of the Holy See. Also, see *John Paul II and the Family of Peoples: The Holy Father to the Diplomatic Corps (1978-2002)* (Pontifical Council for Justice and Peace, 2002) and *Ways of Peace: Papal Messages for the World Days of Peace (1968-86)* (Pontifical Council for Justice and Peace, 1986). More recent statements for the World Day of Peace may be found at the Vatican Website: http://www.vatican.va/holy_father/messages/peace.

6. For a summary of the Church's position on humanitarian intervention, see *The Compendium of the Social Doctrine of the Church* (Pontifical Council for Justice and Peace/United States Conference of Catholic Bishops, 2005) nos. 504-506. Preventive war is treated below. (N. B. References to the documents of Catholic social teaching are commonly made to enumerated sections or paragraphs in the text rather than to pages.)

7. On *Pacem in Terris*, see my "Commentary on *Pacem in Terris*" in Kenneth Himes et al., eds., *Catholic Social Teaching: Commentaries and Interpretations* (Georgetown, 2005), pp. 217-243. On the positive Catholic conception of peace, see National Conference of Catholic Bishops, "The Challenge of Peace: God's Promise and Our Response" (USCC, 1983), nos. 68-69. I trace the concept further in a talk for a panel on Catholic peacemaking for the United States Institute of Peace in "Catholic Peacemaking: From *Pacem in terris* to *Centesimus annus*." The talk was reported in detail by David Smock in "Catholic Contributions to International Peace," U.S.I.P. Special Report 69 (April, 2001).

8. For the principal documents of contemporary Catholic Social Teaching, see David J. O'Brien and Thomas W. Shannon, eds. *Catholic Social Thought: The Documentary Heritage* (Maryknoll, 1995).

9. On the idea of a "convoy concept," see David Braybrooke, *Three Tests for Democracy: Personal Rights, Human Welfare, Collective Preferences* (Random House, 1968), p. 92.

10. "*Gaudium et Spes* (The Pastoral Constitution on the Church in the Modern World)," no. 78, in *Catholic Social Thought.*

11. *Centesimus annus*, no. 23.

12. Ibid., no. 52.

13. See Vatican Council II, *Gauidum et spes*, no. 78, in *Catholic Social Thought.*

14. *Centesimus annus*, no. 52.

15. Ibid.

16. "The Challenge of Peace: God's Promise and Our Response," no.71.

17. "Harvest," p. 12.

18. For the bishops' response to September 11, see http:/www./usccb.org/sdwp/sept11.

19. Address to the Diplomatic Corps, January 13, 2003, no. 4 in *Papal Diplomacy.*

20. *Centesimus annus* (On the Hundredth Anniversary of *Rerum Novarum*) in *Catholic Social Thought*, no. 52.

21. Ibid., no. 25.

22. National Conference of Catholic Bishops, "The Harvest of Justice Is Sown in Peace" (United States Conference of Catholic Bishops, 2001), p. 15.

23. Ibid., p. 16.

24. See http:/www./usccb.org/sdwp/sept11._

25. Bishop Wilton D. Gregory, President, United States Conference of Catholic Bishops, "Statement on Iraq," February 26, 2003: "Based on the facts that are known, it is difficult to justify resort to war against Iraq, lacking clear and adequate evidence of an imminent attack of a grave nature or Iraq's involvement in the terrorist attacks of September 11. With the Holy See and many religious leaders throughout the world, we believe that resort to war would not meet the strict conditions in Catholic teaching for the use of military force."

26. "Harvest," p. 12.

27. "Compendium," no. 501.

28. On John Paul's ministry of forgiveness, see Luigi Accattoli, *When A Pope Asks Forgiveness: The Mea Culpas of John Paul II*, tr. Jordan Ammann, O. P. (Pauline, 1998).

29. See http://www.vatican.va/holy_father/john_paul_i_mes_20011211_world_day_for _peace_en.html.

30. *Compendium*, nos. 428-32.

31. For the foundational theological themes of the unity of the human family and the consequent communitarian nature of the human vocation, see "*Guadium et Spes*," nos. 23-32 and 42. The last identifies "the promotion of unity" in the world community as one of the principal ways in which the Church serves the world.

32. Vatican Council II, *Lumen Gentium* ("The Dogmatic Constitution on the Church") no. 1, in the *Documents of Vatican II*, general editor Walter Abbott, S. J. (America Press, 1966). On the service of the world through the promotion of unity in the human family, see "The Pastoral Constitution on the Church in the Modern World," no. 42, in *Catholic Social Thought.*

33. World Day of Peace Message, 2004.

34. Ibid.

35. Some commentators have perceived a difference of attitude to interreligious dialogue on Pope Benedict XVI's part in his re-assignment of the President of the Pontifical Council for Interreligious Dialogue, Archbishop Michael Fitzgerald, to be nuncio in Egypt and the merging of the council with one dedicated to culture. But see John Borelli, "From Tiber to Nile," *The Tablet*, April 8, 2006, pp. 10-11.

36. Address to the Diplomatic Corps, January 10, 2002, no. 3, in *Papal Diplomacy.*

37. For materials from the first Assisi meeting, see the *Bulletin of the Secretariat for Non-Christians* 22:1 (1987). For use of the Assisi meetings on behalf of peace in the former Yugoslavia, see *Assisi 1993*, also cited in note 2 above.

38. On the Church's role in post-Civil War Lebanon, see Carole H. Dagher, *Bring Down the Walls: Lebanon's Post-War Challenge* (St. Martin's, 2000).

39. For regional views of Christian-Muslim dialogue, see "Ensemble Devant Dieu Pour Le Bien de la Personne et de la Societe: La coexistence entre musulmans et chretiens dans le monde arabe," Third Pastoral Letter of the Catholic Patriarchs of the Middle East (General Secretariat of the Council of Patriarchs of the East [Bkerke, Lebanon] 1994); and Sixth Pastoral Letter of the Patriarchs of the East, "Ensemble pour l'avenir" in "Pour qu'ils aient la vie et qu'ils l'aient en abondance," Acts of the 1st Congress of Catholic Patriarchs and Bishops of the East (General Secretariat of the Council of Patriarchs [Bkerke, Lebanon], 1999), pp. 426-427.

40. "La Nouvelle Espérance pour le Liban" (Vatican, 1997).

41. On Catholic-Muslim dialogue in general, see Michael L. Fitzgerald and John Borelli, *Interfaith Dialogue: A Catholic View*, Part II Christian Muslim

Relations (London: SPCK, 2006), pp. 85-162. Pope John Paul's efforts in opposing the war in Iraq led to the recognition by leading Muslim clerics that the U.S.-led effort was not a Christian or "crusader" war against Islam.

42. Final Declaration of Participants in the Symposium on "The Spiritual Resource of the Religions for Peace," Rome, 16-18 January, 2003. See Vatican Website: http://vatican.va/roman_curia/pontifical_councils/interreligious_dialogue/rc_pc_interlg_doc_20020311_religions-peace_en.html.

A DIPLOMACY OF CANDOR: POPE BENEDICT XVI ON THE GLOBAL STAGE

By Bernard J. O'Connor

American humorist and essayist Elwyn Brooks White seldom bothered to conceal his disdain for conventional diplomacy. In an essay entitled "Compost," White argued that "a nation, like an individual, if he has anything to say, should simply say it." Most practitioners of the diplomatic craft, according to his view, seem almost inherently incapable of clear, coherent, and credible discourse. But White might be pleasantly surprised to learn that the diplomatic style shown by Joseph Cardinal Ratzinger since he assumed the papacy on April 19, 2005, could well be described as a "Diplomacy of Candor."

Berlin-based journalist Vicente Poveda, generally reticent where Benedict XVI is concerned, aptly summarized the first year of his papacy as one which "advocates concentration and contemplation," seeking "profundity and the core." And at this core of the pontiff's relations with the international community is an approach which combines explicit and evident goals, together with a philosophy to ground them based upon human dignity and solidarity, and a straightforward clarity in their articulation. There is nothing of a hidden agenda.

Pope Benedict believes that diplomacy is a public service intended primarily to safeguard the common interests of mankind. He has deplored the folly of diplomatic preference for interests more nationalist than global, more restrictive than broadly applicable. His words, though always chosen carefully and for precision, neither compromise nor apologize for his perception of political reality and morality.

Of what does Benedict XVI's Diplomacy of Candor consist? Five elements may be identified:

Respecting Objective Moral Truth

No nation elevates its status by adopting a selective definition of what constitutes truth, and even less so by schemes to distort interpretation of that same truth. Speaking before a meeting of Vatican representatives to international organizations on March 18, the pope asserted that "when truth is violated, peace is threatened, law is endangered [and] forms of injustice are unleashed."

It is fidelity to truth which characterizes, for example, Pope Benedict's interaction with Jewish political and religious leaders. In his visit to Auschwitz on May 28, the pope insisted that: "I had to come. It is a duty before the truth and the just due of all who suffered here, a duty before God, for me … as a son of the German people—a son of that people over which a ring of criminals rose to power by false promises ... with the result that our people was used and abused as an instrument of their thirst for destruction and power." The Nazis also "ultimately wanted to tear up the taproot of the Christian faith and to replace it with a faith of their own invention: faith in the rule of man, the rule of the powerful."

What the pope implied for our own society is apparent. The denial of the transcendent and campaigns to degrade the holy invariably result in wrongful attempts to substitute man for God. Humanity is never bettered by the tendency to self-deification. The obliteration of the First Commandment leads to a rejection of those remaining. The pope noted that Holocaust victims were considered by their captors as "the refuse of the nation." Yet, "today we gratefully hail them as witnesses to the truth and goodness which even among our people were not eclipsed." The pope also called for forward-looking initiatives such as a Center for Dialogue and Prayer, which will further purify the "memory demanded by this place of horror," with "the aim of imposing a limit upon evil and confirming goodness."

Facilitating Practical Inter-faith Dialogue

Pope Benedict's commitment to using diplomacy to advocate for the incorporation of practical interfaith dialogue in the affairs of state is perhaps best illustrated by his approach to Iraq. On August 25, 2005, Pope Benedict and the Vatican Secretary of State, Angelo Cardinal Sodano, met with Iraq's Foreign Minister, Hoshyar Zebori, to discuss the draft text of Iraq's Constitution. While Islam was designated to be the country's official religion, the pope strongly emphasized the need to provide an ongoing opportunity for all of Iraq's religious communities to contribute input to the Constitutional process. Otherwise, the necessary reconstruction of institutions will be thwarted; suspicion will fuel factionalism and tolerance will become yet another defeated ideal.

The pope's position prefigured a subsequent Statement of the Holy See to the Conference on Tolerance, held in Kazakhstan on June 13. This statement emphasized Pope Benedict's resolve "that no partnership among cultures, religions, and ethnicities can be established in mutual ignorance," especially where "religions are too often manipulated or even misunderstood." A climate of trustful, sensitive, and informed exchange will ensure that a nation such as Iraq may come to esteem the uniqueness as well as the shared heritage of its diverse citizenry. The pope was certainly mindful, as have been Iraq's twelve bishops, that the persecution of minorities could readily follow, for example, as a consequence of the proposed Article 2.1 (a) which states: "No law can be passed that contradicts the undisputed rules of Islam."

Building Realistic Bridges

On October 14, 2005, the President of the Pontifical Council for Interreligious Dialogue sent his annual message "to our Muslim brothers and sisters" as they concluded their observance of Ramadan. He used this message to reiterate Pope Benedict's prior remarks to Islamic delegates who attended the inauguration of his pontificate: "I assure you that the Church wants to continue building bridges of friendship with followers of all religions, in order to seek the true good of every person and of society as a whole." According to the pope, "it is the duty of every one," whether they are motivated by religious or secular tenets, to strive to place the "cause of peace on solid foundations." This responsibility is particularly incumbent upon diplomats.

Daniel Madigan, a consultant to the Pontifical Council for Interreligious Dialogue, notes that Pope Benedict never resorts to the familiar phrase, "clash of civilizations," but rather speaks of "encounter and alliance of civilizations." Madigan rightly adds that the pope "is not simply an easy optimist." Instead, the pope understands that the rhetoric of "clash" can stimulate a self-fulfilling prophecy. He avoids needlessly incendiary language, yet speaks plainly in calling all religious traditions to respect universal human dignity. In an Address to the Pontifical Council for Migrants and Travellers on May 15 this year, for instance, the pope minced no words in urging Islamic countries to refrain from burdening Christians living in their midst with unjust and discriminatory laws and treatment.

Intervening for Peace

The Holy See, responding to the crisis unleashed by Iran's nuclear program, stated on June 6 that it "is firmly convinced that the current difficulties also can and must be overcome through diplomatic channels, using all means at the disposal of diplomacy." The point was unmistakable, and made in the wake of an offer to Iran by the U.N. Security Council along with Germany. There are definite implications beyond Iran itself in any bid for uranium enrichment. Iran cannot and must not pose as a sort of "lone ranger" before the nations of the world. Still, the Holy See also conveyed the outlook of Benedict XVI when it insisted that "care for the honor" of a country has to be maintained. Only then will it be feasible to take steps directed towards rapprochement. Recent expressions by the United States of greater willingness to join face-to-face talks with Iran are consistent with the pope's commitment to peaceful conflict resolution.

The priority on using the skills and tools of diplomacy for active peacemaking is evident in other areas as well. For instance, on August 26, 2005, President Alvaro Uribe of Colombia announced acceptance of the Church's "offer to mediate with leftist guerrilla armies to end the four-decade-old conflict that has crippled the country." Preliminary talks were immediately planned with the Revolutionary Armed Forces of Colombia (FARC) and the National Liberation Army (ELN). Likewise, on May 1 this year the Papal Nuncio to Sri Lanka, reinforced by Caritas International, called for "urgent international mediation" between rebel forces and the Sri Lankan government. And during his General Audience of May 31, the pope mentioned the "grave disturbances" afflicting East Timor. He pleaded that the local Church and both Catholic and international organizations commit themselves to the relief of displaced persons, and to participate in activities designed to elicit peace.

Prioritizing Persons over Markets

On May 18, in an address given while receiving the Credentials of new Ambassadors from India, Australia, Chad, Cape Verde, and Moldova, Pope Benedict forthrightly rejected that "the management of public life" can "be guided solely by economic considerations." Profitability is never a justification for immoral "use of the planet's resources," and which amounts to "running the risk of long-term mortgaging [of] the world's future." Serious reappraisal of the worth of the human person is imperative. With this message in mind, on June 11 the Vatican publication *L'Osservatore Romano* reminded the world's rich nations of their commitment to increase development aid and to help to reduce health costs in poorer countries. In Africa, for example, an estimated 800 children daily "could be saved by meeting basic health expenses."

Diplomacy must remain ever vigilant to the priority of personhood over the supposed dictates of market "efficiency" and convenience. As Pope Benedict argued with eloquent simplicity in an address on May 13, exaggerated materialism and consumerism render damage to those authentic spiritual and moral values which are indispensable for an integrated society.

The thread that runs through all of the current pope's diplomatic priorities is this: a rejection of radical relativism and respect for a transcendent moral order. "Total subjectivism in defining human rights," concludes Pope Benedict, "leads only to 'might makes right'." As the pontiff explained on March 30, each of us, professional diplomats and otherwise, must consent to become a "consistent witness" for "principles which are not negotiable," such as reverence for life at its every stage, the natural structure of the family, and the right of parents to educate their children. Such a witness is not narrowly confined to a specific religious confession, for it is "inscribed in human nature itself." ❖

BENEDICT XVI: PEACEMAKER

By Drew Christiansen, S.J.

A year after Pope Benedict XVI quoted a Byzantine Emperor on the evils of Islam, one hears much less talk of the Vatican's alleged hard new line on Islam. The shift of attention is a tribute to the pope's unexpected success in the unfamiliar roles of diplomat and peacemaker.

After the late Pope John Paul II presided over the fall of Communism in Eastern Europe and set in motion the change of governments from Haiti to East Timor, few anticipated that Benedict, a scholar and church administrator, would similarly influence world affairs. There were indications, moreover, that Benedict would carry into the papacy the suspicions of officials at the Palazzo del Sant' Uffizio, the home of the Congregation of the Doctrine of the Faith, toward the Terza Loggia, the offices of the Secretariat of State, the bastion of the diplomatic corps. But two years into his pontificate it appears that, despite a brief period of turmoil, Pope Benedict has quickly mastered his role as a diplomat and religious peacemaker.

It was a role he could not avoid.

Religious Peacemaking: The Spirit of Assisi

For a thousand years the Holy See has sent diplomats abroad. With the demise of the Papal States in 1870, as Archbishop Celestino Migliore, now the Holy See Permanent Observer at the United Nations in New York, has said, the Holy See was free of "the ball and chain" of ordinary statecraft and could carry out "a diplomacy of conscience" and peace. In the late Pope John Paul II's peripatetic pontificate, the diplomatic role took on new intensity and a new form. The intensity was evident in a flurry of activity from central Europe to the Balkans to the Middle East. The new form came in religious peacemaking, especially John Paul II's convocation of religious leaders in times of conflict to oppose violence and proclaim their common commitment to peace.

John Paul's religious peacemaking came to be known by the popular title "The Spirit of Assisi," referring to the 1986 interreligious prayer for peace held in Assisi. It was followed by two other major gatherings, in 1992 following the outbreak of war in the former Yugoslavia, and in 2002 following 9/11 and the invasion of Afghanistan. In between those events and since 2002, "the Spirit of Assisi" has been kept alive by Rome's Community of Sant' Egidio with an annual day of Prayer for Peace. Last year's gathering met at Georgetown University in Washington, D.C. The presence of Catholic prelates with world leaders of other faiths made it clear religious peacemaking is fully integrated into the life of the Church today.

As Bishop William F. Murphy, the undersecretary of the Pontifical Commission for Justice and Peace at the time of Assisi I in 1986, explained in *America* last year, the whole Roman curia was involved in planning the event.[1] Despite this corporate preparation, John Paul's religious peacemaking, like his steady series of apologies to groups harmed or offended in the past by the church, remained controversial in some corners of the curia. Rumors persisted that Pope Benedict, who had had reservations about the alleged syncretism at Assisi I, continued his opposition as pope. Those rumors gained more weight with an action he took last year, reining in the Franciscans of Assisi, putting activities at the Basilica of Saint Francis under a millstone of ecclesiastical control that included the bishop of Assisi, the Episcopal Conference of Umbria, and the Italian Episcopal Conference.

EARLY IN HIS PONTIFICATE POPE BENEDICT HAD TAKEN A SERIES OF STEPS THAT VATICAN JOURNALISTS PRESENTED AS EVIDENCE OF A NEW HARD LINE TOWARD ISLAM

Though it is hard from this side of the ocean to pierce the veil of Italian church politics, the issue appears to have been just that, one of Italian church politics, specifically an effort to curb the independently progressive Franciscans, who showed excessive sympathy to the Italian left. For, when the 20th anniversary of the first Assisi event was observed in September, Pope Benedict sent warm and encouraging greetings. While gently warning against syncretistic interpretations of the meeting, Benedict reflected at length on the need for such meetings both two decades ago and in our own day. He wrote of the first Assisi convocation,

> It should be stressed that [the] value of prayer in building peace was testified to by the representatives of different religious traditions, and this did not happen at a distance but in the context of a meeting. Consequently, the people of diverse religions who were praying could show through the language of witness that prayer does not divide but unites and is a decisive element for an effective pedagogy of peace, hinged on friendship, reciprocal acceptance, and dialogue between people of different cultures and religions.

Likewise, earlier this year, he praised the charisms of the lay religious movements, including Sant' Egidio, the carrier of "the Spirit of Assisi," and Focolare, whose charism is the promotion of unity. He insisted that the church is enriched by the charisms of popular groups and that the tensions such gifts bring to the larger church must be worked out with patience. In talk after talk, moreover, the Holy Father has endorsed "the dialogue of cultures," embodied in Assisi, as essential to the Church's ministry of peace. Some of the over-interpretation of the disciplining of the Assisi Franciscans came from *Vaticanisti*, journalists covering the Vatican, with an interest bordering on advocacy in the re-shaping of post-9/11 Vatican policy toward Islam. They touted Benedict's new, supposedly hard line toward Islam. In this coverage, one could often detect neo-conservative alliances, with Europeans like Michele Pera and Americans like George Weigel receiving extensive and favorable coverage for publicizing the new pope's alleged toughness on Islam. It was a case of bringing the culture wars into the church. But Benedict did not share their enthusiasm for finding new enemies.

Islam: A Dialogue of Cultures

Early in his pontificate Pope Benedict had taken a series of steps that Vatican journalists presented as evidence of a new hard line toward Islam. Most importantly, he had set "reciprocity" as a goal of Vatican Islamic policy, that is the demand that Christians be allowed the same rights in Muslim countries that Muslims are allowed in the West. By itself, this was a necessary adjustment to the realities of an asymmetrical relationship. Pope John Paul's openness had won the right to open churches in some Gulf States, memoranda of understanding with the PLO and the Hashemite Kingdom of Jordan guaranteeing religious liberty, and cooperation between Christians and Muslims in Lebanon, but in places like Pakistan, Iran, and Saudi Arabia, life for Christians went from very trying to downright oppressive. After 20 years of dialogue, more progress could reasonably be expected. Indeed, Cardinal Francis Arinze, the former president of the Pontifical Council for Interreligious Dialogue, had complained to Muslim interlocutors in the 1990s, before Pope John Paul II had begun his long decline, that the relationship was one-sided, with positive initiatives coming only from the Catholic side.

In another move, the new pope folded the Pontifical Council for Interreligious Dialogue into the Pontifical Council for Culture and missioned the Vatican's leading Islamicist, Archbishop Michael Fitzgerald, who succeeded Arinze as president of the PCID, as nuncio to Cairo and the Arab League. As a result, the Holy See now speaks of "a dialogue of cultures" rather than a dialogue of religions. The cultural dialogue is broader than Catholic-Muslim relations narrowly defined, and, given the size of the two communities, the contemporary global political climate, and the plight of the ancient churches of the Middle East, the Muslim dialogue, it may be argued, has become the most important bi-lateral conversation on the church agenda.

In his end-of-year address to the Roman Curia, December 22, 2006, Pope Benedict expressed sympathy with Islam, which like Christianity, must confront the Enlightenment, both adopting its virtues as Pope John XXIII and the Second Vatican Council did, for example in the field of human rights and religious liberty, and correcting its excesses and deficiencies, like its materialism and moral relativism. Above all, the Holy Father argued, both must address the positivist notion of reason that "excludes God from the life of the community." Likewise, Christians and Muslims must be united in the commitment "to find solutions" in opposing violence and finding a synergy between faith and reason, between religion and freedom. The theme of the common tasks facing people of faith, both Muslims and Christians, in confronting the godlessness of the Enlightenment ran through his essays in his exchange with Michele Pera, *Without Roots* (Basic Books, 2006). In these recent statements, he exhibits no abstract respect for Islam, but rather a sense of spiritual solidarity of people of faith in the face of unbridled secularism.

Accordingly, too much can be made of the transition from interreligious dialogue to a dialogue of cultures. In the Islamic dialogue, as in much of the recent history of the Jewish dialogue, the focus has been on social and cultural issues, rarely on great issues of theology. An exceptionally strong example of this type of undertaking at the international level was the Symposium on the Spiritual Resources of the Religions for Peace hosted by Archbishop Fitzgerald in January 2003. The focus on social issues is likewise characteristic of dialogue with Orthodox Jews, for example, who, because they regard the Torah as unmediated revelation, avoided discussing theology. (Formal theological discussion with Reform Jews in the U.S. only began in the late 1990s.) The same inhibitions hold for discussions with most Muslims for a similar reason, the revelatory status of the Qur'an. So, instead these dialogues tend to focus on great public issues, like war and peace, or other social concerns the two religions share in common, such as defense of the family or support of education. (An exception is the regional dialogues held in the U.S. which focus on issues like prayer.)

In the Mideast, moreover, where the Church and Islam have their most intimate encounters, local church leaders have long spoken of "the dialogue of daily life," referring to the many social interactions in which Muslims and Christians routinely engage one another. Benedict takes this notion a step further, counseling non-violent "conviviality."

"Simply living together and suffering together," he explains, "has a healing effect on wounds and disposes people to thoughts and deeds of reconciliation and peace." In a Christmas 2006 letter, he encouraged Middle East Christians "to continue along the path of trust with acts of friendship and good will (toward Muslims)" in "both the simple daily deeds you have practiced in your region by so many good and humble people who have always treated others with consideration and also those deeds considered heroic, inspired by authentic respect for human dignity and the desire to find solutions to situations of grave hostility."

Where, then, does Pope Benedict's lecture at Regensburg fit with its imputation of violence and irrationality to Islam? For it seemed at the time that the great "clash of civilizations," promoted by Princeton Professor Bernard Lewis and theretofore repeatedly rejected by the Vatican and Benedict himself, had actually exploded across the world stage following the lecture. Parliaments and Islamic scholars denounced the pope. Diplomats were recalled, protesters marched in the streets, and in Somalia, a nun was killed. Through it all, Benedict remained serene; but the new chief of Vatican communications, Father Federico Lombardi, S. J. swung into action, and Vatican diplomats, when they weren't summoned by host governments, buttonholed their colleagues to soothe tempers and answer questions.

It is hard to recall a crisis in which the Roman curia responded so rapidly with such concerted action and in such a short period of time. Explanations of varying degrees of credibility were issued. The pope offered expressions of regret. Though not apologies, they nonetheless count as an unprecedented step taken in record time. Pope Benedict met with Muslim diplomats and other Islamic leaders. Above all, despite a firestorm of controversy stirred by the lecture, he refused to cancel his visit to Turkey planned for late November. The lecture itself may have been poorly staffed (or staff advice overruled), but the comeback was exceedingly well executed. By the time the pope returned from Turkey not only had relations with Islam been genuinely calmed, but Benedict, with the help of his team, had proved himself a consummate diplomat.

The Turkey Visit

Even before the Regensburg lecture, the visit to Turkey looked fraught with trouble. For months, Turkey had been filled with anti-Catholic agitation. As cardinal, Benedict had roiled the waters by declaring his opposition to Turkey's entrance into the EU on the grounds it did not share the (Christian) identity of Europe. In the months leading up to the visit, priests were assassinated and attacked, and a novel depicting the pope's murder during the Turkey visit made the best seller list. The Regensburg lecture, following as it did a summer of protest against the blasphemous Danish cartoons, aggravated existing hostility toward Christianity and toward Benedict in particular. To hold firm to his resolve to visit Turkey in the face of this turmoil showed exceptional courage and trust in providence.

These tension made the primary task of the trip, showing solidarity with the Greek Orthodox Ecumenical Patriarchate of Constantinople, even more difficult. While Turkey is a secular state, government constraints on the patriarchate are especially grave. It sets limits on the election of the patriarch, refuses to recognize the role the patriarch plays among Orthodox Christians, and refuses to allow the patriarchal seminary, closed in 1971, to re-open. As a result of the controversy over Regensburg, the pope's ability to provide a show of unity with the Orthodox appeared greatly weakened.

To its credit, the Turkish government never asked the Vatican to cancel the trip. Prime Minister Tayyip Erdogan, who let it be known he would be out of the country during the papal visit, in the end remained to greet the pope before heading to a European summit. The pope expressed his affection for the Turkish people, quoting the late Pope John XXIII, once nuncio to Ankara: "I am fond of the Turks to whom the Lord has sent me ... I love the Turks." He also expressed his esteem for Turkey as "a noble land" which "has seen a remarkable flowering of Islamic civilization in the most diverse fields, including its literature and art as well as its institutions."

In a meeting with Ali Bardaoglu, the head of the directorate of religious affairs, Benedict, citing Pope Gregory VII, appealed to the "particular charity that Christians and Muslims owe one another 'because we believe in one God, albeit in a different manner, and because we praise him and worship him every day as the creator and ruler of the world.'" At the Blue Mosque, Istanbul's most important shrine, Benedict stood with the city's grand mufti, Mustafa Cagrici, before the "mihrab" niche that marks the direction of prayer facing Mecca. According to one reporter, the pope told the mufti, "Thank you for this moment of prayer." Father Lombardi explained, it was a personal prayer without the outward manifestations of Christian prayer, so as to emphasize what unites Christians and Muslims. Later the pope related that he had prayed there that all believers may see themselves as brothers and sisters. After those encounters, it would be hard any longer to regard Benedict as a "hardliner" on Islam.

By the end of the visit, Pope Benedict had won the hearts of the Turks. As one said, "We are quick to anger and quick to forgive." At the same time, in his quiet, direct manner, Benedict affirmed his core message. Against the background of religious and civilizational violence, he continued to promote a dialogue of cultures, reiterating that it is "a vital necessity, on which . . . our future depends." Faced with the suffering of Turkey's religious minorities, however, he also pleaded for religious freedom and the rights of minority religions. "The civil authorities of every democratic country are duty bound to guarantee the effective freedom of all believers," he told the diplomatic corps in a meeting in Ankara, "and to permit them to organize freely the life of their religious communities." In staying on message, Benedict demonstrated that even while healing and nurturing relationships, a world religious leader can speak the truth in love. In so doing, he proved himself both a diplomat and a peacemaker.

BENEDICT DEMONSTRATED THAT EVEN WHILE HEALING AND NURTURING RELATIONSHIPS, A WORLD RELIGIOUS LEADER CAN SPEAK THE TRUTH IN LOVE

Lebanon: The Israeli-Hezbollah War

Another crisis in which Pope Benedict proved himself a diplomat and religious peacemaker was Israel's war against Hezbollah in Lebanon in July and August of last year. Throughout Benedict's position was sure. With pastoral sensitivity, his first request was to make the first Sunday of the war a day of prayer and fasting—the fasting a sign of the seriousness with which he regarded the conflict. He regularly brought the situation to the world's attention during his Angelus message. Furthermore, his public statements were clear and direct, characteristic marks neither of traditional Vatican diplomacy nor of the pronouncements of John Paul II. From the beginning, he laid out a farsighted program that exceeded any coming out of major foreign ministries. It included an immediate ceasefire and a negotiated settlement, respect for the humanitarian law of war, i.e., immunity from attack for civilians and medical workers, the recognition of humanitarian corridors, so refugees could escape the fighting, and aid for the refugees to sustain them in the emergency.

A month had passed before the world community caught up with the pope and a ceasefire was put in place. Within days of the ceasefire, the U.S. ambassador to the Holy See, Francis Rooney, laid out U.S. plans for reconstruction aid and humanitarian assistance for Lebanon. It was a clear sign that the importance of Lebanon to the Holy See and the future prospects for Christianity in the Middle East had finally, and hopefully not too late, registered with the administration after weeks of delay in agreeing to a U.N. plan to end hostilities and forestall further conflict on the Lebanese-Israeli border. The Maronite Patriarch, the Synod of the Maronite Church, and the Assembly of Catholic

Ordinaries in Lebanon have also been exercising an important mediating role in Lebanon, opposing factionalism and supporting national unity based on Lebanese citizenship. In accord with this position, Maronite Patriarch Nazrallah Pierre Sfeir, at the outset of Lent this year, published an extraordinary pastoral letter, "On Love of Country," reflecting on the nature of genuine patriotism.

Counseling Nonviolence to Victims

Across the Middle East, Christians are facing unprecedented pressures: in Iraq, in Palestine, and in Lebanon as well as in countries which are burdened with refugees from neighboring countries, like Jordan and Syria. In a December 21 Christmas letter to the Catholics of the Middle East, Benedict wrote the faithful across the region in an effort to bolster their perseverance in the midst of their struggles. He recognized that events in the region "naturally give rise in those involved to recriminations and rage leading them to thoughts of retaliation and revenge." While recording grievances, he wrote, might offer an illusory satisfaction, experience had shown the results of such efforts were "disappointing." "When one person suffers he should first of all wish to understand how much someone else in a similar situation suffers." The best hope of healing he advised was in "patient, humble dialogue." Such dialogue he correctly noted "has already [yielded] positive results in many countries previously devastated by violence and revenge." Thus, even to the victims of violence he counseled non-violence.

The Christmas letter is a model of pastoral care that at the same time never fails to uphold the prophetic mission of the church. Fully aware of the politics involved—"dangerous geopolitical situations, cultural conflicts, economic and strategic interests, forms of aggression that claim justification from a social or religious basis"—the pope is concerned to address the immediate pain of the faithful, offset their discouragement, and offer counsel on the choices they face regarding, e.g., acting on impulses of revenge or weighing the possibility of emigration, but he also endeavors to remind individuals of the duties of discipleship and the need to build up the church as an instrument of peace. Accordingly he encourages both individuals and communities to acts of forgiveness, reconciliation, and solidarity.

Benedict: What's In A Name?

Benedict's nonviolent counsel to Middle East Christians is consonant with the path many, especially in Israel and Palestine, have already set for themselves. It is also consistent with the teaching of Pope John Paul II. But it flows as well from Joseph Ratzinger's own models of ministry, symbolized by his choice of Benedict as his papal name. Pundits noted, and Benedict himself later confirmed, that the new pope was invoking the memory of both Saint Benedict, the patron of Europe and the founder of Western monasticism, and Benedict XV, the early 20th century pope who labored in vain to end the First World War. Joseph Ratzinger took on the papacy late in life, but his long attachment to Benedictine spirituality seems to have informed his personal style in international affairs.

During the 2006 Lebanon War, his Angelus messages often reflected on the life of the saint of the day. Two of those reflections seemed to reflect Benedict's view of his own papal ministry and particularly the struggle to keep a balance between contemplation and action in the life of a church leader, those on Gregory the Great Bernard of Clarivaux. Gregory, Benedict remarked, was the model the Second Vatican Council had in mind when it outlined the role of the contemporary pastor, "inspired by the love 'that rises wonderfully to high things when it is compassionately drawn to the low things of neighbors; and the more kindly it descends to the weak things of this world, the more vigorously it recurs to the things on high'."

Similarly, commenting on the pastoral practice of Bernard of Clairvaux, he said, "The life of a pastor of souls must be a balanced synthesis of contemplation and action...." Bernard's advice to Pope Eugenius III, to avoid excessive activity because it leads to hardness of heart, he told his listeners, is advice "to the Pope of that time and to all Popes, to all of us." Bernard, he observed, "knew how to harmonize the monk's aspiration to the solitude and tranquility of the cloister with the pressing needs of important and complex missions at the service of the Church."

With Benedict, diplomacy and the care of souls fit together like hand in glove. Diplomacy is not an add-on or a remnant of days of the temporal power of the papacy. As in the Letter to Middle East Christians, pastoral care for the faithful—their religious and moral affections and their practical personal and political choices—combine effortlessly with counsels to nonviolence and to heroic action in the midst of conflict as well as promoting "solutions to situations of grave hostility." In initiatives like this, one senses a natural, integrated Christian imagination, at home in the world but not of it. Benedict would be the first to admit that not every move he makes may be correct, but if his diplomacy succeeds, it will be because his Christian peacemaking, rooted in the Benedictine spirituality, is so authentic. ❖

1 Bishop William F. Murphy ["Remembering Assisi after 20 Years," 10/23/06].

CATHOLIC SOCIAL TEACHING, MACINTYRE'S SOCIAL THEORY, AND GLOBAL DEVELOPMENT

By Scott M. Thomas

> What is to be done to prevent increased exchange between cultures (which ought to lead to genuine and fruitful dialogue between groups and nations) from disturbing the life of communities, overthrowing traditional wisdom and endangering the character of people? How is the dynamism and expansion of the new [universal] culture to be fostered without losing living fidelity to the heritage of tradition?
> —*Gaudium et Spes*, 1965 (56)

> The integral development of peoples and international cooperation require the establishment of a greater degree of international ordering, marked by subsidiarity, for the management of globalization. They also require the construction of a social order that at last conforms to the moral order, to the interconnection between moral and social spheres, and to the link between politics and the economic and civil spheres, as envisioned by the Charter of the United Nations.
> —Benedict XVI, *Caritas in Veritate*, 2009 (67)

International relations have changed dramatically since the Second Vatican Council, yet there are remarkable continuities in Catholic social teaching and its approach to global development. The changing signs of the times are now apparent: the global resurgence of religion, the spread of globalization, emerging great powers, and the changing nature of conflict and security. During the heady, optimistic times of the 1960s, one of the often overlooked aspects of the magesterial documents was the importance they accorded to culture and religion vis-à-vis the Church's conception of integral human development. The roles of culture and religion in global economics are even more explicit in contemporary Catholic social thought, as can be seen in Benedict XVI's recent encyclical *Caritas in Veritate*, which offers a decidedly moral perspective on the global market economy.

Unfortunately, only recently have the roles of culture and religion become a concern of Western donor governments and aid agencies (including even some Catholic or more broadly Christian ones). Several of the basic principles of Catholic social teaching are related to the main problems of developing countries, so Catholic

Table 1. List of Papal Encyclicals Cited

MM	*Mater et Magistra*, Christianity and Social Progress, 1961
PT	*Pacem in Terris*, Peace on Earth, 1963
LG	*Lumen Gentium*, Dogmatic Constitution on the Church, 1964
GS	*Gaudium et Spes*, Pastoral Constitution of the Church in the Modern World, 1965
NA	*Nostra aetate*, Declaration on the Relations of the Church to Non-Christian Religions, 1965
PP	*Populorum Progressio*, On the Development of Peoples, 1967
EN	*Evangelii Nuntiandi*, Evangelization in the Modern World, 1975
RH	*Redemptor Hominis*, Redeemer of Man, 1979
SS	*Sollicitudo Rei Socialis*, On Social Concern, 1987
RM	*Redemptoris Missio*, Encyclical Letter on the Church's Missionary Mandate, 1990
CA	*Centesimus Annus*, On the Hundredth Anniversary of *Rerum Novarum*, 1991
VS	*Veritatis Splendor*, The Church's Moral Teaching, 1993
CV	*Caritas in Veritate*, On Integral Human Development in Charity and Truth, 2009

social teaching can inform how the development community views culture and religion. In this article, I survey major global trends affecting development since the 1960s, with a particular focus on Catholic social thought as expressed in papal encyclicals during this period (see Table 1) and in the *Catechism of the Catholic Church*.[1] I then discuss how viewing the principles of Catholic social teaching through the lens of Alasdair MacIntyre's social theory helps us to constructively apply those principles to global development policy today.

The Changing Signs of the Times

One of the most significant changing signs of the times since the Second Vatican Council is a global resurgence of religion—which is more wide ranging than a clash of civilizations driven by religious extremism, terrorism, or fundamentalism. In developed countries the global resurgence of religion is part of a larger existential crisis, reflecting a deep and widespread disillusionment with a "modernity" that reduces the world to what can be perceived and controlled through reason, science, technology, and bureaucratic rationality, and leaves out considerations of religion, the spiritual, or the sacred. The "naive mechanistic optimism" of the 1960s, evident in some of the conciliar documents, now seems to have "been replaced by a well-founded anxiety for the fate of humanity" (SS, 27). In so far as postmodernism shows a greater sensitivity to the human limits of the Weberian disenchantment of the world, it shares a basic insight with those theologians, cultural critics, artists, or even activists in the new social movements who recognize the limits of this disenchantment through their concerns about capitalism, the consumer society, materialism, the environment, and the commodification of every day life—problems exacerbated during the global financial crisis (CV, 36, 71).[2]

Even though these concerns may not always be recognized as religious or spiritual concerns (LG, 16; RH, 18, 46), the value of Benedict XVI's encyclical is that its analysis of economic life, domestically and internationallly, is firmly grounded in theology, i.e. in a Christian worldview, and it has firmly put that worldview on the global agenda.[3] In developing countries the global resurgence of religion stems from the secular modernizing state's failure to produce democracy or development and the widespread inequalities in wealth brought by the neoliberal prescription of free markets and open economies. These factors fostered a growing conflict between religious nationalism and secular nationalism—one of the most important developments in the politics of developing countries in the 1990s.[4]

The religious resurgence follows a massive, general demographic population shift from the developed countries in the North (Europe,

North America, the former Soviet Union) to the developing countries. The North accounted for 32 percent of the world's population in 1900, 29 percent in 1950, 25 percent in 1970, about 18 percent in 2000, and it is estimated that the North will account for only 10–12 percent of the world's population in 2050. The trend is led by Europe, where the numbers of people being born are hardly replacing those dying. Prosperity, urbanization, birth control, and female education have all contributed to a declining population in the North. The religious resurgence is related to this demographic shift toward the global South. It turns out that religious people marry younger and reproduce more than liberal or non-religious people. So theology (and how it impacts lifestyle) has emerged as one of the most accurate indicators of fertility, far better than religious, denominational, or ethnic identities.[5]

Given these demographic shifts since the Second Vatican Council, "one of the most serious problems of our time" is no longer atheism nor secularism, but the problem of cultural and religious pluralism (GS, 19–21, 28). What GS prophetically called for in 1965—the "proper development of culture" (GS, 53–62)—was later elaborated on by Pope Paul VI in *Populorum Progressio* as integral human development. It is now more apparent how prescient the magesterial documents were concerning how *culture matters* to politics and economics, and that religion is an inherent part of how development problems are interpreted within poor communities around the world (since most poor communities *are* faith communities).[6] This is now far more widely recognized in the development literature.[7] Taking cultural and religious pluralism seriously is also now recognized as a key global issue by the World Bank, the World Economic Forum, Western donor governments, and the United Nations Development Program. Moreover, the questions that GS, PP, and CV asked regarding the proper development of culture are not only related to authenticity and development (CV, 48, 51, 55, 59, 78). They also now have a grave impact on global security, the war on global terrorism, and international economic development.

A second important change since the Second Vatican Council is globalization, which Benedict XVI has recently examined. Globalization refers to a set of technological processes affecting the world economy, telecommunications, information technology, travel, and growing economic interdependence between states and peoples that is altering our sense of time and space, and is creating (or is at least creating the possibility the world will become) a single social space. Globalization, it is argued, has created a "shrinking world." Some scholars argue that globalization is rapidly dissolving the social and economic barriers between states and transforming the world's diverse populations into a uniform global market, but at the same time ethnic, religious, and racial hatreds are fragmenting the political landscape into smaller and smaller tribal units. Thus, according to some theorists of globalization, the global resurgence of culture and religion is a response to the paradoxical interdependence of these social forces. Globalization is creating a more *unified* and a more *fragmented* or pluralistic world at the same time.

The Second Vatican Council seemingly anticipated the unifying elements of economic interdependence and the idea of an increasingly common or universal form of culture (GS, 54, 61; NA, 1). *Caritas in Veritate* identified these unifying elements of globalization with global interdependence and the related analytical and ethical consequences of globalization (CV, 33). Benedict XVI's further elaboration of these themes was influenced by the Bologna school of economics and Franciscan economic theory.[8] Regarding international ethics and international institutions, *Caritas in Veritate* maintains, "What the Church's social doctrine has always sustained, on the basis of its vision of man and society, is corroborated today by the dynamics of globalization" (CV, 39). In other words, globalization is now bringing into existence the kind of global society of nations or the natural society of nations that the Church *already* anticipated in its doctrine regarding the human person, society, natural law, and the principles of international order. This conception is what contributed to early Catholic support, at least in continental Europe, for the League of Nations and the United Nations (and this underscores why John Paul II and Benedict XVI's support for international institutions is part of European Catholicism).[9]

However, given the Catholic social principles of personalism and subsidiarity, GS warned about the danger of fragmentation. As the unity of humankind is being fostered, it should be expressed in ways "that the particular characteristics of each culture are preserved" (GS, 54). CV expresses a similar concern (CV, 26, 32, 33, 51, 53, 55, 59). In fact, globalization may not mean the world is being swept up by the unrelenting and unstoppable homogenizing forces of a blandly uniform globalization. What is taking place has more accurately, if awkwardly, been described by Roland Robertson as "global localization" or "glocalization." Worldwide processes are being adapted to *local* circumstances, and so globalization may be a self-limiting process insofar as it incorporates locality. Many of the forces that appear to be homogenizing the global market involve subtle, but important cultural differences, and so what is actually occuring is the universalization of particularism and the particularization of universalism.[10]

If religious traditions are being enhanced by globalization in this way, then it may be better to describe religious groups as part of wider transnational religious subcultures. Religious power and knowledge are not solely ideas or belief systems that are free-floating in the ether of some kind of global public sphere. They are rooted or embodied in the virtues and practices of particular religious traditions, embedded in actual faith communities in ways that bring together forms of piety and cultural and religious identity as a basis for political mobilization.[11] If this is the case, then the Catholic social principles of subsidiarity, solidarity, social justice, and the common good may be ways of directing "global localization" in ways that promote authentic human development. A few of these ways are briefly examined later in this article.

The changing nature of international conflict and security is the third important sign of the times since the Second Vatican Council. The Council and much of the post-conciliar social teaching dealt with the social and ethical aspects of nuclear weapons, the East–West axis, and the North–South axis. Since World War II there has been a decline in wars between states. *This may have made states more secure, but it has made people more insecure.* Brutal wars within states—civil wars, guerrilla wars, anti-colonial wars, wars of national liberation, and revolutionary uprisings—characterized the 1960s and 1970s, the heady times of Vatican II and post-conciliar Catholic social teaching. John Paul II's social teaching addressed the time of the "Second Cold War" (e.g. the wars in Central America and southern Africa in the late 1970s and early 1980s), the end of communism, and the end of the Cold War.

Benedict XVI's pontificate has so far been dominated by the dynamics of the war on terrorism, global poverty, global Islamic revivalism, the global financial crisis, and the crisis of the global environment. These interrelated issues are not only occurring simultaneously (CV, 20, 21); they are also occurring amid a global resurgence of religion in international relations—particularly in the global South. This makes inter-religious dialogue and taking cultural and religious pluralism seriously key aspects of international relations and international development.[12]

In the aftermath of the Cold War, new kinds of wars—internal conflicts exacerbated by the effects of globalization, involving entire ethnic, national, or religious communities—coupled with a number of global threats—crime, and trafficking in drugs, women, children, small arms, and conflict commodities, such as oil, timber, and diamonds—are making people more insecure than ever before.[13] What Samuel Huntington called "decaying states" in the 1960s are now called (in a narrative influential since the late 1990s) "weak states," "failed states," or "collapsed states," caught in a spiral of poverty, instability, and conflict. According to this theory, the societies in these states are susceptible to religious extremism, and there are marked tensions between the ethnic and religious groups and communities they contain.[14]

Authenticity and Development

We can now consider how Catholic social teaching can accommodate the changing signs of the times to its policy of global development. In the postmodern era, the Catholic Church's concept of integral or authentic human development can help the Church respond more effectively to the struggles for authenticity and development taking place throughout the developing world. This section will briefly examine how Alasdair MacIntyre's social theory might inform how principles of Catholic social teaching can be applied to global development policy. First, through Christian personalism and a rethinking of religion, civil society, and development; second, through subsidiarity and the role of faith-based organizations; and third, through global justice and the common good in a world of cultural diversity.

THE MODERN CONCEPT OF CIVIL SOCIETY IS THEREFORE INEVITABLY A NORMATIVE CONCEPT AS WELL AS AN ANALYTICAL ONE

Christian Personalism: Rethinking Religion, Civil Society, and Development

The concept of Christian personalism can be interpreted within Alasdair MacIntyre's narrative conception of identity because both conceptions share a relational understanding of identity, rather than a notion of identity rooted in the rational autonomy of the individual in the liberal West. This has crucial implications for how Catholic aid agencies, other faith-based non-governmental organizations (NGOs), and even secular development NGOs understand how religion and civil society are related to democracy and development. After a decade of civil society programs adopted by Western donor governments to promote democracy and development what we now know is that the modern form of civil society is unrecognizable in most parts of the developing world. This is because a new kind of identity, as well as new forms of social and political organization, are required for the modern concept of civil society to succeed.

What the foreign aid and development literature has not emphasized is that the modern concept of civil society (going back to the Scottish Enlightenment) altered the concept of identity on which civil society was based.[15] It was David Hume and Adam Ferguson who helped transform both the concept of the individual and the concept of civil society. They did this, as Alasdair MacIntyre and Charles Taylor have explained, by rejecting Aristotelian morality, with its concept of the *telos*, or ultimate governing principles that guide the moral life, and instead posited the notion of autonomous individuals motivated by moral sentiments—passions, emotions, and desires. Civil society simply became the arena in which each person pursues their own idea of the good life in a utilitarian way.[16]

Ernst Gellner has emphasized that a new kind of person, with a new kind of human identity, accompanied the development of civil society in the 18th century. Gellner calls this new kind of person "modular man," with a bolted-on identity, unencumbered by ethnicity, religion, or other kinds of affective ties.[17] This man is embedded in a new kind of culture, the culture of liberal democracy and capitalist modernity. The modern concept of civil society and the separation of politics and religion are part of a self-congratulatory form of political liberalism, and are often considered to be one of the unique accomplishments of the West.[18] Many scholars and development practitioners have considered Jurgen Habermas' theory of the public sphere to reflect this concept of civil society at its best. However, Habermas has now come to recognize that even in the West religious motivations are important for a vibrant civil society and democracy.[19]

The modern concept of civil society is therefore inevitably a normative concept as well as an analytical one, and this is something the Church can recognize given its concept of authentic human development. The idea of building civil society in developing countries reflects the wider debates over modernization and Westernization. Civil society can not be examined as a value-free, mechanistic, or technical way for Western donor governments and aid agencies to promote freedom, democracy, development, or conflict prevention. The debate over building civil society is part of the struggle in developing countries over religion and state, over the boundaries of the sacred and the profane, and over authenticity and development. In fact, the modern form of civil society is unrecognizable in most parts of the developing world. Religious beliefs and the ascriptive aspects of clan, ethnic, or religion remain a part of the "modernization of tradition" in developing countries.[20] Contrary to modernization theory, the intermingling of ethnic groups and professions in urban life is not leading to the bolted-on, individualized, social conditioning required for the modern kind of civil society Gellner, Habermas, and others have celebrated (although it would seem much of the development community, in their use of Habermas, has not kept up with his recent dialogue on religious resources for civil society with Pope Benedict XVI).[21] Quite the opposite has occurred, for example, in Africa, with the rise of identity politics and the resurgence of ethnic, religious, or regional forms of identity.

> Africans do not conceive of themselves as discrete individuals in the Western mould ... Individuals are not perceived as being meaningfully and instrumentally separate from the (various) communities to which they belong. This means that an individual remains firmly placed within the family, kin, and communal networks which (s)he is issued ... Africans do not now appear to feel that their 'being modern' requires them to be single individuals whose life choices are essentially determined by their own private circumstances and desires. Difficult as it may be for us to conceive of modernity other than in our own terms, it is necessary to understand how Africans can be both modern and 'non-individual(ist)' if we are to make sense of political events on the continent.[22]

We can see more clearly why MacIntyre's narrative conception of the self, his concepts of the virtues, and his understanding of social practices (out of which his understanding of morality, social tradition, and community emerges) may very well be consistent with the intuitive understanding of morality and social practices found in Africa and other parts of the developing world. MacIntyre argues that our values and ethical conceptions—and the rationality on which they are based—are socially embodied in particular social traditions and communities. There is no rationality independent of tradition, no set of moral principles or guidelines which will commend themselves to all independent of their conception of the good.[23]

MacIntyre helps us understand how, compared to secular political theory, Catholic social teaching has a deeper, more coherent account of these human relationships. It understands Christian personalism and the human person in society, in contrast to the "individual" in liberal modernity. This informs the Church's conception of authentic development. The self in this account is a self with a life story, embedded in the story of a larger community. Character is displayed and developed when individuals are inducted into particular communities, which are themselves shaped by larger narratives and social traditions. This continues to be the case in Africa, but the same thing can be said about other parts of the developing world, and also of Japan and East Asia.[24]

If rationality is dependent on tradition, then morality is not detached from historical communities and cultural and religious traditions. Contrary to Weber, what is important are not only the religiously-based values or motives for social change and community development, but the kind of moral reasoning that gives rise to the content of those convictions and the faith communities in which they are embedded. Thus, appeals to the virtues and moral judgements in religion, or to duty, charity, justice, compassion, obligation, tolerance, and the appeals to conscience (John Paul II [SS, 4], and Benedict XVI, recently [CV, 5, 9, 36, 51, 68, 71, 75]) are not free-floating moral propositions to which rational (autonomous) individuals simply give their intellectual assent. What they mean is shaped by the linguistic conventions of different faith communities, connected to the practices of a religious tradition, and their meaning is only intelligible because they are recognized types of behavior (social practices) passed on through the narratives that shape the identity of these communities.

Therefore, for MacIntyre, as for Catholic moral and social teaching, the actions of human persons cannot be isolated from each other, for every act in an act of the whole person. The question is not, "What am I to do?" [in a particular situation] because this is the kind of single question framed in what is called "quandary ethics," which emerges from the moral predicament of the rational and autonomous individual in secular modernity and political liberalism.[25] At issue for faith communities is a more primary question, one that is identified with MacIntyre's narrative understanding of human identity: "Of which stories am I a part?" For, as David Burrell has argued regarding the Israeli–Palestinian conflict, there are "narratives competing for our souls," but the same could be said for the ethical dilemmas in development or the conflicts in developing countries.[26]

WHAT IS DISTINCTIVE ABOUT A VIRTUE-ETHICS APPROACH TO AID POLICY IS THE PLACE IT ALLOWS FOR CHURCHES, MOSQUES, TEMPLES, AND OTHER PLACES OF WORSHIP

The modern virtue-ethics tradition stemming from MacIntyre's social theory, therefore allows for the crucial role of churches, mosques, temples, and other places of worship in building what Stanley Hauerwas has called "communities of character" as a part of foreign aid policy. The virtue-ethics approach argues that the primary task of religious social ethics is not to come up with policies to promote justice, peace, or social change and development. When religious social ethics defines its task in this way the churches, mosques, or temples that make up faith communities in developing countries can easily be marginalized or forgotten, or they simply become another part of civil society, democratic pluralism, and part of a secular, Western development agenda. We see this in the International Committee of the Red Cross's (ICRC) view of ethics and development or the Carnegie Commission's view of religion and deadly conflict. Faith seems to be of secondary importance to the "real" and more general goals of promoting social change, fostering a more just society, preventing deadly conflict, or meeting the World Bank's Millennium Development Goals.

However, virtue-ethics and Christian personalism's narrative concept of identity emphasize that the *truthfulness* of religious convictions cannot be separated from the *kind of community* that the church, the mosque, or temple is, or is trying to become. Liberal notions of freedom, social justice, or peace are not freestanding values to which any one of goodwill can simply give their intellectual assent. How they are interpreted is part of how the virtues and practices of a religious tradition are enacted, embodied, and disseminated by a particular faith community.

Theology and social ethics cannot be separated, as liberal modernity would have it. The "good," therefore, of the Catholic, Islamic, Jewish, Hindu, or Buddhist religious tradition, is the *formation of a particular kind of community*, one that inculcates those virtues and practices necessary for what it means to authentically live out life according to Catholic social teaching or according to the social teaching of any other religious tradition. John Paul II's recovery of moral theology, and the new *Catechism of the Catholic Church* situate the Church's *moral social* teaching—within a moral framework examining what it means to live out life in Christ (Catechism, Part III).

Such a community, contrary to our liberal presuppositions, does not have to be characterized by an oppressive uniformity. The mark of a truthful community is partly seen in its dialogue about what are the primary "goods" of its religious tradition. It is seen in how it enables the diversity of gifts and virtues within it to flourish, for such a community of character is, as

Hauerwas amusingly says, also "a community of characters," and there are enough of those in the Catholic Church.[27] Now, there is nothing to indicate building a community of character is easy. The issues faith communities must deal with in the developing world are complex, and include gender and reproductive issues, HIV/AIDS, religious approaches to work, wealth, and poverty, usury and interest, corruption, state privatization, inter-faith cooperation, and good governance.

Clearly, what is distinctive about a virtue-ethics approach to aid policy is the place it allows for churches, mosques, temples, and other places of worship to participate in these aspects of development policy. This is not the same thing as aid agencies simply working with and through local churches, mosques, or temples, which is already happening (following the shift in aid policy in the 1980s to channel funds through NGOs rather than corrupt governments as part of the privatization of foreign aid). Virtue-ethics and building communities of character, as we will see below, represent a fundamentally different way of working with places of worship in developing countries, and one which can help local Catholic communities to live out the Church's social teaching. It is also particularly important since the foreign aid industry has now recognized the key role faith-based organizations can play in reaching the poor and alleviating world poverty.

Subsidiarity, Faith-based Organizations, and International Development Policy

According to the principle of subsidiarity, "a community of a higher order should not interfere in the internal life of a community of a lower order, depriving the latter of its functions."[28] Rather, it "should support it in case of need and help to co-ordinate its activity with the activities of the rest of society, but always with a view to the common good."[29] The common good is defined as "the sum total of social conditions which enable individuals, families, and organizations to achieve their own fulfillment more fully and easily."[30] Therefore, all power in the Christian community should be exercised at the lowest level compatible with the common good, which is ordered to the end of persons and organizations that make up civil society. The role of the state is to promote the common good of civil society (Catechism, 1910).

Mater et Magistra (Christianity and Social Progress) recognized—in contrast to the mainstream experts on development in the 1960s—that cultural matters should not be ignored amidst the concern for social change and development. In addition, it held that, "in accordance with 'the principle of subsidiary function,' public authority must encourage and assist private enterprise, entrusting to it, wherever possible, the continuation of economic development' (MM, 152).

Fifty years later, we can see more clearly how the principle of subsidiarity can help to maintain a kind of balance in development policies between the state and civil society. The World Bank and Western donor governments have struggled to acheive this balance, emphasizing instead civil society and privatization and only belatedly recognizing the positive role of the state.[31] These ideas are now mainstream, expressed in the current jargon of development discourse as the need for people in developing countries to feel "ownership" over their development programs, the need for "participatory development," (e.g. micro-finance programs), and the support for civil society rather than state-led development (MM, 22, 152, 259).

Given the global resurgence of religion, subsidiarity can be applied to the way power is exercised in other faith communities as well. One of the events that prompted the World Bank's interest in developing a dialogue and partnership with faith-based organizations was the discovery by its research program, "Voices of the Poor," that religious leaders and institutions were often the most trusted people and institutions in developing countries, given corrupt governments and public sector welfare services.[32] The World Bank and development NGOs now recognize that poor communities can also be described as faith communities. It turns out religion—its beliefs, rituals, practices, and institutions—is still central to the social, cultural, and moral life of these communities.[33] Indeed, as this paper has argued, they constitute the real existing communities in international development.

What can be called the new orthodoxy regarding religion and development was stated by Kumi Naidoo, the general secretary of CIVICUS, a global alliance of NGOs committed to strengthening civil action and civil society. In a study on charitable giving in Islam, Naidoo noted the practical result of applying the principle of subsidiarity to foreign aid policy: "[F]aith-based organizations probably provide the best social and physical infrastructure in the poorest communities," he says, "[because] churches, temples, mosques, and other places of worship [are] focal points for the communities they serve."[34]

Thus, the principle of subsidiarity is directly related to the growing recognition by the World Bank, Western donor governments, and development NGOs that faith-based organizations can play a vital role in the delivery of social services, alleviating world poverty, and meeting the Millennium Development Goals.[35] In addition, for faith-based organizations the virtue-ethics perspective can help them see that their role in social service delivery is not only an instrumental one; it is part of grappling with what it means for congregations/faith communities to become the kind of communities of character that display the virtues and practices necessary for authentic human development.

Global Justice, the Common Good, and International Development Policy

Catholic social teaching is about the integral or authentic development of *persons*—persons-in-communities, or persons and peoples—rather than about the economic development of the states that make up international society (Catechism, 1905–1912). What does this actually mean? It may sound more like a radical slogan than a statement of practical policy. How *can* the Church formulate its commitment to global justice and the common good in a world of growing cultural and religious diversity? After all, John Rawls and other political liberals argue that the pluralism of international society means such a project—indebted to Aristotle, Aquinas, and Catholic social teaching—has to be abandoned.[36]

The Church's concept of authentic human development can not be separated from its understanding of global justice and the common good. The Church acknowledges the North–South gap, the need for foreign aid, and the need "to reform international economic and financial institutions so that they will better promote equitable relationships" with developing countries—but it also argues for authenticity and development. Holistic development "reduces dire poverty and economic exploitation," but it also "makes for growth in respect for cultural identities and openness to the transcendent" (Catechism, 2437–2441).

The Church's concept of authentic human development is about promoting authentic social change and development. Catholic social teaching can help churches, temples, and mosques build the kind of communities of character that generate the social capital—ideas and trust linking groups and individuals—important for democracy and development. Greater social capital can change the political culture of societies and local communities. As the Human Development Report on cultural liberty argues, this is what needs to be done to promote freedom and the protection of minorities. The report states that changes in policy, legislation, and constitutional provisions are all important but changing political culture is what allows real change to happen. A change in political culture is what promotes tolerance and cultural diversity as foundational to democracy.[37]

The report says when this does not happen, "the consequences are disturbingly clear." Indeed, it is now more widely recognized that successful development, no matter how it is defined, can only occur if social and economic change correspond with the moral basis of society. This view seeks to connect religious values both to the actual kind of development that takes place and to the meaning of development. When development does not correspond with a society's moral base and a country makes a cruel choice between bread and dignity, between development and authenticity, and promotes a distorted form of modernity and development, it can result not only in policy failure, but also in political instability, revolution, terrorism, and religious extremism.

Given what is at stake, inter-religious dialogue and the Church's vision of how faith, culture, and religion are related have vital implications for the debate over conflict, security, and development (CV, 26, 29, 30, 31, 56, 57, 59, 76). The principles of subsidiarity, solidarity, and the common good fit together (CV, 58, 60, 67). The common good is ordered to the end of the persons and communities that make up the state and civil society, and global justice is the ordering of goods in domestic society and international society in such a way that they contribute to the authentic development of persons and communities.

Conclusion

Alasdair MacIntyre's social theory can help faith-based development NGOs and Western donor governments understand how Catholic social teaching takes inter-religious dialogue and cultural and religious pluralism seriously in global development. Understanding these principles is essential to encouraging stable societies with strong social capital. Security experts and development agencies stress the importance of social cohesion, and they are beginning to recognize how religious people and institutions in local communities are key actors in community development. The principle of subsidiarity, in particular, can help both governmental and non-governmental development agencies recognize the "deeper pluralism" among the different associations or communities that make up civil society in developing countries. This pluralism includes the "thick" practices—the virtues, social practices, and traditions—of the main world religions. This does not mean there are no universal moral values, only that the rationality of the Western Enlightenment is not the only way of arriving at them. Examples include charity (*zakat* in Islam) and hospitality. Conceptions of the common good are embedded in different cultural and religious traditions.

The task not only for Catholic aid agencies but also for other faith-based agencies is to identify those common, "thick" social practices regarding the moral life and the virtues necessary to sustain them. These agencies should apply the principle of subsidiarity and seek these practices and virtues at the community level. This can provide a way for the members of faith-based organizations in different religious traditions to work together to implement the common good in their community. ❖

1. The full text of papal encyclicals is available online at http://www.vatican.va/offices/papal_docs_list.html, and the full text of the *Catechism of the Catholic Church* is available online at http://www.vatican.va/archive/catechism/ccc_toc.htm.
2. Pontifical Council for Culture, "Jesus Christ the Bearer of the Water of Life"; Thomas, "Religious Resurgence."
3. Griffiths of Fforestfach, "Beyond Social Doctrine." Lord Griffiths is currently Vice-President of Goldman Sachs International and is a former director of the London Business School. He was a key advisor to Margaret Thatcher in the 1980s, and he was closely associated with the London Institute for Contemporary Christianity, which John Stott, the famous British evangelical leader, started in the early 1980s.
4. See Thomas, *The Global Resurgence of Religion.*
5. See Kaufman, *Shall the Religious Inherit the Earth.*
6. On Catholic theology and culture see Rowland, *Culture and the Thomist Tradition.*
7. Bosco, "Development and Religion."
8. Finn, "Benedict's Third Way"; Todeschini, *Franciscan Wealth*; Bruni and Zamagni, *Economia civile.* Zamagni stood with two cardinals and a bishop at the press conference when *Caritas in Veritate* was released.
9. See Beales, *The Catholic Church and International Order* and Brown, *International Relations from a Catholic Standpoint.* It would be easy to demonstrate the continuity between this early Catholic tradition on the unity of humankind and what Benedict XVI calls the "metaphysical interpretation of 'humanism'" (CV, 55). See also O'Mahony, "The Vatican and Europe."
10. See Robertson, "Globalization and the Future of 'Traditional Religion.'"
11. See Thomas, "The Soul of the World?"
12. Thomas, "Religions and Global Security."
13. See Commission on Human Security, *Human Security Now.*
14. See Weinstein et al., *On the Brink.* See also Berdal, "Beyond Greed and Grievance," and Berdal, *Building Peace After War.*

15. See Howell and Pearce, "Civil Society, the State, and the Market."
16. See MacIntyre, *After Virtue*; Charles Taylor, *Sources of the Self.*
17. See Gellner, *Conditions of Liberty.*
18. See Hall, "In Search of Civil Society."
19. See Habermas and Ratzinger, *The Dialectics of Secularization.*
20. See Rudolph and Rudolph, *The Modernity of Tradition.*
21. See Habermas and Ratzinger, *The Dialectics of Secularization.*
22. Chabal and Daloz, *Africa Works*, 52–3.
23. See MacIntyre, *Whose Justice? Which Rationality?*, 354–5.
24. See Baldine, "Is Human Identity an Artifact?"
25. See Pincoffs, "Quandary Ethics."
26. See Burrell, "Narratives Competing for Our Souls,"
27. Hauerwas, *A Community of Character.*
28. CA, 48; *Catechism*, 1883–1885.
29. Ibid.
30. GS, 26, 74; *Catechism*, 1877–1948.
31. See The World Bank, *The State in a Changing World.*
32. See Narayan, *Voices of the Poor.*
33. See Belshaw et al., *Faith in Development.*
34. Naidoo, "The Charities Aid Foundation (CAF)."
35. See Marshall and Marsh, eds., *Millennium Challenges* and Marshall and Keough, *Mind, Heart, and Soul.*
36. See Hollenbach, *The Common Good & Christian Ethics.*
37. See Fukuda-Parr, *Cultural Liberty in Today's Diverse World* and Bruce Cronin, *Institutions for the Common Good.*

References

Baldine, Joanne. "Is Human Identity an Artifact?: How Some Conceptions of the Asian and Western Self Fare During Technological and Legal Development." *Phil & Tech* 3,no. 2 (1997): 25–36.

Beales, A.C.F. *The Catholic Church and International Order,* a Penguin Special. London: Penguin Books, 1941.

Belshaw, Deryke, Robert Calderisi, and Chris Sugden, eds. *Faith in Development: Possibilities for Partnership between the World Bank and the Churches in Africa.* Oxford: Regnum Books/Oxford Centre for Mission Studies, 2001.

Berdal, Mats. "Beyond greed and grievance—and not too soon…" *Review of International Studies* 31 (2005): 687–98.

Berdal, Mats. *Building Peace After War.* London: Routledge/International Institute for Strategic Studies, 2009.

Bosco, Robert M. "Development and Religion." In *The International Studies Encyclopedia,* vol. II, ed. Robert A. Denemark, 970–87. Oxford: Wiley-Blackwell, 2010.

Brown, Stephen J. *International Relations from a Catholic Standpoint.* Dublin: Browne and Nolan, Ltd., 1932.

Bruni, Luigino and Stefano Zamagni. *Economia civile. Efficienza, equità, felicità pubblica* [Civil economy, efficiency, equity, and public happiness]. Bologna: Il Mulino, 2004.

Burrell, David B. "Narratives Competing for Our Souls." In *Terrorism and International Justice,* ed. James P. Sterba, 88–100. Oxford: Oxford University Press, 2003.

Chabal, Patrick and Jean-Pascol Daloz. *Africa Works: Disorder as Political Instrument.* London: James Currey, 1999.

Commission on Human Security. *Human Security Now.* New York: United Nations, 2003.

Cronin, Bruce. *Institutions for the Common Good: International Protection Regimes in International Society.* Cambridge: Cambridge University Press, 2003.

Finn, Daniel. "Benedict's Third Way." *The Tablet* (London), March 13, 2010.

Fukuda-Parr, Sakiko. *Cultural Liberty in Today's Diverse World.* Human Development Report 2004. New York: United Nations Development Programme, 2004.

Gellner, Ernest. *Conditions of Liberty: Civil Society and its Rivals.* London: Hamish Hamilton, 1994.

Griffiths of Fforestfach, Brian. "Beyond Social Doctrine: Reflections on *Caritas in Veritate.*" *L'Osservatore Romano,* Weekly Edition in English, December 16, 2009, 12.

Habermas, Jurgen and Joseph Ratzinger. *The Dialectics of Secularization: On Reason and Faith.* San Francisco: Ignatius Press, 2006.

Hall, John A. "In Search of Civil Society." In *Civil Society: Theory, History, Comparison,* ed. John A. Hall, 1–31. Cambridge: Polity Press, 1995.

Hauerwas, Stanley. *A Community of Character: Toward a Constructive Christian Social Ethic.* Notre Dame, IN: University of Notre Dame Press, 1981.

Hollenbach, David. *The Common Good & Christian Ethics.* Cambridge: Cambridge University Press, 2002.

Howell, June and Jenny Pearce. "Civil Society, the State, and the Market: A Triadic Development Model for the Twenty First Century?" In *Civil Society and Development: A Critical Exploration,* ed. Jude Howell and Jenny Pearce, 63–88. Boulder and London: Lynne Rienner, 2001.

Kaufman, Eric. *Shall the Religious Inherit the Earth: Demography and Politics in the Twenty-First Century.* London: Profile Books, 2010.

MacIntyre, Alasdair. *After Virtue: A Study in Moral Theory.* London: Duckworth, 1985.

MacIntyre, Alasdair. *Whose Justice? Which Rationality?* London: Duckworth, 1996.

Marshall, Katherine and Lucy Keough, eds. *Mind, Heart, and Soul in the Fight Against Poverty.* Washington, DC: World Bank, 2004.

Marshall, Katherine and Richard Marsh, eds. *Millennium Challenges for Development and Faith Institutions.* Washington, DC: World Bank, 2003.

Naidoo, Kumi. "Editorial." *Alliance (Charities Aid Foundation)* 5, no. 1 (2000): 1.

Narayan, Deepa. *Voices of the Poor: Can Anyone Hear Us?* Washington, DC: Oxford University Press for the World Bank, 2000.

O'Mahony, Antony. "The Vatican and Europe: Political Theology and Ecclesiology in Papal Statements from Pius XII to Benedict XVI." *International Journal of the Study of the Christian Church* 9, no. 3 (2009): 177–94.

Pincoffs, Edmund. "Quandary Ethics." In *Revisions: Changing Perspectives in Moral Philosophy,* ed. Stanley Hauerwas and Alasdair MacIntyre, 92–112. Notre Dame, IN: University of Notre Dame Press, 1983.

Pontifical Council for Culture. "Jesus Christ the Bearer of the Water of Life, A Christian Reflection on the 'New Age.'" Pontifical Council for Interreligious Dialogue. London: CTS, 2003.

Robertson, Roland. "Globalization and the Future of 'Traditional Religion.'" In *Religion and the Powers of the Common Life.* Vol. 1, *God and Globalization,* ed. Max L. Stackhouse and Peter J. Paris, 53–68. Philadelphia: Trinity Press International, 2000.

Rowland, Tracey. *Culture and the Thomist Tradition After Vatican II.* London: Routledge, 2003.

Rudolph, L. and S. Rudolph. *The Modernity of Tradition: Political Development in India.* Chicago: University of Chicago Press, 1967.

Taylor, Charles. *Sources of the Self: The Making of the Modern Identity.* Cambridge: Cambridge University Press, 1989.

Thomas, Scott M. "Religious Resurgence, Postmodernism, and World Politics." In *Religion and Global Order,* ed. John L. Esposito and Michael Watson, 38–65. Cardiff: University of Wales Press, 2000.

Thomas, Scott M. *The Global Resurgence of Religion and the Transformation of International Relations.* London: Palgrave, 2005.

Thomas, Scott M. "The Soul of the World? Religious Non-State Actors in World Politics." In *The Global Resurgence of Religion and the Transformation of International Relations,* ed. Scott M. Thomas, Chapter 4, 97–120. London: Palgrave, 2005.

Thomas, Scott M. "Religions and Global Security." In "Le religioni nelle relazioni internazionali," [Religions in International Relations] *Quaderni di Relazioni Internazionali* 12 (2010): 4–21. Milano: Istituto per gli Studi di Politica Internazionale (ISPI), April 2010.

Todeschini, Giacomo. *Franciscan Wealth: From Voluntary Poverty to Market Society.* St. Bonaventure, NY: Franciscan Institute, St. Bonaventure University, 2009.

Weinstein, Jeremy M., John Edward Porter, and Stuart E. Eizenstat. *On the Brink: Weak States and U.S. National Security.* Washington, DC: Commission on Weak States and U.S. National Security at the Center for Global Development, 2004.

The World Bank. *The State in a Changing World.* World Bank Development Report 1997. Washington, DC: The World Bank, 1997.

Index

Note: Page numbers in **bold** type refer to tables
Page numbers followed by 'n' refer to notes

Printed in Great Britain
by Amazon

84974045R00113